CONTEMPORARY POLICING

CONTEMPORARY POLICING
Personnel, Issues, and Trends

Edited by M.L. Dantzker, Ph.D.

Georgia Southern University
Department of Political Science
Justice Studies

Butterworth-Heinemann
Boston • Oxford • Johannesburg • Melbourne • New Delhi • Singapore

Butterworth-Heinemann

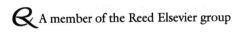 A member of the Reed Elsevier group

Library of Congress Cataloging-in-Publication Data

Contemporary policing : personnel, issues & trends / M.L. Dantzker,
    editor.
        p.   cm.
    Includes bibliographical references and index.
    ISBN 0-7506-9736-9 (alk. paper)
    1. Police—United States.   2. Police—United States—Personnel
management.   I. Dantzker, Mark L., 1958–   .
HV8138.C645   1997
362.2′2′09373—dc21   96–50435
                                                        CIP

British Library Cataloguing-in-Publication Data
A catalogue record for this book is available from the British Library.

The publisher offers special discounts on bulk orders of this book.
For information, please contact:
Manager of Special Sales
Butterworth-Heinemann
313 Washington Street
Newton, MA 02158-1626
Tel: 617-928-2500
Fax: 617-928-2620

For information on all criminal justice publications available, contact our World Wide Web home page at:
http://www.bh.com/sec

10 9 8 7 6 5 4 3 2 1

Printed in the United States of America

CONTENTS

About the Authors

GAIL D. DANTZKER

Gail D. Dantzker is an educational consultant. She received her Ph.D. in educational leadership and policy studies from Loyola University-Chicago in 1996. While completing her dissertation, Dr. Dantzker worked as a lead evaluator of the first round of training given to Chicago police officers as they prepared to enter the community policing era. Results from this opportunity were published in *Police Studies*. Dr. Dantzker's interests include adult education, workplace training and education, educational program evaluation, and curriculum development and evaluation.

M.L. DANTZKER

M.L. Dantzker is an associate professor of political science at Georgia Southern University, teaching in the justice studies program, specializing in policing. In 1989 he received his Ph.D. in administration through the Institute of Urban Studies at the University of Texas, Arlington. He is a former police officer whose research interests include education, stress, and job satisfaction among police officers, about which he has published articles in several journals. His first textbook was *Understanding Today's Police* (Prentice-Hall); he is a co-author of the text *Criminal Justice Statistics* (Butterworth–Heinemann) and is completing a police organization and management textbook for West Publishing Company. He also has several other journal articles and book projects underway.

WILLIAM G. DOERNER

William G. Doerner is currently a professor in the School of Criminology and Criminal Justice at Florida State University. He has also worked as a part-time police officer for the city of Tallahassee, Florida, since 1980. He has written about the area of victimology. His current project is his textbook *Law Enforcement: An Insider's View,* which is to be published by Butterworth–Heinemann.

LORIE A. FRIDELL

Lorie A. Fridell is an associate professor in criminology and criminal justice at Florida State University. She received her Ph.D. in social ecology from the University of California at Irvine in 1987. Her primary research area is police and violence. She has written articles, chapters, and a monograph on police use of deadly and non-deadly force, complaints of excessive force, and violence against police. With Geoff Alpert she co-authored *Police Vehicles and Firearms: Instruments of Deadly Force* and with Antony M. Pate recently completed an NIJ-funded project on the felonious killings of police officers.

ARTHUR J. LURIGIO

Arthur J. Lurigio, a social psychologist, is a professor of criminal justice and member of the graduate faculty at Loyola University. Much of his research is in the areas of drugs and crime, mental disorders and crime, and community corrections. He has co-edited several works such as *Smart Sentencing: The Emergence of Intermediate Sanctions, Drugs and Community Corrections,* and *Victims of Crime.* He has recently co-authored a book called *Community Antidrug Efforts.* His other research interests include probation programs, community policing, crime prevention, and domestic violence.

ELIZABETH MCGRATH

Elizabeth McGrath received her Ph.D. in philosophy from Florida State University in 1982, her J.D. from Loyola University of New Orleans in 1987, and is a member of the Florida Bar Association. She taught philosophy at Spring Hill College in Mobile, Alabama, from 1979 to 1984 and taught criminal justice at Loyola University-Chicago from 1987 to 1994. She is currently associate dean of Mundelein College of Loyola University-Chicago. McGrath is the author of *The Art of Ethics: A Psychology of Ethical Beliefs* (Loyola University Press).

ANTONY M. PATE

Antony M. Pate is a senior research associate at Florida State University in both the College of Social Sciences and the School of Criminology and Criminal Justice. Prior to working at Florida State University he was director of research at the Police Foundation in Washington, D.C. He has more than 23 years of experience in conducting field research and evaluations in law enforcement agencies. He recently co-wrote with Lorie Fridell *Police Use of Force: Official Reports, Citizen Complaints, and Legal Consequences.* Recent articles have appeared in *Crime and Delinquency* and the *American Sociological Review.*

MARILYN B. PETERSON

Marilyn B. Peterson is a management analyst with the Economic Crime Bureau, Division of Criminal Justice, New Jersey Department of Law and Public Safety. She has been a law enforcement analyst since 1980 and has also served with the Pennsylvania Crime Commission and the Middle Atlantic–Great Lakes Organized Crime Law Enforcement Network (MAGLOCLEN). She is a graduate of Thomas Edison State College (BS, criminal justice) and Seton Hall University (MA, education), a lifetime certified criminal analyst, and a certified fraud examiner. She has written and taught extensively in the field of law enforcement analysis, co-edited *Criminal Intelligence Analysis* (Palmer, 1990), and authored *Applications in Criminal Analysis: A Sourcebook* (Greenwood, 1994).

DENNIS P. ROSENBAUM

Dennis P. Rosenbaum is a professor of criminal justice at the University of Illinois at Chicago. He served as director of the Center for Research in Law and Justice on Campus for five years. He has conducted a wide range of evaluations and research projects focusing on police and community efforts to prevent violence, drug abuse, and delinquency through community involvement. Professor Rosenbaum has written extensively on the topic of community-oriented prevention. His books include *Community Crime Prevention: Does It Work?* (1986), *The Social Construction of Reform* (1988), *Drugs and Communities* (1993), and *The Challenge of Community Policing: Testing the Promises* (1994).

STAN K. SHERNOCK

Stan K. Shernock is currently associate professor and chair of the Department of Justice Studies and Sociology at Norwich University in Vermont. He received his Ph.D. in sociology from the University of Virginia. He has published articles on police solidarity, police ethics, police education, and civilianization in police organizations, as well as articles on criminal justice education, crime prevention, bystander intervention, political prisoners, governmental terror, and mobility of revolutionary successors, and numerous book reviews on a diversity of criminological and sociological topics. Most recently he has presented a number of papers on police training based on a job task analysis done for the Vermont Criminal Justice Training Council.

LORETTA STALANS

Loretta Stalans received her Ph.D. in social psychology from the University of Illinois at Chicago in 1990. She is an assistant professor of criminal justice at Loyola University-Chicago. She has published articles on public opinion about justice and on police discretionary decision making in several journals, including *Behavioral Sciences and the Law, Crime and Delinquency, Criminal Justice and Behavior,* and *Law and Society.* Dr. Stalans is currently co-authoring a book with Julian Roberts on *Crime, Justice, and Public Opinion* (Westview Press).

LARRY D. STOKES

Larry D. Stokes is an assistant professor of sociology at the University of Tennessee at Chattanooga. He received his Ph.D. from Howard University. His research interests are race relations, multiculturalism, law enforcement, and the role of racial and ethnic factors in the criminal justice system.

JEFFERY T. WALKER

Jeffery T. Walker, Ph.D. is an associate professor of criminal justice, teaching in the graduate program at the University of Arkansas at Little Rock. Dr. Walker's two primary areas of work are in law enforcement and criminology. In addition to these areas, he has researched and written in the areas of computers in criminal justice, educational and legal issues concerning the police, and gang behavior. He has served as president of both the Arkansas Law Enforcement and Criminal Justice Association and the Southwestern Association of Criminal Justice Educators, and as secretary of the Police Section of the Academy of Criminal Justice Sciences. He is also the editor of the *Journal of Criminal Justice Education.* Previous publications include more than fifty papers, articles, and other publications, including articles in the *Journal of Quantitative Criminology* and the *Journal of Gang Research* and the book *Briefs of Leading Cases in Law Enforcement* (2nd edition).

Preface

Contemporary or modern policing has existed in the United States for more than 150 years. Since its inception, policing has experienced many changes. Growth in the legal arena, technological advances, and the social, racial, ethnic, and cultural changes in our society have brought about changes in policing. While these changes have affected various aspects of policing, this book focuses on the areas of personnel, issues, and trends.

Policing has grown from a white male-dominated occupation where little education or training was required to a more racially, ethnically, and gender-mixed semi-profession with fairly rigorous employment standards and requirements. This change has created a number of issues. Furthermore, change and societal demands and expectations are contributing to several trends in policing.

This text is designed to explore many of the changes, issues, and trends associated with the evolution of policing. Each area or topic is discussed in a manner that provides readers with an in-depth review of the topic's development, application, and results. While not all possible topics could be included, those that have been chosen are extremely relevant to the study of contemporary policing today and for the future because how they impact policing will, in turn, affect how police officers perform their duties. Simply put, the included topics are strongly related to the quality of police service and, therefore, deserve special recognition and attention.

Historically, the police officer was a white male from a blue-collar background, where policing may have been a family tradition, and often represented a major ethnic group such as the Irish. Although a majority of police officers in the United States are still white males, females have joined the ranks. In Chapter 1, *Police Officers: A Gender Perspective,* Loretta Stalans discusses the entry of women into policing; this growth, including problems and issues they have faced; current issues; and future prospects. Gender composition is just one of the changes in police personnel. In Chapter 2, *Minority Groups in Law Enforcement,* Larry Stokes offers an examination of the status of minority group members in policing, historically and at present.

The composition of police personnel has had an interesting effect on policing. In addition to the compositional changes, the progression in hiring and retaining officers has been interesting. In *Recruitment and Retention* (Chapter 3), Bill Doerner observes and discusses changes and patterns in recruitment efforts and the retaining of police personnel. This is supported and expanded upon in Chapter 4, *Education and Training: No Longer Just a Badge and a Gun,* where Stan Shernock and Gail D.

Dantzker explore the efforts and improvements associated with the preparation of police personnel for the performance of their job tasks.

Few occupations are free of job-related stress. Yet, how many occupations are charged with preserving or taking human life, where stress can have severe adverse effects? Many questions about stress and its relationship to policing are addressed by M.L. Dantzker in Chapter 5, *Stress and the Badge.*

How a police officer performs his or her job often receives public scrutiny. When the performance does not meet expectations or when officer behavior is unacceptable, a question of professionalism is often raised. For many years policing has been criticized for its lack of professional standing. In *Being a Police Officer: Part of a Profession?* (Chapter 6), M.L. Dantzker explores the idea of policing as a profession, including the effort to raise policing to this status; the struggles; successes; and solutions.

An important aspect of policing, not only as a profession but with regard to general practices, is the ethical component. Elizabeth McGrath gives an in-depth view of ethics and its role in policing in Chapter 7, *Professional Ethics and Policing.*

An increasingly important means for assisting officers in carrying out their duties is the use of criminal analysis. Although not new to policing, its recognition and usage are relatively new. In beginning the **Trends** section, *Criminal Analysis,* Chapter 8, by Marilyn Peterson, looks at what crime analysis is and how it can be a valuable tool to policing as well as how it relates to all the topics discussed in this text.

Despite how much policing has changed and improved in many areas, some things may be better left unchanged. How police and citizens interact has changed over the years, often with less than positive outcomes. To address this important aspect of policing, many agencies are turning back to a community-oriented practice, which may involve a renewed, people-oriented approach to policing that present-day officers may not be skilled or comfortable in providing. In Chapter 9, *Community Policing: Major Issues and Unanswered Questions,* Arthur Lurigio and Dennis Rosenbaum lead the reader through the definition, growth, and implementation of community policing and what effect(s) it has on police personnel.

Whether we want to admit it or not, our society appears to be slowly becoming more violent. This violence occurs between citizens, against citizens by police officers, and against police officers. Issues surrounding violence and the use of force are increasingly important. Lorie Fridell and Antony M. Pate provide a detailed discussion of use-of-force issues by police officers in Chapter 10, *Use of Force: A Matter of Control.*

Finally, while it does not necessarily impact those who are police officers, technological advances have had an obvious effect on how police officers perform their jobs. Jeffrey Walker, in *Re-Blueing the Police: Technological Changes and Law Enforcement Practices* (Chapter 11), examines how technological advances such as computers, weaponry, and communication devices have added new dimensions to policing, and how they have aided in improving services provided by personnel and how these advances may shape the future of policing.

The contributors to this text have a wealth of knowledge and experience. Their writings provide readers with an extremely timely and useful body of information that will improve one's insights and understanding about important topics surrounding police personnel, issues, and trends. It is the goal of this text and its contributors to give readers a singular source of information that, once read, will allow a more critical, informed examination of these specific topics.

Acknowledgments

No book, whether a solo effort or edited work, can be completed without assistance from others. I would like to acknowledge those who assisted in the completion of this work. To begin, my gratitude to my acquisitions editor, Laurel DeWolf, who has taken more than one chance on me and seems to have a never-ending amount of confidence; to Stephanie Aronson, assistant editor, who on more than one occasion has probably wished I would learn to submit work in the proper format; to Hilary Selby Polk, production editor, whose hard work and guidance brought about a publishable manuscript; and of course, the reviewers, Jim Gilbert and Tom Mijares, whose critiques and feedback provided necessary and welcomed guidance.

A special thanks to my colleagues and fellow contributors, without whom this book would never have been completed. I appreciate their diligence throughout the process and their ability to finish their chapters in spite of my harassment and constant haranguing.

Last, but by no means least, an extra special thanks and my utmost gratitude to my wife, Gail, for all her support and love on every project I have undertaken, despite the time they require and my grouchiness as deadlines get closer.

1

Police Officers: A Gender Perspective

Loretta Stalans, Loyola University of Chicago

> *On 12 September 1910, Alice Stebbins Wells of the Los Angeles Police Department became the first woman police officer. The humiliations began on her appointment. Showing her badge to obtain a free ride on a streetcar, she was accused of misusing her husband's. Despite her uniform, the public was reluctant to accept that she had any powers: the idea of police women had been a joke in comic weeklies since the 1850's* (Linda Grant, *Independent on Sunday,* 9/9/90, p. 23; cited in Walklate, 1992).

The story about Alice Stebbins Wells illustrates the treatment of women in modern policing. It is a treatment that, despite its improvement, still requires change. Although women have come a long way in policing, their quest for acceptance is far from over. This first chapter looks at the progress and status of women as police officers.

HISTORICAL OVERVIEW

From the beginning, the criminal justice system and the public believed that women were ill-suited to investigate gruesome crimes and to handle disputes between physically stronger citizens. Most women who desired to be police officers did not challenge this view. Women instead argued that their unique feminine traits of compassion, morality, and negotiation made them well-suited to handle juvenile delinquency, prostitution, domestic violence, and victims of rape. Female officers dealt with vice crimes such as prostitution and gambling because the majority of men in policing or in the criminal justice system did not see these crimes as "serious" criminal activity. Female officers' focus on the protection of children and women also fitted the stereotypic view of women as more nurturing and compassionate than men. Female officers thus carved out a unique role that would not challenge the duties of male officers.

Even before women were given the official title of officer and the power of arrest, many women either volunteered or were paid for the performance of certain police functions. The wives of police officers often interviewed and searched female suspects

1

and victims (Radford, 1989). In the early 1900s, feminists in Britain formed the Women's Freedom League (WFL). This organization focused on fighting for women's rights and protecting women from the oppression and exploitation of men. The WFL demanded female police officers to combat male violence against women and fought for women's rights to equal status. Other women's organizations, however, were content to establish a place in policing for women through the cooperation of men and to limit women's roles to tasks that did not threaten men. This more conservative agenda won (Radford, 1989).

Both in the United States and in Great Britain women's organizations suggested that female officers would be specialists for tasks that males did not see as real policing. Alice Stebbins Wells organized the International Association of Police Women (IAPW) and became its first president in 1915. The IAPW provided an official position for police women and advocated a separate (but not equal) status for policewomen. Women were to perform duties that facilitated the protection of women and children and the prevention of crime.

This crime prevention model did not fit the vision of policing that male officers held. Between the mid-1920s and 1945, a crime control model emerged that portrayed the police officer as "a crime fighter *extraordinaire,* a seasoned, well-armed, professional soldier in a savage war on crime. The implications of this development for policewomen were plain: women could not be soldiers" (Appier, 1992, p. 28). Male officers accepted this crime control model of policing in which officers reacted with swiftness and harshness to criminal activity. The crime control model was reactionary and oriented toward deterring criminals from further crimes, whereas the crime prevention model was proactive and oriented toward rehabilitating criminals and protecting helpless victims (Appier, 1992). In keeping with the crime prevention model, female police officers performed specialized duties such as patrolling railroad depots for runaway and kidnaped children, patrolling streets in plain clothes to stop prostitution, returning runaway girls to their homes, conducting interviews with rape victims, and conducting investigations in crimes involving women and children (Feinman, 1994). By articulating that they were different from men and did not desire to perform the duties of men, these early policewomen won some acceptance from male officers.

The acceptance won by female officers came at a high cost. This different stance allowed gender stereotypes to remain intact and justified the men's perspective that women's work was not worth as much as men's work. Women were paid substantially less than men, but were required to have more qualifications than men. For example, women were required to have a high school diploma and often required to have college education and work experience, whereas men did not face educational requirements until 1955 (Feinman, 1994). The number of women in police departments was kept low by quotas, and women were given different training from that given to men. Besides the lower pay, departments did not allow women to be promoted, regardless of their ability or experience. By emphasizing how women were different from men, women allowed male officers to view them as necessary tools for the performance of undesirable duties rather than as persons with equal talent and competence.

The women's liberation movement and the consciousness raising of the 1960s and 1970s provided women with the insight that they were equal to and as competent as men. The unequal pay and lack of promotional opportunities also provided women with the motivation to question the substandard specialist status they had acquired. In the late 1960s and early 1970s, women began to challenge male opposition to their full acceptance as equal members in policing. As Lunneborg (1989) notes, Felicia Shpritzer and Gertrude Schimmel served as police officers in the Juvenile Aid Division for nineteen years and were not allowed to take the exams for promotion to sergeant. Officer Shpritzer took the department to court and won women the right to take promotional exams. Both Shpritzer and Schimmel took and passed the exams in 1964. "Gertude Schimmel was the first woman to take and pass all three civil service exams—sergeant, lieutenant, and captain—and to become, in 1971, the first woman deputy inspector in the New York City Police Department" (Lunneborg, 1989, p. 6). The right to promotion, however, was not accepted by many male officers. For example, "Commissioner Patrick, who had entered the department in 1940 at the same time as Schimmel, ceased to talk to Shpritzer and Schimmel after they became sergeants and never truly accepted women as equals in the department" (Feinman, 1994, p. 101).

Other legal changes also provided women officers with additional ammunition to demand opportunities for equal hiring practices, assignments, and promotions. In 1972, Congress passed the Equal Employment Opportunity Act, which expanded the coverage of Title VII to prohibit both public and private employers from discriminating in their hiring and promotional practices on the basis of ethnic origin, race, or gender. After the passage of this act, departments faced greater federal scrutiny and a need to justify decisions that resulted in few female officers on the force. The passage of the Crime Control Act of 1973 also gave police departments additional incentives to hire women. This federal law established that

> any police agency discriminating against women could not receive grant money from the Law Enforcement Assistance Administration (LEAA). And LEAA's money was considerable. One billion dollars a year went to improve 40,000 departments, courts, and correctional facilities. Unfortunately, LEAA, born in 1968, died in 1983, and with it this additional pressure to implement women's equal opportunity plans (Lunneborg, 1989, p. 8).

Despite legal mandates and incentives to provide women with equal opportunity, both supervisors and the rank-and-file male officers resisted and blocked the integration of women. Women have fought for their place in policing and continue to struggle for equal status. The Los Angeles Police Department, for example, practiced blatant discrimination against women.

Illustration: In January 1971, Chief Davis informed approximately one hundred female officers that "women were no longer wanted or needed by the LAPD." Then Chief Davis went on to assert that, "women didn't belong in law enforcement, couldn't do the job, and that men didn't want them there." Later that month Chief Davis presented a new reorganization scheme for the department, called the Jacob's Ladder plan, which prohibited female officers from being promoted above the rank of sergeant or investigator II.

> Between 1970 and 1973, the department hired no new female officers and the approximately two hundred women, who were already serving as sworn officers, were reassigned to receptionist and secretarial jobs without having their formal job classification changed (Felkenes, Peretz & Schroedel, 1993, p. 34, cites omitted).

Fortunately, Fanchon Blake, who had served twenty-five years as a female officer, fought for her right to be promoted to the level of investigator III. She filed a lawsuit in 1973 under the 1972 Equal Employment Opportunity Act and charged that the Los Angeles Police Department discriminated against her on the basis of her gender (*Blake v. Los Angeles City*). In 1979, the Ninth Circuit Court of Appeals ruled in favor of Blake. The Court found that the dual classification system was discriminatory because it could not be justified as necessary for conducting business or for achieving important objectives of the government (Felkenes, Peretz & Schroedel, 1993). Other lawsuits forced departments to remove height requirements, which discriminated against women as a class, to allow women the opportunity to be promoted to detective, and to provide similar training to women. Legal mandates often did not persuade departments to change their discriminatory practices. Departments, for example, were slow to adopt affirmative action policies. By 1986, 43 percent of the departments in cities serving 50,000 or more had no affirmative action policies (Martin, 1990). Individual women have fought for the changes that have occurred, and in the 1990s female police officers are still struggling for equal pay, equal status, and acceptance by male officers.

This history of exclusion and segregation is why the topic of female police officers is so important. Female officers initially were content to be outsiders and to be "tools" for men's housecleaning and dirty work. Women soon realized their own worth and began to demand equal opportunity and a voice in the nature of policing. This brief history of female police officers illustrates that women face unnecessary obstacles in their chosen careers, and these obstacles have also shaped the very nature of policing. The next section examines the extent of exclusion and the many different faces of exclusion from hiring, retention, promotion, harassment, and lack of acceptance by male officers. The remainder of the chapter focuses on the problems female officers face and the issues female officers create for police departments. This chapter concludes with an examination of the causes of exclusion, harassment, and lack of acceptance, as well as future attempts to solve these problems.

THE NATURE OF THE EXCLUSION OF WOMEN FROM POLICING

Over the last fifteen years, Uniform Crime Report Statistics indicate that the percentage of women in law enforcement has increased. Across the nation in municipal departments, women accounted for 3.2 percent of the force in 1978, 7.2 percent in 1986, and 9.4 percent in 1993. Across the nation in state agencies, women accounted for 0.9 percent of the force in 1979, 3.5 percent in 1986, and 5.9 percent in 1993. These figures show some improvement in the hiring and retention of female officers.

For both municipal departments and state agencies, women, however, still are substantially underrepresented.

Women compose about half of the United States' population but account for less than 10 percent of police officers across the nation. The representation of female police officers in police departments shows considerable variation across the United States. In 1993, female officers composed less than 6 percent of the police force in departments with 100 officers or more in most New England states but comprised at least 11 percent of the force in most southern states. In the Midwest, West, and Mid-Atlantic states, women represented about 9 percent of officers in the departments of one hundred or more officers. (See Table 1.1 for a complete description of the percentage of women in police departments within each state.) Earlier research also supports these regional differences. Steel and Lovrich (1987), in 1981, conducted a national survey of police chiefs in cities with populations greater than 24,999. The chiefs indicated the percentage of their officers that were women. Of departments having forces in which women represented 6 or more percent of the sworn officers, the South had the highest number of departments and the Northeast the lowest: 44 percent of the departments in the South, 29 percent in the Midwest, 23 percent in the West, and 17 percent in the Northeast. The Northeast, moreover, had the highest percentage of departments where women represented from 0 to 2 percent of the force: 64 percent in the Northeast, 35 percent in the Midwest, 24 percent in the West, and 18 percent in the South. Research on nineteen major cities across the nation in 1981 also indicated that the South and West hired a greater number of women than did the Northeast (Lunneborg, 1989).

Women also represent a greater percentage of the police force as the size of a city's population increases. At the end of 1986, women nationwide represented 10.4 percent of the force in cities with more than one million people, 6.8 percent of the force in cities with populations between 100,000 and 250,000 persons, and 4.9 percent of the force in cities with populations between 50,000 and 100,000. This variation by size of the city largely reflects changes in the hiring of minority women, who comprised 4.8 percent of the force in cities of more than a million but less than 1 percent of the force in cities with populations between 50,000 and 100,000 (Martin, 1990). Similar differences still existed in 1993: Women composed 15 percent of the police force in cities with populations of one million or more, 12.3 percent in cities with populations between 250,000 and 999,999, 9.0 percent in cities with populations of 100,000 to 249,999, 6.8 percent in cities with populations of 50,000 to 99,999, and 5.8 percent in cities with populations of 25,000 to 49,999. Across the nation, considerable variation also exists between police departments of major cities. Based on 1986 data, the percentage of women in five major cities ranged from 18 percent to 7.1 percent: 18 percent for Detroit, 15 percent for Birmingham, 13 percent for Washington, D.C., 10 percent for Chicago, 7.8 percent for Los Angeles, and 7.1 percent for Phoenix (Felkenes, Peretz & Schroedel, 1993). Interestingly, four of these five cities were sued by female police officers and had to sign consent decrees in which they agreed to increase their hiring of women to meet an annual goal: 25 percent for Birmingham, 33 percent for Chicago, 33 percent for Detroit, and 25 percent for Los Angeles. These cities were required to meet these annual goals until women represented a

Table 1.1 Average Percentage of Women in Police Departments with 100 or More Officers as of August, 1993

New England: 5.7%	% of Women	Southern: 11.5%	% of Women
New Hampshire	1.50%	Mississippi	6.60%
Rhode Island	2.95%	Arkansas	7.26%
New Jersey	3.80%	Missouri	8.07%
Connecticut	6.64%	West Virginia	9.10%
Massachusetts	7.01%	South Carolina	11.12%
Maine	7.10%	Georgia	11.47%
Delaware	11.00%	Kentucky	11.57%
		Virginia	11.58%
Mid Atlantic: 9.4%		Florida	11.96%
Ohio	11.66%	Alabama	12.45%
New York	8.11%	Maryland	13.00%
Pennsylvania	8.55%	Tennessee	13.07%
		Wash. DC	13.20%
		Louisiana	21.16%
Midwest: 8.9%			
Kansas	6.18%	*West: 8.60%*	
Indiana	6.76%	South Dakota	3.40%
Iowa	7.02%	Hawaii	5.37%
Illinois	7.12%	Utah	7.10%
Wisconsin	9.17%	Oklahoma	8.73%
Michigan	10.76%	Arizona	8.89%
Minnesota	10.85%	New Mexico	9.25%
Nebraska	13.55%	Nevada	9.40%
		Texas	9.67%
Northwest: 7.84%		California	10.13%
Idaho	2.80%	Colorado	14.05%
Montana	2.90%		
Washington	8.90%		
Alaska	11.90%		
Oregon	12.70%		

Compiled from Reaves, B.A., & Smith, P.Z. (1995). Law enforcement management and administrative statistics, 1993: Data for individual state and local agencies with 100 or more officers. Washington, D.C.: Bureau of Justice Statistics.

certain percentage of the force: 44 percent for Birmingham, 33 percent for Chicago, 33 percent for Detroit, and 20 percent for Los Angeles (Felkenes, Peretz & Schroedel, 1993). Based on 1993 data, these cities still fall considerably short of the goal: 18.8 percent for Birmingham, 16.6 percent for Chicago, 20.8 percent for Detroit, and 14.4 percent for Los Angeles (Reaves & Smith, 1995).

Police departments in the 1990s still hire and retain fewer women than the Equal Employment Opportunity Act allows. Women as a class generally have not fared as well from the legal changes as have minority men as a class. The Los Angeles Police Department illustrates this point. "By 1990 the number of blacks [sic] in the LAPD was 110 percent of their proportion of the work force in the region, the number of Hispanics was 72 percent of their proportion of the work force, and the number of women was 29 percent of their proportion in the work force" (Felkenes, Peretz & Schroedel, 1993, p. 44). Martin (1990) found that female police officers have higher turnover rates and shorter careers than men, with the women's turnover rate about 2 percent higher than men's. Women also have a higher rate of voluntary separations due to "family problems," because women still have most of the responsibility for child care and household duties. Shift work, uncertain demands for overtime due to court appearances and arrests, and weekend duties create difficulties in finding babysitters and caring for sick children (Martin, 1990). Pregnancy and maternity-related problems also create difficulties for women, because many departments do not have the possibility of assigning officers with disabilities to "light duty" and do not have family leave policies. Martin (1990) found that "more than half the departments give light-duty assignments to pregnant officers but agency practices vary significantly by city size. In 10 percent of the departments in large and medium-sized cities, there is no light duty, and pregnant officers are required to go on paid leave, then unpaid leave until after delivery; in 40 percent of the smaller departments there was no light duty available or no 'usual practice' because the problem of a pregnant officer had not yet arisen" (p. 136). Women, for personal reasons related to societal expectations about child care responsibility, often have shorter careers in policing than do men.

A second feature of exclusion that lowers the number of women who apply, are hired, and remain on the job as police officers are nonsexual and sexual harassment. Some women who are interested in a policing career do not apply to be police officers because they do not want to face the harassment and resistance of male officers (Martin, 1990). Other women become more motivated when faced with disparaging and discouraging remarks from male officers. Heidensohn (1992) describes a female radio dispatcher's experience: "We had a male chauvinist pig, with capital letters as a chief. . . . Women were fine as dispatchers, but not as police officers, well the academy was opening up . . . and I said, 'I want to go' as a jest, and strictly at this point, as a jest. And he says, 'You couldn't make it' and you know what that is to women . . . so here I went" (p. 163). Heidensohn (1992) describes another woman who received resistance when she picked up the application. This woman was not hired but men were. Eventually she was hired after she filed suit under the Equal Employment Opportunity Act.

Once women are hired, they face sexual harassment by some male officers and supervisors (Feinman, 1994; Martin, 1990). Sexual harassment takes many forms. Some male officers keep *Playboy* magazines lying around and sexually-explicit photographs on their desks or make sexually explicit jokes toward female officers (Martin, 1990). Other men make unwarranted sexual advances and requests for dates. For example, one female officer relates this experience: "One supervisor asked me to go out with him. I said, 'No, I don't date my boss.' Suddenly my work was no longer acceptable; he will not speak to me at all now. Up 'til last May, I had rave evaluations; all of a sudden, it changed. I was asked to go to another squad, saw the handwriting on the wall, and I did" (Martin, 1990, p. 145). Other men believe that they have the right to touch female officers and are surprised to find that female officers are angry about the lack of respect for their personal space. For example, "one white woman . . . responded angrily when one of her sergeants put his arm around her, saying 'if you want to put your hands on me, put me under arrest; otherwise, keep your hands off.' The sergeant, who was black, interpreted her response as racially motivated" (Martin, 1980, p. 150). Other men comment on women's uniforms and appearance out of uniform using implied sexual meanings or make explicit comments about female officers' breasts (Martin, 1980).

A third feature of exclusion is the refusal of male officers to train rookie female officers in the field. The most important training for rookies is field experience. During the first year, rookies are assigned to partners who are supposed to serve as field instructors and share knowledge about all aspects of patrol. Female police officers often find themselves ostracized by the male officers and must learn to handle situations without the advice and support of more-seasoned veterans. Research has found that, in some departments, men in the 1970s and early 1980s organized to avoid working with women by calling in sick when they were assigned to a woman partner, and when they had to work with women, they refused to talk to them (Martin, 1990). Today, the resistance is not organized, but many men still resist the integration of women into the profession.

Male officers create three obstacles for female rookie officers that lower the quality of their probationary field experience. First, male officers are quite willing to share information and teach skills to rookie male officers but often withhold information and refuse to teach skills to female officers (Martin, 1990). Female rookies must learn how to deal with angry citizens on their own, to learn the geography of the precinct, the technical reports, a variety of dangerous situations, and the informal norms of the department. Second, male officers will often complete tasks for women and will not allow them to acquire the hands-on experience they need to become comfortable with the job (Feinman, 1994). Third, male officers, if they do not like the female officers, will be slow to respond to a backup call and will be slow to respond when women officers are serving as decoys in stakeouts designed to catch johns, muggers, and rapists (Martin, 1990; Feinman, 1994).

> *Illustration:*   A supervisor/manager, 26–35, three to six years tenure, "big" department, from California: "You have to learn to become an island of your own. I have worked in other nontraditional jobs—I was a copper miner. Not a truck driver like the women hired before me were—I started with a pick and shovel and worked my way up so that I was supervising men that were twice my age. I was the first woman at this mine to do the jobs that I worked up to, and I proved that I could do it. Once I proved myself that was it. I was accepted. Not so [sic] the department I work for now. I have to prove to each and every officer that I can do the job" (Timmins & Hainsworth, 1989, p. 203).

As this woman's history suggests, female rookie officers often are isolated from the close police family that exists among male officers. This isolation creates training of unequal quality and places women in needless danger on the job. As women increase their numbers on patrol assignments, they can serve as field instructors for rookie female officers.

A fourth feature of exclusion is the type of job assignment women receive. Several researchers support the notion that women have more difficulty obtaining certain assignments than do men. Heidensohn (1992) reports, "In my own research, I found that women officers faced barriers to appointment as dog handlers, as mounted police, and as detectives" (p. 63). Martin (1990) found that women are less likely to be assigned to vice or investigative units because of the unit's prestige and possibly because women may find these assignments less attractive because of the extensive overtime and late hours.

One study surveyed 180 members of the International Association of Women Police; the researchers received a low return rate of 38 percent, which indicates cautions in generalizing their findings to the entire population of police women (Garrison, Grant & McCormick, 1988). This study, however, does indicate some discontent among at least some female police officers about their job assignments. Most policewomen surveyed had experienced uniform patrol (78.2 percent). Fewer had assignments to administrative services (35 percent), tactical units (31 percent), crimes against persons (19 percent), vice (14 percent), juvenile (11.7 percent), and crimes against property (5 percent). When asked whether they had the same opportunity for special training as male officers, 54 percent responded yes and 33 percent responded no. When asked whether they had the same opportunity for special assignments as male officers, the sample was more closely split with 45 percent responding yes and 41 percent responding no. Women who felt they had been denied certain job assignments because of their gender indicated that men had the advantage for certain assignments.

Illustration: One woman remarked, "Male officers seem to have early 'knowledge' of plush details such as Grand Prix, plain clothes evening details, convention details when convention is of special interest such as political, and are solely used for escorting celebrities." Another woman commented, "I was denied both K-9 and motorcycle patrol ('not for women') and although I set the highest shooting record ever recorded at the academy (99.2 average), shot on the pistol team, taught professionally and constantly outshoot any man on [sic] the department, I am still being denied training as a firearms instructor because the higher ups feel I wouldn't have control over an all-male department" (Garrison, Grant & McCormick, 1988, p. 69).

Other research supports the fact that men often have knowledge of plush details, because police departments do not post the opportunities but use word of mouth in the locker room to spread the information (Feinman, 1994).

Women's perceptions that men have the advantage in obtaining good assignments, however, are not generally supported by the male officers. A study of 175 male and 42 female officers in the Illinois State Police found that 84 percent of the male officers believed that women were given special assignments because of their sex (Weisheit, 1987). One male officer vividly describes the situation from his perspective: "From my point of view, in the last two years, it appears female troopers are getting better treatment than male troopers. Quick stripes and most other departments chase after them like a dog in heat, either trying to impress them, or just wanting their company. . . . If you're female everybody opens closed doors, to ensure instant job openings" (Weisheit, 1987, p. 142).

The view that women have a much easier time at obtaining special assignments is also echoed by some women, but these women note that typically the woman hired serves as a token; thus, when one woman is hired, departments are not as receptive to other female applicants. One woman's history of assignments illustrates this token status often acquired by female police officers, especially those in special units.

> *Illustration:* "I am the first female in the state police K-9 unit. Although others may have expressed a desire to transfer into the unit, they were usually talked out of it before actually applying. My acceptance was helped by the open-minded progressiveness of those in charge of the unit, although I feel a part of the decision may have been based on the fact that I am a woman. It's possible that I was accepted to avoid a charge of discrimination. I'm also one of the firearms instructors for the department. First female in the history of my department. A great deal of reverse discrimination occurs. I was a detective because I was a female. Usually one position is a token and males are denied it" (e.g., child abuse or often juvenile officers—one of three positions is a woman's) (Garrison, Grant & McCormick, 1988, p. 69).

This woman's career consisted of assignments in which she was the only woman in a certain position—not because other women did not want the assignment, but because the token slot for a woman had been filled. So for one position or some percentage of positions, qualified women may have an advantage over qualified men in order to meet the standards set by consent decrees or the standards implied by the Equal Employment Opportunity Act.

A fifth feature of exclusion is the low number of women who are promoted to higher positions and the difficulties they face in receiving such promotions. Women are making only slow progress toward being promoted to lower supervisory roles in the police hierarchy and are virtually nonexistent in the upper levels of management (Martin, 1990). From 1978 to 1986, the proportion of women in supervisory positions increased for every rank. As of 1986, across municipal departments in the United States, 3.7 percent of women held the rank of sergeant, 2.5 percent held the rank of lieutenant, and 1.4 percent held a rank above lieutenant (Martin, 1990). The percentage of women who held supervisory positions varied by the size of the city. A greater percentage of women held supervisory positions in cities with populations between 250,000 and 1,000,000 than for cities with less than 250,000 people or more than 1,000,000 people (Martin, 1990).

African American female officers are sometimes at a disadvantage in obtaining promotions because departmental rules, derived court orders, and affirmative action plans often count black women as women and not as minorities (Martin, 1994). For example, in the case of *U.S. v. City of Chicago* in 1973, the judge imposed quotas for promotion to sergeant because the exam was found to be discriminatory.

Black women "were represented by the Afro-American Police League and were initially drawn from the promotion list as blacks regardless of gender. When the white women realized some black women were being promoted to sergeant ahead of them, however, they filed a claim asserting that all females should be treated as a single minority group. The judge ruled that the black women could not be given double benefit" (Martin, 1994, p. 389).

The lawyer agreed to count African American women as women without consulting them. This decision put African American women at a disadvantage because they now had to compete with white women, who generally have higher test scores, whereas African American women generally have higher test scores than African American men (Martin, 1994).

Many women who have reached higher ranks have had to fight for their right to be promoted.

Illustration: Harrington's career summarizes the recent history of women in law enforcement. In January 1985, she became the first woman in the nation to head a large city's police department when the mayor appointed her chief of the 767-member Portland Police Bureau. A college graduate, Harrington joined the bureau in 1964 and worked her way up through the ranks. She held the titles of officer, sergeant, lieutenant, precinct captain, and detective before becoming chief. However, she did it the hard way. . . . She had filed numerous complaints in her continuous struggle to end discrimination based on sex and to end practices favoring men in the department (Feinman, 1994, p. 117).

Many women have had to fight for their promotions as Harrington did. Their struggle, however, has allowed some female officers in the 1990s to be promoted without a struggle and with the support of male colleagues (Feinman, 1994).

A sixth feature of exclusion is lack of acceptance by male officers. Numerous studies document that many male officers are unwilling to accept female officers as equals and as partners (Brown, 1994; Belknap & Shelley, 1993; Feinman, 1994; Felkenes & Schroedel, 1993; Heidensohn, 1992; Lunneborg, 1989; Martin, 1980, 1990, 1994). Research indicates that female officers perceive that they are better accepted now than they were a decade ago (Martin, 1994). A recent survey of male officers' attitudes suggests that about one-third of the officers still do not accept female officers. Brown (1994) conducted a survey of 280 male officers in police departments in the state of Washington. Based on a series of attitudinal items, Brown was able to classify officers along the dimension of their acceptance of female officers: "3 percent strongly accepted, 33 percent accepted, 40.3 percent split, 22.4 percent did not accept, and 1.5 percent strongly did not accept women into policing" (p. 51). At least 60 percent of officers did not want their wives to be police officers and did not think women could handle physical conflict. Forty-seven percent of officers would rather have a male backup on a dangerous call, thirty-nine percent would rather have a male sergeant, and 32 percent want a male partner in the same patrol car. The majority of officers (at least 55 percent) believed women were capable of performing all the requirements of patrol work. Men clearly vary in their view toward female police officers.

Martin (1990) has a four-category classification scheme to capture differences among men in their attitudes toward women. The four categories are traditional, principled moderates, individualistic moderates, and moderns. Traditionalists strongly oppose the integration of female officers and adhere to an "aggressive policing." Traditionalists are angry at and critical of female officers, because they believe female officers have undermined the cohesion of the police and are physically weaker, not aggressive, and undependable, all of which does not adhere to the style of "aggressive policing." Somewhat more accepting of women are the moderates. Principled moderates agree that women should have an equal opportunity to be police officers but were not very comfortable working with women. Individualistic moderates did not accept women as a group but sometimes accepted individual female officers who proved themselves to be good cops. Moderns are the most accepting of women. They believed masculinity included sensitivity and did not require a show of strength. Moderns regarded "the less aggressive style of policing characteristic of women officers as an asset rather than a liability" (Martin, 1990, p. 149). Martin (1990) notes that most male officers she interviewed in the late 1970s were traditionalists, the rest were moderates, and a few were moderns; in the late 1980s she found that the proportion and influence of traditionalists had diminished and the proportion of moderates and moderns had increased.

Lack of acceptance by male officers often translates into female officers constantly having to prove themselves and into women officers facing discriminatory treatment in evaluations, promotions, and assistance from fellow officers. Women in the 1990s continue to perceive the pressure of having to prove themselves (Feinman, 1994; Felkenes & Schroedel, 1993; Belknap & Shelley, 1993).

> *Illustration:*   A woman detective on the force in Arizona stated: "I love being a 'cop' but male officers (not all) talk down to the women and you continue to have to 'prove yourself' to some. It's tiring after nine years. You battle with the public ten hours a day, and battle with the 'brass' every time you turn around. I wonder a lot if it's worth it. The rewards aren't there enough— negatives outweigh positives" (Timmins & Hainsworth, 1989, p. 203).

Female officers compared to male officers also may be faced with greater scrutiny when situations get out of hand. One female officer relates a story about a shooting, which illustrates the double standard that female officers sometimes face.

> *Illustration:*   "Years ago there was a female officer that, her partner got hurt, shot, and she missed the suspect when she shot. She was almost crucified in this department. Two weeks ago we had a male officer that missed the suspect. He shot twice and missed the suspect. And there hasn't been said one thing about it, not one thing. Maybe the times have changed, but I think that if it happened to a female officer again, they would crucify her. . . . A couple of years ago, we had a female officer, her partner got shot. . . . She did manage to hit the suspect, and you hear comments, 'Well, I'm surprised it was

a woman.' They were much more meticulous in analyzing that shooting than if it had been two male officers" (Heidensohn, 1992, p. 185).

The many facets of exclusion of women from policing have changed in the past twenty years. Women have made some increases in successfully completing academy training, being hired, being promoted, obtaining special job assignments, and being accepted by male officers. Women, however, still face too much harassment and too much resistance, and lack of acceptance. In the next section, we will examine the issues and problems that have arisen for female officers and the issues that have arisen for police departments as female officers are included in the force.

PROBLEMS AND ISSUES ASSOCIATED WITH FEMALE OFFICERS

Female officers face several problems on the job. Some of these problems have already been covered, including sexual and nonsexual harassment, lack of acceptance by male officers, and barriers to promotion. Some problems associated with lack of acceptance by male officers deserve further exploration; these problems are male officers' perceptions that female officers are less competent, whether women have different role styles than men, and stress associated with the job. Female officers also worry about whether the public fully accepts them as equally competent as male officers. In addition, the presence of women on the police force creates problems for the organization, including police officers' social status, work norms, and group solidarity among officers.

Actual Competence of Women

Many male officers believe that women are less competent than men at handling violent situations and at performing patrolling duties. Several studies have compared men and women on their performance at a variety of policing duties and skills. These studies generally assess performance using field observations, though some research has also used archival data, evaluations by supervisors, and surveys of citizens. Steel and Lovrich (1987) compared cities in which women composed less than 3 percent of the force to cities in which women composed more than 3 percent. They found no difference between cities with low utilization of women and cities with high utilization of women on the rate of crime, the operating costs, or the clearance rates. These findings suggest that women do not appreciably change the overall performance of departments. Studies conducted in nine law enforcement agencies between 1973 and 1978 also indicate that "women can perform the duties traditionally assigned to men and as effectively as men. They also indicated that men are in no more danger with women as partners than with men as partners" (Feinman, 1994, p. 110). Consistent with research studies in Washington, D.C., New York City, and St. Louis County, Snortum and Beyers (1983) found no difference between male and female officers in El Monte, California, on traffic stops, pedestrian checks, vehicle stops, or other patrolling observations. Supervisors in small town police departments also rated a sample of 30 women and 30 men as having equal performance on eleven measures (Bartol et al., 1992).

The nine studies conducted in the 1970s, however, did report some gender differences. For example, several studies showed women to be less proficient in the use of firearms and to have more accidents. Other studies showed that male officers received more citizens' complaints, were more willing to use their guns, and met more resistance than did female officers (Felkenes, 1991; for a review, see Lunneborg, 1989; Morash & Greene, 1986). The interpretation of these differences, however, is plagued by design shortcomings. For example, researchers often failed to adjust for findings of differences due to chance, focused on stereotypical male traits, and used a variety of definitions of what constitutes good performance (Morash & Greene, 1986).

Role Style of Women

Male officers believe that policing requires toughness, bravery, and physical strength. Studies have found that female compared to male officers have a lower arrest rate (e.g., Bloch & Anderson, 1974a,b; Sherman, 1975; for a review, see Martin, 1980). The majority of female officers (81 percent) in one survey also reported that women's style of policing differs from men's style, and that female and male officers handle calls differently. From responses to open-ended questions, the most frequent perceived differences were that female officers are more communicative, less violent, and more respectful toward citizens (Belknap & Shelley, 1993).

Women and men, however, are very similar in the way they see their clientele, their departments, and their roles (Worden, 1993). Both female and male officers were "ambivalent about restrictions on their autonomy and the definition of their role, only mildly positive about their public clientele, complimentary of their colleagues, and unenthusiastic about working conditions and supervisors" (Worden, 1993, p. 229). Female and male officers also have similar levels of cynicism toward the public and their job (Felkenes, 1991; Worden, 1993). Women and men, moreover, have a similar attitude about the importance of arrest (Davis, 1984). Thus, differences in attitudes cannot account for differences in observed behavior.

Several studies, based on agreement to closed-ended questions, also have found that women and men have similar reasons for choosing policing (for a review, see Meagher & Yentes, 1986). Females place importance on service to people, job security, and salary. Female officers place more importance on salary, benefits, and job security, and less importance on career advancement and challenges (as they acquire more experience) (Poole & Pogrebin, 1988). When asked to rank reasons or choose the primary reason, Felkenes and Schroedel (1993) found that a greater number of men than women cited job security as the primary reason, whereas a greater number of women than men cited salary as the primary reason. Other research finds that a greater number of men than women place more importance on job security than service to people, whereas a greater number of women than men place more importance on service to people than on job security (Weisheit, 1987).

Though comparisons between men and women yield few overall differences, female officers show a great deal of variation in how they handle the status inconsistency between the role required by sex-role norms and the role required by occupational norms. Hochschild (1973) characterized women along a dimension of defeminized to deprofessionalized. Defeminized female officers minimized gender differences and attempted to become equal to male officers. Deprofessionalized women emphasized their femininity, did not try to become one of the boys, and accepted receiving treatment and exemptions appropriate for a woman. Martin (1980) describes a similar continuum anchored at one end by POLICEwomen, who emphasize occupational role obligations, and anchored at the other end by policeWOMEN, who emphasize meeting sex role norms while on the job. POLICEwomen, similar to male officers, see their role as the enforcement of laws and the protection of lives and property. POLICEwomen place importance on carrying their fair share of the work and doing their job like male officers. POLICEwomen realize the fact that they must work harder to prove themselves and that they must sometimes become physical. By contrast, policeWOMEN adopt a service-oriented perspective, and make fewer arrests. PoliceWOMEN are "content to attain personal acceptance, willingly acquiescing to the stereotypic roles into which they are cast by men" (Martin, 1980, p. 196). Other research has also supported the continuum between an emphasis on professionalism and an emphasis on sex-role norms (Wexler, 1985).

Additional Stress

Women often face unique sources of stress that men do not. These unique stressors include negative attitudes of male officers toward them, sexual and nonsexual harassment, and being the token female officer in small departments (Yarmey, 1990). Two studies, one conducted in small town police departments and the other conducted in municipal departments, found that men and women reported similar amounts of stress (Bartol et al., 1992; Davis, 1984). One study, however, has found that women experience more physical and psychological symptoms from stress than do men (Silbert, 1982). Moreover, women apparently derive more positive feelings from their lives outside of the department, whereas men derive more positive feelings from their job than from their outside lives (Silbert, 1982).

However, the source of job stress differs. Wexler and Logan (1983) discovered that the primary sources of stress that women experienced were organizational and related to their lack of integration into the police force. The primary sources of women's stress were lack of promotional opportunities, inadequate training, and rumors about them. In addition, women mentioned the negative attitudes of male officers, generalizations by male officers about their ability based on the performance of other female officers, and the lack of female role models.

Several studies have also found that women and men differ in the amount of stress they derive from certain tasks. Women, compared to men, experienced more stress from the constant danger to themselves and colleagues (Bartol et al., 1992; Davis, 1984; Pendergrass & Ostrove, 1984). Women, compared to men, also had more stress associated with the frequent exposure to tragedy and the responsibility of saving lives (Bartol et al., 1992; Pendergrass & Ostrove, 1984).

The most consistent difference in performance between male and female officers is that male officers may receive more citizens' complaints and may be more willing to use their guns. Job burnout may account in part for this difference. Johnson (1991) surveyed more than 700 police officers employed in two major eastern cities about stress and job satisfaction. Both men and women had similar levels of job burnout but handled this burnout differently. Female officers were more likely to report fatigue and difficulty facing their job day after day, whereas male officers "were more likely to externalize their burnout by treating citizens like impersonal objects or becoming callous toward people" (p. 15). Stress and burnout may be handled quite differently by men and women. Women obtain relief from stress by disclosing problems to their spouses and colleagues, while men are less likely to disclose their stress (Ellison & Genz, 1983).

Public Acceptance

Research in the 1970s and 1980s suggests that the majority of the public accepts female police officers and perceives them as competent as men in performing certain duties but less competent in performing other duties. A 1975 survey of residents in a Midwest city clarifies further whether the public perceives women to be as competent as men in performing the duties of a police officer (Kerber, Andes & Mittler, 1977). Over half of the sample had no preference as to whether male or female officers handled most situations, while 38 percent preferred male officers. When the public perceives a difference in competence between male and female officers, it is in the direction of stereotypes about gender roles: Men are perceived as stronger and more aggressive and therefore better able to handle fist fights, whereas women are seen as more nurturing and therefore better with handling young children and rape victims. Patrolling and answering calls for assistance generated the most disagreement among respondents (Kerber, Andes & Mittler, 1977). For patrolling in a squad car, 55 percent believed that men were more competent and 42 percent believed that men and women were equally competent. For answering calls for personal assistance, 45 percent believed men were more competent than women, while 49 percent believed men and women to be equally competent. A survey conducted after encounters with male or female officers also revealed that, overall, citizens were equally satisfied and had similar respect for female and male officers. Citizens also believed that women and men were equally capable of handling patrol situations, except for violent situations. Male officers were perceived to be more able to handle violent situations, and two male partners were perceived as more capable of handling dangerous, angry, and upset citizens than were teams consisting of a male officer and a female officer

(Block, Anderson & Gervais, 1973). In summary, the public appears skeptical of women's abilities to handle violent situations and shows wide disagreement about women's abilities to handle routine police work such as patrolling and answering calls for assistance.

People from different gender, education, and age backgrounds have different perceptions about the competence of female officers. Senior citizens were overwhelmingly skeptical of women's ability to answer calls for assistance or patrolling, with only 17 percent indicating that women and men were equally competent to handle calls or patrol neighborhoods. As with other stereotypes in criminal justice, education also was strongly related to public perceptions. About half of high school educated or college educated respondents indicated that men and women are equally competent at patrolling or answering calls, whereas only 23 percent of respondents without a high school education perceived equal competence. In addition, men were more likely to judge female officers as more competent in these traditional female roles than were women.

Male Officers' Social Status

Martin (1980) provides a succinct description of how the integration of women may threaten male officers' social status. Even without the integration of women into policing, male officers are insecure about whether their occupation puts them in the working class or the middle class. They, of course, desire to be in the middle class. Officers recognize that the public is ambivalent toward them, which further denies them the prestige that they desire. As Martin (p.101) notes, "despite the fact that the officer has power over our highest social values (life and honor, liberty and justice) policing remains a tainted occupation, and the officer is regarded as someone who does society's dirty work" (Skolnick, 1966; Bittner, 1970; Manning, 1977). Female officers further threaten male officers' perceptions of their social status in two ways. First, when women are recruited into an occupation, the occupation generally suffers a decline in prestige. The presence of female officers challenges men's attitudes about gender, such as "a woman's place is in the home taking care of the children." Second, female officers threaten men's image of policing as requiring toughness, physical strength, and bravery, characteristics that men generally attribute to their masculinity. Male officers, thus, feel they are denied professional status and that women threaten to take away the public's image that police officers are an "object of fear, someone with authority, a man to be reckoned with" (Martin, 1980, p. 101).

Hunt (1984) describes the threat to male officers' public image:

Policemen . . . oppose the "moral woman" . . . because she represents the exposure of an informal world of policing on which masculine gender is based. In addition, her presence signifies the exposure of the "police myth" . . . which conceals the demeaning nature of the "private" occupation and maintains the policeman's public image as a successful crime fighter. Symbolically, then, she reminds him that he can only achieve illusory manhood by denying and repressing the essential feminine dimension of police work, which involves social relations, paper work, and housekeeping in the public domain (p. 294).

Male officers, thus, perceive female officers as a threat to their public image as crime fighters.

Work Norms

Police officers obviously rely heavily on each other for protection. Male officers believe that they must protect female officers and that female officers do not provide adequate protection for them (Feinman, 1994; Heidensohn, 1992; Martin, 1980). Male officers voice concern that women's lack of authority with male criminals will also affect their own authority. As one officer noted: "Who's going to listen to a small woman? Small men are different. The men on the street know he means business and will put them in jail. He has a masculine way of conveying authority" (Martin, 1980, p. 94). Because male officers resent women's presence and believe that they do not carry their fair share of the workload, male officers often are slow to respond for calls of backup or when women are serving as decoys (Martin, 1990; Feinman, 1994). Thus, the presence of women serves to disrupt the work norms of backing up one's partner.

"The rule of maintaining respect is also threatened by patrolwomen. Maintaining respect is central to police work yet, as many recognize, the authority of the uniform and the office are often insufficient; the officer's personal authority and manner of conveying it are involved in gaining citizen compliance" (Martin, 1980, p. 94). Male officers also believe that women will not be assertive enough toward citizens when citizens challenge their authority (Martin, 1980). If female officers do not demand respect from citizens, citizens may also conclude that they can be disrespectful toward male officers. In addition, male officers believe that female officers will be unable to handle fights and that they will have to do it. Women are seen as substantially weaker and hesitant about using force. The work norm of being able and willing to get physical is disrupted by the presence of policewomen. One officer stated: "Women can't hold their own end in fights. I'm no babysitter. Equal pay means an equal amount of work. No woman performs the same way or amount as a male. . . . Women are physically inadequate . . . not mentally but physically, and this job is both mental and physical." Even in dealing with problems with other officers, male officers often resort to threats of violence. Male officers, however, cannot resort to threats of violence against women and still retain their masculine image. Thus, female officers also change the rules on how problems with colleagues are handled (Martin, 1980).

In summary, the resistance of male officers to the integration of women in policing often disrupts work norms. Male officers believe that the presence of female officers disrupts the norms of commanding respect from citizens, eagerness to handle a physical situation, and protecting one's partner. Men base their perceptions of women's response on gender stereotypes rather than on how women actually respond to the situation.

Solidarity Among Officers

The police culture emphasizes the importance of camaraderie and a cohesive community among officers. Male officers can develop a bond with each other, because they often enjoy similar outside interests such as sports, hunting, fishing, and working on automobiles (Martin, 1980). Because many police officers come from working class backgrounds, they learn that men cannot develop close nonsexual relationships with women (Martin, 1980). Female officers thus are excluded from the group, and the police force becomes less of a cohesive group. Sometimes this exclusion takes extreme forms. For example, "Black and female officers have complained about the existence of a clique that went by two different names, White Anglo Saxon Police (WASP) or Men Against Women. The first black female rookie assigned to the station claimed . . . that one officer, possibly as part of his initiation rite into the clique, doused her with gasoline" (Felkenes & Schroedol, 1993, p. 82).

Women also often do not form strong bonds with other female officers, because they disagree about what an officer's role should be and what relationship they should have with male officers (Martin, 1994). They also compete with each other for promotions and merit raises. These disagreements and competition contribute to women's reluctance to organize and unite to eliminate gender biases. As Martin (1994) notes,

> a few of the women belong to state or national women's law enforcement organizations, but efforts to organize the women in their own agencies have been short-lived or sporadic. Chicago is the only case study site with an active (but still fledgling) departmental women officers' organization, the Coalition of Law Enforcement Officers (CLEO). . . . Commenting on a recent meeting held by CLEO, one white Chicago officer admiringly observed: "White women won't be organized. [At the CLEO meeting] they were talking about day care! . . . White women have the housewife's syndrome; many black women are single, used to running a family, and are more assertive. . . . Black women have much more consciousness of abuse; white women are less aware of abuse as women" (p. 396).

Martin (1980) describes several ways that women disrupt the solidarity among male officers. The presence of women inhibits men from bonding through telling off-color stories about physical and sexual prowess and from using physical means to settle differences. The presence of women also makes it more likely that men's own sentimentality and emotional failures will be exposed. "The presence of women [also] disturbs the informal distribution of rewards based on the 'buddy system,' in which all compete on the same basis. The men become upset by the fact that women can—and a few policewomen do—gain exemptions and favorable assignments by taking 'unfair advantage' of their sex" (p. 99).

CAUSES OF EXCLUSION

Individual, sociological, and organizational factors contribute to men's resistance, harassment, and negative attitudes toward female officers and explain the under-representation of women in policing. This section briefly describes some of the central known causes for exclusion of women officers.

Individual Contributors

Individual contributors to the exclusion of women include men's attitudes toward women and their stereotypes about sex roles. Sex role stereotypes are beliefs about the appropriate roles and behavior for women. Research has found that male officers generally perceive female officers "as being too soft, too weak, too emotional, and too irrational for contemporary street policing" (Lord, 1986, p. 89). These stereotypes fuel police officers' resistance and negative attitudes toward female officers. One officer provides a clear example of how stereotypes can produce resistance:

> People like myself were brought up in a gracious style of dealing with women; we don't want our women to dirty their hands or do anything strenuous. . . . Guys my age (30) think it's more acceptable for women to work . . . as doctors and teachers. . . . Policing continues to be very physical. A lower percentage of females can do the job. . . . You know, very few women can shoot another person without some hesitation. I don't know many women who will be able to take a preemptive strike. The female mental make-up is slightly different from the male's (Martin, 1990, pp. 149–150).

The influence of gender stereotypes extends to how references for job candidates describe their candidates' characteristics. An analysis of the content of reference letters revealed that "levelheaded" was used to describe male candidates more often than female candidates. Intelligence and a sense of humor were qualities attributed only to male candidates, whereas good moral values, dedicated, and reliable were qualities attributed only to female candidates (Walklate, 1992). Women were more likely to be described as having good moral values because the male referees used this characteristic more often than did female referees. These different images of men and women in reference letters suggest that gender stereotypes affect both the public image of female officers and the departments' image of officers. Sex role stereotypes, as noted earlier, may also contribute to the ambivalence in public perception about the competence of police women to patrol in a squad car and to answer calls for assistance.

Sociological Contributors

Several sociological theories have been proposed to explain why women are harassed in male-dominated occupations and to explain why men resist the full integration of women into a male-dominated occupation such as policing. Gender identification theory attributes men's resistance to sex role stereotypes that they learned in early childhood (Berg & Budnick, 1986). Gender identification theory also can account for why few women apply to be police officers. Women do not apply because their early childhood training teaches them that policing is dangerous and should be men's work (Martin, 1980). Martin (1980) states,

> Many occupations, particularly those offering the greatest income, prestige, and power, call for qualities that are antithetical to the female role and femininity. Most women resolve the potential normative conflict between "appropriate" occupational role and sex role behavior by engaging in jobs in which the tasks involve service to or nurture of others and in which they are subordinate of men (p. 17).

Role theory also assumes that women and men are socialized during childhood about appropriate roles for women and men. "Role theory argues that resistance to women results from a conflict between norms associated with sexual status and occupational roles. . . . Men resolve the ambiguity of women's presence [in policing] by placing them into stereotypic categories such as 'seductress,' 'mother,' or 'lesbian'" (Hunt, 1990, p. 4). Men categorize women into certain stereotypes, because the categorization process resolves the conflict between their gender and their occupational choice and allows men to respond to women using a set of prior beliefs.

Hunt (1990) notes that one limitation of role theory is that it undermines the possible economic reasons behind men's resistance. Two theories, socialist feminism and conflict theory, assert that the primary motivation for men's resistance is to protect their occupational territory and their occupational prestige. Socialist feminist theorists. "argue that sexist ideology functions to legitimate the exclusion of women from high paying 'men's work' and binds them to the home and feminine spheres within the labor market. Sex segregation and the reproduction of gendered institutional structures contribute to the expansion of capital because women provide a reserve army of cheap labor" (Hunt, 1990, p. 5). Conflict theory argues that the powerful members of society (generally white males) make laws and rules to keep the less powerful members (women and minorities) in their place and to protect their own property and position.

Several researchers have advanced a tokenism explanation for why women experience harassment and discrimination in the workplace. Tokens are a single member or a relatively small group of persons who have some characteristic, such as their race or gender, which is different from the majority of workers in an occupation. The tokenism explanation suggests that harassment and discrimination occur because of the small number of women in policing, not because of their gender per se. Kanter (1977) found that token women in male-dominated corporations had to "work twice as hard and expend more energy than the average man to succeed, and in the process felt highly visible and isolated from peers" (p. 207). Researchers have acknowledged that tokenism may account for women's small growth in policing and their inability to overcome male resistance (Belknap & Shelley, 1993; Martin, 1980). Belknap and Shelley (1993) found some support for the tokenism explanation in their survey data from female officers. They compared women in departments where women constituted less than 10 percent of the force (tokens) to women in departments where women constituted more than 10 percent of the force (nontokens). Token female officers were more likely to feel that they were only noticed when they had done a good job and were more likely to report and were more likely to believe that fellow officers saw them as women first than were nontoken female officers.

Organizational Contributors

Several factors associated with organizational practices also contribute to lower-than-expected hiring and retention rates. First, many women never receive information or exposure to policing that will entice them to consider it as a career. Across departments, women typically represent between 13 and 22 percent of the pool of applicants (Kay, 1994). Police departments who have open positions often do not actively attempt to recruit female applicants, which contributes to the low number of qualified female applicants. Timmins and Hainsworth (1989) found that many of the women who completed police officers standards and training (POST) academies were unsure why they were selected and were uncertain how training related to police work. These findings suggest that "POST academies need to be more open and specific concerning law enforcement as a career for women" (p. 201). Women who seek careers in policing typically learn about the job of a police officer either through family members who are police officers or through taking a civilian job in a police department and observing police officers (Heidensohn, 1992).

Another organizational barrier that contributes to the lower hiring and retention rate is police academy training. "One of the primary mechanisms for keeping out women is academy training. Failing women and minorities during training allows one to preserve the myth of open access without having to alter the composition of the permanent force" (Felkenes, Peretz & Schroedel, 1993, p. 44). Women generally have a higher failure rate from the police academy than do men. For example, in the Los Angeles Police Department (LAPD) between 1976 and 1980, 59 percent of the women failed academy training, whereas only 20 percent of Caucasian men failed academy training. After the LAPD implemented changes to their academy training as part of a consent decree, the average failure rate in the period 1981 to 1988 was 29 percent for women and 18 percent for men (Felkenes, Peretz & Schroedel, 1993). Changes to the physical strength tests and the implementation of preacademy programs have begun to close the gap between failure rates of men and women (Felkenes, Peretz & Schroedel, 1993). Minorities and women can now participate in programs that prepare them for academy training. Women who participate have twice the likelihood of successfully completing academy training, compared to women who do not participate (Felkenes, Peretz & Schroedel, 1993). In an evaluation of Michigan State Police academy training in 1977, Charles (1981) found that women and men had similar academic performance, achievement in performing technical skills, boxing ability, and aggressiveness. Instructors, however, rated women as demonstrating lower ability and aggressiveness at defensive tactics. "Male recruits reported that, while the females showed a willingness to strike and be struck without retreating, male recruits, overall, are stronger and more capable in a fighting situation" (Charles, 1981, p. 216).

Male recruits entered the academy with the belief that women are physically weaker and that men perform better in tasks that require physical strength; these beliefs did not change at the end of their academy training (Charles, 1981). Women recruits, however, did not agree that men were superior to women in handling physically demanding tasks. Because of men's beliefs about women's ability, men undergoing training often indicate to women that they are not welcomed and block their integration into the group. In the 1990s, training academies are also hiring women instructors who can serve as important role models for women trainees and provide support to women officers (Heidensohn, 1992).

Another organizational barrier is that some police departments still do not have affirmative action policies for hiring and promotion. Research shows that affirmative action policies improve both the hiring and retention rate of female officers. Martin (1991) analyzed survey data collected from 446 municipal departments in 1986. She compared departments that had voluntary affirmative action policies, departments that had court-ordered affirmative action policies, and departments that did not have any affirmative action policy. She found that the presence of affirmative action policies significantly increased the number of women on the force and the number of female supervisors on the force even after other explanatory concepts were controlled. "At the end of 1986, women made up 10.1 percent of the sworn personnel in agencies under court order to increase the representation of women and minorities, 8.3 percent of the sworn officers in agencies with voluntary affirmative action plans, and only 6.1 percent of personnel in agencies without any affirmative action plan" (Martin, 1991, p. 493). The presence of affirmative action plans also increased the proportion of women among all applicants and the proportion of female applicants accepted as recruits. Affirmative action plans, however, did not affect the rate at which women were promoted to sergeant. The commitment and organized effort to achieve equality for women are important in reducing exclusion of women from policing. Other organizational barriers for retaining women include lack of maternity leave policies, lack of available day care, and shift work (Martin, 1990).

SOLUTIONS

Men's resistance to the integration of women in policing is a longstanding and complex problem. Simple solutions to this problem do not exist. However, police departments have made progress in increasing the number of women who are hired, retained, and promoted. In order for progress to continue, departments must address the causes of men's resistance and negative attitudes toward women. Departments can implement several organizational policies to create an equitable, fair, and non-hostile environment for female officers. First and foremost, departments should establish and follow affirmative action programs that allow women who have qualifications equal to men to be hired and promoted. Police officers should receive training on EEOC guidelines. Second, organizations must remove barriers that discourage and discriminate against female officers.

One clear hurdle women must overcome to enter policing is academy training. Some departments have made much progress in providing women with an equal chance to complete academy training. The failure rates for women and men are much closer now because departments provide women with the opportunity to complete a preacademy training program, have lower height and weight requirements, and have trained some women to be trainers in the academies. To further increase women's chances for successful completion of academy training, departments should encourage women to take additional training in self-defense tactics or karate (Martin, 1990). Female leaders and instructors are especially important during academy and field training because these women can help female rookies develop skills and confidence (Martin, 1990). Academy training should also include a course that challenges male officers' sex role stereotypes and negative attitudes toward women. Research suggests that instructions about how stereotypes bias evaluations of job performance and hiring decisions may reduce the biasing nature of these stereotypes (see Fiske & Taylor, 1991).

Departments can also implement clear policies that prohibit sexual and nonsexual harassment. In order to be effective, departments must specify adequate sanctions for sexual harassment and consistently enforce a policy that prohibits sexual and nonsexual harassment. Female officers can also reduce harassment and sexual harassment once appropriate policies are in place by making complaints against offenders. When one woman is willing to complain and the complaint is taken seriously by the department, this reaction encourages other women to come forward with complaints against men who are harassing them. Martin (1990) describes one such success story told by a female sergeant:

> A male officer made an obscene gesture to me just after I'd made sergeant. The department righted the wrong quick and fired him. . . . When he made that gesture to me, I brought it to my supervisor's attention; they investigated, and found he'd been doing it for years. Women try to get accepted; they don't want to make waves. Once I brought it to light . . . then other victims came forth (p. 154).

Women often threaten to file grievances to obtain some redress for the injuries, and these threats have often been successful (Martin, 1990). Establishment and enforcement of a policy may not curtail sexual harassment. In addition, departments should establish commitment-based training programs (Tomman & Serritella, 1994). In commitment-based training,

> the trainer involves individuals in a participative learning process where they examine the underlying cultural values and beliefs that influence their socio-sexual interactions at work. The ultimate objective is to create shared commitment to a harassment-free environment. This is accomplished by establishing shared meanings and definitions of sexual harassment, common understanding about the human toll and institutional implications, and a diverse set of communal responses to remedy and prevent sexual harassment incidents (Tomman & Serritella, 1994, p. 32).

In addition, supervisors and line managers should receive additional training on how to respond to sexual and nonsexual harassment (Tomman & Serritella, 1994).

Another problem that contributes to women leaving a policing career is conflict between work and family life. Departments can take several steps to reduce the conflict between an officer's work life and his or her family life. Departments can implement family leave policies for pregnancy, adoption of a child, care of an infirm family member, or death in the family. These policies should allow women and men to take unpaid leaves of absence and should also provide a specified paid leave of absence period. The Family Leave Act implemented by the federal government requires that organizations allow three days for death in the immediate family and allow workers to obtain an unpaid leave of absence for births. In addition, departments need maternity policies that allow women to be assigned to light duty (Martin, 1990). Moreover, "departments should review their shift rotation policy in order to make it more compatible with the family needs of officers" (Martin, 1990, p. 170).

Female officers often do not hear about plush details or opportunities for special assignments because they are not in the inner circle. Departments can eliminate this problem by posting openings for special assignments. In additions, departments should have clearly written criteria for the selection to special assignments and should conduct periodic audits to ensure that the selection criteria are being used in decisions to ensure that women are not disproportionally being assigned to clerical duties and to other stereotypic female assignments such as a juvenile unit (Martin, 1990).

Departments can also take more initiative in informing potential applicants that policing is an appropriate career option for women. Female and male police officers can visit high schools and provide informative lectures about policing and the requirements to become a police officer. This educational approach may increase the number of women who apply to become police officers. Departments should also make efforts to increase the number of women who are promoted. Departments can give all officers eligible for promotion written notification of the date of the promotion exam and a sign-up period at least several months in advance (Martin, 1990).

From the 1970s to the 1990s, female officers have made great progress. A greater number of female officers hold supervisory positions, compared to the number of female supervisors a decade ago. Women who obtain promotions feel more empowered to challenge discriminatory treatment, which should help female patrol officers (Martin, 1990). Moreover, as the number of women increases in departments, tokenism theory suggests that harassment and discrimination should decrease. Several additional steps should be taken to ensure that female officers become fully integrated members. Departments should encourage female officers to form support groups, mentor relationships, and to facilitate participation in state and national organizations such as the International Association of Women Police and the National Organization of Black Women in Law Enforcement (Martin, 1990). As the number of women increases on the force and women become more empowered to challenge discriminatory treatment, men's resistance to women will begin to crumble. Much of the burden of fully integrating women into policing, however, rests with departments. Perhaps then a greater number of departments will begin to implement policies that can remove the barriers that block women's integration into policing.

SUMMARY

Female officers are still underrepresented in police departments and are under-represented in supervisory positions. Though some progress has been made during the 1980s and 1990s, much more work remains to fully integrate women into policing. Some male officers still resist the inclusion of women, hold negative attitudes toward female officers, and harass female officers in an attempt to keep policing an all-male occupation. However, the tide has clearly turned, and male officers are ultimately fighting a battle that cannot be won: Women have the legal right to be officers and now have the motivation and determination to fight for that right. The future should see an increase in the number of female officers who are hired, retained, and promoted.

Men's resistance to female officers, does raise several problems for women. Female officers face additional stress owing to harassment and discrimination by male officers. Female officers also must continuously prove themselves and are under much more scrutiny than male officers. Even though officers learn from first-hand experience that some female officers are competent, they conclude that women are not as competent as men because they generalize from the few female officers who make mistakes. Research further shows that female officers are as equally effective as male officers. Female officers also have the difficult task of trying to address the per-ceived conflict between their chosen occupational role and their prescribed sex role.

The presence of female officers also raises issues for departments. In particular, the presence of female officers has disrupted the solidarity among officers. Depart-ments can take several steps to increase the solidarity among all officers and reduce incidents of nonsexual and sexual harassment. First, all officers should receive commitment-based training on sexual and nonsexual harassment and should receive training on how inaccurate stereotypes influence their interactions with each other. Second, departments should establish clear policies and should consistently enforce these policies. Third, departments should establish policies that reduce the conflict between an officer's work life and family life.

The integration of women in policing is a long and slow process. It requires chal-lenging sex role stereotypes. As boys and girls are socialized to appreciate and acquire both expressive and instrumental skills, fewer individuals will judge officers based primarily on their gender. Martin (1990) found that fewer men held traditional atti-tudes about women's roles in the 1980s compared to the number of men who held tra-ditional attitudes about women's roles in the 1970s. In addition, as female officers and supervisors become more prevalent on the force, they can begin to change poli-cies by voicing discontent about the discrimination and harassment of women. Suc-cess stories for female officers have already occurred, and hopefully the trend will be that these success stories will multiply.

DISCUSSION QUESTIONS

1. How similar are women to men in how they approach policing, especially confrontational encounters with citizens?
2. Do you think female police officers, compared to male police officers, are more responsive and sympathetic toward battered women?
3. Do you think men's resistance toward women is better explained by individual characteristics or by features of the organization?
4. Will female officers gain more equity in pay and assignments if they band together?
5. In trying to reduce harassment by men, should female officers emphasize how they are similar to men or should they emphasize how they are different from men?

REFERENCES

Appier, J. (1992). Preventive justice: The campaign for women police, 1910–1940. *Women and Criminal Justice, 4,* 3–36.

Bartol, C.R., Bergen, G.T., Volckens, J.S., & Knoras, K.M. (1992). Women in small town policing: Job performance and stress. *Criminal Justice and Behavior, 19,* 240–259.

Belknap, J., & Shelley, J.K. (1993). The new lone ranger: Policewomen on patrol. *American Journal of Police, 12,* 47–75.

Berg, B.L., & Budnick, K.J. (1986). Defeminization in law enforcement: A new twist in the traditional police personality. *Journal of Police Science and Administration, 14,* 314–319.

Bittner, E. (1970). *The functions of police in modern society.* Chevy Chase, MD: National Institute of Mental Health.

Bloch, P.B., & Anderson, D. (1974a). *Policewomen on patrol: Final report: Methodology, tables, and instruments.* Washington, D.C.: Urban Institute.

Bloch, P.B., & Anderson, D. (1974b). *Policewomen on patrol: Final report.* Washington, D.C.: Urban Institute.

Bloch, P.B., Anderson, D., & Gervais, P. (1973). *D.C. Policewomen evaluation vol. III: Major findings: First report.* Washington, D.C.: Urban Institute.

Brown, M.C. (1994). The plight of female police: A survey of NW patrolmen. *The Police Chief, 61*(9), 50–53.

Charles, M.T. (1981). The performance and socialization of female recruits in the Michigan State Police Training Academy. *Journal of Police Science and Administration, 9,* 209–223.

Davis, J.A. (1984). Perspectives of policewomen in Texas and Oklahoma. *Journal of Police Science and Administration, 12,* 395–403.

Ellison, K.W., & Genz, J.L. (1983). *Stress and the police officer.* Springfield, IL: Charles C. Thomas.

Feinman, C. (1994). *Women in the criminal justice system.* Westport, CT: Praeger.

Felkenes, G.T. (1991). Affirmative action in the Los Angeles Police Department. *Criminal Justice Research Bulletin, 6*(4), 1–9.

Felkenes, G.T., Peretz, P., & Schroedel, J.R. (1993). An analysis of the mandatory hiring of females: The Los Angeles Police Department experience. *Women and Criminal Justice, 4,* 31–64.

Felkenes, G.T., & Schroedel, J.R. (1993). A case study of minority women in policing. *Women and Criminal Justice, 4,* 65–89.

Fiske, S.T., & Taylor, S.E. (1991). *Social Cognition.* New York: McGraw-Hill.

Garrison, C.G., Grant, N., & McCormick, K. (1988). Utilization of police women. *Police Chief, 55,* 32–35, 69–73.

Heidensohn, F. (1992). *Women in control? The role of women in law enforcement.* Oxford, UK: Clarendon.

Hochschild, A.R. (1973). A review of sex role research. *American Journal of Sociology, 78*(4), 1011–1029.

Hunt, J.C. (1990). The logic of sexism among police. *Women and Criminal Justice, 1,* 3–30.

Hunt, J.C. (1984, winter). The development of rapport through the negotiation of gender in fieldwork among police. *Human Organizations, 43,* 283–96.

Johnson, L.B. (1991). Job strain among police officers: Gender comparisons. *Police Studies, 14,* 12–16.

Kanter, R.M. (1977). *Men and women of the corporation.* New York: Basic Books.

Kay, S. (1994). Why women don't apply to be police officers. *Police Chief, 61*(9), 44–45.

Kerber, K.W., Andes, S.M., & Mittler, M.B. (1977). Citizen attitudes regarding the competence of female police officers. *Journal of Police Science and Administration, 5,* 337–347.

Lord, L.K. (1986). A comparison of male and female peace officers' stereotypic perceptions of women and women police officers. *Journal of Police Science and Administration, 14,* 83–97.

Lunneborg, P.W. (1989). *Women police officers: Current career profile.* Springfield, IL: Charles C. Thomas.

Manning, P.K. (1977). *Police work: The social organization of policing.* Cambridge, MA: Massachusetts Institute of Technology Press.

Martin, S.E. (1980). *Breaking and entering: Policewomen on patrol.* Berkeley, CA: University of California Press.

Martin, S.E. (1990). *On the move: The status of women in policing.* Washington, D.C.: Police Foundation.

Martin, S.E. (1991). Effectiveness of affirmative action: The case of women in policing. *Justice Quarterly, 8,* 489–504.

Martin, S.E. (1994). "Outside within" the station house: The impact of race and gender on black women police. *Social Problems, 41,* 383–400.

Meagher, M.S., & Yentes, N.A. (1986). Choosing a career in policing: A comparison of male and female perceptions. *Journal of Police Science and Administration, 14,* 320–327.

Morash, M., & Greene, J.K. (1986). Evaluating women on patrol: A critique of contemporary wisdom. *Evaluation Review, 10,* 230–255.

Pendergrass, V.E., & Ostrove, N.M. (1984). A survey of stress in women in policing. *Journal of Police Science and Administration, 12,* 303–309.

Poole, E.D., & Pogrebin, M.R. (1988). Factors affecting the decision to remain in policing: A study of women officers. *Journal of Police Science and Administration, 16,* 49–55.

Radford, J. (1989). Women and policing: Contradictions old and new. In J. Hanmer, J. Radford, & E.A. Stanko (Eds.), *Women, policing, and male violence: International perspective.* New York: Routledge.

Reaves, B.A., & Smith, P.Z. (1995). *Law enforcement management and administrative statistics, 1993: Data for individual state and local agencies with 100 or more officers.* Washington, D.C.: Bureau of Justice Statistics.

Sherman, L.J. (1975). An evaluation of policewomen on patrol in a suburban police department. *Journal of Police Science and Administration, 3,* 434–438.

Silbert, M.H. (1982). Job stress and burnout of new police officers. *Police Chief, 49*(6), 46–48.

Skolnick, J. (1966). *Justice without trial.* New York: John Wiley & Sons.

Snortum, J.R., & Beyers, J.C. (1983). Patrol activities of male and female officers as a function of work experience. *Police Studies, 6,* 36–42.

Steel, B.S., & Lovrich, N.P. (1987). Equality and efficiency tradeoffs in affirmative action, real or imagined? The case of women in policing. *Social Science Journal, 24,* 53–70.

Timmins, W.M., & Hainsworth, B.E. (1989). Attracting and retaining females in law enforcement. *International Journal of Offender Therapy and Comparative Criminology, 33,* 197–205.

Tomman, D.A., & Serritella, T.M. (1994). Preventing sexual harassment in law enforcement agencies. *Police Chief, 47,* 31–35.

Walklate, S. (1992). Jack and Jill join up at sun hill: Public images of police officers. *Policing and Society, 2,* 219–232.

Weisheit, R.A. (1987). Women in the state police: Concerns of male and female officers. *Journal of Police Science and Administration, 15,* 137–144.

Wexler, J.G. (1985). Role styles of women police officers. *Sex Roles, 12,* 749–755.

Wexler, J.G., & Logan, D.D. (1983). Considerations in the training and development of women sergeants. *Journal of Police Science and Administration, 13,* 98–105.

Worden, A.P. (1993). Attitudes of women and men in policing: Testing conventional and contemporary wisdom. *Criminology, 31,* 203–242.

Yarmey, A.D. (1990). *Understanding police and police work: Psychological issues.* New York: New York University Press.

2

Minority Groups in Law Enforcement*

Larry D. Stokes, University of Tennessee at Chattanooga

The underrepresentation and underutilization of minority group members in police agencies have been controversial issues since 1803, beginning in New Orleans (Dulaney, 1996). However, minority group members' underrepresentation did not receive scrutiny until after the 1963 Watts riot and 1967 summer civil disorders in major cities. Because employment discrimination was not sufficiently addressed by policy makers and administrators during the past several decades, the hiring of minority group members remains a problematic issue not only in law enforcement but also in most public and private sectors. Thus, minority group members' underrepresentation might be explained by a history of institutional racism and institutional discrimination in the United States. The criminal justice system, moreover, functions equitably for middle and upper class Euro-Americans but inequitably for people of color and the poor (Brown, 1977). African Americans, for instance, compose approximately 12.8 percent of the U.S. population, but they are more likely to be arrested, convicted, and sentenced than any other racial group. Consequently, people of color are least likely to find employment in the criminal justice system. The police social structure does not have its roots in the protection of the rights of people of color, and these people have had little participation in determining police departments' functions.

Despite a history of racial and employment discrimination in this country, people of color have reluctantly pursued professions in law enforcement. Those who did enter law enforcement were interested in providing protective services in their community, lessening the degree of police brutality, and for financial gain (Myrdal, 1944). Thus, this chapter provides a brief socio-historical discussion and contemporary examination of African Americans' representation in police departments. It will

---

*This chapter is built upon excerpts from the articles, "Affirmative Action and Selected Minority Groups in Police Forces" *Journal of Criminal Justice, 24,* pp. 29–38 (1996), and "Affirmative Action Policy Standards and Employment of African Americans in Police Departments," *Western Journal of Black Studies, 17,* pp. 135–142 (1993).

also examine the extent to which Asian Americans and Hispanic American officers are represented in municipal police departments.

A SOCIO-HISTORICAL PERSPECTIVE OF AFRICAN AMERICAN POLICE OFFICERS

In antebellum New Orleans "free men of color" served on the city guard and constabulary forces as early as 1803. African Americans held these positions because of their status in the city's unique multiracial society and because they wanted to establish their loyalty and ties to the city's white population rather than its black slave population (Rousey, 1978). In most southern cities, white citizens resented the authority of black officers, even though their authority was similar to white officers'. Yet, in most southern cities their authority was restricted to the African American community (Dulaney, 1996). By the 1870s, African Americans were also serving as police officers in Montgomery, Mobile, and Selma, Alabama; Vicksburg, Meridian, and Jackson, Mississippi; Jacksonville, Florida; Charleston, South Carolina; Chattanooga, Tennessee; and Austin and Houston, Texas (see Table 2.1). Most often, African American police officers were appointed by Republican administrations to protect blacks from white violence and terrorism that characterized the Reconstruction era. Similarly, as in New Orleans, African Americans' presence on police forces was resented by whites, and the exercise of police powers by African Americans became one of the most hated features of the Reconstruction governments (Rabinowitz, 1976).

During this period, the city of New Orleans had more African American officers than any other city. Following Redemption, whites began to initiate a movement to eliminate African American police officers from New Orleans' department (Dulaney, 1996). In defense of the African American officers, editors of the *New Orleans Tribune,* the first African American newspaper in the United States, wrote:

Table 2.1 African American Police Percentages in Selected Southern Cities during Reconstruction

City	1870		1880	
	% of Police	% of Pop	% of Police	% of Pop
New Orleans	28	26	07	27
Charleston	42	54	19	55
Mobile	37	44	0	42
Memphis	0	39	23	44
Montgomery	50	49	0	59
Vicksburg	50	55	15	49
Norfolk	3	46	0	46
Portsmouth	29	35	0	34

Source: Rousey, "The New Orleans Police," p. 329.

What good and solid objection can be made to the appointment of people of colored police officers? Will it be said that the population of African descent does not bear a sufficient proportion to the whole population, to entitle them to any share on the police force? This would be absurd, since everybody knows that one-half of the inhabitants of Crescent City have more or less African blood in their veins and, moreover, three-fourths of the qualified voters of the city, as far as registration goes today, belongs to Africans. These three-fourths are deprived of their share of representation on the police force (*New Orleans Tribune,* 1867 as cited in Dulaney, 1996).

Despite such endorsement of support, African Americans were eliminated from New Orleans' police department as racism and discrimination intensified. By 1877, most southern states had "redeemed" their governments and had driven African Americans and their white Republican allies from office. Thus, African Americans holding minor political offices, such as police officers, were eliminated. By the 1890s, police officers in most cities in the South were again all white (Dulaney, 1996). However, in 1895, coalition politics between African Americans and the Populists allowed some African Americans to recapture police jobs in Wilmington and New Bern, North Carolina. A few African American police also continued to serve in Houston, Austin, and Galveston, Texas. However, in the post-Reconstruction period, racial proscriptions were placed on police agencies—to limit the authority of African American officers. They could not arrest whites, and they patrolled only African American communities (Dulaney, 1990).

Contrary to practices of racial discrimination and institutional racism exhibited by whites toward African Americans in the South, African Americans were police officers in the District of Columbia in 1861 (Johnson, 1947). In an examination of the personnel records of the Washington, D.C. police force during Reconstruction, Alfers (1976) found no significant difference between the performance of African American and white officers. Evidence also suggests that African American officers were on the New York Police Department (NYPD) in 1865 but entered as a group between 1891 and 1910 (Alexander, 1978). The earliest evidence of an African American police officer in New York is contained in a photograph dated 1865. It is speculated that this officer may have served in the Union Army, and was probably part of the "Old Mounted Squadron" attached to the 32nd Precinct (Alexander, 1978). The entry of African Americans to police departments is known as "getting one's foot in the door." This expression applied to African Americans' efforts to secure employment in police departments (Handlin, 1950). To this end, African Americans began to find employment in police departments as precincts' door attendants (*Brooklyn Daily Eagle,* 1890 as cited in Alexander, 1978). The principal reason for hiring African American officers was political. White politicians promised the African American community that African Americans would be hired as police officers if they won and carried most of the African American votes. Where African Americans were not allowed to vote, they were not allowed to serve as police officers (Banton, 1964). Responding to the question in Kephart's study, *Why do you think there are so few Negroes on the forces?* an African American officer noted "politics." It is who one knows, not what one knows

(Kephart, 1957). Despite political patronage, African Americans were prohibited from serving on police forces in most southern cities and, for that matter, some northern ones (Fogelson, 1977). Consequently, the position of African Americans and the law can be understood by alluding to southern mores.

> The police are functionaries not only of just but of the racial code that is an unwritten law. The view of the white officer is that he is to enforce all written regulations including the provision that there should be no disturbance of the peace. This latter provision includes all violations of race etiquette so that all well-recognized southern customs with the local variations become extensions of the law. When it is remembered that policemen are recruited from the classes in the community with low education and insecure economic status, and from the groups that are frequently forced into competition with Negroes for unskilled positions, the exercise of authority over Negroes is apparently more than a routine matter and is one in which resentment, vengeance, and satisfaction of proving superiority take many sadistic forms (Schermerhorn, 1959, pp. 124–125).

AFRICAN AMERICAN OFFICERS IN POLICE AGENCIES IN THE NORTH AND SOUTH

In spite of the degree of racial discrimination whites harbored toward African Americans, they comprised a total of 1,818 law enforcement officials in the United States in 1930; the majority were in northern cities (U.S. Bureau of the Census, Negroes in the United States: 1920–1932, pp. 322–324). In Philadelphia, African Americans comprised a total of 203 police officers in 1944 (Brown, 1947, p. 88). Even so, Kephart (1957) observed that African Americans were underrepresented to a greater degree than they had ever been in Philadelphia's police department. In northern cities, African American police officers were of southern heritage; they had migrated with their families (Alexander, 1978) in search of better employment opportunities and living conditions, and to avoid racial injustice in the southern states (Myrdal, 1944). African Americans who joined were not only ostracized but also suffered severe psychological stress from European American officers (*New York Post,* 1938 as cited in Dulaney, 1996; McDonagh & Simpson, 1965). Only on official duty did European American officers interact or speak to African American officers; even so, their interactions were limited. Physical intimidation was also contrived to dissuade others from joining police departments. Thus, African Americans seeking employment in police departments were uncommon and those applying for the position of patrol officer were "going against the system" (Alexander, 1978). An African American officer in Detroit recalled how he almost did not get on the police force in 1947. After passing the civil service examination and the oral interview, the police department forwarded the applicant a correspondence rejecting his application. The letter advised him that he had failed the medical examination; he had tuberculosis. Chest x-rays taken by his physician revealed otherwise. Such evidence compelled the police department to accept his application and admit him as an officer (Report of the United States Commission on Civil Rights, 1971). Once hired, however, the authority of African American officers varied regionally. In most northern and western communities, African Americans patrolled any part of town but their assignments were confined to the African American community (Myrdal, 1944). African American officers were often confronted with physical and verbal abuse when assigned to a European American community. They often were subject to unusual provocations if offenders were African Americans. If they overreacted when arresting a Caucasian, they were subject to complaints and charges. If they needed to make an arrest or investigate in a white neighborhood, they needed a white officer to verify their official status (Alex, 1969).

In most southern cities, African American officers' authority to apprehend suspects was restricted to African Americans and the African American community. When offending whites needed to be arrested, white officers were called to make the arrest (U.S. Bureau of the Census, Negroes in the United States: 1920–1932, pp. 322–324). Only on an emergency basis did African Americans work in European American districts. Some police administrators permitted African American officers to arrest only European American felons (Rudwick, 1960). A survey of southern police departments found that twenty-eight police departments reported restrictions on arrest powers of African American officers (*Ebony*, 1966 as cited in Roberg & Kuykendall, 1993). In 18 of the 28 departments, administrators lamented that if a white officer were not available, the African American officer could apprehend a white suspect. Ten departments permitted no arrest by an African American officer of a white suspect under any circumstances; three departments required African American police officers to keep a white suspect under surveillance but not have direct contact with the suspect until a white officer arrived. Usually, white offenders had more status than the African American officer (*Ebony*, 1966 as cited in Roberg & Kuykendall, 1993). Banton (1964) observed that in two southern cities, African American officers arrested whites without difficulty; African Americans, he asserted, were more conversant with whites than the antithesis. Elise Scott, the executive director of the National Organization for Black Law Enforcement Executives (NOBLE), recalls that African American officers rode in patrol cars marked "Colored Police" and were allowed to arrest only "colored" people (cited in Sullivan, 1989). Routinely, police administrators assigned African Americans to foot patrol instead of in a vehicle; the only time they were allowed to use a patrol car was in case of an emergency (Kephart, 1957). Banton (1964) further observed that, in one southeastern city, African American officers were assigned to patrol cars, but only with another African American officer and only in the African American community. On the other hand, some departments' policies did not allow "Negro police officers to wear uniforms home as did the white officers" (U.S. Bureau of the Census, Negroes in the United States: 1920–1932, pp. 322–324).

Moreover, African Americans participation as police officers was nonexistent in southern states. Fewer than fifty African Americans were police officers in the entire South, even though over three-fourths of all African Americans lived in this region (Rudwick, 1962). Hiring African American officers was viewed by southern white officials and citizens as an experiment that demanded meticulous treatment and training. Thus, they were more cautiously screened and selected than were European American officers.

> In many communities colored recruits were more educated and intelligent than their white counterparts. For example, in 1947 the six African American patrol officers in Greensboro, North Carolina, were college men. Once appointed to the force, the Negroes frequently received more adequate recruit training than the whites (Rudwick, 1960, p. 274).

On the other hand, an African American interviewee, in Kephart's study, noted that college-educated African Americans were often rejected by the department. Many qualified African American candidates took the civil service examination; some were college graduates or had some level of college education. What happened? When the results were posted, the first three hundred names were all white, not an African American in the first three hundred (Kephart, 1957).

Since the 1950s African Americans have increased their representation not only in law enforcement but also in other areas of the criminal justice system; nonetheless, the African American community remains unconvinced that the system is impartial. The generally held belief in the African American community is that if an African American is accused of a crime, he or she will not receive fair treatment from the criminal justice system. This apprehension is based upon a history of police brutality and malfeasance by the judicial system. In every city, for instance, that experienced racial disruption during the summer of 1964, abrasive relationships between the police and the black community were a major source of grievance, tension, and ultimate disorders (National Advisory Commission on Civil Disorders, 1968). Police brutality resulted in riots between African Americans and white police officers in New York City during the 1930s and 1940s. In the 1960s and 1970s more than twelve American cities experienced African American uprising against local symbols of white authority (i.e., police officers).

Illustration: Three uprisings occurred in Miami between 1982 and 1991, all triggered by incidents involving white or Latino police officers shooting to death an African American or being acquitted for such a killing (Feagin & Hahn, 1973). A white photographer in Los Angeles captured on videotape the beating of Rodney King by white police officers, while more than a dozen other officers watched. Initially the Los Angeles police chief did not condemn the officers, saying only the beating was an "aberration" (Leerhsen, 1991).

Additionally, in a search of articles appearing in major newspapers between January 1990 and May 1992, Lersch found reports of 130 incidents of serious police brutality against citizens. White police officers were involved in more than nine in every ten of these cases: African American or Hispanic citizens were the victims in 97 percent of police incidents. Significantly, an officer was punished in only 13 percent of the incidents, and the usual punishment was slight (Lersch, 1993).

Further, police officers charged with the duty of preventing crime and apprehending criminals are in nearly all cases European Americans who share the general idea that African Americans are criminals or potential criminals (Reuter, 1970). African Americans feel that they are being leaned upon and that the police are the agents of repression, tending toward defiance of what they regard as order, maintained at the expense of justice. To many African Americans, police have come to symbolize white power, white racism, and white repression (Roberg & Kuykendall, 1993). In the African American community, European American officers' "presence is an insult, and it would be, even if they spent their entire day feeding gumdrops to children. They represent the force of the white world, and that world's criminal profit and ease, to keep the black man corralled up here, in his place. The badge, the gun in the holster, and the swinging club, makes vivid what will happen should his rebellion become overt" (Baldwin, 1962).

RECRUITMENT AND AFRICAN AMERICANS' REPRESENTATION IN POLICE AGENCIES

Police departments began desegregating police units from all African American and all white in the early 1960s. However, it was not until 1963 that departments began to abolish segregated police units. Until this period, African Americans were not permitted to attend the police training academy. African Americans were usually given the rank of *patrolman*—a level lower than the lowest rank of *officer* held by whites. Since this time, the opportunities for African American police officers have improved considerably (U.S. Commission on Civil Rights, 1971).

Before the civil disorders of the 1960s, African Americans composed a total of 106 police officers in northern cities and a total of 2,937 in western cities. African Americans average one officer for every 3,125 blacks, compared with a ratio of one white officer to every 442 whites (Roberg & Kuykendall, 1993). An attempt to reform policies of institutional discrimination and institutional racism in America's police departments engendered resentment and hostility by whites toward African Americans. Reform meant challenging the hegemony of white officers for positions and promotions in policing. Recruitment and promotion of African American officers were attempts to reform long-standing policies that had excluded African Americans from partici-pating as police officers in urban areas (Dulaney, 1996). After the civil disturbance of the 1960s, efforts were undertaken by politicians and police administrators to increase the representation of African Americans and other minority groups as police officers. Thus, the National Advisory Commission on Civil Disorders suggested that every police agency should engage in employing ethnic minority groups' members. When a substantial ethnic minority population resides within particular jurisdiction, the police agency should take affirmative action to achieve a ratio of minority group employees in approximate proportion to the makeup of the population (National Advisory Commission on Civil Disorders, 1968). Yet, people of color did not exactly flood police departments for jobs. The results of recruitment efforts by police departments were mixed. Some cities experienced substantial increases in the percentage of people of color on their police forces, other cities experienced only a slight increase, while still other cities experienced decreases (Goldstein, 1977).

During the 1970s, African Americans continued to confront various forms of discrimination to prevent them from joining police departments. One technique employed was the rejection of African American candidates on the grounds that they generally could not be good officers; they did not have forbears as officers from whom they could have inherited motivating traits for police work (Wilson, 1968). Police departments also excluded African Americans by requiring a college degree of prospective candidates. Some police administrators further argued that African American and Hispanic applicants are unqualified for police work, and that hiring qualified applicants of any ethnic background for police work is something of a challenge, with the difficulty being particularly acute for African Americans and Hispanics (Radelet, 1980). Improvement in the relationship between police departments and minority communities continues to be hampered by the resistance of police departments to hire and promote minority police officers. The Report of the National Advisory Commission on Civil Disorders (1968) found that

> Despite efforts to hire more Negro police, the proportion of Negroes on police forces is still far below the proportion of Negroes in the total population. Of 28 departments . . . the percentage of Negro sworn personnel ranged from less than 1 percent to 21 percent. The median figure for Negro sworn personnel on the force was 6 percent; median figures for the Negro population were approximately 24 percent. In no cases were the proportion of Negroes in the police department equal to the proportion in the population (National Advisory Commission on Civil Disorders, 1968, p. 165).

Patrick Murphy (an ex-commissioner of the New York City Police Department) suggested that one serious problem facing police departments is the lack of adequate representation of African Americans in police departments. Police agencies have not recruited enough African Americans in the past and are not recruiting enough of them today. Police administrators would be less than honest if they did not admit that African Americans have been prevented from joining police forces for reasons of racial discrimination (National Advisory Commission on Civil Disorders, 1968). So, from the 1968 Report of the National Advisory Commission on Civil Disorders (see Table 2.2), the Commission formulated a recommendation that read in part: "It should be a high priority objective of all departments in communities with a substantial minority population to recruit minority group officers, and to deploy and promote them fairly" (National Advisory Commission on Civil Disorders, 1968, p. 102).

As of 1978 and 1990, only two police agencies had been successful in meeting the recommendation of the 1968 National Advisory Commission on Civil Disorders (see Table 2.2). In 1978, only Phoenix's police department employed African American officers in twice their proportion within the local population (NOBLE, 1978). By using Walker's compliance index to analyze these departments, the data in Table 2.2 show that in 1978 these police departments had a mean EEO compliance index of 0.43. This suggests that most of the police departments had a low level of sworn African American officers. The employment of African American officers was 57 percent below an acceptable EEO compliance index level. Only the Detroit police department had a high index. Eight departments had a moderate compliance index, 11 had a low compliance index, and both Tampa and Pittsburgh police departments had a noncompliance index. Additionally, data in Table 2.2 shows that the mean com-

Table 2.2   Compliance Index of African American Representation in 26 Police Departments

Depts	1968 Percent Pop	Index	1978 Percent Pop	Index	1990 Percent Pop	Index
Atlanta	38	0.26	51	0.61	67	0.81
Baltimore	35	0.20	35	—	57	0.46
Boston	10	0.20	16	0.25	26	0.67
Buffalo	14	0.21	20	—	31	0.57
Chicago	24	0.71	33	0.64	39	0.62
Cincinnati	22	0.27	28	0.46	38	0.46
Cleveland	29	0.24	38	0.29	—	—
Dayton	22	0.18	31	0.32	40	0.34
Detroit	29	0.18	44	0.77	76	0.68
Hartford	16	0.69	28	0.46	39	0.42
KC, MO	18	0.33	22	0.55	29	0.43
Louisville	18	0.34	24	0.29	—	—
Memphis	37	0.14	39	0.41	55	0.60
New Haven	15	0.47	26	0.69	—	—
New Orleans	37	0.11	45	0.26	62	0.52
New York	15	0.33	21	0.38	29	0.39
Newark	34	0.29	54	0.33	—	—
Oakland	26	0.15	35	0.54	44	0.58
Ok City, OK	13	0.31	14	0.42	—	—
Philadelphia	27	0.74	34	0.58	39	0.59
Phoenix	6	0.17	5	2.00	5	0.80
Pittsburgh	17	0.41	20	0.10	26	0.96
St. Louis	29	0.38	41	0.32	47	0.51
San Fran	18	0.33	13	0.54	11	0.81
Tampa, FL	17	0.18	20	0.20	—	—
Wash, D.C.	55	0.38	71	0.62	66	1.01

—Indicates departments did not report data.

Sources: *Report of the 1968 National Advisory Commission on Civil Disorders,* National Organization of Black Law Enforcement Executives (1978) and Stokes & Scott (1993) Affirmative Action Standard & African American Representation in Municipal Police Departments, *Western Journal of Black Studies.* Note: For analytical purposes, Samuel Walker's hypothetical Equal Employment Opportunity Index is used to decide compliance by police departments with the affirmative action standard (see Walker, 1983).

pliance for 20 municipal police departments in 1990 was 0.61, showing a 90 percent increase in compliance (Stokes & Scott, 1993). Although numbers of African American police officers have increased, 39 percent of the police departments had an unacceptable compliance level. The highest compliance level of 1.01 was found in the District of Columbia. This compliance index may reflect African Americans' political longevities as mayor and city councilpersons and their commitment to following the recommendation of the National Advisory Commission on Civil Disorders. The

Dayton, Ohio, department had the lowest compliance index of 0.34. In 1990, five departments were classified as having high compliance, nine moderate, and six low compliance. Since 1968, four cities (New York, Hartford, Dayton, and Cincinnati) have not gone beyond low compliance with the affirmative action standard (Stokes & Scott, 1993). Walker (1992b) revealed that the percentage of African American officers in the NYPD had not increased since 1983. However, the NYPD compliance level remained unchanged from 1978 to 1990; the compliance index was 0.38 in 1978 and 0.39 in 1990. Thus, the number of African American officers increased only 3 percent in 14 years in the NYPD.

MINORITY HIRING CONTROVERSY

Strategies and methodologies used to increase the representation of police departments have met with opposition from various sectors, including police union officials, police administrators, and policy makers charging *reverse discrimination*. The gains made by minority group members in law enforcement have not been without controversy and resistance (Stokes & Scott, 1993; Walker, 1992a, 1992b; Hochstedler, 1984; Stewart, 1985; Martin, 1980). The debate over the role of affirmative action policies in achieving social equity will continue (Warner, Steel & Lovrich, 1989). For example, in *United States v. Paradise* (1987), the Justice Department brought the Alabama State Troopers' case to the United States Supreme Court, challenging its affirmative action plan. As late as 1972, not one Alabama State Trooper was African American. That year a federal court ordered the force to integrate. By the mid-1980s, 27 percent of the state's troopers were African American; however, no African American ranked higher than sergeant. Civil rights advocates charged the Alabama State Police with racism. The lower court agreed and developed an affirmative action plan so that African American troopers might be promoted. The Justice Department argued that the one-for-one quota was excessive and profoundly illegal. By a vote of five to four, the Supreme Court disagreed (*United States v. Paradise,* 1987). Justice Brennan wrote the majority opinion in which he stated that such longstanding, stubborn racism of the Alabama State Police Department justified a *race-conscious* remedy. He further noted that whites were not necessarily penalized by the plan, since it only postponed the promotion of qualified white candidates. Additionally, Justice Stevens wrote that, in cases of proven discrimination, courts have "broad and flexible authority to remedy wrongs" (*United States v. Paradise,* 1987).

However, in the *Adarand Constructors v. Pena* (1995) decision, Adarand was the losing bidder for a subcontract to build the guardrail on a federal highway project in southern Colorado, though it had submitted the lowest bid. The court held in favor of Adarand, but the court did not strike down the program; the Supreme Court sent the case back to a lower court to be reexamined under a "strict scrutiny standard." This test will force federal officials to decide whether an affirmative action program is narrowly tailored to serve a compelling government interest. In writing for the majority, Justice O'Connor noted that all governmental action based on race should be subjected to detailed judicial inquiry to ensure that the personal right to equal protection of the law has not been infringed. However, Justice Stevens, dissenting, lamented that the strict scrutiny standard "has been understood to spell the death of any governmental action" (*Adarand Constructors v. Pena*, 1995).

Despite some gains made in the employment of minorities as police officers, as noted by the National Minority Advisory Council (1980), the United States Commission on Civil Rights found that the "underutilization of minorities and women in local law enforcement agencies continues to hamper the ability of police departments to function effectively in and earn the respect of predominantly minority neighborhoods by that increasing the probability of tension and violence" (U.S. Commission on Civil Rights, 1981, p. 5). To increase minority group members' representation in governmental organizations and municipal police departments, the United States Employment Services, in the early 1980s, began using various tests to refer job seekers to potential employers. The United States Employment Services converted these standardized scores to percentiles because African Americans' and Hispanic Americans' mean scores are usually lower than European Americans' scores. The same raw score would be converted to a markedly different percentile score if the examinees were European Americans, African Americans, and Hispanic Americans. Candidates' scores were compared with the scores of candidates from various ethnic groups and were referred to employers at comparable rates. Thus, an employer requesting candidates scoring at or above a preferred percentile would receive a list made up of these ethnic groups' applicant pool members scoring above the requested percentile within their own group (Sackett & Wilk, 1994). This method of referral and scoring stimulated the conflict between African American and white officers.

Illustration: The controversy surrounding "race norming" and affirmative action erupted in Chicago's police department when the department announced the scores on an exam taken by candidates competing for the position of sergeant. Of 500 officers who scored high enough to win promotion, only 40 were African American and 22 Hispanic American in a city that is 39 percent African American and 19.6 percent Hispanic (Thin White Line, 1994). African American officers questioned whether the examination predicted *job performance* and whether the test were *culturally biased.* Racial bias remains a possible explanation in the low scores; however, it is alleged that some European American officers may have obtained study materials that duplicated the test format (Thin White Line, 1994). Similarly, in St. Louis, Missouri's police department, the head of the local African American police organization was given copies of the confidential sergeant's exam. A copy of the examination was forwarded to him after being circulated among white officers before the test was given (Black and Blue, 1995). Additionally, in federal district court a retired police sergeant of Boston's police department admitted he had given officers the answers to a civil service examination in the 1970s. Other defendants involved in the selling or conspiracy to sell examinations included a police superintendent, a lieutenant, a retired captain, a former state Senate aide, and a brother and son of an officer (Ex-Sergeant Says He Aided Bid to Sell Exams, 1987). Amid similar controversy, the Chicago police department became the first department in the country to drop "race norming," as a practice for hiring and promoting officers.

The United States Department of Justice in 1986 challenged the practice of within-group norming as unfair to European American candidates. However, the National Academy of Sciences (NAS) committee that investigated this practice concluded that the U.S. employment test scores were "scientifically justified" because the modest validity of standardized tests (General Aptitude Test Battery) causes selection errors that weighed more heavily on minority workers than on majority workers (Hartigan & Wigdor, 1989). Although not supported by Congress and the courts, police administrators viewed race norming as a part of an affirmative action program to increase minority groups' representation in law enforcement.

POLITICAL ISSUES AND LAW ENFORCEMENT

As race norming and affirmative action provoke increasing public scrutiny and resistance, both Democrats and Republicans in Congress joined in supporting a ban on race-conscious score adjustment in the Civil Rights Act of 1991 (Gottfredson, 1994). This bill passed without any opposition because presidential and congressional politics are polarized on racial grounds. For instance, five of the six presidential elections between 1968 and 1988 were won by Republican candidates who received virtually no African American support. Republicans hardly contend for African American votes, and increasingly view civil rights legislation and affirmation action as a form of reverse discrimination. By pursuing an anti-civil rights "southern strategy" in 1968, Richard Nixon carried ten of eleven southern states (Dent, 1978). Both the Reagan and Bush administrations were also hostile to affirmative action and lacked vigorous enforcement of the civil rights laws.

In 1994, Republicans gained control of both the Senate and House of Representatives; in doing so, they exploited white fears by using racial code words. These words included "strong anti-crime bill," "law and order," "welfare queen," and "affirmative action quotas" (Piliawsky, 1994). In California, conservatives placed affirmative action on the 1996 ballot to outlaw affirmative action. As the 1996 presidential race began, affirmative action became a key issue for Republican candidates, even for those who once supported strong civil rights legislation. Bob Dole suggested that after 30 years of affirmative action laws "the race counting game has gone too far" (Affirmative Action Faces New Pressures, 1995). Subsequently, Dole requested an investigation into affirmative action to decide whether the original purpose of the program had been accomplished, whether reverse discrimination exists, and whether alternative methods should be devised to ensure equitable opportunity for all citizens (Affirmative Action Hearings Sought, 1995).

In attempting to remake the party's image, Democrats belittled the concerns of minorities and stressed "welfare reform" and "tough crime" legislation, issues with strong racial overtones (Piliawsky, 1994). Fighting for the support of European American suburbanites, Democrats had no incentive to raise issues that threaten to divide their constituencies (Harris & Wilkins, 1988). President Clinton ordered a review of affirmative action programs to assess employment discrimination allegations against all citizens (Affirmative Action Faces New Pressures, 1995). It was this type of hyperbole and demagoguery playing on the fears of European Americans that led to the enactment of the 1991 Civil Rights Act. This act stated that it is an unlawful practice for an employer,

In connection with the selection or referral of applicants or candidates for employment or promotion to adjust the (test) scores of, use different cutoffs for, or otherwise alter the results of employment-related tests on the basis of race, color, religion, sex or national origin (Section 106).

The issue of testing was addressed in Section 703h, known as the Tower Amendment, which states: "Nor shall it be unlawful employment practice for an employer to give and to act upon the results of any professionally developed ability tests, if such a test, its administration or action upon the result is not designed, intended, or used to discriminate because of race, color, religion, sex, or national origin" (Title VII of the 1964 Civil Rights Act).

Minority preference remains permissible under a variety of circumstances involving either (a) a finding of discrimination, (b) a court-monitored plan to remedy an imbalance, or (c) a voluntary plan to remedy an imbalance. When a firm has engaged intentionally in unlawful employment practices, the court may grant any form of equitable relief it deems appropriate (Title VII, Section 706g). A consent decree is an admission of wrongdoing (employment practices) by an agency or institution. An employer tenders with the court agreement to rectify its illegal activity. Which is to say, given a pattern of minority employment discrimination, an employer agrees to a plan for future minority hiring rather than continuing with litigation (Sackett & Wilk, 1994). In a voluntary affirmative action plan, the courts have ruled that if employers observe that minority groups are underutilized in the work force, they can carry out an affirmative action plan with a minority preference component to remedy the situation. Although the act outlawed race-norming, it did nothing to correct the previous and present methods of discrimination. Nonetheless, Senator Jesse Helms introduced a bill to eliminate all federal affirmative action programs, and House Speaker Newt Gingrich noted to reporters that he considered affirmative action to be a form of "government racism" (U.S. Sues Ill. Schools on All-Black Janitor, 1995, p. A2). An ex-presidential candidate, Senator Phil Gramm, also noted that if he had been elected president, he would have issued an executive order eliminating federal hiring and contract practices based soley on race or gender (Affirmative Action Faces New Pressures, 1995).

Affirmative action refers to the positive efforts taken to end race and gender discrimination in employment. When affirmative action is applied to hiring practices, for example, employers are asked to inventory all employees. After they have identified areas in which few minorities and women are employed, employers are to set goals for the employment of members of such groups. Goals are a way of assessing an employer's commitment, but they are not quotas: "The employer is not compelled to hire unqualified persons or to compromise genuinely valid standards to meet the established goals. If goals are not met, no sanctions are imposed, if the contractors can demonstrate that he made good faith efforts" (U.S. Commission on Civil Rights, 1977, p. 6).

HISPANIC AND ASIAN AMERICAN POLICE OFFICERS

Since the adoption of Title VII of the 1964 Civil Rights Act, as amended in 1972, prohibiting discrimination based on race, color, religion, sex, or national origin, minorities have generally made gains, but slight ones, in employment by law enforcement agencies in the United States. To date, most studies of minority representation on police forces have focused on African Americans (Kaminski, 1993; Stokes & Scott, 1993; Lewis, 1989; Hochstedler, 1984; Hochstedler, Regoli & Poole, 1984; Walker, 1983, 1985), largely because of the tensions and conflicts that have existed and continue to exist between police and African American communities. The relative absence of overt strife between police and certain other minorities, such as women, Hispanic Americans, and Asian Americans, has meant that the underutilization of these minorities in police work has been less visible and, therefore, has received less systematic attention. The existence of such a situation has increased the difficulty of looking comparatively at the relative progress made by various minority groups. Walker's study of the largest cities in the United States showed that Hispanic and Asian officers are vastly underrepresented to their proportion in the community. Some forces, however, since the 1960s and 1970s, have made modest gains in making departments more representative of their community (Walker, 1992b). Despite these gains, Asian and Hispanic officers remain underrepresented in police forces in America. Usually, these groups are similar to or even more underrepresented than African Americans respective to their proportions in the population.

Walker (1983) suggests that Hispanic Americans are more successful in obtaining police employment in cities where they represent a significant proportion of the population than Asian Americans, African Americans, and women. In New York City, for instance, Hispanic officers increased from 10.4 percent in 1983 to 13.6 percent in 1992. Despite this increase, the president of the Hispanic Police Association noted that the percent of Hispanic American officers is hardly where it should be with a Hispanic population of 25 percent (Walker, 1992b). Alexander (1978) also notes that racial discrimination is a significant factor in determining the outcome of Hispanics and other minority groups' representation in the New York Police Department. He further articulates that an independent agency is warranted to correct employment discriminatory practices.

In Table 2.3, 15 police departments recorded moderate compliance indexes of Hispanic/Latino Americans, whereas Asian Americans obtained either a noncompliance or low compliance index. Buffalo's police department reported a higher compliance level of Hispanic American officers than their proportion in the population. Additionally, in Dayton's department, Hispanic American police officers were proportionate to their percent in the population. The compliance index for the Buffalo and Dayton police forces might be explained by the small percentage of Hispanic Americans in the population, political pressure, or an aggressive hiring policy of the police department. On the other hand, the Boston police force reported only one Hispanic American officer, even though Hispanic Americans represented 11 percent of the population. Only two cities, Pittsburgh and Memphis, reported not having any Hispanic American officers. Of these police departments, 58 percent had a noncompliance or low noncompliance index levels, 31 percent had moderate to high compliance levels, and 11 percent had high compliance levels. For the nineteen departments that had moderate to high compliance levels, the mean compliance index was 0.493. Overall, this is considered a low compliance level with respect to the affirmative goal.

TABLE 2.3   Hispanic and Asian American Compliance Index in 19 Police Departments

Depts	1990		1990	
	Percent Hispanic Population	Compliance Index	Percent Asian Population	Compliance Index
Baltimore	1	*	1	1.00
Boston	11	*	5	0.80
Buffalo	5	1.14	1	*
Chicago	19	*	4	*
Cincinnati	1	*	1	*
Dayton	1	1.00	1	—
Detroit	3	*	1	*
Hartford	31	*	1	*
KC, MO	4	0.57	1	*
Memphis	1	—	1	*
New Orleans	3	0.67	2	*
New York	24	0.50	7	*
Oakland	14	0.78	15	0.60
Philadelphia	5	0.60	3	*
Phoenix	20	0.55	2	0.50
Pittsburgh	1	—	2	—
St. Louis	1	*	1	*
San Francisco	14	0.73	29	*
Washington, D.C.	5	0.60	12	*

* Indicates a noncompliance index less than 0.25.
—Indicates departments did not report data.
Note: The percent in the population and compliance index were rounded.

In other words, the employment of Hispanic American officers was 50.7 percent below the hypothetical Equal Employment Opportunity (EEO) compliance level. Moreover, five departments (Chicago, New York, Oakland, Phoenix, and San Francisco) surveyed by Walker (1983) were also examined in this study. In only Oakland and Phoenix did the departments reflect a decline in Hispanic American officers. Walker observed a compliance index of 0.96 in 1983 in Oakland but in 1990 the compliance index decreased to 0.77. This compliance index represents a 19 percent decrease of Hispanic American officers. The compliance index in 1983 was 0.63 and in 1990 the index was 0.55. In both cities, a decrease in the compliance index might reflect a dramatic increase of the Hispanic population rather than the hiring practices of the departments. Walker (1983), in contrast, noted a 1983 compliance index of 0.36 in New York; the index increased to 0.50 in 1990. Among the three cities (Chicago, New York, and San Francisco) that experienced an increase of Hispanic American officers, the city of New York reflected the largest compliance index increase. Additionally, both the Chicago and San Francisco police departments had small incremental changes in their compliance index (Walker, 1983).

Similarly, Table 2.3 shows the percent and compliance index of Asian Americans in the respective cities. The mean compliance index was 0.295 for Asian American officers in these cities. Thus, the employment of Asian American officers was 69.5 percent below the EEO compliance standard. Even in urban areas with sizable Asian American proportions in their population (San Francisco, New York, and Washington, D.C.), the compliance indexes are not reflective of their proportion in the population. For instance, although Asian American police officers are not reflective of San Francisco's population, they registered a high compliance index of 0.73. Similarly, in Oakland, Asian Americans represent 8.6 percent of the officers; they also registered a high compliance index of 0.77.

In 1987, Winters' study noted a total of twenty-six sworn officers on Chicago's police force (Winters, 1990). This number nearly tripled in three years (see Stokes & Scott, 1994). These increases might be explained by an increase in Asian American applicants, a rise in the Asian American population, political pressure exerted by the Asian American community on the department to hire more Asian Americans, and the tendency of the department to see the employment of Asian Americans as a way to counteract the rise of Asian gang violence. Despite these increases and although Asian Americans represent 4 percent of the city's population, Asian Americans still represented only ½ of 1 percent of the officers in the Chicago police department.

CLOSING

What began in the 1960s as a struggle for equal employment continues in the 1990s because of political and administrative attacks and general lack of support for equal employment opportunity for ethnic minority groups. The economy of the United States is contracting and, as such, the issue of equal employment has been exploited for purely political purposes in an attempt to divert public attention from the real sources of economic difficulty (Stokes & Scott, 1993). Thus, the standard set forth in the National Advisory Commission on Civil Disorders that the percent of minority group members in the community should be the target percent for that minority's representation on the police force, appears far from being realized. Apparently, the application of affirmative action policy even in a quasi-military organization like the police is influenced by many political, economic, legal, and ideological factors (Stokes & Scott, 1993). The United States Commission on Civil Rights notes that "serious under utilization of minorities and women in local law enforcement agencies continues to hamper the ability of police departments to function effectively in and earn the respect of predominantly minority neighborhoods, thereby increasing the probability of tension and violence" (U.S. Commission on Civil Rights, 1981). Consequently, the Los Angeles riot incident heightened the debate surrounding police officers' abusive nature, the inequity in the judicial system, and the awareness of minority underrepresentation in police departments. As the affirmative action debate is heightening and charges of police brutality increase, police–community relations will continue to erode, especially in ethnic group communities.

Minority groups have made significant gains in employment in municipal police departments. The gains, however, have not come without resistance. President Clinton lamented that the *Adarand Constructors v. Pena* decision, which holds affirmative action efforts to stricter legal standards, must not be used as a reason to abandon the fight for equal opportunity. He noted further that, *with ink barely dry,* some will use the decision as a reason to stop fighting discrimination (Clinton: Equal Opportunity Still Valid Despite Ruling, 1995). Thus, the continued employment of minorities in police forces is in jeopardy considering the current political assault upon affirmative action from the Republican party, and given President Clinton's lack of vigorous support. A "changing of the guard" has not occurred but the effect of affirmative action has been an inclusion of minority and ethnic groups previously denied employment in law enforcement. For instance, a recent bipartisan federal panel, U.S. Labor Department's Glass Ceiling Commission, reported that women and minorities rarely go beyond the "glass ceiling" into the top levels of business (Glass Ceiling Report Adds Fuel to Debate, 1995). U.S. Labor Secretary Robert Reich lamented that the Glass Ceiling Report should dispel the views of those who believe that employment discrimination has been eradicated with regard to women and ethnic groups in the United States (Glass Ceiling Report Adds Fuel to Debate, 1995, p. 4A).

Data in this chapter provide support for Walker's (1983) findings that show Hispanic Americans are much more successful than Asian Americans and women (as noted in the previous chapter) in translating their sizable community population into higher levels of representation on municipal law enforcement agencies as sworn police officers. When viewed proportionately, Hispanic Americans have been more successful in becoming sworn officers than have women. However, in absolute numbers more women have been hired as police officers than Hispanic Americans. Even so, women and minority groups continue to be underrepresented on municipal police forces (Stokes & Scott, 1994; Walker, 1992b & 1983; Hochstedler, 1984; Winters, 1990). Additionally, some police departments use similar discriminatory practices to exclude Asian Americans from consideration as sworn police officers. However, the tendency for Asian Americans is generally to view police work as an undesirable occupational choice. For Asian Americans, police work might not be looked upon as a valued career option (Kozel & Tennant, 1992).

Despite the underrepresentation of minority groups as sworn police officers, some police departments across the country have begun the implementation of cultural diversity and sensitivity training for police officers. Obviously, the objective of police administrators is improvement of police relations with minority communities. It is possible that sometimes the application of such urgent programs could dissuade some policy makers and police administrators from pressing aggressively for an employment policy that would bring minorities into police forces in proportion to their representation in the general population.

The critical issue involved in this analysis is whether cultural diversity, as it applies to employment in municipal police organizations, is a political or ideological slogan or whether it has become an approach by which the police can improve their effectiveness in communities. As with other organizational groups in society, a fundamental point to be made about police is the fact that goal achievement is inextricably linked to their ability to work with various groups within the communities they serve. Often this ability depends on neutralizing mutually held negative perceptions between the police and other community groups. Where community groups, including the police, become isolated from one another, such perceptions reinforce their alienation, leading to serious breakdowns in intergroup communication and interaction. Harmonious intergroup relations, on the other hand, are more likely to occur in situations where groups share perspectives and outlooks. Intergroup understanding is also enhanced where opportunities exist for members of groups to participate in each other's activities. The high incidence of crime and violence, which has reached epidemic proportions in many American communities, underscores the need for police to work more closely with community groups by demonstrating, in tangible ways, their commitment to nondiscriminatory employment practices. Effective police work, then, will increasingly demand closer relationships between the police and the community in crime control and prevention.

There exists an inherent tension between the performance of the police role and the exercise of democratic principles in American society. It is therefore essential that police organizations avoid employment practices that would exclude possible employment of otherwise qualified persons. In fact, public legitimation of the police role is often contingent upon how the makeup of police organizations is viewed compared with the communities' own racial, ethnic, and gender compositions. When data for the three groups—African Americans, Asian Americans, and Hispanic Americans—are analyzed, the findings show that their representations on municipal police forces are not impressive, especially when viewed in relation to the employment set by the United States Commission on Civil Rights (1981).

DISCUSSION QUESTIONS

1. Suggest several ways to limit any form of employment discrimination in law enforcement agencies.
2. Should ethnic groups have adequate representation in law enforcement? Explain.
3. Discuss the political controversy surrounding race norming and affirmative action.
4. How may the *Adarand* case decision affect minority hiring in law enforcement? Explain.
5. Define strict scrutiny. How does this notion apply to race, ethnic, or gender-based programs supported by the government?

REFERENCES

Adarand Constructors v. Pena, 115 S.Ct. 1841 (1995).
Affirmative action hearings sought. (1995, March 7). *Chattanooga Free Press,* p. A5.
Affirmative action faces new pressures. (1995, March 18). *Chattanooga Free Press,* p. A1.

Alfers, K.G. (1976). *Law and order in the capital city: A history of the Washington police, 1800–1886.* GW Washington Studies, 5. Washington, D.C.: George Washington University.

Alex, N. (1969). *Black in blue: A study of the negro policeman.* New York: Appelton-Century-Cross.

Alexander, J.I. (1978). *Black coats: Black skin.* Hicksville, New York: Exposition Press.

Banton, M. (1964). *The policeman in the community.* New York: BasicBooks.

Baldwin, J. (1962). *Nobody knows my name.* New York: Dell.

Black and blue. (1995, February 13). *U.S. News & World Report,* pp. 43–44.

Brown, G.G. (1947). *Law administration and negro–white relations in Philadelphia.* Philadelphia, PA: Bureau of Municipal Research.

Brown, L. (1977). Bridges over trouble waters: A perspective on policing in the black community. In R.L. Woodson (Ed.), *Black perspectives on crime and the criminal justice system.* Boston: GK Hall.

Clinton: Equal opportunity still valid despite ruling. (1995, June 14). *USA Today,* p. 8A.

Dent, H.S. (1978). *The prodigal south returns to power.* New York: John Wiley & Sons.

Dulaney, W.M. (1996). Black police in America. Bloomington, IN: Indiana University Press.

Dulaney, W.M. (1990). The Texas negro peace officers' association: The origins of black police unionism. *Houston Review, 12,* 60–61.

Ex-sergeant says he aided bid to sell exam. (1987, February 26). *Boston Globe,* p. 61.

Feagin, J.R., & Hahn, H. (1973). *Ghetto revolts.* New York: Macmillan.

Fogelson, R.M. (1977). *Big-city police: An Urban Institute study.* Cambridge, MA: Harvard University Press.

Glass ceiling report adds fuel to debate. (1995, March 17). *USA Today,* p. 4A.

Goldstein, H. (1977). *Policing a free society.* Cambridge, MA: Ballinger Books.

Gottfredson, L.S. (1994). The science and politics of race-norming. *American Psychologist, 49,* 955–963.

Handlin, O. (1950). *Race and nationality in American life.* New York: Doubleday & Company.

Harris, F.R., & Wilkins, R.W. (1988). *Quiet riots: Race and poverty in the United States.* New York: Pantheon Books.

Hartigan, J.A., & Wigdor, A.K. (1989). *Fairness in employment testing: Validity generalization, minority issues, and the General Aptitude Test battery.* Washington, D.C.: National Academy Press.

Hochstedler, E. (1984). Impediments to hiring minorities in public police agencies. *Journal of Police Science and Administration, 12,* 227–240.

Hochstedler, E., Regoli, R.M., & Poole, E. (1984). Changing of the guard in American cities: A current empirical assessment of integration in twenty municipal police departments. *Criminal Justice Review, 5,* 8–14.

Johnson, C.S. (1947). *Into the mainstream: A survey of best practices in race relations in the south.* Chapel Hill, NC: University of North Carolina Press.

Kaminski, R.J. (1993). Police minority recruitment: Predicting who will say yes to an offer for a job as a cop. *Journal of Criminal Justice, 21,* 395–409.

Kephart, W.M. (1957). *Racial factors and urban law enforcement.* Philadelphia, PA: University of Pennsylvania Press.

Kozel, P., & Tennant, W. (1992). Attitudes of Asian SFPD officers. Unpublished paper prepared for the Personnel Division, San Francisco Police Department.

Leerhsen, C. (1991, March 18). L.A.'s violent new video. *Newsweek,* pp. 33, 53.

Lersch, K. (1993). *Current trends in police brutality: An analysis of recent newspaper accounts.* Master's thesis, University of Florida.

Lewis, W.G. (1989, May/June). Toward a representative bureaucracy: Blacks in city police organizations, 1975–1985. *Public Administration Review,* pp. 257–267.

Martin, S.E. (1980). *Breaking and entering: Policewomen on patrol.* Berkeley, CA: University of California Press.

McDonagh, E.C., & Simpson, J.E. (1965). *Social problems: Persistent challenges.* New York: Rinehardt & Winston.

Myrdal, G. (1944). *An American dilemma.* New York: Harper & Row.

National Advisory Commission on Civil Disorders. (1968). *Report on civil disorders.* Washington, D.C.: U.S. Government Printing Office.

National Minority Advisory Council on Criminal Justice. (1980). *The equality of justice: A report on crime and the administration of justice in the minority community.* Washington, D.C.: Law Enforcement Assistance Administration of the U.S. Department of Justice.

National Organization of Black Law Enforcement Executives (NOBLE). (1978). *Minority police officers.* Washington, D.C.: Unpublished.

Piliawsky, M. (1994). Racism or realpolitik?: The Clinton administration and African-Americans. *The Black Scholar, 24,* 2–9.

Rabinowitz, H.N. (1976, November). The conflict between blacks and the police in the urban south, 1865–1900. *The Historian, 39,* 64–66.

Radelet, L. (1980). *The police and the community.* New York: Macmillan.

Reuter, E.B. (1970). *The American race problem.* New York: Thomas Y. Crowell.

Roberg, R.R., & Kuykendall, J. (1993). *Police and society.* Belmont, CA: Wadsworth Publishing Company.

Rousey, D.C. (1978). The New Orleans police, 1805–1889: A social history. Doctoral dissertation, Cornell University.

Rudwick, E. (1960). The negro policeman in the south. *Journal of Criminal Law, Criminology, and Police Science, 11,* 273–276.

Rudwick, E. (1962). *The unequal badge: Negro policemen in the south.* Report of the Southern Regional Council. Atlanta: Southern Regional Council.

Sackett, P.R., & Wilk, S.L. (1994). Within-group and other forms of score adjustment in pre-employment testing. *American Psychologist, 49,* 929–954.

Schermerhorn, R.A. (1959). *These our people: Minorities in American culture.* Boston: D.C. Heath & Company.

Stewart, C.E. (1985, spring). Multiple claims under rule 54(b): A time for reexamination? *Brigham Young University Law Review,* (2), 327–346.

Stokes, L.D., & Scott, J.F. (1993). Affirmative action policy standard and employment of African-Americans in police departments. *The Western Journal of Black Studies, 17,* 135–142.

Stokes, L.D., & Scott, J.F. (1994). Affirmative action and selected minority groups in law enforcement. *Journal of Criminal Justice, 24,* 29–38.

Sullivan, P.S. (1989). Minority officers: Current issues. In R.G. Duham, & G.P. Alpert (Eds.), *Critical issues in policing: Contemporary readings,* Prospect Heights, IL: Waveland Press.

Thin white line. (1994, August 15). *U.S. News & World Report,* pp. 53–54.

United States v. Paradise, 106 S.Ct. 3331 (1987).

U.S. Bureau of the Census. *Negroes in the United States: 1920–1932,* pp. 322–324. Washington D.C.: U. S. Government Printing Office.

U.S. Commission on Civil Rights. (1971). *Report of a study of minority recruitment efforts in protective services: Who will wear the badge?* Washington, D.C.: U.S. Government Printing Office.

U.S. Commission on Civil Rights. (1977). *Statement on affirmative action for equal employment opportunities.* Washington, D.C.: U.S. Government Printing Office.

U.S. Commission on Civil Rights. (1981, October). *Who is guarding the guardians? A report on police practices.* Washington, D.C.: U.S. Government Printing Office.

U.S. sues Ill. schools on all-black janitor. (1995, March 4). *Associated Press,* p. A2.

Walker, S. (1985). Racial minority and female employment in policing: The implications of "glacial" change. *Crime and Delinquency, 31,* 555–572.

Walker, S. (1983). Employment of black and Hispanic police officers. *Review of Applied Urban Research, 5,* 1–6.

Walker, S. (1992a). *The police in America: An introduction,* (2nd ed.). New York: McGraw-Hill.

Walker, S. (1992b, October 8). NYPD black hiring "worst" Los Angeles best in 50-city survey. *Associated Press.*

Warner, R.L., Steel, B.S., & Lovrich, N.P. (1989). Conditions associated with the advent of representative bureaucracy: The case of women in policing. *Social Science Quarterly, 70,* 562–578.

Wilson, J.Q. (1968). *Varieties of police behavior.* Cambridge, MA: Harvard University Press.

Winters, C.A. (1990). Hispanics and policing in Chicago and Cook County, Illinois. *The Police Journal, 64,* 71–76.

3

Recruitment and Retention

William G. Doerner, Florida State University

All formal organizations, if they are to survive for any length of time, must provide for the orderly transition of new incoming personnel to replace departing members. Colleges and universities, for example, have set up a series of mechanisms aimed at replenishing the student body every year. There are policies that govern the admission of first-year and transfer students, along with procedures for graduating seniors and terminating nonproductive students. Governmental entities, such as law enforcement agencies, also focus upon similar membership concerns. They must induct new workers periodically to succeed former employees and to fill expanding personnel allocations. Part of what we will do in this chapter, then, is to provide a broad overview of the hiring process that law enforcement agencies typically have in place.

Law enforcement, by its very nature, is a coercive function (Muir, 1977). The police have the unique authority to deprive citizens of their cherished freedom. This awesome role carries some broad implications for personnel selection. Unbridled power, especially among novices in an unstructured setting, can deteriorate quickly into aberrant behavior (Haney, Banks & Zimbardo, 1973). One counteracting safeguard to offset this tendency is to erect an elaborate screening process to cull undesirable applicants. The hope, of course, is that hiring the "cream of the crop" will act as a first line of defense against police misconduct and abuse (Sechrest & Burns, 1992).

There has been a growing recognition over the years that police recruitment efforts were not generating a candidate pool completely representative of the larger population. Around the turn of the century, for example, police officers were essentially political appointees. Occupationally relevant selection standards were absent. As Chapters 1 and 2 explained, women and minorities were conspicuously absent from the rank and file until recently. This lack of access for many minority members broadened the chasm between the police and the policed. It fanned interracial tensions, spawned civil disruption, and strained police–community relations. Left to their own devices, though, many police administrators steadfastly refused to budge. Achieving significant personnel reform was like trying to bend granite (Guyot, 1979; Hale & Wyland, 1993; Walker, 1985). It simply did not occur. As a result, it took the prodding of the courts and other external forces to usher in changes that have shaped current police hiring and selection practices. What we need to do later in this chapter, then, is to identify these mechanisms and look at how they have molded the employment process.

While recruitment serves as an important catalyst for change, one must be careful not to overlook retention practices. Turnover can unravel any apparent gains associated with recruitment. Although a certain amount of voluntary employee turnover can be a healthy development, an excessive departure rate may signal some fundamental flaws within an organization. Consequently, we will take a brief look at what agencies are doing to keep employees who are already on board and the ramifications of premature employee turnover.

THE POLICE SELECTION PROCESS

Typically, the police selection process involves several stages or steps. These phases include the written application, the written aptitude or psychological test, the background investigation, polygraph testing, the psychological interview, the oral board interview, and the medical check (Ash, Slora & Britton, 1990; Hogue, Black & Sigler, 1994; Sanders, Hughes & Langworthy, 1995). Applicants who fail to survive a step are eliminated from any further consideration. An outstanding score at one stage does not offset or average out a poor grade elsewhere. Survivors advance to the next phase only to endure more rigorous scrutiny. As you can see, the candidate pool shrinks in size with each subsequent stage of this multiple-hurdle selection process.

This funneling procedure operates under the premise of "weeding out" candidates as opposed to a "screening in" orientation. The phrase "weeding out" means that investigators comb through each application looking for grounds to disqualify the job-seeker. The final eligibility pool, then, does not consist of people who positively match some previously articulated profile of what it takes to be a good officer. Instead, it houses only applicants whom the agency has failed to reject.

There are at least three reasons for this seemingly negative approach. First, the initial applicant pool is usually so big that agencies have the luxury of choosing from a large number of qualified persons to fill the empty slots. If a qualified person is mistakenly eliminated from further consideration, plenty of attractive candidates still remain in the eligibility pool. The downside is that too lenient a screening procedure runs the risk of becoming too costly without a commensurate return. What agencies need, then, is a balanced approach.

Illustration: Let us assume, hypothetically, that the cost of processing one police recruit from application to placement on the eligibility list is five hundred dollars. Suppose that the agency attracts fifty applicants for the one vacancy available, and suppose that forty of the fifty applicants pass all the tests given in the early stages of the selection process. When the agency conducts background investigations of those who have successfully completed the tests, however, it is discovered that ten of the applicants have prior felony convictions. In essence, the municipality has wasted the money spent on testing these individuals since, in most jurisdictions, they could not be hired as police officers regardless of performance on the tests. Again, suppose that ten more of the applicants really have no interest in police work once they discover something about its nature and would not accept a police position if it were offered. The time and money spent on these individuals are also wasted. Now there are thirty applicants remaining, but the agency has only one vacancy. As you can see, the cost of recruiting the one individual who is selected is quite high (Cox, 1996, p. 102).

Second, there is no universally agreed upon definition of what qualities make a good police officer. A quip from August Vollmer, the "father" of American policing, sheds some light on these expectations. He writes, "The citizen expects police officers to have the wisdom of Solomon, the courage of David, the strength of Samson, the patience of Job, the leadership of Moses, the kindness of the Good Samaritan, the strategical training of Alexander, the faith of Daniel, the diplomacy of Lincoln, the tolerance of the Carpenter of Nazareth, and, finally, an intimate knowledge of every branch of the natural, biological, and social sciences. If he had all these, he *might* be a good policeman" (1936, p. 222).

This lack of specificity has haunted policing since its inception. Despite the body of research that has accumulated to date, police officer selection is not yet a science. As we will see later, the development of relevant occupational criteria is of recent vintage in law enforcement.

Third, it is very time-consuming and expensive to process every candidate through the entire selection process. Agencies usually save the most expensive stages for last. Thus, eliminating candidates early in the review process is a more economical practice for the agency.

Because different criteria are used to weed out candidates at various stages, it makes sense to talk about what occurs at each point in the hiring process. The next few pages, then, provide more detail about what takes place at each juncture.

The Written Application

The first step toward receiving consideration for a sworn position is to submit a written application. Agencies use the information provided on this form to help decide whether a person meets all the state-mandated minimum standards. For example, there will be questions concerning citizenship, age, educational attainment, military records, driving background, social security number, criminal involvement, medical history, academy training, certification exam results, and other pertinent areas.

Table 3.1 displays the minimum entrance requirements that Florida demands of all incoming law enforcement officers. Other states may have their own special prerequisites. Minnesota and Wisconsin, for instance, specify the number of college credits that recruits must have completed prior to employment (Buerger, 1996). Although there may be slight differences from one state to the next, the bulk of these criteria remain very similar.

Table 3.1   Minimum Entrance Requirements for Law Enforcement Officers in Florida

To become a law enforcement officer in the state of Florida, a person must satisfy the following minimum entrance requirements:
- be at least 19 years old;
- be a United States citizen;
- hold a high school diploma or its equivalent;
- hold an honorable discharge, if a previous member of the armed forces;
- pass a fingerprint check for a criminal history;
- not have any prior felony convictions;
- not have any prior misdemeanor convictions involving moral turpitude;
- be of good moral character;
- successfully complete a basic police training course; and
- successfully complete the state law enforcement certification examination.

Source: Florida Statutes, Chapter 943.13, 1995.

Illustration: In the June 1996 and July 1996 issues of *Police,* several police departments posted employment notices. Each advertisement listed the minimum qualifications required. The Montgomery, Alabama, police department advised that applicants must be U.S. citizens, at least 21 years old, possess a high school diploma or GED, and have vision correctable to 20/20 with no color blindness. The Detroit, Michigan, police department states that applicants must be U.S. citizens, at least 18 years old, have a high school diploma or GED, and be Detroit residents. Interested candidates must also have vision correctable to 20/20, no felony convictions, and a valid driver's license. Finally, the Jackson, Tennessee, police department applicant must be a U.S. citizen in good health, of good moral character, and at least 21 years old. Candidates must also have a high school diploma or GED, vision correctable to 20/20, and an honorable discharge from the military. Both Detroit and Jackson require the candidate to take a written exam.

Agencies cannot employ anybody in a sworn capacity if they fall below these minimum standards. On the other hand, departments are free to exceed these basic requirements. As Table 3.1 shows, Florida wants its police officers to have at least a high school diploma or its equivalent. Some Florida municipalities, though, hold incoming personnel to a higher educational standard. They may require recruits to have a two-year college degree or a comparable number of college credit hours. This practice is acceptable even though it surpasses state provisions.

One point made earlier was that agencies operate under a weeding out philosophy. Once an application is logged in, office workers will compare its contents against state minimum standards. If the applicant does not meet these specifications, he or she is weeded out, or dismissed from the eligibility pool. If all the state criteria are met, the next step is to match the applicant against the agency's own hiring provisions. Applications that meet these conditions receive a green light and remain eligible for further consideration.

Operating a police vehicle is a significant part of a patrol officer's duty assignment. Administrators are acutely aware that improper or negligent vehicular operation is a high liability area (Alpert & Fridell, 1992; Kappeler, Kappeler & del Carmen, 1993). Police officers often drive under extraordinary conditions when responding to calls in an emergency or when they engage in pursuit driving. Knowing this, police managers look for ways to reduce their financial exposure due to improper officer behavior. As a result, agencies routinely reject applicants who present an unacceptable driving history. Being ticketed for a moving traffic violation in the past two or three years may be grounds for weeding out an otherwise seemingly acceptable candidate.

Psychological Testing

Selecting police officers can be a risky venture. Some applicants may harbor undue resentment toward certain racial groups. Other candidates may exhibit violent tendencies, dishonesty, or try to mask signs of other inappropriate behavior. Administrators are keenly aware that they may incur civil liability should they hire a person who is not fit for duty or who misbehaves while on duty (del Carmen, 1989; Kappeler, Kappeler & del Carmen, 1993). Thus, many agencies rely upon psychological testing to help weed out undesirable or unsuitable applicants.

Many agencies require prospective employees to complete a paper-and-pencil test to help determine psychological fitness. The Minnesota Multiphasic Personality Inventory (MMPI) and the California Personality Inventory (CPI) are the two most commonly used nonprojective pre-employment devices throughout this country (Ash, Slora & Britton, 1990; Johnson, 1983).

Despite this popularity, these instruments suffer from a major limitation. They were created and normed on an institutionalized population. In other words, these tests were devised to distinguish pathological from normal persons. Thus, their basic utility lies in reaching a clinical assessment as to the applicant's mental health.

As we will see later, though, an unwarranted expectation concerning just what these psychological tests are capable of doing has developed among police administrators. As long as these test results are used to weed out unstable candidates, they work well. It is when these same test results are used for "screening in" purposes that a substantial number of weaknesses emerge.

The Background Investigation

Many agencies conduct a cursory background check at this point and postpone a more deliberate inspection until the candidate pool shrinks further. Other departments may elect to carry out a more extensive probe early in the process. In any event, investigators are searching for any abnormalities that may indicate the presence or potential of a character defect.

Usually the information on the written application provides the starting point for this inquiry. Investigators will run a credit check to see whether the person has his or her financial affairs in order. For example, being the subject of an automobile repossession, constantly overdrawing a checking account, failing to make child support payments, or missing credit card installment payments are possible indicators that one's personal life is in disarray. The worry, of course, is that these behaviors may make the person more susceptible to various temptations or corrupting influences once on the job.

Former employers will be contacted about job performance. Past neighbors may receive a visit and be asked about the applicant's life style. School yearbooks may provide leads as to acquaintances and the type of reputation the person accrued. In short, the agency wants assurances that potential officers are upstanding and have no character flaws that would preclude them from active employment.

Polygraph Testing

The polygraph, or what some people call the lie detector, is used to capture biographical data that may have escaped earlier detection. Like drug screening, polygraph testing has come under fire. Because the accuracy of the test results depends upon many factors, critics claim it can be an invalid screening device. While the Employee Protection Act of 1988 forbids most private sector employers from conducting such pre-employment testing, public safety agencies generally do not fall under this umbrella. However, the debate over whether polygraph testing is a proper screening tool continues (Ash, Slora & Britton, 1990).

The polygraph is a machine that registers changes in heart rate, blood pressure, respiration, and galvanic skin respiration when responding to questions. It is based upon the notion that lying or making deceptive statements triggers unseen physiological changes in a subject. The beginning of a session concentrates on establishing an individual's baseline against which to compare subsequent responses.

Many agencies are very sensitive to prior drug use. Some agencies refuse to employ anybody who admits to recreational use or experimentation, even if such incidents took place only a handful of times and in the distant past. Other agencies may be more tolerant. However, they too will probe this area during polygraph testing.

The problem with much drug testing is that the results cover only a limited period. Metabolic methods, which include a urinanalysis, may be subject to tampering and yield reliable results for only a matter of days. Structural methods, such as hair analysis, may extend this window up to two or three months after ingestion (Mieczkowski, 1995). Thus, the polygraph allows agencies to investigate a much lengthier interval.

Other observers argue there are some very desirable latent, or unintended, benefits to polygraph testing. Swanson and his associates (1993, p. 241), for instance, maintain that applicants with questionable credentials or checkered histories will not bother applying when they learn about the polygraph provisions. In addition, reliance upon the polygraph broadcasts the message that an agency is interested in hiring only the most upright persons to work in the community.

The Psychological Interview

The psychological interview is a critical phase in the hiring process. Prior to this meeting, the psychologist will review all the recorded information the agency has gathered concerning the applicant. A check of the profiles generated during the written psychological tests may alert the psychologist to areas that are vague and require some probing. This pre-interview planning sets the stage for the face-to-face encounter.

The psychologist will ask the candidate a multitude of questions. Some inquiries will focus upon why the person has selected a law enforcement career and what type of job the candidate would look for if he or she did not get a position in policing. Other areas may include the kind of hobbies in which the applicant engages, what techniques the person uses to handle stress, and why the agency should select this person over anybody else in the pool.

The psychologist probes to see if there are any signs that indicate that the interviewee is not a well-adjusted person. Is the candidate easily intimidated, overly hostile, short-tempered, or too aggressive? Is there any evidence of authoritarianism, deception, or other undesirable traits? In short, the assessor is trying to determine whether any reason exists to weed out this person.

The important point to recognize is that the psychologist is not trying to match the candidate against some profile of what the ideal law enforcement officer should be. In fact, there is some literature that suggests that faith in these assessments is unfounded. In one study, a third of the hired officers whom a psychologist rated as suitable candidates earned unsatisfactory job performance ratings at the end of their first year of service (Hiatt & Hargrave, 1988). Another project found that the psychological recommendations were not related to evaluations received during the rookie training period (Wright, Doerner & Speir, 1990). Of course, these results are not surprising if one remembers the goal is to weed out unsuitable candidates and not to screen in prospective employees.

The Oral Board Interview

The capstone or final pre-employment hurdle in the police selection process is the oral board interview. The oral board usually consists of a panel of veteran officers who meet with each surviving member of the pool in a question-and-answer forum. Board members present a series of questions to the job-seeker and then grade the candidate's responses. The goal is to determine whether the person would make a suitable recruit.

The session usually opens with a request for a short autobiographical statement from the applicant. After the candidate finishes, board members will ask more specific questions. Some areas that the panel will touch upon include reasons for becoming a police officer, what occupational preparation the person has undertaken to prepare for this career, a self-assessment about the candidate's best and worst traits, and why the applicant thinks the agency should hire him or her over other people. In addition, the board may ask the candidate to explain how he or she would handle several hypothetical situations. Usually, these circumstances involve some type of moral or personal dilemma in which there is no right or wrong answer. The panel is interested in seeing how the candidate responds in a stressful setting.

After the candidate departs, each oral board member completes an evaluation of how well he or she thinks the person performed. The grading components usually reflect the applicant's appearance, self-confidence, ability to field questions and to express himself or herself, understanding of the job, and the work history or educational background. The final score reflects an assessment of whether the individual would make a suitable law enforcement officer.

While this procedure may appear to be reasonable, there are some doubts as to its inherent objectivity. One study discovered significant variability among raters (Gaines & Lewis, 1982). In other words, it appeared that some board members were using criteria that differed from what other panelists were invoking. Another project determined that board member characteristics predisposed the ratings that some candidates received (Falkenberg, Gaines & Cox, 1990). Female raters, in particular, had a tendency to downgrade minority participants. Thus, the literature suggests that one should refrain from blindly assuming that the oral board procedure automatically yields the most reliable and valid results.

There are indications, though, that these obstacles are surmountable. Gaines and Kappeler (1992) suggest that administrators should take the time to train oral board members prior to conducting any actual face-to-face interviews. Quite often, oral board members assemble on short notice and are not provided much in the way of instructions or guidance. Instead, emphasis should go to explaining what the panelists should look for in a candidate, how to assign numerical scores to their observations, having a standardized set of questions for all applicants, and afterwards assessing reliability and validity. Adherence to these guidelines should make oral board outcomes more trustworthy.

The Eligibility List

Once this entire process is completed, agency personnel will review the scores and compile an eligibility list of prospective police recruits. Conditional job offers will be extended and those who accept move onto the next stage.

The Medical Check

Police work, as you will see in Chapter 5, can be strenuous and quite stressful at times. If left unchecked, occupational demands eventually can take their toll and exact a hefty price on an officer's health. Shift work, dietary habits, the strain on interpersonal relationships, continuous exposure to danger, the abrupt way in which officers must spring into action, and experiencing the General Adaptation Syndrome over and over again without sufficient relief can be detrimental to one's well-being. In fact, these hazards and the ravages of stress are so well known that many agencies routinely send veteran employees to a physician for an annual physical.

Because there is a high incidence of cardiovascular and gastrointestinal disorders among police officers (Violanti, Vena & Marshall, 1986), the medical evaluation looks for any preexisting or abnormal physical conditions. Injuries, physical disabilities, worker's compensation, and early retirements are high-cost items in policing. Thus, weeding out medically unfit applicants becomes a top priority at this point.

Another facet of the medical check involves screening for illicit drug use. While drug testing was popular in the private sector during the 1980s, this practice raised significant issues concerning confidentiality, employee rights under collective bargaining agreements, and Fourth Amendment protection against unreasonable intrusions (Kirk, 1989; Orvis, 1994). Today, court rulings have narrowed the legal basis for drug detection tests in the civilian work place.

Public sector employees, on the other hand, operate under a much-diminished expectation of privacy (Orvis, 1994). Law enforcement members serve in such a critical capacity that it is fair to hold them to a more rigorous standard. While certain protections are afforded to in-service personnel, pre-service applicants do not enjoy similar privileges. In other words, governmental interests far outweigh the individual's claim to privacy. Thus, the rules regarding drug screening of prospective and current criminal justice employees are far less stringent than what is in place for the private sector (Gaines & Kappeler, 1992).

In summation, successful survivors of the selection process now shed their candidate's status and become police recruits. As the following chapter explains, these new inductees still face a barrage of occupational hurdles before they become full-fledged police officers. They must attend the pre-service training academy, earn state certification as law enforcement officers, and complete the agency's rookie training program. Rather than pursue those topics at this point, we should first look at how various legal requirements have impacted the recruitment and selection process already outlined.

EXTERNAL LEGAL PRESSURES

Earlier the comment was made that changing the police recruitment and selection process was akin to trying to bend granite. A number of legal developments in recent years have forced administrators to modify their hiring practices. This section will look at how three tools have been used to pressure law enforcement officials into complying with a much broader mandate.

The Civil Rights Act

The 1964 Civil Rights Act, along with its 1972 Title VII Amendment and the Civil Rights Act of 1991, are federal efforts to monitor unfair labor practices. These legal guidelines bar employers from rejecting a potential employee because of the person's race, color, religion, sex, or national origin. Instead, employers must apply the test of a *bona fide occupational qualification* (BFOQ). A BFOQ means that a hiring practice is legitimate as long as an employer can demonstrate a valid reason for its existence. This standard means that an entrance norm must be job-related in order to be an acceptable requirement. For the very first time, then, legal principles dictated that one should evaluate job applicants solely on the basis of whether they can discharge the duties of the position rather than some remote or tangential criterion.

At one time, many agencies subscribed to the notion that applicants should be at least a certain height to become a police officer. The thinking was that shorter officers were incapable of handling suspects and they lacked sufficient strength to handle other aspects of the job (Gaines, Falkenberg & Gambino, 1993). However, the courts later determined that this screening requirement disproportionately eliminated protected classes such as women and Hispanic males from police job offers. Since there was no empirical proof connecting the height requirement to job performance, height was not a valid BFOQ and agencies could not use it as part of their screening process.

As time went by, court rulings expanded upon this theme. Eventually, these decisions gave rise to the concept of *prima facie discrimination.* In other words, a hiring practice would be considered invalid if it disproportionately excluded members of a protected class from being hired. More important, though, the burden of proof shifted away from the plaintiff and onto the employer in these instances. What this switch means is that the employer now has to demonstrate that the hiring standard is a valid job-related criterion.

A plaintiff seeking relief under the civil rights provisions has to pass four tests. First, the person raising the complaint must belong to a protected class. Second, the complainant must satisfy the minimum requirements for the job. Third, even though the applicant did meet the minimum requirements, the employer must have rejected that person. Fourth, the employer had to continue the hiring process by interviewing other applicants after turning down the plaintiff as a viable candidate for the vacancy.

This new emphasis on hiring criteria's being job-related sparked considerable research interest. Concerned administrators wondered whether they should expect pre-employment psychological testing to focus more upon screening in than weeding out candidates. Psychologists countered that these expectations were misplaced and that they exceeded the capabilities of the instruments in use. However, these protests did little to discourage researchers from examining the relationship between psychological testing and subsequent job performance.

The first step in this endeavor was to identify what characteristics distinguished good police officers and how best to measure these traits. As one commentator put it, "before tests and measures can be accepted to predict who will or will not make a good police officer . . . it is necessary to agree on *what it is that makes a good police officer*" (Alpert, 1991, p. 262). As a result, a whole body of literature developed that concentrated on how best to measure police performance.

The lack of a consensus over how to best measure police performance did not prevent an extensive research effort. No matter how sophisticated the performance measure became, a consistent pattern emerged from the findings. Pre-employment psychological testing was not capable of predicting subsequent on-the-job performance (Dwyer, Prien & Bernard, 1990; Super et al., 1993; Wright, Doerner & Speir, 1990). In fact, the verdict reached by one police expert is quite revealing: "the usefulness of psychological testing for police officer selection is, at best, questionable" (Alpert, 1991, p. 266).

What needs to be done at this point in light of the present conclusion is to focus on building more appropriate screening in assessment devices while retaining the effective weeding out instruments. This strategy is precisely the direction that current research is now taking.

The Americans with Disabilities Act

The Americans with Disabilities Act (ADA) of 1990 is a federal law that makes it unlawful for employers to discriminate against qualified individuals who have a disability. A person is considered disabled if he or she falls into any of three categories: (1) he or she has a physical or mental impairment that severely limits a major life activity, (2) he or she has a record of such an impairment, or (3) he or she is thought to have a disability. As Table 3.2 illustrates, the ADA has also spawned some new terminology that reflects its concerns.

Table 3.2 Common Terms Associated with the Americans with Disabilities Act

Disability	(1) A mental or physical impairment that substantially limits a major life activity; (2) a record of having such an impairment; (3) being regarded as having such an impairment.
Major life activity	Basic functions that the average person in the general population can do with little or no difficulty such as walking, seeing, hearing, breathing, speaking, procreating, learning, sitting, standing, performing manual tasks, working, or having intimate sexual relations.
Otherwise qualified	A person with a disability who satisfies all of the requirements of the job such as education, experience, or skill and who can perform the essential functions of the job with or without reasonable accommodation.
Essential functions	The fundamental, not marginal, duties of a job.
Reasonable accommodation	A change in the application process, work environment, or job descriptions involving marginal functions of the job, or the use of modified or auxiliary devices that enable a person with a disability to perform the essential functions of the job without causing an undue hardship or direct threat to the health and safety of herself or himself or of others.
Undue hardship	Significant difficulty or expense relative to the size and overall financial resources of the employer.

Source: Rubin (1993, p. 4).

To be protected under the ADA, a person with a disability must also be qualified to perform the essential functions of the position with or without reasonable accommodation. In other words, the applicant must satisfy the minimum entrance requirements for the vacancy and be able to do the job with or without reasonable accommodation.

> ***Illustration:***   Suppose, for the moment, that a police department advertises an opening for a 911 telecommunications operator. The essential functions of this position would include answering incoming telephone calls and talking with callers. After screening all the applications to ensure that the candidates meet the minimum qualifications (high school diploma, English speaking, no significant criminal history, and so forth), the agency learns that one applicant has a reduced hearing ability. However, this person wears a hearing aid which amplifies sound and has no difficulty using a regular telephone on a daily basis. While ADA does not extend a hiring preference to this person, it does prohibit the agency from rejecting this otherwise qualified person on the grounds that he or she wears a hearing device.

The two areas with the most potential to impact law enforcement are substance abuse and the medical evaluation. In the past, drug and alcohol abuse, both commonly regarded as illnesses, have been sufficient grounds for being weeded out of the police selection process. The ADA does not change this practice (Smith & Alpert, 1993, p. 518). It specifically excludes current users from coverage, but does protect prior users who have recovered or are rehabilitated. However, several courts have ruled that the ADA does not require law enforcement agencies to abandon this standard. The prevailing view is that policing is such a critical function to society that character and trustworthiness are important employee attributes (Chaires & Lentz, 1994; Orvis, 1994; Smith & Alpert, 1993).

While the ADA has not affected the validity of the medical examination, this statute does regulate its timing (Schneid & Gaines, 1991; Smith & Alpert, 1993). Since the purpose of the ADA is to protect against unwarranted discrimination, employers may not schedule a physical testing prior to rendering an actual hiring decision. Instead, agencies must complete all the other relevant screening procedures first, reach a hiring decision, and then extend an offer of employment pending the outcome of the medical examination. Thus, the ADA has changed the point at which the medical screening takes place, but has not necessarily altered how these results are used.

How can an agency insulate itself from legal action under the ADA? In order to demonstrate compliance, the potential employer must inventory the basic job duties of the position before undertaking an advertisement or recruitment campaign (U.S. Equal Employment Opportunity Commission, 1991). In other words, this legislative mandate continues the theme of articulating job-related criteria that we have encountered already in previous legal developments. When viewed in this context, the ADA is simply an evolution and not a revolution.

Consent Decrees

One tool that the courts have used to prod police departments into complying with affirmative action mandates has been the consent decree. Whenever a class action lawsuit is resolved, such as in a negotiated settlement or court ruling, a consent decree will be forged between the parties or imposed by the court. A consent decree usually spells out the concessions won by the plaintiffs and also includes an affirmative action plan for hiring members of that protected class in the future.

Quite often, the terms of a consent decree address four areas (Doerner & Patterson, 1992; Felkenes, Peretz & Schroedel, 1993). The first area itemizes the monetary damages owed to each member of the class action. This calculation compares the salary that the person would have made in the law enforcement position against what the person actually did earn during that same period. Assume, for example, that the average annual salary of a police officer was $20,000 over a five-year interval. A class action member received an annual salary of $15,000 during that time. Because that person was unfairly discriminated against and did not land a law enforcement job, he or she incurred an annual loss of $5,000 in wages. That $5,000 difference, when multiplied by the five years, means that the person is entitled to a lump-sum payment of $25,000 plus interest to reach parity.

The second area in this kind of an agreement normally deals with preferential hiring rights. Since the agency rendered an unfair determination during the original hiring process, it now must extend job offers as vacancies arise to each member belonging to the class action. The department cannot place any other applicants on its roster until all these participants have exercised the first right of acceptance or refusal.

The third consideration revolves around any job benefits that have accrued during the period under litigation. All seniority rights are restored to each class member who accepts an employment offer. These items include salary increases, pension benefits, vacation leave, sick time, and promotional credits. As you can see, the goal is to reinstate the affected person without any penalty whatsoever.

Finally, the consent decree will outline an affirmative action program aimed at increasing the number of affected class members in the employee pool. This arrangement imposes a quota, as well as a timetable, upon the agency. For instance, the consent decree may state that thirty of the next sixty people hired will be females. Or, the agreement may announce that the goal for the agency is to have a specific percentage of women or minority members on board in a sworn capacity within so many years.

The court will retain jurisdiction over the case and continue to monitor the agency's hiring practices to ensure compliance. The department will submit periodic reports to the judge explaining the progress to date in all four areas. Once the agency has reached the goals outlined in the consent decree or whenever the judge is satisfied that the agency has achieved sufficient "good faith" progress, the consent decree is dissolved.

Given this background, the obvious question is whether consent decrees work. Employment figures for sworn personnel at the local level in 1990 show that less than 10 percent were female while 17 percent were nonwhite (Reaves, 1992, p. 5). These numbers do not impress critics who view this change as proceeding at a snail's pace.

Martin (1991), however, counters that one can trace the recent surge in female representation to the imposition of consent decrees. She notes that at the end of 1986 "15 percent of the departments in cities serving populations of more than 50,000 (and 40 percent of the 53 agencies in jurisdictions with populations of more than 250,000) were operating under court orders or consent decrees, 42 percent had adopted voluntary affirmative action plans, and 43 percent had no affirmative action policy" (Martin, 1991, p. 491).

Martin (1991), though, goes one step further. She conducted a national survey of police agencies and paid particular attention to whether an agency had an affirmative action policy in effect and if it was court-ordered or initiated by the agency. The results revealed that affirmative action policies are responsible for increasing the presence of women, especially black females, among the rank and file. Since agencies tabulate race and gender employment figures separately, minority women permit the agency to satisfy both race and gender quotas simultaneously.

Examinations of the Los Angeles Police Department personnel operations in the wake of a consent decree provide similar findings (Felkenes, 1991; Felkenes & Schroedel, 1993). The biggest affirmative gains came in the form of nonwhite women. Other indirect evidence offers additional support for this line of thinking. Several studies indicate that agencies with a firm minority presence are also able to attract more female officers (Hochstedler & Conley, 1986; Martin, 1989; Martin, 1991; Warner, Steel & Lovrish, 1990). Thus, it would appear that affirmative action mandates have been successful in inducting previously underrepresented groups and in producing a more diverse police presence. Whether these efforts persist only for the short run or are more durable is the focus of the next section.

TURNOVER AND RETENTION

As Chapter 1 demonstrated, the introduction of female officers into the police world initially met with a hostile reaction and resentment from co-workers. We also learned from Chapter 2 that the influx of minorities into policing drew a similar resistance from white incumbents. Despite this formidable opposition, though, affirmative action efforts appear successful. The number of minority members and women entering law enforcement is on the rise and the police service is becoming more diversified.

These same affirmative action reports, however, can be misleading because they focus exclusively on the front end of recruitment and hiring efforts. Simple demographic "bean counting," tallying the number of African Americans and females an agency hires, overlooks the essential ongoing question of employee retention. A more important issue, and one that more accurately maps the internal organizational atmosphere, is how many African American and female officers remain in continuous service within the agency from year to year (Doerner, 1995).

A troubled agency that has not dealt thoroughly with affirmative action concerns will post a relatively high employee turnover rate. However, if the personnel director quickly replenishes the agency roster with new hires from protected classes, the bean counting monitoring strategy can generate a false sense of accomplishment. To avoid any distortion, one must move beyond simple recruitment and look at employee retention patterns. Given this orientation, the following sections address turnover experiences with recruits, rookies, and veteran officers.

Recruit Turnover

One reform that arose from the movement to establish minimum standards for sworn personnel was the requirement for recruits to attend the police academy before assuming police duties. Over the years, most states have developed a standardized recruit curriculum, specified the number of instructional hours devoted to various topics, licensed police trainers, and outlined learning objectives for each academy module. Despite these advances, one regular complaint is that many academy graduates lack basic skills. The washout rate that many agencies register during the initial rookie training phase and the perceived lack of a connection between academy lessons and what officers do in the field have made some people wonder just what is imparted at the training academy (Ness, 1991).

As one might imagine, a number of recruits drop out or are terminated from the pre-service training academy. Felkenes, Peretz, and Schroedel (1993, p. 46) learned that the failure rate at the Los Angeles Police Academy was 20 percent for white males and 59 percent for women prior to a consent decree's taking effect. After the consent decree, the failure rate diminished to 29 percent for women. These and other observations led the research team to comment that "Failing women and minorities during training allows one to preserve the myth of open access without having to alter the composition of the permanent force" (Felkenes, Peretz, & Schroedel, 1993, p. 44).

Unfortunately, no uniform statistics are kept on academy turnover. However, a recent development may shed some additional light on this neglected area. The latest wrinkle is the certification examination. As of July 1, 1993, Florida began requiring all police recruits to pass a state board examination after completing the academy training program. A passing score is a prerequisite to becoming licensed as a law enforcement officer. In fact, agencies are barred from placing anybody who fails this test into a sworn position.

Test scores vary throughout the state. While some academies boast of a perfect pass rate, other locations have logged pass rates as low as 61 percent on a single test administration. Failure rates hovering around a quarter of the recruits are common. More recently, the washout rates appear to have stabilized around the 10 percent mark. For our immediate purposes, these failure rates are not broken down by race or by gender. In any event, it should be clear that attending the police academy offers no guarantee that one will shed the recruit label and move up to rookie status.

Rookie Turnover

Consent decrees have ushered in many organizational changes. One of these developments involved restructuring the rookie training program that new officers faced after graduating from the police academy. Since Chapter 4 looks at training practices, a detailed description of the Field Training Officer (FTO) program is not appropriate here. For our purposes, though, it is important to understand how FTO programs came into existence.

Post-academy training was quite informal in the old days. Rookies were paired with senior officers for their first tour of duty. For a month, the novice would accompany the veteran and observe the older officer handling calls for service. The rookie would ask questions and soak up the mentor's philosophy and style of policing. At the end of this indoctrination period, the senior officer would give his opinion about the younger officer's suitability for police work. If the old-timer gave a positive report, the recruit moved up to permanent status. Should the veteran officer express any doubts or reservations about the rookie, this person was terminated from the police service.

A number of flaws tainted this procedure. There was no standardized lesson plan or standardized instruction from one recruit to the next. Senior officers received very little guidance about how to evaluate newcomers. Documentation to substantiate the veteran officers' assessments was absent. Since most veteran officers were white males, this practice amounted to nothing more than an indefensible perpetuation of the "good old boy" system. Obviously, such a practice was not receptive to affirmative action concerns (Doerner, Speir & Wright, 1989, p. 104).

Agencies faced with consent decrees found it necessary to dismantle this antiquated training procedure and to substitute a more valid appraisal mechanism that could withstand judicial scrutiny. The need for a performance evaluation based upon job-related behavior was recognized. The result was the widespread adoption of a training module created by the San Diego Police Department (Bradley & Pursley, 1987).

When the FTO program was devised, its producers expected there would be a 35 percent flunk-out rate. One study, though, did document actual officer turnover. Doerner, Speir, and Wright (1989, p. 104) reported that 81 percent of the male rookies and 79 percent of the female trainees successfully completed one agency's FTO program. In terms of race, only 64 percent of the black rookies, compared to 88 percent of the white officers, made it through this period.

While Doerner, Speir, and Wright (1989) were not able to pinpoint an exact reason for this differential attrition, other studies have uncovered some disturbing habits. They reveal that female officers often complain bitterly of sexual harassment and intimidation (Doerner & Patterson, 1992; Fagan, 1985; Felkenes & Schroedel, 1993). In fact, some training officers confided that, in their opinion, hiring females and blacks reduced the quality of service delivery on the streets (Fagan, 1985, p. 143). As one research team put it, "While judicial intervention can ensure that protected classes do attain visibility on agency rosters, it cannot legislate the type of reception these new employees receive" (Doerner & Patterson, 1992, p. 31).

Whether attrition during the FTO program reflects inadequate employee screening practices during the hiring phase or discontent with the inner workings of the training program, there is a very clear loss here. Affirmative action goals are sabotaged. In addition, locating and training suitable replacements translates into a considerable delay in filling authorized positions. Understaffing, of course, means a greater workload for existing personnel. One can only conjecture about whether personnel shortages affect citizen perceptions of service delivery, rudeness complaints, and allegations of excessive force.

Veteran Turnover

Despite being an important concern, the literature is very quiet when it comes to veteran officer attrition. However, this topic has garnered some attention in the correctional field. Wright (1993), for example, reports that the voluntary employee turnover in corrections hovers around the 20 percent mark. Experts usually advise that attrition is excessive once it reaches a level of 10 percent (Dantzker, 1992; Fry, 1983; Martin, 1990). When compared to other occupations, criminal justice employee separation figures are alarmingly high.

One study tracked 134 police officers who were hired by a municipal agency during 1981–1986 to see what their employment status was in 1994 (Doerner, 1995). Officers who left the agency were dubbed "quitters." Those who remained in continuous employment during this period became the "stayers." Almost three-quarters of the African American females had departed by their eighth year of service. Overall, the female separation rate was twice as high as the corresponding male figure.

Correctional research shows that quitters tend to be very productive workers with impressive credentials (Wright, 1991, 1993). While there is some concern that state and federal agencies are luring away outstanding African American and female local officers to satisfy their own affirmative action mandates, that fear seems to be misplaced. In fact, Doerner (1995) found that quitters who were white or male were more likely to relocate to a state or federal agency than quitters who were African American or female. Thus, it does not appear that state and federal agencies are draining away local talent to satisfy their own equal opportunity mandates.

The upward march toward hiring officers with more educational credentials may also contribute to employee turnover. One research team (Buckley, McGinnis & Petrunik, 1992) learned that officers with college degrees regarded themselves as prime promotional material. Of course, there are so few opportunities for advancement within policing that most officers never progress beyond their entrance rank.

In a related vein, Dantzker (1992) reports that college-educated officers expressed greater interest in abandoning their police jobs and switching careers once they hit the five-year mark. As he puts it, "departments that want to promote college education for their officers need to examine their organizational structure and its potential for providing avenues that will assist in maintaining satisfied officers" (Dantzker, 1992, pp. 114–115).

CLOSING COMMENTS: THE IMPENDING CHALLENGE OF POLICE PERSONNEL

As the 21st century approaches, several dark clouds are looming ominously on the horizon when it comes to police personnel matters. The scant literature that is available suggests that competent criminal justice employees are the ones who relocate to pursue better job prospects. What does this trend mean for the pool of officers who are left behind? Do stayers remain in policing because they have no other viable career options? If so, what kind of police service do they deliver? Police typologies readily recognize a disenchanted employee category as bordering on being dysfunctional. Whether we call these officers "rule-appliers" (White, 1972), "realists" (Broderick, 1977), "avoiders" (Muir, 1977), or "shirkers" (Hochstedler, 1981), they all exhibit a common trait. They are burned out and do just enough to get by on the job.

These observations lead to other worries. Do stayers make a conscious decision to pursue a law enforcement career or do they become "careerists" by default? If we think that older officers who have grown jaded and cynical are more likely to cling to misanthropic views, will they end up imparting their outlooks and infecting new officers entering the ranks? The major concern, of course, is that we do not know how this configuration will affect police–citizen interaction.

Another development destined to impact the area of police personnel is President Clinton's crime bill. The President proposes to augment the police strength in this country by putting an additional 100,000 federally funded officers on the streets for three years. Since it takes about a year to fully train a recruit, this new cadre has a usable street-life of two years. What is the long-term payoff to the agency? As one observer put it, "It takes several years of seasoning to make a good law enforcement officer. . . . If 22-year-olds are hired as officers, and they leave at 25 or 26, they mature at the expense of the agency and give no real benefit in return" (Buerger, 1996, p. 13).

Still other issues abound. For example, what is the impact of mixing careerists with "terminalists"? Will the level of service that the community receives from this temporary contingency of terminalists differ from what ordinary careerists offer? How will this influx of terminalists affect citizen dissatisfaction, civil liability, and complaints of police misconduct? Can two separate tracks of officers hinder or promote affirmative action efforts? Will these efforts lead to a gentrification or graying of careerists? Will this institutionalized employee turnover have a positive or negative effect on police professionalization?

As these concerns demonstrate, current personnel policies carry the potential to generate some very deep and far-reaching repercussions well beyond the turn of the century. While this chapter may not have provided any firm answers to the impending dilemmas that law enforcement faces, it has exposed you to some of the contemporary personnel issues that will frame the composition of police agencies in the near future.

DISCUSSION QUESTIONS

1. Suppose that your college or university plans to start a public safety department that will provide law enforcement and police services for the campus. Administrators come to your class seeking advice about how to select new officers. After much discussion, these administrators ask you to write a job advertisement for these openings. What items would you include in the job announcement?
2. Continuing the previous question, the university or college officials arrange for members of the psychology department to meet with members of the criminal

justice department to discuss how to select and hire these new officers. You are asked to chair this meeting and to prepare an agenda that will guide this group's deliberations. What topics will appear on the agenda and why?

3. Continuing the previous question, the director of personnel services at your university or college telephones you and asks how the eyesight and hearing standards for prospective police officers will comply with civil rights regulations and the Americans with Disabilities Act. How would you respond?

4. Continuing the previous question, the director of personnel services also inquires as to what steps you would take to ensure that the university or college does not come under a consent decree in the future. What would you tell this person?

5. Continuing the previous question, the personnel director explains that every unit within the university or college must submit an annual report describing its employment patterns and practices. What kind of topics would you recommend that the public safety department include in its annual report?

REFERENCES

Alpert, G.P. (1991). Hiring and promoting police officers in small departments—The role of psychological testing. *Criminal Law Bulletin, 27*(3), 261–269.

Alpert, G.P., & Fridell, L.A. (1992). *Police vehicles and firearms: Instruments of deadly force.* Prospect Heights, IL: Waveland Press.

Ash, P., Slora, K.B., & Britton, C.F. (1990). Police agency officer selection practices. *Journal of Police Science and Administration, 17*(4), 258–269.

Bradley, D.E., & Pursley, R.D. (1987). Behaviorally anchored rating scale for patrol officer performance appraisal. *Journal of Police Science and Administration, 15*(1), 37–45.

Broderick, J.J. (1977). *Police in a time of change.* Morristown, NJ: General Learning Press.

Buckley, L.B., McGinnis, J.H., & Petrunik, M.G. (1992). Police perceptions of education as an entitlement to promotion: An equity theory perspective. *American Journal of Police, 12*(2), 77–100.

Buerger, M., (Ed.). (1996). Police education and the crime bill. *Police Forum, 6*(1), 1–16.

Chaires, R.H., & Lentz, S.A. (1994). Criminal justice employees' rights: An overview. *American Journal of Criminal Justice, 18*(2), 259–288.

Cox, S.M. (1996). *Police: Practices, perspectives, problems.* Needham Heights, MA: Allyn & Bacon.

Dantzker, M.L. (1992). An issue for policing—Educational level and job satisfaction: A research note. *American Journal of Police, 12*(2), 101–118.

del Carmen, R.V. (1989). Civil liabilities of police supervisors. *American Journal of Police, 8*(1), 107–135.

Doerner, W.G. (1995). Officer retention patterns: An affirmative action concern for police agencies? *American Journal of Police, 14*(3/4), 197–210.

Doerner, W.G., Speir, J.C., & Wright, B.S. (1989). An analysis of rater-ratee race and sex influences upon field training officer program evaluations. *Journal of Criminal Justice, 17*(2), 103–114.

Doerner, W.G., & Patterson, E.B. (1992). The influence of race and gender upon rookie evaluations of their field training officers. *American Journal of Police, 11*(2), 23–36.

Dwyer, W.O., Prien, E.P., & Bernard, J.L. (1990). Psychological screening of law enforcement officers: A case for job relatedness. *Journal of Police Science and Administration, 17*(3), 176–182.

Fagan, M.M. (1985). How police officers perceive their field training officer. *Journal of Police Science and Administration, 15*(1), 138–152.

Falkenberg, S., Gaines, L.K., & Cox, T.C. (1990). The oral interview board: What does it measure? *Journal of Police Science and Administration, 17*(1), 32–39.

Felkenes, G.T. (1991). Affirmative action in the Los Angeles police department. *Criminal Justice Research Bulletin, 6*(4), 1–4.

Felkenes, G.T., & Schroedel, J.R. (1993). A case study of minority women in policing. *Women and Criminal Justice, 4*(2), 65–89.

Felkenes, G.T., Peretz, P., & Schroedel, J.R. (1993). An analysis of the mandatory hiring of females: The Los Angeles police department experience. *Women and Criminal Justice, 4*(2), 31–63.

Fry, L.J. (1983). A preliminary examination of the factors related to turnover of women in law enforcement. *Journal of Police Science and Administration, 11*(2), 149–155.

Gaines, L.K., & Lewis, B.R. (1982). Reliability and validity of the oral interview board in police promotions: A research note. *Journal of Criminal Justice, 10*(5), 403–419.

Gaines, L.K., & Kappeler, V.E. (1992). Selection and testing. In G. Cordner & D. Hale (Eds.), *What works in policing? Operations and administration examined.* Cincinnati: Anderson Publishing Co.

Gaines, L.K., Falkenberg, S., & Gambino, J.A. (1993). Police physical agility testing: An historical and legal analysis. *American Journal of Police, 12*(4), 47–66.

Guyot, D. (1979). Bending granite: Attempts to change the rank structure of American police departments. *Journal of Police Science and Administration, 7*(3), 253–284.

Hale, D.C., & Wyland, S.M. (1993). Dragons and dinosaurs: The plight of patrol women. *Police Forum, 3*(2), 1–6.

Haney, C., Banks, C., & Zimbardo, P. (1973). Interpersonal dynamics in a simulated prison. *International Journal of Criminology and Penology, 1*(1), 69–97.

Hiatt, D., & Hargrave, G.E. (1988). Predicting job performance problems with psychological screening. *Journal of Police Science and Administration, 16*(2), 122–125.

Hochstedler, E. (1981). Testing types: A review and test of police types. *Journal of Criminal Justice, 9*(6), 303–323.

Hochstedler, E., & Conley, J.A. (1986). Explaining underrepresentation of black officers in city police agencies. *Journal of Criminal Justice, 14*(4), 319–328.

Hogue, M.S., Black, T., & Sigler, R.T. (1994). The differential use of screening techniques in the recruitment of police officers. *American Journal of Police, 13*(2), 113–124.

Johnson, E.E. (1983). Psychological tests used in assessing a sample of police and fire fighter candidates. *Journal of Police Science and Administration, 11*(4), 430–433.

Kappeler, V.E., Kappeler, S.F., & del Carmen, R.V. (1993). A content analysis of police civil liability cases: Decisions of the federal district courts, 1978–1990. *Journal of Criminal Justice, 21*(4), 325–337.

Kirk, G.T. (1989). Employee drug testing: Federal courts are redefining individual privacy; will labor arbitrators follow suit? *University of Miami Law Review, 44*(2), 489–538.

Martin, S.E. (1989). *Women on the move? A report on the status of women in policing.* Washington, D.C.: Police Foundation.

———. (1990). *On the move: The status of women in policing.* Washington, D.C.: Police Foundation.

————. (1991). The effectiveness of affirmative action: The case of women in policing. *Justice Quarterly, 8*(4), 489–504.

Mieczkowski, T. (1995). Hair analysis as a drug detector. *Research in Brief.* Washington, D.C.: National Institute of Justice.

Muir, W.K., Jr. (1977). *Police: Streetcorner politicians.* Chicago: University of Chicago Press.

Ness, J.J. (1991). The relevance of basic law enforcement training—Does the curriculum prepare recruits for police work: A survey study. *Journal of Criminal Justice, 19*(2), 181–193.

Orvis, G.P. (1994). Drug testing in the criminal justice work place. *American Journal of Criminal Justice, 18*(2), 289–305.

Reaves, B.A. (1992). State and local police departments, 1990. *Bureau of Justice Statistics Bulletin.* Washington, D.C.: U.S. Department of Justice.

Sanders, B., Hughes, T., & Langworthy, R. (1995). Police officer recruitment and selection: A survey of major police departments in the U.S. *Police Forum, 5*(4), 1–4.

Schneid, T.D., & Gaines, L.K. (1991). The Americans with disabilities act: Implications for police administrators. *American Journal of Police, 10*(1), 47–58.

Sechrest, D.K., & Burns, P. (1992). Police corruption: The Miami case. *Criminal Justice and Behavior, 19*(3), 294–313.

Smith, M.R., & Alpert, G.P. (1993). The police and the Americans with disabilities act: Who is being discriminated against? *Criminal Law Bulletin, 29*(6), 516–528.

Super, J.T., Blau, T.H., Wells, C.B., & Murdock, N.H. (1993). Using psychological tests to discriminate between "best" and "least best" correctional officers. *Journal of Criminal Justice, 21*(2), 143–150.

Swanson, C.R., Territo, L., & Taylor, R.W. (1993). *Police administration: Structures, processes, and behavior* (3rd ed.). New York: Macmillan.

The Americans with Disabilities Act, 42 U.S.C. 12101-12213 (Supp. II 1990).

U.S. Equal Employment Opportunity Commission. (1991). *The Americans with disabilities act: Your responsibilities as an employer.* Washington, D.C.: U.S. Equal Employment Opportunity Commission.

Violanti, J.M., Vena, J.E., & Marshall, J.R. (1986). Disease risk and mortality among police officers: New evidence and contributing factors. *Journal of Police Science and Administration, 14*(1), 17–23.

Vollmer, A. (1936). *The police and modern society.* Berkeley, CA: University of California Press.

Walker, S. (1985). Racial minority and female employment in policing: The implications of "glacial" change. *Crime and Delinquency, 31*(4), 555–572.

Warner, R.L., Steel, B.S., & Lovrish, N.P. (1990). Economic, political, and institutional determinants of minority employment in municipal police departments. *American Journal of Police, 9*(2), 41–61.

White, S.O. (1972). A perspective on police professionalization. *Law and Society Review, 7*(1), 61–85.

Wright, B.S., Doerner, W.G., & Speir, J.C. (1990). Pre-employment psychological testing as a predictor of police performance during an FTO program. *American Journal of Police, 9*(4), 65–84.

Wright, T.A. (1991). The level of employee utilization and its effect on subsequent turnover. *Journal of Applied Business Research, 7*(1), 25–29.

————. (1993). Correctional employee turnover: A longitudinal study. *Journal of Criminal Justice, 21*(2), 131–142.

4

Education and Training: No Longer Just a Badge and a Gun

Stan Shernock, Norwich University
Gail D. Dantzker, Georgia Southern University

In the early stages of policing in the United States, there was much to be desired in the quality of those who became police officers. Obtaining a job as a police officer was often the result of political patronage, and preparedness was limited to the provision of a badge and a gun. Police officers sometimes were not the most respected or trustworthy individuals.

However, as society began to change, the call came for change in policing. Although that call was first heeded in the early 1900s by August Vollmer, the issue did not receive national attention until the late 1920s, with the formation of the first national commission charged with examining and suggesting ways to improve policing.

In 1931, the final report of the Wickersham Commission noted that "the great majority of police are not suited either by temperament, training, or education for their position" (National Commission on Law Observance and Enforcement, 1931). Since the time of the Wickersham Commission report, successive commissions and many police administrators have recommended that reform and professionalization among police officers be pursued through improved education and training. They emphasized that education and training are critical because they are among the most important variables having direct effect on police officers' role perceptions and behavior.

There has been a tendency to assume a blurring and cross-fertilization between law enforcement training and higher education (Haley, 1992). Although often treating them as twin processes directed at similar ends, some students of policing have identified important distinctions between the two concepts. For example, Massey (1993) argues that the hallmark of an education, as distinct from training, is that it promotes understanding rather than merely the ability to master a range of skills and techniques. Thomas Dull (1982, p. 316), quoting Sam Souryal, states that training is giving narrow, specific, and one-best-way information that can be used on the job, and education is the presentation of basic principles and broad concepts to offer a wide variety of decisions.

Thus, when educated people are faced with a novel situation, they should be able to analyze, interpret, and make judgments about the situation themselves, rather than rely on others to tell them what to do. Moreover, educated people should be able to justify their actions by applying reason and reasonableness rather than appealing to authority to justify their decisions by succumbing to the familiar and discredited "I was just following orders" argument. A person who has been merely trained, on the other hand, is more likely to rely on others to tell him or her what to do in a particular situation and is less likely to understand the reasons for doing what he or she is directed to do. Therefore, education is intended to promote autonomy and deliberate judgment while training may create dependency, conformity, and working to rule.

The importance of both education and training in policing has long been debated. This chapter explores the two concepts, their critical distinctions, and their status and development. Each concept will be treated separately before we explore the relationship between the two in the conclusion.

POLICE EDUCATION: HISTORY AND BACKGROUND

The belief in the importance of a college education for police officers today derives from two main movements. The first and most longstanding source of this belief is the perceived need to reform the police by professionalizing them, and the second source, the perceived need to change police attitudes. The movement to professionalize the police by requiring a college education for police began with August Vollmer, who, in 1917, proposed a thirty-six month college level program in police education (Hudzik, 1978). Vollmer envisioned higher education for police primarily as a vehicle for converting the police occupation into a prestigious profession (Goldstein, 1977; Sherman, 1978; Sherman et al., 1978). The purpose of higher education to improve the professional prestige of the police, rather than to promote professional behavior, has been the overriding objective of the police reform movement since World War II and remains a major concern of police officials (Greene & Cordner, 1980; Sherman et al., 1978). It was felt that education would not only improve the professional behavior and increase the effectiveness or expertise of police, but would also upgrade the nature of the job or occupation of policing in the eyes of the public (Bittner, 1970; LeDoux et al., 1984; Scott, 1986; Sherman et al., 1978; Smith, 1978).

Even though a police training school was established in 1917 on the University of California campus, it wasn't until 1931 that Vollmer, a professor in the political science department and still chief of police of Berkeley, was asked to create a degree program (Griffin, 1980). By 1960, twenty-six institutions offered full-time law enforcement programs.

The major impetus for implementing Vollmer's idea of higher education for police came in the late 1960s (Sherman et al., 1978). This was, for the most part, due to negative relationships between the police and minorities and to harsh police responses to the civil unrest during that period (Carter & Sapp, 1990; Jacobs & Magdovitz, 1977). The concern with the role of education shifted during that time to viewing education as an instrument for inculcating democratic and progressive social values of equality, mutual accommodation, and adaptation in the police, rather than imparting necessary skills (Smith & Ostrom, 1974; Worden, 1990). Greene and Cordner (1980) have described this role for higher education as one of promoting the process of social change, especially when officers with higher education act as change agents as they move into positions of leadership and authority in police agencies.

Consequently, a number of different national commissions during this period recommended that police agencies require a baccalaureate degree of new recruits, to help them deal with their complex role. The most significant of these commissions was the President's Commission on Law Enforcement and the Administration of Justice, which issued a report in 1967 calling not only for a baccalaureate degree but emphasizing the value of a liberal arts education (Brown, 1974; Sherman et al., 1978). Although this need for college education was reiterated in reports by other national commissions (Beckman, 1976), the President's Commission was probably the most effective of all the commissions. It was the President's Commission on Law Enforcement and the Administration of Justice report that led to the Omnibus Crime Control and Safe Streets Act of 1968. From this act came the creation of the Law Enforcement Assistance Administration (LEAA). A tool of the LEAA was the Law Enforcement Education Program (LEEP), which provided monies to universities and colleges to create police-related programs and scholarship monies for students to enroll in these programs (Sherman et al., 1978). The LEAA and LEEP programs were a boon to programs of higher education at colleges and universities.

As previously noted, in 1960 only twenty-six police-related programs existed. In 1978 the International Association of Chiefs of Police (IACP) estimated that more than 1,000 associate and almost 600 baccalaureate criminal justice programs existed (Dull, 1982).

Profound changes occurred in police education programs as a result of LEAA's demise in 1981. Technical-type programs that attracted large numbers of in-service, part-time students declined dramatically in enrollments, while the broader, more rigorous academic programs that attracted pre-service, full-time students stabilized or increased in enrollments (Weirman & Archambeault, 1983). As these programs became less technical, broadened their curricula and perspectives, and began to offer courses on the other components of the criminal justice system besides the police, the names of these programs changed from police science or law enforcement to criminal justice.

THE CURRENT STATUS OF POLICE EDUCATION

Despite the commissions' recommendations and predictions, the educational level and educational requirements for positions in policing have not been upgraded substantially during the intervening decades. The recommendation in the 1967 President's Commission on Law Enforcement and the Administration of Justice that general law enforcement officers and their supervisors be required to have at least a bachelor's degree was regarded negatively and generally not implemented (Beckman, 1976). A national survey for the Police Executive Research Forum (PERF) on police education found that 22.6 percent of the officers in their survey had earned a baccalaureate degree (Carter, Sapp & Stephens, 1988). This survey, however, was biased toward the middle and larger sized departments, where officers were assumed to be more likely to possess a bachelor's degree. While these results showed an increase over the 10 percent of all officers who had bachelor's degrees in 1981 (Taft, 1981), it certainly did not fulfill the expectations of the National Advisory Commission on Criminal Justice Standards and Goals. Even more disturbingly, only 0.4 percent of the departments surveyed required a baccalaureate degree, and only 13.8 percent of the departments had a requirement for education beyond the high school diploma (Carter & Sapp, 1990; Carter, Sapp & Stephens, 1988).

In a subsequent Law Enforcement Management and Administrative Statistics survey (Reaves, 1992), of 1,830 local police departments, 840 sheriff's departments, 226 special police departments, and the 49 primary state police departments, about 6 percent of local departments required recruits to have some college education, as did 18 percent of state departments. Again, this is not much of an improvement over what the National Manpower Survey of the Criminal Justice System found in 1978: of the 2,639 police agencies responding, only 5.5 percent had any college requirement as a condition of entry level employment (Green & Cordner, 1980, p.14). Efforts and educational requirements by police departments do not seem to indicate a commitment to raising educational levels of police officers.

It should be noted, however, that there are exceptions to the low level of higher education reported in these studies. For example, in Colorado, nearly six times as many agencies as those in the PERF study required a bachelor's degree for recruits (Copley, 1992). Still, only two states, Minnesota and Wisconsin, currently have education standards (*Police Forum,* 1996).

THE EFFECTS OF HIGHER EDUCATION

Instead of entry level educational requirements, police agencies have provided incentives for educational achievement, either providing immediate material reward for college credit or providing for more long-term rewards (Greene & Cordner, 1980). Greene and Cordner cite two separate studies finding that 60 percent of the agencies they surveyed provided educational incentives for their officers. In Colorado, the two most frequently cited means of support for officers attending college classes were tuition assistance and the ability to attend classes on duty, each means provided by 51 percent of the agencies responding to the survey (Copley, 1992).

Desirable educational levels of police officers continue to be a highly debated topic owing to the limited data pertaining to how effective education really is for police officers. This section explores current beliefs and findings about the effect of higher education on policing.

On Police Attitudes and Professional Orientations

The arguments provided in commission reports indicating the value and effects of higher education for the police and policing were generally rhetorical and intuitive, rather than based on empirical evidence (Carter & Sapp, 1990; Finckenauer, 1975; Greene & Cordner, 1980; Griffin, 1980; Worden, 1990), as was the earlier literature on police education (Griffin, 1980; Swanson, 1977). Nevertheless, both the commissions' reports and the increasing federal funding of criminal justice research did lead to a number of subsequent empirical studies that attempted to examine the effects of college education on the police.

The first studies undertaken were largely studies of the difference in attitudes between college educated officers and those without college educations. Studies examined whether college education had positive effects in changing the dogmatism, authoritarianism, cynicism, prejudice and intolerance, and punitive orientation of police (Alpert & Dunham, 1988). Studies indeed found that the college-educated officer was less authoritarian (Smith, Locke & Fenster, 1970; Dalley, 1975), more attuned to social and ethnic problems (Weiner, 1976), less dogmatic (Parker et al., 1976), more open-minded and less punitively oriented (Guller, 1972). There is also a preponderance of research findings, albeit not conclusive evidence, that college educated officers are more responsive to the public, are better decision makers, are more innovative and flexible in problem-solving, show greater empathy toward the disenfranchised, are more responsible in exercising police authority, are less cynical, and exhibit a more goal-oriented and professional attitude (Carter & Sapp, 1990).

Since, with a few exceptions (Worden, 1990), attitude studies largely have focused on the inculcation of global democratic values and general social psychological traits, they not only have ignored examining attitudes relevant to professional values, but for the most part also have ignored how these attitudes are related to policing. For instance, while authoritarianism is viewed negatively, the very nature of police work may require it at some minimum level (Swanson, 1977).

Smith (1978) treated both college education and police training as measures of professionalization. He further noted that the attributes of a profession include

1. full-time career work (for pay), which would lead to a commitment or sense of calling;
2. a formalized code of ethics, which would result in a service orientation of commitment or sense of calling;
3. a professional organization or association, which would foster group identity; and
4. autonomy, which would lead to peer review and enforcement of standards besides group identity.

This and other recent definitions of professionalization (Shernock, 1992), differ from that of O.W. Wilson, whose view of professionalization involved the organization rather than the individual becoming professionalized, which is better identified as bureaucratization.

Shernock (1992) examined the relationship between higher education as an independent variable and professional orientations as dependent variables. He found that college education is not related strongly to most of the attitudinal attributes of professionalism that have been identified in the literature on police professionalism. Higher educational level was not related significantly to the measure of commitment to the service ideal or to suspicion of the outside world. Higher educational level was also not related to the exercise of greater discretion as indicated by a greater tendency to take informal action in order-maintenance cases and by greater support for independence from the supervision or authority of nominal superiors, nor to the comparative value placed on efficiency in work. It was related positively to the importance of ethical conduct, but not to self-regulation. Higher educational level was related to a less parochial organizational identity because it apparently decreases insularity within police departments.

Miller and Fry (1976) examined the relationship between higher education and the endorsement of the professional model. They did not find that increased education, as measured by degrees held and units of college work, led to a greater likelihood of endorsement of the professional model of law enforcement.

On Work Performance

In addition to finding education the strongest factor related to a certification examination, a basic competency level test administered to new peace officers at the end of recruit training (Schwartz & Stucky, 1993), and examining overall success as a police officer (Copley, 1992), studies have found positive relationships between college education and fewer civilian complaints (including fewer physical force allegations), quicker response time, fewer injuries and accidents, less likelihood of being assaulted, more parking tickets issued, more arrests, and greater activity in detection practices such as stopping vehicles and checking businesses (Bowker, 1980; Carter & Sapp, 1990; Cascio, 1977; Finckenauer, 1975; Hudzik, 1978; Sherman, 1980; Sparling, 1975; Taft, 1981). Hooper (1988) found that criminal justice majors were more proficient than majors in other subjects in the majority of job performance measures he examined.

Other studies (e.g., Kedia, 1985; Griffin, 1980) found no relationship between police officers' performance and level of education, and contradictory results on the correlation between college education and police effectiveness (Carter, Jamieson & Sapp, 1978). The basic conclusion to be drawn appears to be that evidence on the impact of higher education on police behavior is decidedly mixed (Sherman & Blumberg, 1981). For example, findings vary among indicators used to measure the use of force. Thus, depending on where and how police use of force is measured, more-educated police officers tend to use force less often, more often, or just as often as less-educated officers.

Studies attempting to link educational level and many of these job performance measures have been criticized for a plethora of contradictory findings (Alpert & Dunham, 1988; Eskridge, 1989; Scott, 1986; Sherman, 1980), for not being longitudinal studies that examine changes in behavior over time (Jacobs & Magdovitz, 1977; Sherman, 1978), and for failure to control adequately for both extraneous and component variables (Hudzik, 1978). There has been a lack of consensus or inter-rater reliability, a great degree of subjectivity, discrepancies between supervisor and citizen ratings, and traditional biases of the agency's performance criteria reflected in supervisor evaluations used to determine performance (Jacobs & Magdovitz, 1977; Goldstein, 1977; Griffin, 1980; Sherman, 1978; Scott, 1986; Swanson, 1977); too many extraneous factors involved that influence citizen complaints (Goldstein, 1977); and poor records maintained on officer performance in police departments (Smith & Ostrom, 1974). There is even evidence of bias against education in performance ratings by supervisors (Sherman, 1978). Moreover, there have been problems in deciding whether more or less of a given measure, such as arrests, should be interpreted as good or bad performance (Jacobs & Magdovitz, 1977; Sherman, 1978; Worden, 1990).

On the Police Organization

Other studies have examined the relationship between higher education and personnel issues, and have found college education to be related to lower absenteeism, fewer disciplinary actions, faster career advancement, greater proficiency in paperwork and report completion, and fewer complaints (Cascio, 1977; Daniel, 1982; Griffin, 1980; Gross, 1973; Hooper, 1988; LeDoux et al., 1984; Southerland, 1984). Those exploring the value of college education have suggested that college educated officers would expect to be promoted quickly and would be more likely to criticize management (Dantzker, 1993). Swanson (1977) has pointed out that the opportunities for upward mobility are increasingly delimited as one moves toward the top of the pyramid; since many will be called, but few chosen, better-educated officers who fail to rise to the top may tend to be dissatisfied. Southerland (1984) found that police chiefs surveyed thought college educated officers get promoted faster, and Smith (1978) found that college educated officers felt that some college education should be required for promotion to supervisory ranks. However, Greene and Cordner (1980) found that promotion policies in the departments they studied relied very little on the formal education of the candidate, and Fischer, Golden, and Heininger (1985) found that possessing a college degree was not significantly related to promotion and that the proportion of officers with degrees was somewhat constant across all ranks.

In contrast to Miller and Fry's (1976) and Lefkowitz's (1974) studies that did not find a positive relationship between higher education and satisfaction with work, Dantzker (1993) found that the higher the level of education, the greater the job satisfaction. However, this was only true for patrol officers with up to five years of experience; after five years of patrol service, job satisfaction dropped as educational level increased.

Examining the compatibility between higher education and current police organizational structure, Swanson (1977) argued that college educated police may not be beneficial to police departments because they may not fit into the traditional organizational structure of police departments. Miller and Fry (1976), however, noted no relationship between higher education and satisfaction with the police organization. Smith (1978) found that police officers with higher levels of education, as well as training, were not more resistant to bureaucratic authority, did not manifest more labor union-type militancy, were not more likely to perceive their work environment as unsupportive and hostile, and were not less receptive to external review. Shernock (1992) found that education was not related to the comparative value placed on efficiency in work, while Worden (1990) claimed that college education is only weakly or unrelated to more work-related attitudes. Still, in a later study with a different data set, Shernock (1994) found that, as education level increased, the evaluation of different police tasks as critical tended to decrease.

Carter and Sapp (1990) contend that college education of police reduces the police organization's liability risk from (1) failure to train, (2) failure to supervise, (3) failure to protect, (4) negligent entrustment, and (5) failure to direct, and thus could affect insurance availability and cost for police agencies. According to them, college educated officers have a broader comprehension of civil rights issues from legal, social, historical, and political perspectives. Moreover, they have a broader view of policing tasks and a greater professional ethos. These views presumably indicate that their actions and decisions tend to be driven by conscience and values and, consequently, lessen the chance of erroneous decisions. Furthermore, Carter and Sapp cite their previous research, in which they found that 98.4 percent of the responding departments indicated that officers with two or more years of college received fewer citizen complaints than their less educated counterparts and that 96.3 percent indicated there were fewer disciplinary problems with officers having more than two years of college.

PROPOSED TYPE OF EDUCATION FOR POLICE OFFICERS

While both attitude and performance studies were supposed to examine the way in which higher education improved professionalism, distinctions have not been made between pre-service and in-service students, types of educational institutions attended, and types of major. Most of the performance studies, as well as many of the attitude studies, have not differentiated the type of education that officers have received (Smith, 1978). Many of the officers who were subjects of performance studies were enrolled in college programs during the LEEP years, which appeared to be "training" rather than "educational" in nature, and offered an assortment of courses that had little to do with the social sciences, let alone the liberal arts (Brown, 1974; Goldstein, 1977; Sherman, 1978). Despite the fact that the National Advisory Commission on Higher Education for Police Officers (Sherman et al., 1978) recommended that vocational training courses be replaced by a curriculum providing a more broad-based education, researchers studying the relationship between college education and police performance and attitudes continue to fail to distinguish between vocational and liberal arts programs.

Most of these narrow vocational programs are offered at two-year community colleges (Carter, Sapp & Stephens, 1988; Jacobs & Magdovitz, 1977; Worden, 1990) and which, according to Sherman (1978) and Scott (1986), are associated with education for skilled labor and paraprofessionals, not professionals. Not only have these two-year programs been criticized as failing to fulfill academic needs (Carter, Sapp & Stephens, 1988), but the time spent in acquiring associate degrees contradicts the spirit of recommendations by various national commissions, which explicitly called for a *four-year* baccalaureate college education, abolition of terminal two-year degree programs, and the further development of transfer programs (involving articulation agreements) between two- and four-year schools. These became the most controversial of the National Advisory Commission on Higher Education for Police Officers' recommendations (Dull, 1982).

The Law Enforcement Assistance Administration supported a broad education for police (Langhoff, 1972). It was recommended that curricula should not be based on the facts of any single discipline, but on models of education featuring inquiry rather than rote memorization. In his study for the National Advisory Commission on Higher Education for Police Officers, Sherman (1978, pp. 1–17) recommended that

1. the majority of federal funds for police higher education should go to programs with broad curricula and well-educated faculty rather than to narrowly technical programs;
2. no college credit should be granted for attending police training programs;
3. community colleges should phase out their terminal two-year degree programs in police education;
4. colleges should primarily employ full-time police education teaching staffs, seeking faculty members with Ph.D. degrees in arts and sciences disciplines;
5. prior criminal justice employment should be neither a requirement nor a handicap in faculty selection; and
6. government policies at all levels should encourage educating police officers before they begin their careers.

In the latest effort to set standards for the higher education of police officers and other criminal justice practitioners, the Northeastern Association of Criminal Justice Sciences' (NEACJS) *Minimum Standards for Criminal Justice Education: Guidelines for College and University-Level Programs* (1995) strongly warns that programs in criminology and criminal justice should not offer courses, nor award credit, for vocational training courses designed for specific job skills, or advanced job training. The NEACJS proposes that educational institutions evaluate courses offered by non-educational institutions on a case-by-case basis, assessing both the content of the course and the background of the instructor before awarding academic credit. The NEACJS also concurs with the recommendation that prior employment in the criminal justice system is not an academic qualification by itself.

Sherman and McLeod (1979) note that training-type police education programs are much more likely than liberal arts programs to be taught by less educated, highly experienced, and predominantly part-time faculties. With neither the command of a scholarly body of knowledge nor the time afforded a full-time instructor to read scholarly literature, these instructors are said to teach what they know from their work experience. The result may be basic training similar to that provided in police academies.

Many of those who support a strong general education disagree over the National Advisory Commission on Higher Education for Police Officers' conclusion that a criminal justice major is no more desirable than a major in one of the other social sciences (Dull, 1982). According to Fox (*Police Forum,* 1996), Adam Walinsky, who originated the idea of a Police Corps that was intended to be part of the Clinton crime bill, preferred a broad-based group of diverse individuals— diverse in their interests, backgrounds, and education (not just in criminal justice, but music and art as well)—who would spend four years in policing to improve the level of professionalism, the quality of police forces, and then leave. Sherman (*Police Forum,* 1996) retorts that encouraging a non-criminal justice education for cadets implies that police work is simple but value-driven, merely requiring sensitivity, humanity, and tolerance.

A related issue is whether the criminal justice doctorate should be emphasized in recruitment of faculty in police education. Dull (1982) suggests that the answer to this question is related to the question of what is the best major for police: Does criminal justice education offer something unique and valuable that cannot specifically be found in other fields of study? These issues continue to be debated and consensus appears unlikely in the immediate future.

In terms of appropriate teaching methods, Miller and Braswell (1986) found that students using an experiential case study model of learning, presumably providing a meaningful balance between theory and practice, tended to examine the police-oriented side of issues, exhibited more awareness of subtle implications of police work, and were more realistically aware of police actions than the control group of other criminal justice students. According to Miller and Braswell (1986) and Massey (1993), criminal justice students, particularly those in law enforcement, dislike courses weighted toward theory and conceptual application (e.g., human behavior, research, and management) while enjoying practical course material offering applied skills (e.g., criminal investigation, forensic science, and technical courses). Since students feel that they will not use knowledge from theoretically based courses in the field, they depend more on the experience of other practitioners and colleagues in field conflict situations than upon their own academic preparation. It may be that a more meaningful, yet comprehensive, curriculum is needed.

Since what constitutes an appropriate core curriculum for the criminal justice major is currently being debated (Northeastern Association of Criminal Justice Sciences, 1995), very little consensus has been reached about appropriate coursework for police officers, other than gaining a broader knowledge of the entire criminal justice system. Finally, it has been argued that—given the desires of the community, the expectation of police services and the inherently moral nature of police work— ethical education should be a necessary component of police education programs (Massey, 1993).

NEW ISSUES AND DEVELOPMENTS IN POLICE EDUCATION

One of the latest trends in policing is the adoption of some form of community-oriented policing. While numerous books have been written on community policing, very little if anything has been published on how to incorporate this approach in the curriculum. An important consideration about the relationship betwen higher education and police organization is how the two will be related in the new era of community policing. Swanson (1977) gives us a clue in describing the change from a mechanistic line and line-staff organizational model to an organic organizational model with lower centralization, reduced formality, fewer levels of hierarchy, higher flexibility, maximum opportunity for creative contributions by low-ranking personnel, and higher job satisfaction. This type of team-policing organic model would be more complex and would require the employment of high-growth-need employees, which would presumably make necessary the recruitment of college educated persons. At the least, a completely satisfactory in-service educational or training program to prepare current officers for community-oriented policing would have to be developed. To date, that has not occurred.

Ultimately, the issue comes down to whether to require police officers to possess a college degree. Both sides of the debate raise valid arguments. However, the fact is that policing requires a better educated individual than when it began its modernization. Still, education, in and of itself, is only part of the answer to creating more efficient police personnel. The other important part is training.

POLICE TRAINING: HISTORY AND STRUCTURE

It was not until 1935, at the convention of the Peace Officers Association of the State of California, that a resolution was adopted providing for a committee to assist in formulating a statewide training program for peace officers. The committee came to be known as the California Program for Peace Officer Training, the predecessor of the modern-day police officer standards and training councils (POSTs). In 1973, the National Advisory Commission on Criminal Justice Standards and Goals attempted for the first time to formulate national criminal justice standards and goals for state and local levels. Today, in general, all POSTs have followed the various commission recommendations and have established basic training programs for entry-level police officers (Christian & Edwards, 1985).

In the United States a variety of academies exist at the national, state, regional, and local levels of government and all have some role in the total education and training of police officers. No single academy or educational institution has control over the required training of all higher ranking officers throughout the United States as does the National Police Command Academy in Germany (Stevens, 1983). Finally, while universities in the United States have a significant involvement in police education, they have little part in police training, unlike those in countries such as Germany (Stevens, 1983).

PROBLEMATIC RELEVANCE OF POLICE ACADEMY BASIC TRAINING

Bayley and Bittner (1989) state that the training given at the police academies is universally regarded as irrelevant to "real" police work. From the perspective of the recruits themselves, the formal content of the quasi-military academy generally does not answer the many questions that may trouble them (Lundman, 1980; Van Maanen, 1973). Niederhoffer (1967) found that, after only two months of training, fewer than a quarter of the recruits believed that police academy training does a very good job of preparing the recruit for life in the precinct. Harris (1973) goes even further in arguing that the police academy seems to institutionalize role distance by reinforcing and sanctioning the belief that the police academy is irrelevant to police work. He states that

> some of the recruit's instructors fed his belief that the role he was supposed to play during his 12 weeks of training was not appropriate to the patrolman image. Various instructors would interrupt their lectures to make snide comments about the content of their lectures or to mention that the recruit would learn how to con people or evade due process of law once he left the academy (p. 201).

Upon leaving the academy one of the tasks of the field training officer (FTO), according to Lundman (1980), is to capitalize on the rookies' disenchantment with their training experiences and finalize the rookies' break with the academy experience.

There is near consensus among social scientists who have studied police socialization that FTOs tell rookies that the academy experience is a "waste of time" and to "forget all that crap they were told in the academy" (Kirkham, 1977; Lundman, 1980; Walker, 1992). It appears that a stronger value is placed on field experience than classroom instruction, that the job of policing is viewed as unteachable without contact with the public, and that learning from practice is easier than attempting to learn in the academy (Fielding, 1988). Fielding (1988) quotes a 1982 Police Foundation study finding that 30 percent of respondents in one police division felt training only prepared them for street duty to the most limited extent and that too little time was spent on dealing with people (73 percent), working a beat (70 percent), crime prevention (58 percent), law and the court system (58 percent), and dealing with racial problems (51 percent).

Recruits find how great their ignorance of practice is in their first encounters with police who have detailed knowledge of local terrain and population (Bennett, 1984; Fielding, 1988; Harris, 1973; Niederhoffer, 1967; Van Maanen, 1973). Thus, while recruits may believe during the time they are at the academy that force and a non-arrest orientation serve as solutions to problems (McNamara, 1967; Meadows, 1985), after one year in the field they assume a different view (McNamara, 1967). However, according to Lundman (1980, p. 88), "rookies forget only certain parts of the training. They feel they must remember how to use their weapons although they may never have the occasion to do so. . . ."

Because police behavior is most likely determined more by what happens after the officer is on the job, training program experiences may have little long-term impact on the adjustments to work (Roberg & Kuykendall, 1993). Additionally, if learning occurs through experience rather than through training in a formal setting, then development of occupational skills is likely to be a lengthy process (Bayley & Bittner, 1989). However, although police often claim that "every situation is different," thus denying that policing is amenable to rational analysis and, consequently, to formal learning, they contradict themselves when they simultaneously emphasize the importance of experience in policing (Bayley & Bittner, 1989). The very fact that police base subsequent behavior on its effectiveness in previous situations indicates that learning through experience involves a discernible pattern.

In fact, according to Bayley and Bittner (1989), learning through experience offers much that can be translated to and transmitted in a formal setting. They note that experience on the job contributes to learning about (1) goals, (2) tactics, and (3) presence. Furthermore, they advise that experience teaches police how to juggle complex priorities in action and what goals can reasonably be achieved at the least cost to the officer. It also sharpens the ability to read potential violence in an encounter and teaches them what works in circumstances that vary enormously. It is through experience that police officers cultivate "presence," an inward equanimity leading to outward poise that is learned through practice, a trait neither inborn nor taught (Bayley & Bittner, 1989, pp. 90–103).

In a more specific investigation of the relevance of training, Shernock (1994) found while categorizing the functional groupings of police tasks that most officers felt that encounters with people from diverse groups, physical fitness activities and defensive tactics, and community policing should be learned—and competence in these functions achieved—strictly on the job. Most officers believed some academy preparation was necessary, but competence should be achieved on the job for police functions that include patrol tasks, control of civil disorders, report writing and field note taking, crime prevention, and enforcement of minor motor vehicle violations. Finally, most officers believed that competence must be achieved in the academy for arrest procedures, testifying in court, first aid, mediation in domestic conflicts, the safe use and care of firearms, the use of force, criminal investigation, accident investigation, the enforcement of serious motor vehicle violations, and the collection and preservation of evidence prior to assignment as a working police officer.

RECENT CHANGES IN THE POLICE ACADEMY

With recent changes in the status, length, and content of training, one might expect a different perspective from recent recruits to their basic training at the police academy. As Frost and Seng (1984a) write in their review of changes in the police academies for twelve cities over a thirty-year period (1952–1982), the status of the police academy has changed, as indicated by police entry training becoming an important function in a department's administrative structure. It rose from a unit to a division within the departments studied, changing from relatively limited facilities to extensive, often separate facilities, and from a small to a large full-time staff, with administrators at the command rank and distinguished from instructors. At the same time, the length of the police academy has been dramatically extended. In further review, Frost and Seng (1984b) found an 86 percent increase in the length of the academy among the 18 departments they studied (from an average of 340 hours in 1952 to 633 hours in 1982), with similar increases for officers from small, medium, and large departments.

Most significantly, there have been very dynamic changes in curriculum and pedagogical methods (Frost & Seng, 1984b), which previously "consist[ed] of a few standardized lectures taught by rote memory plus firearms training and physical training to fill up the remaining hours" (Broderick, 1987, p. 221). Critics complained that recruit training consisted primarily of nonhumanistic indoctrination, technical preparation, and rudimentary on-the-job training. There was a focus on crime fighting and technical skill development instead of conflict management and social relations (Meadows, 1987a). Now new courses of instruction have been introduced. For example, the Los Angeles Police Department's academy curriculum includes Jewish and Spanish culture, Spanish language, etiology of homosexuality, labor relations, and interpersonal relations (Meadows, 1985). Generally, more time and attention has been given to human relations, constitutional issues, and the rights of citizens, and special courses or instruction are now offered on arson, sexual assault, narcotics investigation, first response to emergency situations, accident investigation involving hazardous materials, DWI testing, etc. (Frost & Seng, 1984b).

There have also been changes made in the content of previously offered courses. For instance, there has been a move away from physical training under the military model, which encouraged aggressive punishment-oriented programs, promoted participant injuries, and had a negative influence on continued fitness (Charles, 1983), to programs that emphasize long-term commitment to physical fitness, which would lower the high police incidence of heart attacks and other maladies (Charles, 1983; Cooke, 1989; Lilley & Greenberg, 1984; Regali, 1988). The time devoted to drill has also decreased. Further, instead of emphasizing the procedures for arrest, new training stresses the range of dispositional options available in resolving disputes, such as mediation, negotiation, arbitration, and referrals.

Because more attention is given to the problem-solving nature of police work (Bayley & Bittner, 1989), there has been a move away from the traditional lecture- or instructor-centered mode of instruction, a passive means of communication, toward performance-oriented instruction (Molden, 1982; Smith, 1990). Performance-oriented instruction involves role playing (Chaney, 1990; Dantzker et al., 1995; Frost & Seng, 1984b; Smith, 1990); interactive audiovisual programs, and other types of simulation for decision-making training (Frost & Seng, 1984a; Smith, 1990; Chaney, 1990), especially in the use of deadly force; and frank discussion of case studies of the realities of field decisions (Bayley & Bittner, 1988). In the case of the interactive audiovisual programs, some recruits have claimed that it has been the best practical training they ever had (Chaney, 1990). Role playing has replaced physical and verbal abuse in many academies as the method of instruction because it has been shown to be a more effective way to teach recruits how to handle tough situations like a domestic dispute or a pulled-over motorist who turns hostile (Cooke, 1989).

In addition to looking at changes in the administration, curriculum, and pedagogy of recruit training, Frost and Seng (1983) also examined changes in instructors from 1952 to 1982. Prior to 1950, a few veteran police officers were assigned the task of informing groups of police recruits about the elementary functions of their jobs, and at the end of the indoctrination were sent back to their permanent assignments. For 1952, Frost and Seng found that permanently assigned skeleton staffs augmented by temporary instructors were detailed to the training school until the program was completed. They note that the most significant factors for selection as an instructor were active police experience, conscientiousness, and dedication to the assignment. In 1952, at least some of the instructors in 56 percent of the departments had some college education. By 1982, education was mentioned by a majority of departments in addition to the two aforementioned factors. Other factors, such as speaking ability, subject knowledge, and departmental record, were mentioned by about 40 percent of the departments, while teaching ability and interest in teaching were mentioned by about a third. By 1982 all of the departments had staff with some college education. The majority of departments reporting staff with advanced degrees were also the departments with the most civilian instructors. The majority of police recruit instructors did not have any teaching experience prior to their assignment as police instructors, but 25 of the 28 responding departments ensured that their instructors received training in teaching techniques. Instructor certification, which did not exist in the 1950s, was a requirement in 22 of the 28 departments studied in 1982. Twenty-one departments evaluated their instructors formally, and six did so informally (Frost and Seng, 1983).

RELEVANCE AND EFFECTIVENESS OF POLICE ACADEMY TRAINING

A major question asked regarding training is whether it prepares recruits adequately for the police role. Meadows (1987b) attempted to determine whether police training followed a model of crime control or one of service and order maintenance, and whether police entry level training curricula compare with the research findings on the police role. He found that training in patrol and investigation, force and weaponry, and law consumed 83 percent of training time compared to human relations, administration, communication, and criminal justice system, which comprised 17 percent of training time. This indicated that entry-level police training has a crime-control, legal, and technical orientation rather than a service, order maintenance, and criminal justice system orientation. While he found that there are some humanistic and discretionary aspects of force taught, he noted the need for more training in interpersonal communications, human relations, and ethics.

In terms of specific types of training, Levinson and Distefano (1979) indicated that officers' knowledge and attitudes concerning mental illness are improved immediately after a brief mental health orientation program. They go on to state that the results of their research suggest that job-related training limited to specific social service functions may be a useful model for designing and evaluating other components of police academy curricula. There is scattered evidence indicating that crisis intervention training has yielded some measurable increases in officer effectiveness in handling disturbance calls (Pearce & Snortum, 1983). Driscoll, Meyer, and Schanie

(1973) found that officers trained in family crisis intervention managed to resolve the immediate conflict in the crisis situation more adequately than did untrained policemen. Hughes (1972) noted that police recruits can be stimulated to examine their attitudes toward the humanity of their clients and to develop skills in peacekeeping rather than mere apprehension of offenders.

Overall, there has been limited research evaluating the relevance or effect of academy training. There is little doubt that training, whether academy or field training, is important to policing. However, the ultimate issue is whether the training is applicable and relevant to what police officers do. This has led to developing training standards based upon the relevant tasks associated with policing.

DEVELOPMENT OF RELEVANT TRAINING STANDARDS: THE JOB TASK ANALYSIS

The current trend of police academies, whether independent or POST-certified, appears to be toward more empirically-based approaches to the development of standards and training. POSTs are themselves undertaking or contracting out such activities as training needs assessment, selection validation, manpower inventory, and job analysis (Christian & Edwards, 1985).

A task analysis can be very helpful in determining what should be emphasized in the curriculum in the basic training program in terms of what is actually done in the field and what officers feel is critical knowledge. Job analysis specialists have validated methodologies for documenting what a worker does in a job and for prescribing the necessary knowledge, abilities, skills, and other personal characteristics that a worker must possess to do the job well. Police Officer Standards and Training Councils (POST) are using job analysis to set minimum employment and training standards (Christian & Edwards, 1985).

Christian and Edwards (1985) noted that courts have accepted the concept of job analysis as a method for determining the BFOQ for the position of law enforcement officer. From the standpoint of the police academy, it is absolutely necessary to develop training requirements very carefully because Congress has passed two federal laws in which fulfillment of training requirements is interpreted as a selection procedure, and the federal courts have defined type and quality of training itself as a legal issue. On the one hand, Congress has enacted two pieces of legislation, the Americans with Disabilities Act, in 1990, and the Federal Equal Employment Opportunity Uniform Guidelines on Employee Selection Procedures, in 1978, which interpret training requirements as selection procedures. On the other hand, the courts have developed the relatively new legal concept of negligent failure to train, in which liability can result from a government's failure to train its personnel adequately for their work.

In order to train a law enforcement officer, it is first nececssary to develop a job description for the basic law enforcement officer position which, in turn, can help state and local law enforcement agencies respond to the demands of the Americans with Disabilities Act (Title 1), which became effective in 1992. According to the ADA, disabled individuals cannot be excluded from job opportunities unless they are unable to perform the essential functions of the job, which can be determined by a task analysis. Thus, it is absolutely necessary to demonstrate what the essential tasks of a given job are, insofar as disabled individuals may not be disqualified because they cannot perform nonessential or marginal job functions.

Essential functions have been interpreted to mean fundamental, basic, necessary, or vital tasks of the job. These functions do not include tasks that are incidental to the job, or which are performed infrequently or not at all. However, infrequency is not in itself tantamount to being nonessential, since some tasks are performed infrequently but are nevertheless critical, such as an officer's use of his or her firearm. Criteria cannot be used to exclude disabled individuals unless the criteria are job related and consistent with business necessity. If a disabled person is otherwise qualified, an employer must provide reasonable accommodations, unless this would cause undue hardship to the employer. Under certain circumstances, an employer may even be required to change a job's present configuration in order to accommodate an individual's disability. A task analysis should produce a written job description that would be considered evidence of the essential functions of a job.

In addition to the Americans with Disabilities Act, the Federal Equal Employment Opportunity Uniform Guidelines on Employee Selection Procedures (1978), which are supposed to be used as a basis for any employment decision, interpret successful completion of training as a selection procedure. It is therefore necessary to undertake a task analysis, insofar as Section 14, Part A of the guidelines states: "Any validity study should be based upon a review of information about the job for which the selection procedure is used" and that "the review should include a job analysis." To assure compliance with the EEO guidelines, the selection/training process must be "content validated," which essentially means showing that basic law enforcement selection methods and training curricula relate to the actual job police officers perform.

The courts have established the following four-fold test of defensibility regarding type and quality of training:

1. Is the program based on a job analysis, thus ensuring job relatedness?
2. Are there demonstrably valid learning (performance) objectives that substantiate that learning occurred rather than the exposure to a specified number of hours of training?
3. Are the instructors qualified to teach a particular subject?
4. Are there records of student performance?

In sum, to improve the quality and relevance of training, job task analyses are necessary. These analyses will provide a guideline for what officers are expected to do and thus assist in creating a training curriculum best suited for the tasks at hand. These analyses should also shed additional light on the educational debate by indicating what skills and knowledge, available through education and training, are required of police officers.

EDUCATION AND TRAINING: CURRENT RELATIONSHIP

Few police academics would argue for replacing training programs with higher education for police. Although it has been assumed that criminal justice practitioners favor the vocational type programs, a recent national study of police education conducted by the Police Executive Research Forum found otherwise.

As reported in the January/February issue of *ACJS Today* (Sapp, Carter & Stephens, 1989):

> Contrary to what some would expect, police chiefs, sheriffs, and heads of state police agencies do not want the colleges and universities to teach "police skills"; rather, they have expectations for a graduate who can integrate the duties of a police officer with a clear understanding of democratic values, tolerance, and integrity. The general consensus is that a broad-based liberal arts curriculum should be part of every criminal justice program at colleges and universities (p. 1).

The respondents in the study also said that "other skills needed . . . include the ability to integrate materials, critical thinking, decision-making skills, conceptual skills, and the ability to think clearly" (p. 1). In addition to democratic values, "suggested needs included . . . understanding human nature and social problems, value choices, ethics, tolerance and integrity. Still other areas where criminal justice curricula are seen as lacking center around understanding different cultures and how others think, attitudes toward the law . . . and participating in society" (Sapp, Carter & Stephens, 1989, p. 5). Academics, moreover, from the National Advisory Commission Report to the latest Northeastern Association of Criminal Justice Sciences Minimum Standards and Guidelines Committee Report have consistently opposed vocationalism in their college criminal justice programs. While criminal justice faculty have been welcomed by practitioners to teach basic and advanced classes at police academies and study of law enforcement training programs, former and current police officers without the acceptable credentials will not be recruited to the rosters of criminal justice faculty, as Haley (1992) has asserted.

Much has been written about what criminal justice educators and practitioners think education for police officers should be. Still, very few have examined whether there is a difference between criminal justice educators and practitioners regarding police training. Meadows (1987a) found that both criminal justice educators and police administrators ranked patrol and investigation, force and weaponry, and communications as the most important areas and human relations as least important in police training. Criminal justice educators and police administrators did not agree on the value of time needed for training, with the exception of law and written and oral communications training. Meadows also recommends that police curriculum decision making should include persons with academic as well as practical experiences.

Despite academics' concerns of vocational encroachment, some states influenced by their peace officer standards and training council have combined training and education in college criminal justice programs. In Minnesota, the POST, in cooperation with criminal justice educators, has developed and published academic objectives and goals for potential law enforcement officers in their pre-employment educational program. A majority of educators in degree-granting programs in Minnesota, for example, have included both academic and skills objectives in their courses. The Michigan POST prescribes in detail exactly what subject matter each academic program must include and how it must incorporate the required hours of law enforcement training subject matter into its academic curriculum (Christian & Edwards, 1985). In Florida, James Stinchcombe (*Police Forum*, 1996) points out, not a single police agency conducts basic training. It is run through an education system that is funded by the Department of Education. In Colorado it is possible to attend a certification academy conducted by at least two community colleges, with college credits often awarded upon completion (Copley, 1992).

CONCLUSIONS

Both education and training are important aspects of policing. Although their importance is recognized, debates continue over what type of education and training should be required. Training continues to grow because of federal statutes and court decisions requiring police departments to provide adequate and relevant training. Higher education for police officers, while often considered desirable, is still very much in the process of evolving. As empirical evidence about policy, practice, and pedagogy in higher education becomes available, criminal justice curricula may be expected to continue to change. In an effort to join the two, some states have begun to combine education and training programs, hoping to produce the best qualified police applicant possible.

DISCUSSION QUESTIONS

1. Considering the long-standing debate over educational requirements for police officers, what side would you take? Why?
2. How important is measuring the effect of education on police performance? Shouldn't the intrinsic value be enough to support it for police officers?
3. If educational requirements ever become a standard, what type of education should be required?
4. Since training is the applied knowledge officers must have to be effective, is it more important than formal knowledge? Of what should training consist?
5. Assume you are conducting a job task analysis for your local city police department. What are ten major tasks officers perform for which training and education must be established?

6. Should police agencies and academic institutions create programs in which individuals can attain both a degree and the requisite practical training necessary to become police officers? Why?

REFERENCES

Alpert, G., & Dunham, R. (1988). *Policing urban America.* Prospect Heights, IL: Waveland Press.

Bayley, D., & Bittner, E. (1989). Learning the skills of policing. In R.G. Dunham & G.P. Alpert (Eds.), *Critical issues in policing: Contemporary readings,* pp. 87–111. Prospect Heights, IL: Waveland Press.

Beckman, E. (1976). Police education and training: Where are we? Where are we going? *Journal of Criminal Justice, 4*(4), 315–322.

Bennett, R.R. (1984, March). Becoming blue: A longitudinal study of police recruit occupational socialization. *Journal of Police Science and Administration, 12,* 47–58.

Bittner, E. (1970). *The functions of the police in modern society.* Rockville, MD: U.S. Government Printing Office.

Bowker, L.E. (1980). A theory of the educational needs of law enforcement officers. *Journal of Contemporary Criminal Justice* (1), 17–24.

Broderick, J.J. (1987). *Police in a time of change* (2nd ed.). Prospect Heights, IL: Waveland Press.

Brown, L.P. (1974). The police and higher education: The challenge of the times. *Criminology, 12*(1), 114–124.

Carter, D., Jamieson, J.D., & Sapp, A.D. (1978). Issues and trends in criminal justice education. *Criminal Justice Monographs, 8*(5). Huntsville, TX: Sam Houston State University Institute of Contemporary Corrections and the Behavioral Sciences.

Carter, D., & Sapp, A. (1990). The evolution of higher education in law enforcement: Preliminary findings from a national study. *Journal of Criminal Justice Education, 1*(1), 59–85.

Carter, D., Sapp, A., & Stephens, D. (1988). Higher education as a bona fide occupational qualification (BFOQ) for police: A blueprint. *American Journal of Police, 7*(2), 1–27.

Cascio, W. (1977). Formal education and police officer performance. *Journal of Police Science and Administration, 5*(1), 89–96.

Charles, M.T. (1983, September). Police training: A contemporary approach. *Journal of Police Science and Administration, 11,* 251–263.

Chaney, R. (1990, July). Judgment training in the use of deadly force. *Police Chief, 57,* 40–44.

Christian, K., & Edwards, S. (1985). Law enforcement standards and training councils: A human resource planning force in the future. *Journal of Police Science and Administration, 13*(1), 1–9.

Copley, W.H. (1992). Police education in Colorado. *American Journal of Police, 11*(2), 55–64.

Cooke, A. (1989, March). Recruit training reform. *Law and Order, 37,* 47–50.

Dalley, A.F. (1975). University vs. non-university graduated policeman: A study of police attitudes. *Journal of Police Science and Administration, 3*(1), 458–468.

Daniel, E.D. (1982). The effect of a college degree on police absenteeism. *Police Chief, 49*(9), 70–71.

Dantzker, G.D., Lurigio, A.J., Hartnett, S., Houmes, S., Davidsdottir, S., & Donovan, K. (1995). Preparing police officers for community policing: An evaluation of training for Chicago's alternative policing strategy. *Police Studies, 18*(1), 45–69.

Dantzker, M.L. (1993). An issue for policing: Educational level and job satisfaction. *American Journal of Police, 12*(2), 101–118.

Driscoll, J.M., Meyer, R.G., & Schanie, C.F. (1973). Training police in family crisis intervention. *Journal of Applied Behavioral Science, 9*(1), 62–82.

Dull, T. (1982). Current issues in criminal justice education: The aftermath of the Sherman Report. *Journal of Police Science and Administration, 10*(3), 315–325.

Eskridge, C. (1989). College and the police: A review of the issues. In D.J. Kenney (Ed.), *Police and policing: Contemporary issues*, pp. 17–25. New York: Praeger.

Fielding, N. (1988). *Joining forces: Police training, socialization, and occupational competence.* London: Routledge.

Finckenauer, J.O. (1975). Higher education and police discretion. *Journal of Police Science and Administration, 3*(4), 450–457.

Fischer, R., Golden, K., & Heininger, B. (1985). Issues in higher education for law enforcement officers: An Illinois study. *Journal of Criminal Justice, 13*(4), 329–338.

Frost, T.M., & Seng, M. (1983). Police recruit training in urban departments: A look at instructors. *Journal of Police Science and Administration, 11*(3), 296–302.

———. (1984a, March). The administration of police training: A thirty-year perspective. *Journal of Police Science and Administration, 12*, 66–73.

———. (1984b, September). Police entry level curriculum: A thirty-year perspective. *Journal of Police Science and Administration, 12*, 251–259.

Goldstein, H. (1977). *Policing in a free society.* Cambridge, MA: Ballinger.

Greene, J.R., & Cordner, G.W. (1980). Education and police administration: A preliminary analysis of impact. *Police Studies, 3*(3), 12–23.

Griffin, G.R. (1980). *A study of the relationship between level of college education and police patrolmen's performance.* Saratoga, CA: Century Twenty One Publishing.

Gross, S. (1973). Higher education and police: Is there a need for a closer look? *Journal of Police Science and Administration, 1*(4), 477–483.

Guller, I. (1972). Higher education and policemen: Attitudinal differences between freshmen and senior police college students. *Journal of Criminal Law, Criminology, and Police Science, 63*(3), 396–401.

Haley, K.N. (1992). Training. In G.W. Cordner & D.C. Hale (Eds.), *What works in policing? Operations and administration examined*, pp. 143–155. Cincinnati: Anderson Publishing Co.

Harris, R.N. (1973). *The police academy: An inside view.* New York: John Wiley & Sons.

Hooper, M.K. (1988). *The relationship of college education to police officer performance.* Doctoral dissertation, Claremont Graduate School.

Hudzik, J.K. (1978). College education for police: Problems in measuring component and extraneous variables. *Journal of Criminal Justice, 6*, 69–81.

Hughes, J. (1972). Training police recruits for service in the urban ghetto: A social worker's approach. *Crime and Delinquency, 18*(2), 176–183.

Jacobs, J.B., & Magdovitz, S.B. (1977). At LEEP's end?: A review of the law enforcement education program. *Journal of Police Science and Administration, 5*(1), 1–17.

Kedia, P.R. (1985). *Assessing the effect of college education on police performance.* Doctoral dissertation, University of Southern Mississippi.

Kirkham, G. (1977). *Signal zero.* New York: Ballantine.

Langhoff, N.T. (1972). An essay: Police education and training: A foundation for change. *Criminal Law Bulletin, 8*(4), 321–328.

LeDoux, J.E., Tully, E., Chronister, J.L., & Gansneder, B.M. (1984). Higher education for law enforcement: Half a century of growth. *Police Chief, 51*(4), 22–24.

Lefkovitz, J. (1974). Job attitudes of police: Overall description and demographic correlates. *Journal of Vocational Behavior, 5*(2), 221–230.

Levinson, M., & Distefano, M.K. (1979). Effects of brief training on mental health knowledge and attitudes of law enforcement officers. *Journal of Police Science and Administration, 7*(2), 241–244.

Lilley, J., & Greenberg, S.F. (1984, January). Physical training program addresses long-term attitude toward fitness. *Police Chief, 51,* 47–49.

Lundman, R. (1980). *Police and policing: An introduction.* New York: Holt, Rinehart & Winston.

Massey, D. (1993). Why us and why? Some reflections on teaching ethics to police. *Police Studies, 16*(3), 77–83.

McNamara, J.H. (1967). Uncertainties in police work: The relevance of police recruits' backgrounds and training. In D. Bordua (Ed.), *The police: Six sociological essays,* pp. 163–252. New York: John Wiley & Sons.

Meadows, R.J. (1985, September). Police training strategies and the role perceptions of police recruits. *Journal of Police Science and Administration, 53,* 195–200.

———. (1987a). An assessment of police entry-level training in the United States: Conformity or conflict with the police role? In D.B. Kennedy & R. Homant (Eds.), *Police and Law Enforcement,* vol. V, pp. 145–157. New York: AMS Press.

———. (1987b). Beliefs of law enforcement administrators and criminal justice educators toward the needed skill competencies in entry-level police training curriculum. *Journal of Police Science and Administration, 15*(1), 1–9.

Miller, J., & Fry, L. (1976). Reexamining assumptions about education and professionalism in law enforcement. *Journal of Police Science and Administration, 4,* 187–198.

Miller, L.S., & Braswell, M.C. (1986). The utility of experiential case studies in police education: A comparative analysis. *Criminal Justice Review, 11*(2), 9–14.

Molden, J. (1982, June). Training firstline police supervisors: A new approach. *FBI Law Enforcement Bulletin, 51,* 10–15.

National Commission on Law Observance and Enforcement [1931]. (1971). *Report on the police.* New York: Arno Press & *New York Times.*

Niederhoffer, A. (1967). *Behind the shield: The police in urban society.* New York: Doubleday.

Northeastern Association of Criminal Justice Sciences. (1995). *Minimum standards for criminal justice education: Guidelines for college and university level programs.*

Parker, L.C., Donnelly, M., Gerwitz, D., Marcus, J., & Kowalewski, V. (1976). Higher education: Its impact on police attitudes. *Police Chief, 43*(7), 33–35.

Pearce, J.B., & Snortum, J.R. (1983). Police effectiveness in handling disturbance calls: An evaluation of crisis intervention training. *Criminal Justice and Behavior, 10*(1), 71–92.

Police Forum. (1996). Police education and the crime bill. *Police Forum, 6*(1), 1–8.

Reaves, B.A. (1992). State and local police departments. *BJS Bulletin,* 14.

Regali, J.E. (1988, June). Athletic injuries: A comparative study of municipal/county basic police cadets at the Maine Criminal Justice Academy. *Journal of Police Science and Administration, 16,* 80–83.

Roberg, R., & Kuykendall, J. (1993). *Police and society.* Belmont, CA: Wadsworth.

Sapp, A., Carter, D., & Stephens, D. (1989). Police chiefs: CJ curricula inconsistent with contemporary police needs. *ACJS Today, 7*(4), 1, 5.

Schwartz, M.D., & Stucky, T.S. (1993). Predicting success on the Ohio Police Training Examination. *The Justice Professional, 7*(2), 35–45.

Scott, W.R. (1986). College education requirements for police entry level and promotion: A study. *Journal of Police and Criminal Psychology, 2*(1), 10–28.

Sherman, L. (1978). College education for police: The reform that failed. *Police Studies, 1*(4), 32–38.

———. (1980). The causes of police behavior: The current state of quantitative research. In A. Blumberg & E. Niederhoffer (Eds.), *The ambivalent force: Perspectives on the police,* (3rd ed., pp. 183–195). New York: Holt, Rinehart & Winston.

Sherman, L., & Blumberg, M. (1981). Higher education and police use of deadly force. *Journal of Criminal Justice, 9*(4), 317–331.

Sherman, L., & McLeod, M. (1979). Faculty characteristics and course content in college programs for police officers. *Journal of Criminal Justice, 7*(3), 249–267.

Sherman, L., & The National Advisory Commission on Higher Education for Police Officers. (1978). *The quality of police education.* San Francisco: Jossey-Bass.

Shernock, S.K. (1992). *Report on task analysis and evaluation survey of basic training at the Vermont Police Academy.* Montpelier, VT: Vermont Center for Justice Research.

———. (1994). The differential value of training on criticality evaluations of police tasks and functions. Paper presented at the 1994 annual meeting of the Academy of Criminal Justice Sciences, Chicago.

Smith, A.B., Locke, B., & Fenster, A. (1970). Authoritarianism in policemen who are college graduates and non-college police. *Journal of Criminal Law, Criminology, and Police Science, 61*(2), 313–315.

Smith, D.C., & Ostrom, E. (1974). The effects of training and education on police attitudes and performance: A preliminary analysis. In H. Jacob (Ed.), *The potential for reform of criminal justice,* pp. 45–81. Beverly Hills, CA: Sage.

Smith, D. (1978). The dangers of police professionalization: An empirical analysis. *Journal of Criminal Justice, 6*(3), 199–216.

Smith, S.S. (1990, March). How to achieve more learning in your academy. *Law and Order, 38,* 40–43.

Southerland, M.D. (1984). *The active valuing of education by police organizations.* Doctoral dissertation, University of Kentucky.

Sparling, C. (1975). The use of educational standards as selection criteria in police agencies. *Journal of Police Science and Administration, 3*(3), 332–334.

Stevens, J.W. (1983). Basic and advanced training of police officers: A comparison of West Germany and the United States. *Police Studies, 6*(3), 24–35.

Swanson, C.R. (1977). An uneasy look at college education and the police organization. *Journal of Criminal Justice, 5*(4), 311–320.

Taft, P.B. (1981). College education for police: The dream and the reality. *Police Magazine, 4*(6), 8–12.

Van Maanen, J. (1973, Winter). Observations on the making of a policeman. In W.C. Terry, III (Ed.), *Policing society,* pp. 203–215. New York: John Wiley & Sons.

Walker, S. (1992). *The police in America* (2nd ed.). New York: McGraw-Hill.

Weiner, N. (1976). The educated policeman. *Journal of Police Science and Administration, 4*(4), 450–457.

Weirman, C., & Archambeault, W.G. (1983). Addressing the effects of LEAA demise on criminal justice higher education. *Journal of Criminal Justice, 11,* 549–561.

Worden, R.E. (1990). A badge and a baccalaureate: Policies, hypotheses, and further evidence. *Justice Quarterly, 7*(3), 565–592.

5

Stress and the Badge

M.L. Dantzker, Georgia Southern University

While no occupation or profession is without its stress, the stress linked to policing often requires closer attention. The reason for more scrutiny revolves around the fact that few occupations require split-second decision making that affects life or liberty. Therefore, aspects of the job, such as stress, that can have negative repercussions must be recognized and addressed. This chapter examines stress and its relationship to policing. Why this topic is important may be best illustrated by the following news article.

OFFICER KILLS HIMSELF

ELKHART, Ind.—A police officer upset because he was taken off the street and given a desk job shot himself to death in front of the police chief and others. Sgt. Ernest Hill killed himself on Friday. He apparently thought he was ready to go back to his regular duties and asked the chief, J.J. Ivory, in a telephone conversation whether he could be taken off the front desk, Capt. Larry Towns said on Saturday. After Hill hung up suddenly, the chief went out to talk to him in the department's lobby. As Ivory approached, Hill shot himself in the head (*Sun-Sentinel,* Sunday, May 22, 1994, p. 3A).

For a number of years, the issue of police stress has received considerable attention (Bonifacio, 1991). It has been usual for lists identifying the most stressful occupations in the United States to show "police officer" near the top. For example, according to the American Institute of Stress (AIS), the only job tougher than police officer is inner city school teacher. The AIS identified the top ten most stressful jobs as

1. inner city high school teacher,
2. police officer,
3. miner,
4. air-traffic controller,
5. medical intern,
6. stockbroker,
7. journalist,

8. customer service/complaints worker,
9. waiter/waitress, and
10. secretary (*Police Beat,* May/June, 1994 p. 6).

Although stress is a phenomenon experienced by people in every occupation, there are some who believe its presence in law enforcement is of greater concern than in other occupations. For example, longtime Los Angeles Police Department psychologist Marty Reiser has noted, "Police work is a high stress occupation that affects, shapes and also scars the individuals and families involved" (1974, p. 156). Reiser's position has been supported by others: "It is usually assumed that police work is particularly stressful because of the severe psychological and physiological problems experienced by police employees, such as marital strain, alcohol and drug abuse, heart disease, and suicide" (Gaines & Jermier, 1983, p. 569).

Recent experiences of the New York City Police Department (NYPD) could lend support to such conclusions. In April 1994, Ronald Gouch was the third NYPD officer to kill himself that year, allegedly because he was despondent over his recent divorce. By August 1, 1994, NYPD experienced its eighth officer suicide when Captain Terrence Tunnock shot himself in what was believed to be the result of job stress. The 1994 NYPD suicides matched the total number of NYPD officer suicides for all of 1993 in only eight months; by the end of 1994, 12 NYPD officers had committed suicide. In 1995, another 11 NYPD officers took their own lives, and midway through 1996, 3 NYPD officers had committed suicide.

Others have also noted the importance of recognizing and acknowledging stress in policing because police officers perceive many aspects of their work as stressful (Terry, 1983). It has been noted that stress can "encroach most profoundly on decision-making" (Janis, 1982), an extremely important task of police officers. There is little debate about the prevalence of decision-making dilemmas in police work. Whether to issue a ticket, make an arrest, or use deadly force are just a few of the many dilemmas faced by police officers. Furthermore, decision making in policing is especially significant when one considers that policing is the primary occupation with the legislative power to make an instantaneous decision to take away an individual's liberty or life.

Los Angeles Police Department (LAPD) psychologist Reiser and fellow researcher A. Honig (1983) suggested that economic concerns could be a primary reason for recognizing and attempting to reduce stress in policing. They observed that early retirement disability pensions resulting from stress were escalating. In a study of the LAPD, they found that 55 stress-related pensions were granted from July 1, 1972, through June 30, 1977. During 1981, 63 such pensions had been granted. Furthermore, there was sufficient evidence to predict that this number would continue to escalate. Although no published source currently exists to substantiate this, conversations this author has had with police personnel throughout the country indicate the number of such pension requests has risen as predicted. Moreover, the courts have supported employees' attempts to seek compensation based on their perception of stressful events (Blank, 1987). As Conroy and Hess (1992) noted,

Stress has become a problem of increasing proportion. Business, industry, and health insurance firms are concerned about costs of employee disability as the courts award larger and larger monetary settlements for injury from work stress and allow payment for anxiety, depression, and post-traumatic stress disorder (p. 23).

Because of the nature of police work, there are a number of inherent conditions that may be perceived as stressful, such as threat to one's safety, boredom, responsiblity for others, and various unsolvable problems (Conroy & Hess, 1992; Goolkasian, Geddes & De Jong, 1985). In addition, stress can arise from organizational, environmental, and legal sources, which will be explored later in the chapter.

Police officers are constantly barraged with situations that may be perceived as stressful. Yet, considering the image associated with policing—macho, tough, crime fighter—it is difficult for individuals and agencies to admit that police officers are vulnerable, that they can be affected by the job. However, reality has shown otherwise. Stress can have a negative effect on the officer and others she or he interacts with.

Illustration: In September 1994 Milwaukee patrol officer William Robertson was killed when a bullet was fired by an unknown sniper at the van he was driving. Robertson was the first Milwaukee officer to be killed in what appears to have been a random act. A University of Wisconsin-Milwaukee psychologist who works with officers on stress-related issues predicted that the stress of patrol duty for other officers will increase as a result of Robertson's murder, that it will be even more scary for them. Therefore, negative changes in how officers respond to calls and individuals could occur.

Stress and its associated elements must be recognized and understood. The remainder of this chapter provides a simple yet informative introduction to stress and its relationship to policing. What stress is, what causes stress, the effects of stress, and coping with stress are examined so as to promote the recognition of this phenomenon and its many facets among students of policing or among police personnel.

STRESS: WHAT IS IT?

Despite the fact that "Just what police stress really is and what the term really means remains a puzzle" (Bonifacio, 1991, p. 126), recognition of stress is not new. The general concept of stress has existed since the early 14th century. However, it has received substantial attention only since World War II (Lazarus & Folkman, 1984; Muchinsky, 1993).

According to Hans Selye, who might be considered the founding father of modern studies in stress, "Although the word stress was originally used as an expression of human difficulties caused by outside forces beyond one's control, it became formalized in science to mean any change within a system induced by an external force" (1980, p. 26). Formalization of a concept generally includes a definition. With stress, however, several definitions have arisen and, to date, there doesn't appear to be one generally accepted definition (Gaines, 1993; More, 1992; Northcraft & Neale, 1994).

For example, Selye defined stress as "the state manifested by a specific syndrome which consists of all nonspecifically induced changes within a biological system" (Selye, 1956, p. 54). He later shortened this definition to "a nonspecific response of the body to any demand" (1980, p. 55; 1983, p. 2). Selye's definitions are just two of the many found in the literature.

Cox advises that stress "can only be sensibly defined as a 'perceptual' phenomenon arising from a comparison between the demand on the person and his ability to cope. An imbalance in this mechanism, when coping is important, gives rise to the experience of stress, and to the stress response" (1978, p. 25). Sewell (1981) notes that stress is the result of some type of physical, mental, or emotional reaction to a situation. This reaction is believed to cause the individual to experience such feelings as fear, uncertainty, danger, excitement, or confusion. Coleman, in Territo and Vetter, offers that stress refers to "the adjustive demands made upon the individual to the problems in living with which he must cope if he is to meet his needs" (1981, p. 18).

Violanti describes stress as "a 'perceived imbalance' between demands and 'perceived capability' to respond to those demands" (1983, p. 219; Violanti & Marshall, 1983, p. 389). Burchfield (1985) simply views stress as a process that explains why a given stressor acts as a specific stimulus which elicits the stress response.

Luthans defines stress as an "adaptive response to an external situation that results in physical, psychological, and/or behavioral deviations for organizational participants" (1985, p. 130). Finally, the last definition to be offered is found in Asterita: "Stress pertains to a state produced within an organism subject to a stimulus 'perceived' as a threat" (1985, p. 3).

In lieu of definitions offered, there are scholars who believe that stress may be a "rubric," a rule of conduct or procedure, consisting of a variety of variables and processes (Lazarus & Folkman, 1984). Others view stress in terms of a construct rather than a single entity (Terry, 1983). Ultimately, the best view of stress may be, "Stress is difficult to define—it is not strictly an independent, dependent, or intervening variable. Rather, it is a collective term denoting demands that 'tax' a system (physiological, social, or psychological) and its responses" (Muchinsky, 1993, p. 275).

Considering the plethora of definitions, it is no wonder that defining police stress is difficult. However, there is an underlying theme to all the definitions that applies to policing: stress is a phenomenon, whether physical, psychological, or sociological, which produces some type of effect within an individual (Ayres & Flanagan, 1990; Conroy & Hess, 1992; More, 1992). *Therefore, for the purpose of this discussion, police stress is defined as any experience or situation, physical, emotional, and social, that affects a police officer's well-being.*

The definition offered appears to be properly suited for describing police stress. However, I believe that one last definition should be included, a psychodynamic definition, which views stress in police officers as a "by-product of conflict" (Bonifacio, 1991).

The psychodynamic definition of police stress is that:

> It is the result of the policeman's emotional conflicts. One part of his conflict results from feeling overwhelmed by a cruel, uncivilized environment that is too powerful for him to master. The result is feelings of objective anxiety. The second part results from being gratified by the work in ways that threaten his moral code. He is deriving immoral pleasure that threatens to make him uncivilized and cruel. This conflict leads to superego anxiety. These two forms of anxiety—objective and superego—are at the heart of what is described as police stress. The police officer's stress is really his feelings of distress trying to cope with anxiety (Bonifacio, 1991, p. 133).

Regardless of the legitimacy of the psychodynamic definition of stress, its idea of police stress being related to unconscious conflict and defense mechanisms is not a very popular position among police stress researchers (Bonifacio, 1991). Three reasons given for its lack of popularity are:

1. Research designs do not apply very well to explorations of the unconscious;
2. The idea of unconscious motivation, conflict, and anxiety does not sit well with the police community; and
3. The psychodynamic view of police stress does not lend itself to coming up with simple solutions to the problem (Bonifacio, 1991, pp. 133, 134).

To somewhat further complicate matters, there are also several theories, perspectives, and philosophies of stress within the definitions. Each is found to focus on stress from a slightly different angle. A variety of professions and occupations have been examined, identifying differing causes or sources of stress; yet, researchers generally find that there are similar results or outcomes of stress. The one theme that appears to be consistent is that, regardless of the occupation or profession in question, stress exists (Muchinsky, 1993; Robbins, 1993).

Within the last ten years the literature on occupational stress has grown quite rapidly. But why? Probably the best response is because job stress adversely affects employees (Ayres & Flanagan, 1990). Therefore, it is important to understand occupational stress.

What Is Occupational Stress?

While definitions of occupational stress are not as plentiful as those for more generalized stress, there is still a fairly formidable variety. It should be noted that in definitions of work-related stress, occupational and organizational stress appear synonymous. The following are a few examples of occupational stress definitions:

1. "an imbalance between demand, both external and internal, and the capability in meeting the demand when coping is important" (Cox, 1978, p. 150);

2. "the general, patterned, unconscious mobilization of the individual's energy when confronted with any organizational or work demand" (Quick & Quick, 1984, p. 9); and

3. "various degrees of compatibility (or incompatibility) between the individual and his work environment" (Humphrey, 1986, p. 37).

Based on these, and similar, definitions, with respect to policing, occupational stress might best be viewed as *the demands of the job, organizationally, environmentally, socially, and legally; the officers' responses to the demands; and the outcomes.*

Thus far, it has been acknowledged that policing is stressful. Furthermore, several definitions of stress and occupational stress have been offered. This information has been important; yet, a question that was briefly alluded to in the beginning of this chapter and requires further exploration is, why bother to study stress and its relationship to policing?

Why Study Stress?

The same reasons one would study stress in other occupations also apply to policing; that is, stress has been linked with several identifiable physiological, psychological, and sociological problems that can affect performance on the job, as well as being life-threatening to some individuals (Dewe & Guest, 1990; More, 1992; Northcraft & Neale, 1994). The adverse effects of stress appear to be capable of severely limiting an individual's ability to function. Furthermore, with the extensive findings of the effects of stress, it is logical that the study of stress in the work arena would grow. As McLean points out "work occupies a major part of most of our lives, in terms of both time spent and importance. It contains the potential for many forms of gratification and challenge—and harm" (1979, p. 1). Stress has been identified as an extremely important element of work (Reiser, 1974; McLean, 1979; Levi, 1981; Terry, 1983; Gaines & Jermier, 1983; Quick & Quick, 1984; Everly & Sobelman, 1987). Therefore, it is extremely important to organizations and individuals to be able to recognize and understand stress.

From an occupational perspective, reasons for studying stress include

1. Mismanaged organizational stress can produce individual strain and distress which is detrimental to an organization's human resources (can lead to negative economic implications); and

2. When organizational stress is expertly managed, it can lead to improved performance, worker satisfaction, and productivity (Quick & Quick, 1984, p. 10).

French, Caplan, and Harrison (1982) note that there is a need for studies that focus on the relationship of job demands and worker health as it pertains to productivity and economic outcomes. The term *health* is defined by Levi as "not only an 'absence of disease or infirmity' but also 'a state of physical, mental, and social well-being'" (1981, p. 1). He adds that "Promoting health in this broad sense must be one of the principal aims of all social activity, both central and local, including the important sector of working life and its conditions" (1981, p. 1).

For some, a primary concern with occupational stress is the monetary value attached to its effects (Honig & Reiser, 1983; Conroy & Hess, 1992; Robbins, 1993). For example, information from the National Council on Compensation Insurance indicated that, "Claims involving mental disorders caused by stress accounted for nearly eleven percent of all occupational claims between 1980 and 1982. Moreover, claims in which stress causes a physical disability are now recognized in all compensation jurisdictions except Ohio" (Hurrell, 1987, p. 31).

A friend of the author is an example of such action. As an LAPD officer, she received a stress-related medical disability because of rheumatoid arthritis, which was said to have been caused from the stress of the job. While rheumatoid arthritis is not a common stress-induced ailment, it is one of many outcomes of occupational stress, which has been said to be "one of the most debilitating medical and social problems in the U.S. today" (Everly & Sobelman, 1987, p. 7).

Compensation claims are and will continue to be a concern for employers (Blank, 1987). However, compensation claims are not the only area producing economic hardships in organizations. Additional problems, such as absenteeism, turnover, low morale, and job dissatisfaction resulting from occupational stress, also increase an organization's costs and negatively affect its efficiency (Mann & Neece, 1990; Robbins, 1993). Ultimately, it's been noted that stress-related problems are costing businesses as much as $15 billion in lost productivity and other organizational problems (Northcraft & Neale, 1994). Law enforcement is increasingly experiencing such costs, too (Mann & Neece, 1990).

Finally, occupational stress also has individual costs. Work stresses have been associated with a variety of health problems, such as the example previously noted of the officer with rheumatoid arthritis, and others that will be discussed shortly, and with causing hardships in family life, such as marital strain. Therefore, due to the various costs, especially personal and work-related consequences, the stress associated with policing requires recognition and study. Before we further examine the effects of stress, it would help to know what causes stress.

OCCUPATIONAL STRESS AND POLICING

Policing has been viewed as an extremely stressful occupation and appears to dominate the occupational stress literature (Kroes, Hurrell & Margolis, 1974; Reiser, 1974; Sewell, 1981; Territo & Vetter, 1981; Daviss, 1982; Terry, 1981, 1983; Ellison & Genz, 1983; Wexler & Logan, 1983; Jackson & Maslach, 1983; Goolkasian, Geddes & De Jong, 1985; Dantzker, 1986; Murphy & Schoenborn, 1987). Why policing has drawn so much attention is no mystery. Reiser points out that "Police work is a high stress occupation which affects, shapes, and also scars the individuals and families involved" (1974, p. 156). Gaines and Jermier lend support to this belief: "It is usually assumed that police work is particularly stressful because of the severe psychological and physiological problems experienced by police employees, such as marital strain, alcohol and drug abuse, heart disease, and suicide" (1983, p. 569). They do clarify that these problems are not necessarily direct measures of the stress experienced at work "but instead are presumed consequences of the work-related problems" (1983, p. 569).

Terry advises that, "Many aspects of police work and many events encountered by individual police officers are viewed as stressful; these perceptions affect the performance of the police duties" (1983, p. 156). Wexler and Logan state that, "This concern with stress has developed out of the awareness of its personal and work-related consequences, and of the high levels of stress inherent in police work" (1983, p. 46).

Goolkasian, Geddes, and De Jong identified the following elements as inherent to police work that might easily be considered the main components of police stress:

1. the constant threat to an officer's health and safety;
2. boredom, alternating with the need for sudden alertness and mobilized energy;
3. responsibility for protecting others' lives;
4. continual exposure to people in pain or distress;
5. the need to control emotions, even when provoked to anger;
6. the presence of a gun, sometimes even during off-duty hours; and
7. the fragmented nature of police work (1985, p. 4).

An element extremely important to policing is decision making. Janis advises that, "Stress encroaches most profoundly on decision-making when the decision-maker is in a dilemma about what to do about imminent threats of physical suffering, bodily injury, or death" (1985, p. 70).

Honig and Reiser (1983) cite economics as a primary reason for recognizing stress in policing. They state that "Police distress has gained notoriety due to the outgrowth of escalating costs of early retirement disability pensions" (1983, 385). This increase is not a result of police agency generosity.

Blank (1987) claims that the increase in stress-related pensions is primarily attributable to the interpretations of the courts. Apparently the courts have begun to allow employees to seek compensation based on their perception of stress or what they constitute as a stressful event or situation. However, the effects of stress are not always immediately recognizable and may be greater than those initially perceived.

To this point, this chapter has described what stress is in both general terms and as it relates to one's occupation. There undoubtedly is growing concern over the ramifications of stress-related disorders. Yet, in order to address the outcomes of stress, one must understand what causes stress.

CAUSES OF STRESS

It was noted earlier that, regardless of the nature of one's occupation or profession, there is stress; yet, how stress is formulated or perceived varies by individual. For example, having to give a speech may be extremely stressful to one person while it is almost fun to another, or the police officer having to respond to a domestic disturbance call might find this very stressful, while another simply looks at it as part of the job. The point is, stress obviously can take several forms and may not always be negative. Yet, one thing is certain, stress doesn't simply appear out of nowhere—there is generally some root cause. The causes of stress are more commonly referred to as stressors (Ayres & Flanagan, 1990; Conroy & Hess, 1992; Muchinsky, 1993; Northcraft & Neale, 1994). According to Asterita, "Any stimuli which an organism perceives as a threat is termed a stressor. Stressors may be physical, psychological, or psychosocial in nature" (1982, p. 4).

Many professions and occupations share similar stressors—such as shift work, supervisory problems, improper and inadequate equipment, and insufficient reward or reinforcement systems—but there are stressors that are unique to law enforcement, such as responding to unpredictable situations, role conflict (e.g., law enforcer vs. social servant), society's hypocritical demands, and the court system. A result of research in this area has led to several categorizations of police-related stressors. The most popular categorizations appear to be external, internal, law enforcement itself, and individual (Ayres & Flanagan, 1990; Conroy & Hess, 1992; Goolkasian, Geddes & De Jong, 1985).

A general review of the police-stress literature revealed a respectable quantity of publications that attempt to identify police stressors. The majority of stressors associated with law enforcement fall into four broad categories:

1. organizational practices and characteristics;
2. criminal justice system practices and characteristics;
3. public practices and characteristics; and
4. police work itself (Territo & Vetter, 1981).

In general, the literature revealed a number of stressors associated with law enforcement. Therefore, for the purpose of this chapter, stressors are examined from four categories: external, internal, law enforcement work, and individual.

External Stressors

External stressors are those outside of the police organization. Examples include frustrations from the court system, such as plea bargaining and cases dismissed because of a "legal technicality;" the lack of public support and unreasonable demands; and the unfair or negative image attributable to unrealistic media depiction.

Internal Stressors

Internal stressors are stressors that stem from within the police agency. Examples of these stressors include: policies and procedures that negatively affect the officer, such as not allowing officers to work off-duty jobs; limiting the type of weapon the officer can carry; promotional systems that are unfair and heavily favor certain individuals; and poor equipment, benefits, pay, etc.

Law Enforcement Work Stressors

Police work itself provides a plethora of stressors, from responding to unknown situations to the potential for danger and injury. Other stressors include: the rigors of and rotation of shifts; exposure to the worst sides of human nature; going from a state of boredom to sudden alertness; and the unpredictability of daily activities.

Individual Stressors

Each officer is different and brings with him or her characteristics and problems that can be stressful. For example, family, personal health, or financial problems can cause stress for police officers. Furthermore, the effects of the police role itself, such as having to alter one's social status or conform to the police subculture for acceptance can be stressful to individuals.

One of the first, and probably foremost, studies on police stress was conducted by Kroes, Hurrell, and Margolis (1974). Upon interviewing 100 Cincinnati, Ohio, police officers, they found the following elements to be most frequently cited as stressful: the court system, the administration, faulty equipment, and community apathy. Changing shifts, relations with supervisors, non-police type work, boredom, and pay were other stressors identified by these officers. Since this study, others have found that police stressors are born out of a multiplicity of influences that include those from within oneself, from the police organization, and from the working environment.

In an effort to further study causes of stress among police officers, this author conducted a study (Dantzker, 1987a) of a police department of more than four hundred officers that appeared to be representative of a typical police department serving a population of more than 250,000. The top five stressful factors or situations (in order of stressfulness) mentioned by officers were (1) low salaries causing a need to work part-time jobs, (2) understaffing, (3) violent injury or death of a fellow officer, (4) inadequate equipment, and (5) overall failure of the criminal justice system (Dantzker, 1987a).

Ultimately, it is the perception of the individual officer that determines what is stressful and to what extent. Despite the individualization of stress, it is important for police agencies to educate officers on the various facets of stress, particularly its effects, which could be a matter of life and death.

THE EFFECTS OF STRESS

Although it is difficult to define stress, there is unanimous belief that stress has some effect on the living organism. Excessive stress has been found to result in physical, social, and psychological damage. All three can culminate in what has been referred to as "burnout." However, prior to further investigation of this stage it is necessary to examine how one reaches this stage.

The first individual to recognize the interrelationships between stressful conditions, their onset, and the progression of many illnesses was Hans Selye, a Canadian physiologist and physician. Selye discovered that the nervous system automatically recognizes change and immediately initiates a group of biochemical activities to stimulate a set of protective body reactions (Hageman, 1982; Milsum, 1984; Selye, 1956, 1980, 1983). As a result of his research, Selye (1956) identified the three-step biological process a body follows in its reaction to stressful situations. He referred to this process as the General Adaptation Syndrome (GAS) (Conroy & Hess, 1992; More, 1992; Selye, 1956, 1980, 1983).

Stage one of the GAS is the alarm stage. The alarm stage is "the organism's reaction when it is suddenly exposed to diverse stimuli to which it is not adapted" (Kutash & Schlesinger, 1980, p. 129). The primary element in this stage is the shock of the situation. An example related to policing is the response of the rookie officer when confronted with the first exposure to a dead body. Depending on the state of the corpse, the officer may initially need to look away or leave the area. Furthermore, the officer may have an adverse physical reaction, such as nausea.

The second stage of GAS is resistance. This is "the organism's full adaptation to the stressor and the consequent improvement or disappearance of symptoms" (Kutash & Schlesinger, 1980, p. 129). It is within this stage that there appears to be a concurring decrease in resistance to most other stimuli (Selye, 1956). For example, the officer who has responded to several death scene investigations, regardless of the nature of death or victim, finds ways to make light or create some humor about the situation. This mechanism helps separate the officer from the reality of the situation, causing emotional distancing, so to speak.

The third and final stage of the GAS is exhaustion. "Since adaptability is finite, exhaustion inexorably follows if the stressor is sufficiently severe and prolonged symptoms reappear, and if the stress continues unabated, death ensues" (Kutash & Schlesinger, 1980, p. 129). It is in this third stage that the majority of severe illnesses, such as coronary problems, diabetes, and ulcers begin to occur (Asterita, 1982; Selye, 1956, 1980); it is also the stage that is best recognized as burnout.

The effects of burnout are known to include attitudinal problems, such as cynicism, apathy, and failing to respond to certain demands of the job; judgment problems, such as responding to a call of a man with a gun and not taking appropriate care in approaching; impairment of reflexes; and not recognizing danger signs as quickly as in days prior to burnout (Bonifacio, 1991; Conroy & Hess, 1992; Maslach, 1976, 1982; More, 1992).

Many police psychologists seem to agree that burnout is claiming more police officers than ever. Like stress, there are a variety of definitions of burnout and no one definition has been universally accepted (Maslach, 1982; Muchinsky, 1993). Definitions identified in the literature generally seem to include: a syndrome of emotional exhaustion, depersonalization, and reduced personal accomplishment occurring among individuals who do "people work" of some kind; and a state of physical, emotional, and mental exhaustion marked by physical depletion and chronic fatigue, feelings of helplessness and hopelessness, and the development of a negative self-concept and negative attitudes toward work, life, and other people (Gaines & Jermier, 1983; Perlman & Hartman, 1982; Quick & Quick, 1984).

No definition of burnout has been completely accepted, yet three areas of consensus are recognizable. Burnout occurs at an individual level; it is an internal psychological experience involving feelings, attitudes, motives, and expectations; and it is a negative experience for the individual in that it concerns problems, distress, discomfort, dysfunction, or negative consequences (Maslach, 1982).

Concerning policing, professor and police psychologist W. Mullins (1986) found that burnout had a direct negative effect on the police officer. The results of his study indicated that the greater the degree of burnout, the more severe the behavior of the officer in dealing with everyday patrol activities.

Fortunately, burnout is recognizable and there are several identifiable factors that make an officer susceptible to burnout. They are: naivete and enthusiasm, measurement of performance, lack of organizational support, distribution of resources, and dealing with the public in an adversarial manner (Conroy & Hess, 1992).

As for naivete and enthusiasm, many individuals, upon entering law enforcement, often have illusions about helping society. Yet, after a short time reality clouds and even destroys many of these illusions, leaving many officers feeling bitter and wondering why they do this job at all. Therefore, the police officer who has gone from being "gung ho" and dedicated to derelict and less cautious may very well be suffering from the effects of stress.

Illustration: Officer Smith had been one of the most active officers on the midnight shift. Usually the first to arrive for role call and the last to leave, Smith was a model of professionalism both in appearance and performance. However, after several years of being the model police officer, Smith began to change: late to roll call, slovenly dress, not responding to calls, and citizens starting to complain about how Smith talked to them or responded to their problems. It was eventually discovered that Smith was experiencing a number of problems. First, Smith's spouse was threatening divorce if Smith didn't change shifts or transfer to detectives (both of which had been denied by the department). Smith had also begun experiencing severe headaches. No one seemed to recognize the symptoms or indicators.

How an officer's performance is measured can be problematic. Although a number of activities an officer performs can be tracked statistically, such as writing tickets, making arrests, and writing reports, there are many activities that cannot be quantified. These activities, such as giving directions, assisting a motorist, or simply discussing a matter with a citizen, will often make up the bulk of an officer's daily regime. The inability to measure these activities often leaves an officer appearing as if she or he is not doing the job, leaving the officer vulnerable to criticism and ridicule from supervisors and other officers.

In any organization, the lack of support for its members can cause problems. Individual burnout can be caused by the belief that the police organization does not support the officer and is not interested in him or her as an individual but as a mere cog in a machine. This lack of support tends to lead officers to believe they are on their own and that there is little to no assistance available.

How resources are distributed can be linked to burnout. An overwhelming use of resources for special units or a lack of support personnel can create the perception that no one is really interested in how well the patrol officer does his or her job. Lack of resources, leading to extremely heavy workloads, adds to the possibility of burnout.

Finally, perceived lack of citizen support can cause burnout. Although police officers exist to assist in the betterment of society and for improving or maintaining quality of life, they are not superbeings. Yet citizens often perceive that police officers can do anything, solve any problem, and are the saviors of the world. Unfortunately, officers cannot live up to these perceptions or expectations and are unable to solve everyone's problems. This can result in police and citizens becoming adversaries instead of teammates. This adversarial relationship can lead to burnout.

It is obvious that stress, particularly in the form of burnout, appears to have an extremely debilitating effect on an individual, regardless of occupation or profession. Therefore, recognizing the signs or indicators that stress is present or that burnout has been reached becomes important to individuals and the police organization. Fortunately, recognizing the indicators of severe stress or burnout is relatively easy, since there are many obvious physiological, sociological, and psychological signs or indicators.

Physiological Indicators.   The most obvious and detectable area of stress impact is found in the physiological arena. Over the years, stress researchers have found that stress is directly related to several diseases and illnesses. Probably the most prevalent and readily recognized stress-related maladies are peptic ulcers and migraine headaches. Hypertension, backaches, asthma, and even diabetes have all been linked to stress (Asterita, 1982; Martin, 1987). These physiological problems appear to arise as the result of the chronic elicitation of the stress response (Ayres & Flanagan, 1990; Burchfield, 1985).

Stress has also been linked to skin disorders and disorders and diseases of the cardiovascular system (Milsum, 1984). It has even been suggested that the effects of stress may be linked to diseases of the immune system, such as cancer (Asterita, 1982), although this last claim is still under investigation. Overall, stress has been found to play an important role in the causation of physical disorders. The role of stress is not limited to physiological effects, however.

Sociological Indicators.   Stress has been found to be linked with sociological as well as physiological problems. These too, like physical effects, can have serious implications for an officer (see Conroy & Hess, 1992; Robbins, 1993).

It has long been recognized that many police officers find it difficult to socialize outside the ranks of policing. Thus, there appears to be a tendency toward isolation from others not directly involved in law enforcement in the community. Several hypotheses have been offered in an attempt to explain this phenomenon. One explanation arises from the stigma and multiple roles related to being a police officer (More, 1992). Individuals not involved in policing either want to discuss policing, complain, or simply break off all relations with the officer (Dantzker, 1986). Regardless of the reasons for difficulty in relationships, the officer loses contact with and may even begin to feel like an unwanted member of the general society.

Social activities are also difficult to plan due to the logistics of the job. For example, rotating schedules, overtime, and working on holidays, often interfere with social plans; furthermore, even in the most casual of off-duty circumstances, it is difficult to stop thinking or acting as a police officer (Dantzker, 1986, 1989). As a result of the associational difficulties and the social activities' problems there are additional strains on the functioning of the officer as an individual.

This is especially true for the married police officer (Conroy & Hess, 1992; Gaines, 1993; Jackson & Maslach, 1982; More, 1992). One of the most common sociological problems among police officers is divorce.

> Despite the lack of a consensus about the divorce rate in police families, there is nearly unanimous agreement that the job imposes considerable stress on the family unit. Perhaps the most significant stress described in the literature is change in the policeman's self-disclosure and emotional involvement with his family (Bonifacio, 1991, p. 174).

From personal experience, I can honestly say that police officers, in an attempt to shield their families from the negatives of their jobs, tell their families little. This results in less and less communication between officers and family members. Eventually, this causes more and more strain, often leading to divorce. It is easy, especially in larger metropolitan departments, to find several officers who are in the midst of their third marriage and have not yet reached the age of thirty (Schwartz & Schwartz, 1981).

Although the number of factors involved and the degree of difficulty in evaluating the effect of each make it difficult to pinpoint the exact cause or causes, the stressors associated with being a police officer weigh heavily on family life.

> Officers who have dealt with physical confrontations (stress) appear to have a higher risk for interpersonal difficulties in his [sic] home life; and he [sic] possesses a more heightened sense of anger, suspiciousness, criticism, and social discomforts both on the job and in his [sic] personal life (Singleton & Teahan, 1978, p. 360).

Why officers respond to their family in this manner is not difficult to understand. As researchers Jackson and Maslach found, "Exhausted police officers are more likely to bring with them the tensions caused by their job; are likely to return from work upset or angry, tense and anxious, and in a complaining mood" (1982, p. 74). When the officer comes home and begins to treat family members as the "bad guys," it is a good indicator that job stress is taking its toll. A large part of the difficulty may very well be the result of the police officers' dealing on a daily basis with the problems of other people and then having to spend off-duty hours dealing with their own family and personal problems. This may become too much for some officers to handle and, rather than giving up the job, they find it easier to give up the family and its problems. Some officers, however, are lucky enough to recognize this transition and leave the job rather than the family.

Illustration: An academy classmate of the author was an easygoing, good-natured individual with strong religious convictions. Despite his current nature, another classmate and I (both of whom had been police officers elsewhere) tried warning him that his disposition would change as his experiences as a police officer increased. This individual advised us both not to worry— that this would never happen. He would always be the way he was now. Less than three years after graduating from the academy, this gentle, good-natured officer resigned because he did not like what he had become. No longer gentle, easygoing, or good-natured, this officer had come to treat everyone like scum, including his wife and daughters. However, the final blow to this officer was assisting in the arrest of his sergeant, who had been burglarizing pharmacies. If he couldn't even trust his supervisor, whom could he trust?

The last of the sociological problems associated with police stress that requires mentioning is cynicism. Although it has yet to receive the same level of attention as other problems, cynicism is a definite problem. Arthur Niederhoffer (1967) was the first to discuss cynicism in policing. Instead of using the term "stress" as the cause of cynicism, he used the term "anomie" as a direct equivalent. When cynicism sets in, the police officer begins to see everyone as selfish. Interest in the job is reduced to nothing more than financial support and the drive to do a good job is no longer there. Unfortunately, cynicism does not stay behind at the end of the shift; it carries over into the officer's personal life. This makes it extremely difficult for the police officer to get along in any situation. However, it has been noted that cynicism seems to be a common result of job stress in many of the people-oriented service professions (Maslach, 1976).

Overall, attributes of the job can cause stress in police officers, which in turn, can cause sociological problems for a police officer. Unfortunately, it becomes something of a vicious circle in that sociological problems can cause problems for the officer on the job, which only increases the problems off the job.

Psychological Indicators.   Although the physiological and sociological effects of stress contribute their share of problems, it may be possible that the most

devastating effects of stress are psychological problems, especially the psychosomatic problems, influencing the health of the police officer (Conroy & Hess, 1992;
Selye, 1956, 1980).

It has been suggested that general psychosomatic disorders appear to involve

1. sustained emotional arousal to stress—the degree and duration of arousal depending both on the nature of the stress and the individual's perception of it;
2. response stereotypy in which the damaging effects of chronic emotional arousal
   are concentrated in a specific organ system, presumably one that is more vulnerable than others as a result of heredity, illness, and conditioning; and
3. the overall role of sociocultural factors in relation to the stresses characteristic of
   a given society and the patterns of psychosomatic disorders most likely to occur
   (Coleman, 1981, p. 29).

In general, psychosomatic problems include essential hypertension, ulcers, colitis,
asthma, and mental illness (Levi, 1981a; Simpson, 1980; Stratton, 1981).

Psychological stress has been viewed as "a particular relationship between the
person and the environment that is appraised by the person as taxing or exceeding his
or her resources and endangering his or her well-being" (Lazarus & Folkman, 1984,
p. 19). Problems associated with psychological stress include alcoholism, drug
dependency, depression, and suicide (see Bonifacio, 1991; Conroy & Hess, 1992;
Dash & Reiser, 1978; Haynes, 1978; Martin, 1987).

It is fairly common to find police officers who abuse alcohol. While limited,
those surveys that have examined police problem drinking indicate that it is prevalent throughout the United States and Canada, with estimates of alcohol abuse as high
as 25 percent (Bonifacio, 1991). Why is alcohol abuse so prevalent among police officers? Several possible reasons exist. The first is availability. Officers regularly find
themselves in situations where alcohol is readily available; whether it's in a tavern,
nightclub, liquor store, restaurant, or private party, officers frequently find themselves
surrounded by alcohol and, because of the nature of the job (lack of supervision), may
find it easy to accept a drink.

A second reason for alcohol abuse by police officers may stem from the police
subculture. It is usual for officers to stop and have a drink or two after a shift. One
way to solidify one's stand in the culture is to go out drinking with the guys. Failing
to participate could lead to questions as to one's worthiness to be part of the subculture. The reality of this situation stems from peer pressure and the necessity of being
in good standing with fellow officers to maximize job safety.

Finally, what might be the most realistic and legitimate excuse for alcohol abuse
is that alcohol is perceived as the only way to relieve the stress of the job. When all
else fails, alcohol becomes the tool for alleviating the anxiety, frustration, and depression of the job. Simply, alcohol is quick, effective, and legal and is one of the few
coping methods approved by fellow officers (Bonifacio, 1991).

The major concern with alcohol abuse is when it becomes a part of the job.
Although not a circumstance many police agencies or officers will admit to, it is com-

mon to find one or two officers who drink on the job. Unfortunately, when alcohol abuse reaches this state it can be detrimental to everyone who must work with or come into contact with the officer. Therefore, recognition of such abuse must be made and assistance provided.

As for drugs, the relationship and use are very similar to that of alcohol abuse. However, what makes drug dependency worse are the illegality surrounding drugs and drug usage. Despite drugs' longtime existence and availability for police officers, few surveys are available to substantiate or demonstrate how much drug use occurs among police officers.

Last, but by no means least, is suicide. Police observers and ethnographers frequently note that there are high suicide rates among police officers (More, 1992; Gaines, 1993; Violanti, 1995). For example, a study conducted by the National Fraternal Order of Police found in its analysis of 38,800 FOP members' insurance policies (1992–1994), 37 percent of accidental deaths were attributed to suicide. This compares to 26 percent who were victims of homicides or vehicular accidents (National FOP Looks at Police Suicide and How to Prevent It, 1995). However, despite this study and a few similar ones, the literature on suicide among police officers is still rather limited. Since police agencies and fellow officers often want to protect their own, especially officers' reputations and family survivors' benefits, solid information about why and how officers actually commit suicide is sparse (Violanti, 1995).

Unfortunately, we know suicides occur (as indicated at the beginning of this chapter), maybe with a growing frequency. Further confirmation of this phenomenon is demonstrated in a September 26, 1994, *Newsweek* article, "Cops Who Kill—Themselves," where it was noted that more officers are dying by suicide than as a result of duty-related incidents. The article advised that approximately 300 police officers commit suicide annually, noting that, in 1993, 67 officers were killed in the line of duty. Although there are a number of psychodynamic reasons given as to why an officer commits suicide, such as frustration and helplessness, access to firearms, alcohol abuse, and a fear of separation from the police subculture (Violanti, 1995), it would appear that inability to cope with surroundings and accompanying stresses will often lead an officer to commit suicide.

The effects of stress thus far have been briefly examined from a physiological, sociological, and psychological perspective. However, prior to leaving this area of discussion, there is a relatively new concern to policing that should be mentioned: post traumatic stress disorder (PTSD). PTSD has been described as "development of characteristic symptoms following a psychologically traumatic event that is generally outside the range of usual human experience" (Mann & Neece, 1990, p. 449).

Although PTSD was first associated with war veterans, there are those who argue that police officers can be afflicted as well (see McCafferty et al., 1989a; McCafferty, Domingo & Palahunic, 1989; More, 1992). As Mann & Neece (1990) have stated, "Due to the nature of the stressors in the law enforcement environment, the likelihood of PTSD in police officers may be greater than those in many other occupations" (p. 449). While two of the most traumatic events an officer can experience are having a partner killed or having to take someone else's life, an accumulation of lesser events also could lead to PTSD.

Among police psychologists, PTSD has become recognized as a leading cause of burnout (Conroy & Hess, 1992). Therefore, recognition of its symptoms is imperative. Symptoms can include all of the previously noted physio-, socio-, and psychological afflictions as well as flashbacks, hypervigilance, insomnia, and avoidance (Mann & Neece, 1990; More, 1992; Gaines, 1993).

There is one more psychological symptom or indicator deserving recognition: anger. It has been noted that stress and anger "can go hand-in-hand" (Shockley, 1994, p. 20). Since most of us are well aware of what may happen when a police officer is provoked or made extremely angry (e.g., excessive use of force) and if stress is a catalyst of anger, then obviously stress must be dealt with. As Shockley noted, "learning how to recognize stress and effectively diffuse [sic] anger can help police avoid potentially dangerous situations" (1994, p. 20).

Overall, it should be noted that, regardless of the level of stress experienced (physio-, socio-, or psychological), the stress experienced will not necessarily exist or occur at another level. That is, "a person who experiences physiological stress does not necessarily experience psychological stress—stress at the social level does not mean that it will also be experienced at the psychological or physiological levels, or in the same way" (Lazarus & Folkman, 1984, p. 325). Moreover, stress will not necessarily be experienced in the same manner at future times or by others experiencing the same stress.

The Positive Side of Stress

To this point, stress has been discussed from a negative perspective. At this juncture it should be noted that stress is not always a negative factor. Although the negative aspects receive, and unquestionably deserve, the majority of recognition, no discussion of stress is complete without at least a brief mention of the positive aspects of stress.

Selye (1956) was the first to identify stress from both a positive (eustress) and negative (distress) perspective. He describes eustress as pleasant or curative, while distress is unpleasant. "Not all stress is bad, good stress does however have its wear and tear affect on the living organism. Stress can even have curative value, as in shock therapy, bloodletting, and sports" (Selye, 1956, p. 1). Others add that "Stress does not have to be a 'bad thing.' There is only one kind of person without conflicts—a dead one. What matters is the degree and quality of stress which the individual is undergoing in the particular situation he is in" (Bridger, 1980, p. 245). Bridger concludes, "Stress can be as appropriate and normal as inappropriate" (1980, p. 247).

You might ask why eustress generally does not produce the same reaction (illnesses) as distress. "Perhaps 'good' stress does not produce illness because typically the events associated with it are planned in advance (predictable) or otherwise scheduled or integrated (controlled) into the individual's life" (Humphrey, 1986, p. 14).

By its nature, eustress is not generally a concern or focus of stress researchers and therefore receives minimal attention. However, its existence is duly noted. There are also two other forms of stress similar to eustress that should be mentioned: hyperstress and hypostress. Selye advises that "We must recognize 'overstress' (hyperstress), when we exceed the limits of our adaptability; or 'understress' (hypostress), when we suffer from lack of self-realization (physical immobility, boredom, sensory deprivation)" (1980, p. 141). With respect to policing, an uneventful patrol shift could cause understress.

To this point, the discussion has focused on defining stress, identifying the causes of stress and stress' effect on the individual. Throughout, it has been established that stress often has a negative impact on individuals and can impair job performance, lead to family and health problems, or even cause a person to take his or her own life. Therefore, it seems imperative that police officers learn how to recognize and cope with stress.

COPING, MANAGING, AND EDUCATION

It was noted earlier that police officers may attempt to cope with stress through the use of alcohol, drugs, or suicide. But this is not the way we would want our police officers to deal with their problems. Although the formal study of stress has been around since the late 1940s and early 1950s, it has only been within the last 10 to 15 years that stress management has received substantial attention in policing literature. It is a relatively new field of study in which new ways to cope or manage stress are constantly being sought. Regardless of the methods eventually used to deal with stress, it is helpful to first understand what is meant by coping with or managing stress.

Since the trend for definitions associated with stress has been plentiful, it should be no surprise that several are offered for coping with or managing stress. Here are but a few examples,

1. "constantly changing cognitive and behavior efforts to manage specific external and/or internal demands that are appraised as taxing or exceeding the resources of the person" (Lazarus & Folkman, 1984, p. 141);
2. "recognition and acceptance by society that stress exists, that ignoring fears and conflicts will not help them go away, that they must be faced and coped with" (Grencik, 1981, p. 55);

and what appears to be the more popular of the stress management definitions,

3. "concerned with dealing with and attempting to overcome problems of stress" (Humphrey, 1986, p. 19).

Obviously, the underlying focus of stress management is confronting the problem and dealing with it. Furthermore, there appear to be two overriding functions of stress management: managing or altering the the distress-causing environment and regulating emotional responses to the problem. Selye (1956, 1980, 1983) simply suggests that the ultimate goal of stress management is to achieve the pleasant stress of fulfillment (eustress) without the harmful consequences of damaging stress (distress).

A variety of suggestions for coping with or managing stress have been offered. Selye (1980) suggests removing unnecessary stressors from our lives, not allowing particular events to become stressors, becoming proficient in dealing with those situations that we cannot or might not want to avoid, or seek a diversion from the stress. Others have made the following suggestions:

1. enhancement of awareness and self-esteem, physical fitness, relaxation training, and peer counseling (Stratton, 1981);
2. eliminating the stressor, increasing stress-coping abilities, and provision of counseling can assist in the reduction of stress (Ayres, and Flanagan 1990);
3. self-coping measures and employee assistance programs (More, 1992);
4. proactive and reactive stress reduction methods (Gaines, 1993); and
5. dividing management of stress into two areas (a) individual (which includes exercise, social support, relaxation techniques, and time management) and (b) organizational (which includes selection/placement, goal setting, job redesign, participative decision making, communication, and wellness programs) (Robbins, 1993).

There appears to be a general consensus in the stress management literature on such coping methods as goal setting, physical fitness, biofeedback, social support, self-esteem, locus of control, education, and training (see Ayres & Flanagan, 1990; Bonifacio, 1991; Conroy & Hess, 1992; Gaines, 1993; More, 1992; Muchinsky, 1993; Northcraft & Neale, 1994).

In recent years, education and training have grown in popularity as combative strategies to stress. It has been noted that coping skills and education may reduce stress by limiting the probability of negative life events (Simpson, 1980). The idea is that education reduces anxiety and ego involvement, which in turn, "reduce the stress experienced when negative life events occur" (Simpson, 1980, p. 460). Concurrence with these conclusions can be found in many of the sources cited in this chapter and others listed in the references.

Finally, there are some police researchers (see Ayres & Flanagan, 1990; Conroy & Hess, 1992) who have suggested that increasing awareness of the nature of stress and the stressors unique to policing, teaching police officers specific strategies that can be used to combat stress, awareness of the warning signs that indicate the possible need of intervention as the result of a stress-related problem, and the provision of information about resources and programs available to troubled officers, should be the broad objectives of any stress management education or training program. Many police departments are now offering stress management to academy curricula and rookie training. By offering this training early in an officer's career, it is believed that the recognition of stress will occur before it reaches a critical point and officers will seek assistance from specially created units or programs, which are beginning to be more readily available. For example, departments in Boston (which is credited with creating one of the first police stress programs), Dallas, Albuquerque, Austin, and Los Angeles offer peer counseling "rap sessions" and access to outside agencies.

Illustration: As noted, the Boston Police Department is recognized for being one of the first police agencies to offer a comprehensive stress management program for its police officers. The program is staffed entirely by specially trained Boston police officers. It offers preventive stress management to new recruits and their spouses, as well as to veterans, through in-service programs and in supervisor training courses. Support groups include: alcohol and drug abuse, post-traumatic stress, marital and family problems, job stress and burnout, suicide in the police family, women in policing, retirement, and death and bereavement.

In all, it is extremely important that officers and agencies recognize and address the fact that police work can be stressful and the importance of dealing with stress. The suggestions given thus far have all been internal to the agency and external to the officer. However, it is possible that a means of coping with or managing stress exists inherently in police officers—that is, the officers' level of education.

Based upon the literature, one could cite education as a stress-reduction technique. Yet this should be qualified in that the education recommended in most of the literature is stress-related education or training and not academic preparation (i.e., a college degree). However, the results of a study by this author tend to suggest that a higher level of education, in itself, may provide a mechanism for perceiving stress and is a stress-reducer (Dantzker, 1989). In that study it was demonstrated that a limited relationship exists between a patrol officer's level of education and his perception of the stressfulness of various facets of policing, such as responding to certain types of calls, supervisors, fellow officers, and family life. Patrol officers with a college degree reported lower perceived stressor values than officers with only a high-school education. These findings tend to indicate that a college degree is a stress modifier for police officers (Dantzker, 1989).

There is a plethora of possibilities for the reduction, coping, and management of stress. Unfortunately, there is yet little empirical data to demonstrate how successful any of the suggested techniques are in dealing with stress. The fact is many of the suggestions offered for coping are relatively new and therefore, research and study are still required before any definitive answers are provided. However, if anything is going to be successful in combating stress among police officers, the police organization and individual officers have to be willing to (1) acknowledge the need for stress-related programs, (2) implement such programs, and (3) make use of such programs. Failure to do so may be the difference between life and death.

SUMMARY

Policing is a stressful occupation. There are a variety of factors that cause stress. Stress, in turn, can cause a variety of psychological, physical, or social problems.

These problems affect job performance and family life. Therefore, the existence of stress in policing must be recognized. Once the existence of stress is recognized, coping methods can be employed. Yet, considering the image associated with policing, it is difficult for individuals and agencies to admit that police officers are vulnerable, that they can be negatively affected by the job.

Regardless of how calm and collected they may appear externally, experience finds that, if asked, most officers will admit to the internal churnings. It is believed that officers who seek out ways to release and cope with the stresses will be more effective and live longer (see Bonifacio, 1991; Conroy & Hess, 1992; Dantzker, 1989; Gaines, 1993; More, 1992). Officers who ignore how stress affects them will probably eventually suffer unnecessary consequences and so might people around the officer. Therefore, recognition of, acknowledgment of, and coping with stress is an important issue for policing and for police personnel.

DISCUSSION QUESTIONS

1. From your own experiences with stress, how would you define it?
2. Is policing really a stressful occupation or simply one that is rife with possible stressors?
3. Why do you think it is so difficult for police officers to recognize and admit to being "stressed out"?
4. How should police agencies approach the subject of stress? Academy training? In-service? What would you suggest as an approach by which officers might not feel threatened?
5. Despite the alarming number of police suicides, the causes for many are not often directly linked to policing but to an external stressor (e.g., family problems). If these individuals who take their lives were not police officers (with readily accessible weapons), do you think they would have still taken their own lives?

REFERENCES

American Institute of Stress: Top ten most stressful jobs. (1994, May/June). *Police Beat, 6.*

Asterita, M.F. (1982). *The physiology of stress.* New York: Human Sciences Press, Inc.

Ayres, R.M., & Flanagan, G.S. (1990). *Preventing law enforcement stress: The organization's role.* Washington, D.C.: U.S. Department of Justice.

Becker, H., & Whitehouse, J. (1979). *Police of America.* Springfield, IL: Charles C. Thomas.

Beehr, T.A., & Newman, J.E. (1978). Job stress, employee health, and organizational effectiveness: A facet analysis, model, and literature review. *Personnel Psychology, 31,* 665–698.

Bettinger, K.J. (1985, April). After the gun goes off. *Police,* pp. 35–37, 52.

Blank, D. (1987, October). Workers seek payment for job-related stress. *American Banker,* pp. 19, 26, 28.

Bonifacio, P. (1991). *The psychological effects of police work.* New York: Plenum Press.

Bridger, H. (1980). The increasing relevance of group processes and changing values for understanding and coping with stress at work. In C.L. Cooper & Payne (Eds.), *Stress at Work,* pp. 245, 247. New York,: John Wiley & Sons.

Brousseau, K.R., & Mallinger, M.A. (1981). Internal-external locus of control, perceived occupational stress, and cardiovascular health. *Journal of Occupational Behavior, 20,* 65–71.

Burchfield, S.R. (Ed.). (1985). *Stress: Psychological and physiological interactions.* New York: Hemisphere Publishing Co.

Burke, R.J. (1987). Burnout in police work. *Group and Organization Studies, 12*(2), 174–188.

Coleman, J.C. (1973). Life stress and maladaptive behavior. *The American Journal of Occupational Therapy, 27*(4), 169–180; L. Territo, & H.J. Jetter (Eds.). (1981). *Stress and police personnel.* Boston: Allyn & Bacon.

Conroy, D.L., & Hess, K.M. (1992). *Officers at risk.* Placerville, CA: Custom Publishing Co.

Constant, R.T. (1984, September). Not so obvious police stress. *Law and Order,* pp. 65–68.

Cooper, C.L., & Payne, R. (1980). *Current concerns in occupational stress.* New York: John Wiley & Sons.

———. (1981). *The stress check.* Englewood Cliffs, NJ: Prentice-Hall.

———. (Ed.). (1983). *Stress research.* New York: John Wiley & Sons.

Cops who kill—themselves. *Newsweek* (1994, September 26) p. 58.

Cox, T. (1978). *Stress.* Baltimore, MD: University Park Press.

Dantzker, M.L. (1986). A view into police stress. *Journal of Police and Criminal Psychology, 2*(1), 36–43.

———. (1987a). Police-related stress: A critique for future research. *Journal of Police and Criminal Psychology, 3*(3), 43–48.

———. (1987b, March). *Sources of stress in policing.* Paper presented at the Academy of Criminal Justice Sciences Annual Conference, St. Louis, MO.

———. (1987c, October). *Police stress: Continuing the dialogue.* Paper presented at the Society of Police and Criminal Psychology Annual Conference, New Orleans, LA.

———. (1989). *The effect of education on police performance: The stress perspective.* Ann Arbor, MI: UMI. Dissertation Service.

Dash, J., & Reiser, M. (1978). Suicide among police in urban law enforcement agencies. *Journal of Police Science and Administration, 6*(1), 18–21.

Daviss, B. (1982). Burnout: No one can imagine what the costs really are. *Police Magazine,* pp. 10, 11, 14.

Dewe, P.J., & Guest, D.E. (1990). Methods of coping with stress at work: A conceptual analysis and empirical study of measurement issues. *Journal of Organizational Behavior, 11,* 135–150.

Dohrenwend, B.S., & Dohrenwend, B.P. (Eds.). (1974). *Stressful life events: Their nature and effects.* New York: John Wiley & Sons.

Ellison, K.W., & Genz, J.A. (1983). *Stress and the police officer.* Springfield, IL: Charles C. Thomas.

Eth, S., Randolph, E.T., & Brown, J.A. (1989). Post-traumatic stress disorder. In J.G. Howells (Ed.), *Modern perspectives in the psychiatry of the neuroses,* pp. 210–234. New York: Brunner/Mazel, Inc.

Evans, G.W. (1982). *Environmental stress.* New York: Cambridge University Press.

Everly, G.S., Jr., & Sobelman, S.A. (1987). *Assessment of the human response.* New York: AMS Press.

Fell, R.D., Richard, W.C., & Wallace, W.L. (1980). Psychological job stress and the police officer. *Journal of Police Science and Administration, 8*(2), 139–144.

French, J.R.P., Caplan, R.D., & Harrison, R.V. (1982). *The mechanisms of job stress and strain.* New York: John Wiley & Sons.

Gaines, J., & Jermier, J.M. (1983). Emotional exhaustion in a high stress organization. *Academy of Management Journal, 26*(4), 567–586.

Gaines, L.K. (1993). Coping with the job stress in police work. In R.G. Dunham & G.P. Alpert (Eds.), *Critical issues in policing* (2nd ed., pp. 538–550). Prospect Heights, IL: Waveland Press.

Goolkasian, G.A., Geddes, R.W., & De Jong, W. (1985). *Coping with police stress.* Washington, D.C.: U.S. Government Printing Office.

Grencik, J.M. (1981). Toward an understanding of stress. In L. Territo & H.J. Vetter. (Eds.), *Stress and police personnel.* Boston: Allyn & Bacon.

Gross-Farina, S. (1986, November). What's new in stress: Training the recruit to seek help. *Police Chief,* pp. 41–46, 62, 63.

Hageman, M.J.C. (1978). Occupational stress and marital relationships. *Journal of Police Science and Administration, 6*(4), 402–412.

———. (1982). Response of police rookie officers to stress. *Journal of Police Science and Administration, 10*(2), 235–236.

Haynes, W.D. (1978). *Stress related disorders in policemen.* San Francisco: R & E Research Assocs.

Honig, A., & Reiser, M. (1983). Stress disability pension experience in the Los Angeles Police Department: A historical study. *Journal of Police Science and Administration, 11*(4), 385–388.

Hood, J.C., & Milazzo, N. (1984, December). Shiftwork, stress, and well-being. *Personnel Administrator,* pp. 95–105.

Humphrey, J.H., & Stroebel, C.F. (1982). *A textbook on stress.* Springfield, IL: Charles C. Thomas.

Humphrey, J.H. (1986). *Profiles in stress.* New York: AMS Press.

Hurrell, J.J., Jr. (1987). An overview of organizational stress and health. In L.R. Murphy and T.F. Schoenborn (Eds.), *Stress management in work settings.* Washington, D.C.: U.S. Department of Health and Human Services.

Jackson, S.E., & Maslach C. (1982). After-effects of job-related stress: Families as victims. *Journal of Occupational Behavior, 3,* 63–77.

———. Schwab, R.L., & Schuler, R.S. (1986). Toward an understanding of the burnout phenomenon. *Journal of Applied Psychology, 1*(4), 630–640.

Janis, I.L. (1982). Decision making under stress. In L. Goldberger & B. Shlomo (Eds.), *Handbook of stress,* pp. 69–72. New York: Macmillan.

Keane, T.M., Litz, B.T., & Blake, D.D. (1990). PTSD in adulthood. In M. Herson & C.G. Last (Eds.), *Handbook of child and adult psychopathology.* New York: Pergamon Press.

Kobasa, S.C. (1979). Stressful life events, personality, and health: An inquiry into hardiness. *Journal of Personality and Social Psychology, 37*(1), 1–11.

Kroes, W.H., Hurrell, J.J., & Margolis, B.L. (1974). Job stress in policemen. *Journal of Police Science and Administration, 2*(2), 145–155.

———, & Hurrell, J.J. (1975). *Job stress and the police officer: Identifying stress reduction techniques.* Washington, D.C.: U.S. Department of Health, Education and Welfare.

———. (1985). *Society's victim: The police.* Springfield, IL: Charles C. Thomas.

Kutash, I.L., & Schlesinger, L.B. (1980). *Handbook on stress and anxiety.* San Francisco: Jossey-Bass.

Lazarus, R.S., & Folkman, S. (1984). *Stress, appraisal, and coping.* New York: Springer Publishing.

LeDoux, J.C., & McCaslin, H.H., Jr. (1981). Designing a training response to stress. *FBI Law Enforcement Bulletin, 50,* 11–12.

Levi, L. (1981). *Preventing work stress.* Reading, MA: Addison-Wesley.

———. (1981a). Stress as a cause of disease. In L. Territo & H.J. Vetter (Eds.), *Stress and police personnel.* Boston: Allyn & Bacon.

Luthans, F. (1985). *Organizational behavior.* New York: McGraw-Hill.

Mann, J.P., & Neece, J. (1990). Workers' compensation for law enforcement related post traumatic stress disorder. *Behavioral Sciences and the Law, 8,* 447–456.

Martin, R. (1987, March). Stress and police work: An overview of general responses. Paper presented at the Academy of Criminal Justice Sciences Annual Conference, St. Louis, MO.

———, Keyser, A.D., & Kirkpatrick, K.R. (1987, March). Police officer perceptions of job stress and stress management training issues. Paper presented at the Academy of Criminal Justice Sciences Annual Conference, St. Louis, MO.

Maslach, C. (1976, September). Burned-Out. *Human Behavior,* pp. 16–22.

———. (1982). Understanding burnout: Definitional issues in analyzing a complex phenomenon. In Paine (Ed.), *Job stress and burnout.* Beverly Hills, CA: Sage.

McCafferty, F.L., Domingo, G.D., & McCafferty, M.J. (1989a). Understanding PTSD. *The Police Chief, 56,* 22, 24.

———, Domingo, G.D., & Palahunic, L. (1989). Manifestations of PTSD in police officers. *The Police Chief, 56,* 24, 27–28.

McFarlane, A.C. (1991). Post-traumatic stress disorder. *International Review of Psychiatry, 3,* 203–213.

McLean, A.A. (1979). *Work stress.* Reading, MA: Addison-Wesley.

Milsum, J.H. (1984). *Health, stress, and illness.* New York: Praeger.

Modlin, H.C. (1977, September/October). Does job stress alone cause health problems? *Occupational Health and Safety,* pp. 38–39.

More, H.W. (1992). *Special topics in policing.* Cincinnati: Anderson Publishing Co.

Muchinsky, P.M. (1993). *Psychology applied to work* (4th ed.). Pacific Grove, CA: Brooks/Cole Publishing.

Mullins, W.C. (1986, March). The relationship between police officer job burnout and job behavior. Paper presented at the Academy of Criminal Justice Sciences Annual Conference, Orlando, FL.

Murphy, L.R., & Schoenborn, T.F. (Eds.). (1987). *Stress management in work settings.* Washington, D.C.: U.S. Department of Health and Human Services.

National FOP looks at police suicide and how to prevent it. (1995, April 30) *Law Enforcement News,* pp. 1, 8.

Niederhoffer, A. (1967). *Behind the shield.* Garden City, New York: Doubleday.

Northcraft, G.B., & Neale, M.A. (1994). *Organizational Behavior* (2nd ed.). New York: The Dryden Press.

Norvell, N., & Belles, D. (1988, January). A stress management curriculum for law enforcement personnel supervisors. *Texas Police Journal,* pp. 11–14.

Officer kills himself. *Sun-Sentinel* (1994, May 22), p. 3A.

Perlman, B., & Hartman, E.A. (1982). Burnout: Summary and future research. *Human Relations, 35*(4), 283–305.

Petrone, S., & Reiser, M. (1985). A home visit program for stressed police officers. *Police Chief, 52*(2), 36–37.

Phillips, E.L. (1982). *Stress, health, and psychological problems in the major professions.* Washington, D.C.: University Press of America.

Pines, A., & Kafry, D. (1978). Occupational tedium in the social services. *Social Work, 23,* 499–507.

Quick, J.C., & Quick, J.D. (1984). *Organizational stress and preventive management.* New York: McGraw-Hill.

Reese, J.T. (1986). Policing the violent society: The American experience. *Stress Medicine, 2,* 233–240.

Reiser, M. (1974). Some organizational stresses on policemen. *Journal of Police Science and Administration, 2*(2), 156–159.

Robbins, S.P. (1993). *Organizational behavior* (6th ed.). Englewood Cliffs, NJ: Prentice-Hall.

Roth, S., & Cohen, W. (1986). Approaches, avoidance, and coping with stress. *American Psychologist, 41*(7), 813–819.

Schaefer, R. (1985). Maintaining control: A step toward personal growth. *FBI Law Enforcement Bulletin, 55*(3), 10–14.

Schwartz, J.A., & Schwartz, C.B. (1981). The personal problems of the police officer: A plea for action. In L. Territo & H.J. Vetter (Eds.), *Stress and police personnel.* Boston: Allyn & Bacon.

Selye, H. (1956). *The stress of life.* New York: McGraw-Hill.

———. (1980). *Selye's guide to stress research* (vol. 1). New York: Van Nostrand Reinhold.

———. (1983). The stress concept: Past, present, and future. In C.L. Cooper (Ed.), *Stress research.* New York: John Wiley & Sons.

Sewell, J.D. (1981). Police stress. *FBI Law Enforcement Bulletin, 50,* 7–9.

———. (1983). The development of a critical life events scale for law enforcement. *Journal of Police Science and Administration, 11*(1), 109–116.

Shockley, S.M. (1994, September). Mad as hell. *Police,* pp. 20–21, 90.

Shostak, A.B. (1980). *Blue-collar stress.* Reading, MA: Addison-Wesley.

Simpson, M.E. (1980). Societal support and education. In I.L. Kutash & L.B. Schlesinger. (Eds.), *Handbook on stress and anxiety.* San Francisco: Jossey-Bass.

Singg, S. (1984). Toward an understanding of PTSDs: An historical and contemporary perspective. *Journal of Sociology and Social Welfare, 11,* 763–777.

Singleton, G.W., & Teahan, J. (1978). Effects of job-related stress on the physical and psychological adjustment of police officers. *Journal of Police Science and Administration, 6*(3), 355–361.

Somodevilla, A. (1986, March). Dealing with stress. *Texas Police Journal,* pp. 15–16.

———. (1986, May). Guidelines for stress prevention. *Texas Police Journal,* p. 5.

Stratton, J.G. (1981). Police stress: An overview and police stress: Part II: considerations and suggestions. In L. Territo & H.J. Vetter (Eds.), *Stress and police personnel.* Boston: Allyn & Bacon.

———, Parker, D.A., & Snibbe, J.R. (1984). Post-traumatic stress: Study of police officers involved in shootings. *Psychological Reports, 55,* 127–131.

Territo, L., & Vetter, H.J. (1981). *Stress and police personnel.* Boston: Allyn & Bacon.

Terry, W.C. (1981). Police stress: The empirical evidence. *Journal of Police Science and Administration, 9*(1), 61–73.

———. (1983). Police stress as an individual and administrative problem: Some conceptual and theoretical difficulties. *Journal of Police Science and Administration, 11*(2), 156–163.

Violanti, J.M., (1983). Stress patterns in police work: A longitudinal study. *Journal of Police Science and Adminstration, 11*(2), 156–163.

Violanti, J.M., & Marshall, J.R. (1983). The police stress process. *Journal of Police Science and Administration, 11*(4), 389–394.

Violanti, J.M., Marshall, J.R., & Howe, B. (1985). Stress, coping, and alcohol use: The police connection. *Journal of Police Science and Administration, 3*(2), 106–110.

Violanti, J.M. (1995). The mystery within: Understanding police suicide. *FBI Law Enforcement Bulletin, 64*(2), 19–23.

Wagner, W., & Larson, J. (1982, September). Stress: Cause, symptoms, illness. *Law and Order*, pp. 66–75.

Wexler, J.G., & Logan, D.D. (1983). Sources of stress among women police officers. *Journal of Police Science and Administration, 11*(1), 46–53.

6

Being a Police Officer: Part of a Profession?

M.L. Dantzker, Georgia Southern University

The professionalization of policing has been constantly debated since the early 1900s. When officers' behaviors are not consistent with societal expectations (e.g., the beating of Rodney King in Los Angeles or Malice Green in Detroit or the question of racially motivated criminal investigations—O.J. Simpson and Mark Fuhrman), the question "Why does this happen?" arises. Critics often claim that unprofessionalism among police officers is the main reason and argue for the professionalization of policing. Despite the recommendations of commissions such as Wickersham and the President's Commission on Law Enforcement and Administration of Justice, whose findings suggested that the lack of a "professional" standing was a major reason for the problems in policing, the professionalization of policing has been difficult to accomplish.

Since the establishment of this country's first official police department, policing has experienced numerous changes (e.g., technological advances, improved administrative practices, formal training, and increased hiring requirements) that can be credited for assisting in the development of policing toward becoming a true profession. However, the debate as to whether policing should be considered a profession continues. There are some who would argue that policing is a craft (Wilson, 1968) and not capable of becoming a profession.

> The generalist, task-oriented work performed by police, their subordinate position in a bureaucratic, quasi-militaristic organization, a tradition of learning police work through apprenticeship practices, and an absence of professional referents guiding the development of values and ideas yield an image of police work that is more consistent with notions of craftsmanship than professionalism (Crank, 1990, p. 333).

Although policing may very well lend itself to fit the orientation associated with a craft, studies have revealed that police officers do not view their occupation in terms of craftsmanship (Crank, 1990) and consider themselves a profession (Dantzker, 1986). Unfortunately, not everyone has the same view as police officers. This chapter focuses on several issues associated with the development of policing as a profession.

127

HISTORICAL OVERVIEW

A historical review of policing finds that formal policing in this country began in the 1830s. The earliest efforts to begin moving policing toward professionalism began in the 1890s in response to strong political influences (Crank, 1990). However, it was not until the early 1900s that the terms professional and professionalism were attached to policing. This was primarily because of the efforts of one man, August Vollmer (Carte, 1973).

A self-educated individual, August Vollmer first became involved in law enforcement when he was elected "marshal" of Berkeley, California. Eventually, this position evolved into the first chief of police for the Berkeley Police Department, as which Vollmer served from 1905 to 1932. As police chief, Vollmer advocated that technology, combined with honest and efficient officers, would bring professionalism to policing. He argued that changes in society would require policing to change and that this change would require more educated individuals with greater skills.

In 1908, Vollmer broke from the tradition of simply giving a physically strong individual a gun and badge and telling him to go out and enforce the law. Instead, he introduced the first formal police training school with a curriculum that included general police subjects, such as criminal law and procedures, police psychiatry, criminal identification, and police organization and management (Carte, 1973). By 1930, recruits attending this school received more than 300 hours of police-related education.

Formal training was only Vollmer's first move toward professionalizing his department. Despite his own formal education limitations, Vollmer was a strong believer in a college education for police officers and by 1919 began hiring college students as police officers. Although this was the first time any police agency hired individuals with an advanced education, it was by no means the last.

Ultimately, Vollmer's career and influence would have far-reaching implications. As the president of the International Association of Chiefs of Police (1922) and a member of the Wickersham Commission (1931), Vollmer's educational beliefs and genuine concern about the need to professionalize policing throughout the country would be influential. However, while Vollmer's focus was on the officer, it was departmental efforts to eliminate politics and to become more bureaucratic that tended to receive more attention.

An early approach by many of the police organizations was to become more bureaucratic (i.e., more organizationally complex) in structure, to develop specialized sections, create and enforce policies and procedures, define a hierarchial structure, and provide for career movement (Dantzker, 1995). The view was that bureaucracy led to professionalism. A part of the bureaucratic movement even included the introduction of various aspects of the military. As Bittner (1985) notes,

> it is no exaggeration to say that through the 1950s and 1960s the movement to "professionalize" the police concentrated almost exclusively on efforts to eliminate political and venal corruption by means of introducing traits of military discipline (p. 174).

Though organizational change toward professionalism may have improved the organization, it tended to have minimal effect on the line officer (Brown, 1981). This outcome continues today. Many police departments easily meet the criteria of being organizationally professional (e.g. paramilitary, bureaucratic). Manning (1995) advises that "The guise of professionalism embodied in a bureaucratic organization is the most important strategy employed by the police to defend their mandate and thereby to build self-esteem, organizational autonomy, and occupational solidarity or cohesiveness" (p. 112). Unfortunately, the question of individual professionalism and occupational professionalism continues to exist. Perhaps examining how professionalism is defined and applied to policing may offer some insight into why policing remains outside the realm of professions.

PROFESSION: DEFINED

To effectively examine this area, an understanding of what a profession is and how policing fits this description is required. One of the biggest difficulties in the police profession debate is reaching a consensus on the definition. If the standard definition of a profession is applied to policing as it is currently recognized, then policing does not fit as a profession.

Webster defines a profession as "an occupation, especially one requiring extensive education in a branch of science or liberal arts." *Black's Law Dictionary* defines a profession as "a vocation or occupation requiring special, usually advanced, education and skill; e.g., law or medical profession." *Black's* definition continues with, "The labor and skill involved in a profession is predominantly mental or intellectual, rather than physical or manual." Applying either definition to policing reveals a poor fit. However, perhaps no one definition is applicable as suggested by Swanson, Territo, and Taylor (1993) who advise that the term profession should be viewed as a collection of elements. These elements include

1. an organized body of theoretical knowledge,
2. advanced study,
3. a code of ethics,
4. prestige,
5. standards of admission,
6. a professional association, and
7. a service ideal.

In addition to these elements, autonomy should be included (Dantzker, 1995). For the purpose of this discussion, these elements are accepted as a means to examine policing as a profession and will receive closer scrutiny shortly.

The defining of profession is just one problem with police professionalism. The term professionalism creates an additional problem. Realistically, the crux of the profession issue might very well be a semantic problem.

Applying the standard definitions of a profession ultimately eliminates policing as a profession. Yet many police agencies consider themselves professional or products of professionalism. Therefore, the semantic debate encompasses the terms, profession verses professional or professionalism.

Using current definitions, a professional is an individual who conducts himself or herself professionally or with professionalism. Professionalism is best viewed as the conduct, aims, or qualities that characterize or identify a profession or a professional person. The application of these terms to policing creates a dilemma. Police officers may act professionally and police agencies may promote professionalism, but policing is not recognized as a profession. Obviously, actions in themselves are not enough to give policing the status of a profession. If we use Swanson and co-workers' elements of a profession, we are provided a better picture of why policing does not yet fit the profession mode.

POLICING AS A PROFESSION

The application of formal definitions of a profession to policing eliminates policing as a profession because of their limited scope. Therefore, the elements of a profession offered by Swanson et al., because of their specificity, provide a clearer path to understanding why policing does not yet meet the requirements of a profession.

Organized Body of Theoretical Knowledge

A prevalent element of a true profession (e.g., law or medicine) is a well-developed, complex, theoretical body of knowledge. Persons interested in entering those fields designated as professions are required to absorb and prove their understanding of the body of knowledge, often through a comprehensive licensing or certification exam. Generally, failing to demonstrate a complete understanding and comprehension of the required body of knowledge bars the individual from the profession.

Policing uses a very broad body of knowledge that incorporates both training and academic studies. The major problem is that there is no commonly agreed upon body of knowledge that every officer should possess. Each police agency is allowed to define what it deems an appropriate body of knowledge. This is also true of colleges and universities offering a law enforcement, police science, or criminal justice curriculum. The lack of agreement as to what every person who becomes a police officer should know makes it difficult to establish a professional body of police knowledge. It has been suggested that for policing to be considered a profession "it must exhibit a unique and specialized body of knowledge that is written down and can be transmitted abstractly" (Price, 1985, p. 320). Despite concerted efforts to establish such a body of knowledge, gaining a consensus remains a barrier.

Advanced Study

Becoming a lawyer, doctor, certified public accountant, or a member of any of the many other professions often requires years of study. On the average, it takes a minimum of seven years of college study for lawyers and 11 years for doctors just to officially enter the profession. Furthermore, a continuing course of study is usually required. Policing, with a few exceptions, such as most federal police agencies and some local agencies with some type of college hours' requirement, requires no advanced study. As a rule, the only requirement (above a high school diploma or equivalency) is the training academy most recruits are required to attend, which averages from 18 to 20 weeks, and the occasional in-service training program. Otherwise, policing as a whole does not require any advanced study.

Code of Ethics

All professions have a code of ethics that relates the expected moral action, conduct, and characteristics of its members.

> A code of ethics is a formal statement of a group's ethics, whether a description of a preexisting practice (like a dictionary definition) or a formula creating the practice (like a definition in a contract) (Davis, 1991, p. 17).

This is one element that does appear to exist in policing. However, there does not seem to be just one code for all of policing.

Example of a Code of Ethics

AS A LAW ENFORCEMENT OFFICER, my fundamental duty is to serve mankind; to safeguard lives and property; to protect the innocent against deception, the peaceful against violence and disorder; and to respect the Constitutional rights of all men to liberty, equality, and justice.

I WILL keep my private life unsullied as an example to all; maintain courageous calm in the face of danger, scorn, or ridicule; develop self-restraint; and be constantly mindful of the welfare of others. Honest in thought and deed in both my personal and official life, I will be exemplary in obeying the laws of the land and the regulations of my department. Whatever I see or hear of a confidential nature or that is confided to me in my official capacity will be kept ever secret unless revelation is necessary in the performance of my duty.

I WILL never act officiously or permit personal feelings, prejudices, animosities or friendships to influence my decisions. With no compromise for crime and with relentless prosecution of criminals, I will enforce the law courteously and appropriately without fear or favor, malice or ill will, never employing unnecessary force or violence and never accepting gratuities.

I RECOGNIZE the badge of my office as a symbol of public faith, and I accept it as a public trust to be held so long as I am true to the ethics of the police service. I will constantly strive to achieve these objectives and ideals, dedicating myself before God to my chosen profession, law enforcement.

(For comparison purposes, see the code of ethics provided in Chapter 7.)

This code of ethics identifies a variety of actions and behaviors that a police officer should attest to uphold when accepting the role of a police officer. Yet, this code is not mandatory. The use and acceptance of a code of ethics are still mostly limited to individual agencies attempting to enhance their professional status.

Prestige

It was once believed that policing had considerable prestige and that police officers could rely upon the respect and influence their position held with the general public. However, one could easily argue that the prestige of policing has dwindled since the 1960s. Being a doctor or lawyer, despite all the jokes made about lawyers, carries a certain respect and prestige that seems to be lacking with policing. Nowhere does this seem more evident than in the college criminal justice classroom, where it is usual to find more students interested in employment in any other facet of criminal justice than policing. The exception is federal law enforcement, which still carries some respect and prestige despite some well-publicized incidents such as Ruby Ridge, Utah (FBI), and Waco, Texas (ATF).

Standards of Admission

A true profession advocates universally accepted standards for admission. State or nationally certified requirements and licenses are found in the true professions. For example, lawyers, doctors, elementary and secondary school teachers, certified accountants, and even several trades (e.g., an electrician or auto mechanic) must meet certain educational requirements and pass a certification examination before being allowed to practice the profession. Many states require state licensing for police officers, but this license is usually good only in the issuing state. This means that if a police officer licensed in California moved to Texas, the state of Texas would require the individual to pass the Texas licensing exam. This often requires having to go through a state recognized training program before the test can be taken. Doctors, lawyers, accountants, teachers, and other such professionals can more frequently plan on being able to practice their professions anywhere in the country without having to retrain. They too, however, may have to apply for certification, licensure, or take a state examination for which previous preparatory schooling or training is often sufficient. This is seldom the case for police officers.

Illustration: "My law enforcement career began as a state licensed police officer in Terre Haute, Indiana. After a few years I decided to move to Texas where I became an officer with the Fort Worth Police Department. However, to become a licensed officer in Texas, I was required to complete another training academy (where a majority of the information was quite similar to that in the Indiana academy) before I was able to take the state examination for licensure. On the other hand, my wife, who was a certified teacher in Indiana, received a temporary Texas teacher's certificate almost immediately upon request and was required to take only two Texas history courses before a permanent certificate was awarded."

In addition to licensure or certification, policing, unlike other professions, has no nationally consistent entry standards. Age, education, residency, physical/mental, and test results are some of the elements used to determine entry into policing. These differ from state to state, even from agency to agency within a given state. Although a general consensus on age and physical characteristics exists, each police agency sets its own standards. The failure to support a standard of admission is a major factor keeping policing from being recognized as a profession.

A Professional Association

The American Bar Association acts as a watchdog for the legal profession; the American Medical Association oversees the medical profession; the American Psychiatric Association provides guidance to the psychiatric and psychological profession; but policing has no such national association. The International Association of Chiefs of Police would argue that they are such an association, but this association has yet to establish national standards for knowledge or admissions to entry level positions which all police agencies would be required to follow.

In addition, there are several other national organizations that provide input, such as the Fraternal Order of Police, the National Organization of Black Law Enforcement Executives, the National Sheriffs' Association, and others. Reality finds that the fragmentation problem in policing continues to hamper the formation of one national association and, consequently, professionalization. Furthermore, there might be some who would question whether one national organization is really necessary and whether it might actually hamper the growth of policing as a profession.

A Service Ideal

The service ideal is the obligation of a profession to serve the best interests of its clientele and its acceptance of a formal code of ethics. It is the one other element, besides the code of ethics, that is associated with policing. Regardless of the criticism it receives, policing as a whole and many individual agencies appear to operate in a manner that best fits the needs of the public. Critics will argue that it is an extremely limited service ideal; nonetheless, a service ideal does exist.

Autonomy

Autonomy in a profession relates to the manner in which the members of the profession are allowed to conduct their own affairs. It is the ability to control who gets into the schools, licensure requirements, professional recognition, and definition of the base of knowledge. Policing has not yet been able to obtain this autonomy, and because it is so publicly regulated, there is a chance that it may never become completely autonomous. But, policing should be able to gain autonomy with respect to establishing criteria that would make it acceptable as a profession.

In sum, whether applying traditional definitions or elements of a profession, policing does not yet seem to make the grade. Having been the target of criticism for many years for not being a profession, the belief must exist that professionalization of policing is important. The question is "Why?"

THE IMPORTANCE OF POLICING'S BECOMING A PROFESSION

It was Vollmer's view, as well as those of past commissions, that by professionalizing policing, a better quality officer would result. This, in turn, would improve how the community was served. It is this latter part that probably continues to drive policing toward professionalism.

> public confidence in the police is essential for order maintenance and stability in the community. When the police are distrusted, government itself is undermined. Professionalism instills confidence and respect because it means to the public that the practitioners have internalized values of service, even altruism, self-control and commitment to high ideals of behavior (Price, 1995, p. 8).

Accepting that the future of policing as a profession revolves around how it is perceived by the community, the current trend of community policing may be a big step in the right direction. However, simply changing the approach to dealing with society and all its ills will not be successful until the ideal of a profession is addressed by integrating or accepting at least some of the elements of a profession.

PROFESSIONALIZING THE POLICE

As this chapter was written, community policing continued to be the current trend. Operating under the condition that community policing requires professionalization, it has been suggested that three conditions be met: (1) a reduced hierarchy and skill enrichment, (2) reorganizing for empowerment, and (3) selection and development of new professionals (Meese, 1993). However, not every agency will adopt community policing nor has community policing been shown to be the saving grace of policing. Therefore, a different recommendation for professionalizing is offered.

In order for policing to reach the status of a true profession there are four fundamental criteria that must be met, each of which could only enhance community policing, too. These criteria must be met in order to assist in categorizing policing as a profession. They are: education, training, lateral transfer, and accreditation.

Education

The one consistent element that separates policing from all other true professions is education. There is no other true profession willing to rely on a high school education as an adequate entry level requirement. Despite the continuing growth of college educated officers, in 1993 more than 70 percent of police departments employing 100 or more officers only required a recruit to possess a high school diploma or its equivalent (Reaves & Smith, 1995).

The requirement of higher education has long been supported. Starting with August Vollmer in the early 1900s, and followed by a number of national commissions—the Wickersham Commission (1931), the President's Commission on Law Enforcement and the Administration of Justice (1967), and finally, the National Advisory Commission on Criminal Justice Standards and Goals (1973)—support the suggestion that higher levels of education is a necessity to policing persists. In fact, the mentality and support have not seemed to waver and are consistent with the statement offered by Professors Caldwell and Nardini (1977):

> If a police force is to become professional, it must require higher educational
> degrees. That this is essential is evidenced by the development of other professions
> such as teaching, social work, chemistry, medicine, law, psychology, and many
> others (p. 89).

The sentiment of this statement has been echoed by others.

More (1985) notes, "The need for police officers who are intelligent, articulate, mature, and knowledgeable about social and political conditions is apparent" (p. 306). R.V. Mecum (1985) advises, "Education is an integral part of gaining the status of 'professionalism' and if the police are to become professional, they must accept the requirements of some formal, higher education as a minimum standard for their occupation" (p. 316). Finally, Carter, Sapp, and Stephens (1989) suggested that, "The college-educated force sets higher professional standards and goals, which, in turn, command public respect and help shape public opinion" (p. iv).

Supporting the quest for higher education is one thing. Establishing it is another. It seems that in the continuing press for higher education, scholars, academicians, and commissions have been unable to reach a consensus as to what level of education is necessary and what the contents of that education should be. For example, the National Advisory Commission recommended that all police agencies, by 1982, require a minimum of a baccalaureate degree of its recruits. As of 1996, less than 5 percent of all police agencies (excluding the federal agencies) appear to require such a degree.

Failure to agree on what knowledge should be required exacerbates the problem. There are more than one thousand police-related college degree programs in this country. No two have the same requirements or offer the same curriculum. Even states like Texas, whose institutions of higher learning have agreed on a "transfer core" of courses, are unable to say that every student who takes a course with the same title at different places or times receives the same information. The result is a fragmentation of knowledge and a debate over what is relevant and what is not.

Additional arguments over this issue include associate versus bachelors degree, criminal justice versus criminology, and criminal justice-related versus liberal arts.

While police agencies continue to struggle with the concept of higher educational requirements for entry level officers, it should become fairly obvious to the most casual observer that higher levels of education for police officers are becoming a necessity. Modern technology, laws and the legal system, the nature of our society, and the change to community policing all dictate a need for better-educated officers. As Meese (1993) points out,

> The changed strategy of policing alters in important ways the content of the police officer's job. Police responsibilities expand beyond attempting to control criminal activity—to preventing crime, promoting order, resolving disputes, and providing emergency assistance in social crises. The officer's methods and resources extend beyond arrests and citations. They now include mediation and negotiation, referrals to other municipal agencies, and community mobilization. As police activity focuses on the neighborhood, the demands on the basic police officer increase, as do the scope of responsibility and skills required (p. 2).

The bottom line is that the importance of higher education, in itself, is recognized. Furthermore, as a condition to being accepted as a profession, the pursuit of establishing an acceptable body of knowledge and a specific degree level is inevitable; yet, an accord between police practitioners and educators must be reached. Once the consensus on education has been attained, policing will be a giant step closer to being recognized as a true profession.

Training

Education is not the only area that fosters debate and a lack of a consensus. From the time of Vollmer's first formal training efforts, debate has continued regarding the kind and amount of training that should be required. Despite its growth in some areas, it has stagnated in others.

While education can be viewed as the formal university or college classroom attainment of knowledge, training is viewed as the method of developing practical or hands-on knowledge of policing. Formal education focuses on the social and behavioral sciences, training focuses on techniques and procedures. Although policing techniques and procedures do not differ greatly from agency to agency, there is no nationally recognized standard, curriculum, or method of training: what is taught, how it is taught, and how much is taught still vary greatly. Table 6.1 offers a demonstration of the diversity in required training hours among selected police agencies employing a minimum of one hundred police officers. Note the wide disparity.

Traditionally, the arena for training has been the police academy. This is where the new recruit is supposedly schooled in all necessities for working the streets. Although the street requirements differ very little from city to city, academies differ, in some instances dramatically. Referring back to Table 6.1, we find that the number of academy hours differs from zero (0) to a high of 1,248. Furthermore, it can be seen

Table 6.1 Training Requirements for New Officers in Selected
Municipal Law Enforcement Agencies (Over 100), 1993*

Agency	Number of training hours		
	Total	Class	Field
Mobile, AL	1120	640	480
Phoenix, AZ	920	440	480
Concord, CA	320	0	320
Long Beach, CA	2080	880	1200
Los Angeles, CA	1011	971	40
Denver, CO	1593	1033	560
E. Hartford, CT	80	80	0
Miami, FL	1480	840	640
Daytona Bch, FL	760	200	560
Honolulu, HI	1768	1248	520
Chicago, IL	1100	700	400
Muncie, IN	80	40	40
Shreveport, LA	1960	520	1440
Holyoke, MA	16	16	0
Somerville, MA	1760	720	1040
Battle Creek, MI	520	0	520
Detroit, MI	530	530	0
Minneapolis, MN	1120	320	800
St. Paul, MN	400	400	0
Springfield, MO	1300	800	500
St. Louis, MO	640	640	0
Omaha, NE	459	459	0
Lincoln, NE	1522	482	1040
Albuquerque, NM	2080	1040	1040
Mt. Vernon, NY	320	0	320
Portland, OR	3096	960	2136

*Source: Law Enforcement Management and Administrative Statistics,
1993: Data for Individual State and Local Agencies with 100 or More
Officers. BJS (September, 1995).

that field training, an extension of the academy, also varies in the number of hours required. Again, the problem is the inability of police practitioners to agree on how much training is truly required, which continues to be a major barrier to policing's becoming a profession.

The inability to agree on the number of training hours is only one part of the problem. What really appears to be a stumbling block is the failure to establish what should be taught, how much should be taught, and who is going to teach it. This failure creates the majority of the training differences. Historically, subjects such as arrest procedures, firearms, self-defense, penal code, patrol procedures, and search and seizures have comprised the majority of the academy curricula. These courses have traditionally been taught by veteran police officers who, more often than not, spend a large quantity of time telling "war stories." This is not training, yet it is accepted as such. What should be taught and who should teach it continues to cause debate. Until this problem is solved, policing will continue to suffer from a lack of training standardization associated with the true profession.

There has been some movement toward eliminating this problem. For example, California, Colorado, Florida, Indiana, Ohio, Texas, and Washington have established licensing mandates for all police officers. This requires that officers pass a state examination that is developed from a recognized body of information. If the body of knowledge from state to state were the same, policing would be one giant step closer to a major requisite of a profession.

In addition to state licensure, another possibility is the establishment of college programs that combine training and the formal college classroom so that graduates not only attain a college degree but have all the initial training, too. Minnesota is the first state to attempt such a program.

If training and educational requirements become consistent, then the next element associated with a profession would become much easier. An activity that is well accepted among other professions, but is sorely lacking in policing, is lateral transferring.

Lateral Transfer

Lateral transferability truly separates policing from other professions. Although not completely impossible, especially at the federal level and within certain states such as Florida, California, Ohio, and Washington, intrastate lateral transfers are rare, with interstate transfers even rarer.

Lateral transfer is the opportunity for an officer to leave one police agency to work for another, within the same state or in another state, without having to retrain or lose seniority. Unfortunately, the current practice for many police agencies is to require all individuals, previously trained or not, to attend their "sanctioned" academy and start as a probationary officer with no seniority.

It would appear that the primary reason for this practice, as previously noted, is the lack of standardization in training. Obviously, a nationally recognized training curriculum would help eliminate this problem. It might also help eliminate a concern associated with lateral transfers, in particular accepting training from another agency, that is, liability.

The courts have already established that police agencies can be held liable for lack of or improper training. It has been held that a police agency can be held liable if inappropriate or no training in certain areas leads to an injury of a citizen or a violation of rights. With lateral transfer there is the question of whether previous training was sufficient and, therefore, defensible in a civil suit arising from a transferred officer's actions. Because the transferred-to department did not originally train the officer and accepts in good faith previous training, there is that question of liability. Rather than take the chance of inadequate or improper training, police agencies would rather retrain the officer. This is yet one more reason to support a national, standardized training program.

Illustration: States such as California, Florida, Ohio, and Washington have essentially eliminated training concerns associated with lateral transfer through state-mandated licensure. By completing the state's required program, which is a standardized curriculum all officers must pass, officers become eligible for positions anywhere in the state. Acceptance of this requirement has left little concern throughout the state over training liability and has made lateral transfer a viable action for officers and agencies. This acceptance is generally evident in recruitment ads that seek police officers for lateral entry where the primary qualification is possession of the state's police officers standards and training (POST) certificate or be a graduate of a POST-approved academy within a specific set of previous years.

Although standardized training would assist in eliminating the training concerns associated with lateral transfers, there are additional issues that require attention. One such issue is that of seniority and promotions.

While doctors, lawyers, and other professionals seldom need to worry about a loss of rank or seniority when they move from one place of employment to another, police officers do. Often when an officer leaves one agency for another, there is a loss of rank and seniority. On many occasions, the officer must start out as a rookie officer again, regardless of previous experience. Lateral transfers usually allow officers to retain seniority, if not rank, too. This would appear to be advantageous to the receiving agency. Yet, the average police administrator avoids lateral transfer. If asked why they do not support lateral transfer, responses often include a concern over the expense of training and employing an individual, only to have that person leave the agency for another, taking the expensive training already provided. Still, as budgets are cut, more police agencies will begin to advertise for officers who possess state certification, which could lead to a bidding war for trained officers that many police departments may not be able to compete in, let alone win.

There is also a concern with how lateral transfers, especially of ranking officers, might affect department morale. This is particularly true regarding promotions.

Illustration: Suppose an officer with ten years' experience and the rank of sergeant transfers to a department where the officer is credited with all ten years of seniority and the sergeant rank. This officer may now be in a much better position for promotion to lieutenant than other officers with less seniority, but who have been on the department much longer and believe they are in line for promotion. Their inability to receive the promotion because it was given to the officer who transferred in can lead to morale problems.

To eliminate unnecessary expenditures or promotional problems of lateral transfers, many police executives simply will not allow them. But lateral transfers are a necessity to help professionalize policing. Therefore, solutions to the problems associated with lateral transfers must be found. One suggestion is the standardization of training and educational requirements. Furthermore, creating parity in salaries and promotional opportunities, and the creation of a national pension and retirement system, would help establish lateral transfer and push policing closer to the status of profession.

Accreditation

The previously discussed elements for a police profession were individual-oriented, as the concept of a profession tends to dictate. However, there is also the need for an agency-oriented change—an element that the professional organizations recognize and require—accreditation.

Accreditation and professionalism are far from being strangers. All organizations associated with a profession, such as hospitals, school districts, colleges and universities, and many other institutions employing professionals, have required mandatory agency accreditation for years. For these organizations, failure to meet accreditation criteria results in the loss of accreditation, which leads to a loss of standing in the profession. Losing accreditation often leads to the shutting down of the organization because it can no longer attract consumers. For example, a college that loses its accreditation would eventually lose all its students, because students are aware that degrees from unaccredited colleges will not help them obtain employment in their respective fields. Therefore, accreditation has extremely powerful implications.

Police organizations did not have the option for accreditation until 1979, when through the efforts of several groups—the International Association of Chiefs of Police, the National Organization of Black Law Enforcement Executives, the National Sheriffs' Association, and the Police Executive Research Forum—an accrediting agency was established. The Commission on Accreditation for Law Enforcement Agencies (CALEA) was created to develop a set of nationally applicable standards for policing. Agencies that meet these standards are granted accreditation. The original criteria had more than 900 standards categorized into the following six major areas:

1. role, responsibilities, and relationships with other agencies;
2. organization, management, and administration;
3. personnel administration;
4. law enforcement operations, operational support, and traffic law enforcement;
5. prisoner and court-related services; and
6. auxiliary and technical services (*Accreditation Program Review,* 1989).

However, as of this writing, the number of standards has been reduced to 436.

The accreditation process is not yet mandatory; police agencies voluntarily seek accreditation. As of October 31, 1995, 368 agencies have been accredited, while several hundred more were pursuing accreditation. By achieving accreditation, police agencies are demonstrating to their communities their drive toward recognition as a profession.

Many practitioners and academicians see accreditation as a key to the professionalization of policing. Considering the relative newness of this process in policing, no consensus exists as to whether this process will truly propel policing into the status of a profession. In the meantime, accreditation continues to be one of the more popular means for police agencies to gain recognition as professional.

Prior to leaving the discussion of efforts to professionalize policing through higher education, lateral transfer, standardized training, and accreditation, we must acknowledge individual efforts to become professional. Attaining a college degree is undoubtedly a positive step toward individual professionalization. Another major step toward individual professionalization is completion of a well-recognized training program such as the Federal Bureau of Investigation's academy.

Each year, the FBI invites a select group of local and state police officers to attend its academy. Participants are chosen from a pool of candidates submitted by police executives across the country. This pool often represents those identified by executives as outstanding officers. Being selected to and completing the academy is highly regarded by fellow officers as well as community leaders. For example, it is usual to see advertisements for police chiefs that require graduation from the FBI academy of the potential applicant. The status of this accomplishment is a result of the aura that has surrounded the FBI since its achievement of professional status many years ago when a college degree became a requirement and training became standardized.

CONCLUSION: THE IMPLICATIONS OF PROFESSIONALIZING

Whether it is accomplished at an individual, organizational, or national level, the rise of policing to the status of a profession seems a matter of time. How this is accomplished requires a number of changes. Yet, even if the suggested changes occur and policing receives professional status, will it truly impact policing in the manner that is so highly desired? The answer may best lie with this statement by Bittner (1995),

> It must be said, however, that the true professionalization of police work, in and of
> itself, is no weapon against sloth and corruption, no more than in the case of medi-
> cine, the ministry, law, teaching, and social work. That is, the professionalization
> of police work still leaves open the matter of its control (p. 181).

Nowhere does this statement ring truer than with the changeover to community policing, which requires the police to have more control over what they are and how they operate, and which has been touted as the future for professionalization.

> If there is a future to the professionalization of policing, many in law enforcement
> believe it rests in pursuing community policing. But others insist that it is an
> impossible dream—from the community's standpoint there is little cohesion or
> ability to respond to police initiatives; from the police standpoint, the requisite
> skills are difficult to obtain and require mid-management support and facilitation
> that has, to date, been notably lacking (Price, 1995, p. 8).

Community policing will require a change in how the police organization operates and controls its employees. In itself, community policing will force the issue of professionalism because of what it will require.

By lifting some of the constraints under which police officers in the field now operate, and by giving them the freedom to make decisions, innovate, and be problem solvers, community policing promises great benefits for the community in terms of quality of life and for the officers in terms of job satisfaction (Meese, 1993, p. 10).

Community policing aside, policing will require change. Professionalization is part of that change and incorporates such elements as education, training, lateral transfers, and accreditation. Furthermore, how policing operates, as in community policing, will be a key to forcing professionalization. Perhaps former FBI Director William Sessions said it best when he stated, "As we look toward the future, advanced and specialized law enforcement training will be the cornerstone of professionalism" (1991, p. 13).

DISCUSSION QUESTIONS

1. If the application of the formal definitions of a profession eliminates policing, is it possible that the definitions require changing and not policing?
2. You have been requested to rewrite the definition of a profession so that policing, in its current state, would meet the criteria. How would you redefine a profession?
3. Would policing be better off as a craft than as a profession? What is the difference?
4. How important is it that policing attain the status of profession? Would it really make any difference to society? Policing itself?
5. Do you believe that community policing will force policing to become a true profession? Explain.
6. What would you suggest is needed to bring policing from a skilled occupation to the status of profession?

REFERENCES

Accreditation Program Review. (1989). Fairfax, VA: Commission on Accreditation for Law Enforcement Agencies.

Bittner, E. (1995). The quasi-military organization of the police. In V.P. Kappeler (Ed.), *The police and society: Touchstone readings,* pp. 173–184. Prospect Heights, IL: Waveland Press.

Brown, M.K. (1981). *Working the street: Police discretion and the limits of reform.* New York: Russell Sage Foundation.

Caldwell, R.G., & Nardini, W. (1977). *Foundations of law enforcement and criminal justice.* Indianapolis: Bobbs-Merrill.

Carte, G.E. (1973). August Vollmer and the origin of police professionalism. *Journal of Police Science and Administration, 1,* 274–281.

Carter, D.L., Sapp, A.D., & Stephens, D.W. (1989). *The state of police education: Policy direction for the 21st century.* Washington, D.C.: Police Executive Research Forum.

Crank, J.P. (1990). Police: Professionals or craftsmen? An empirical assessment of professionalism and craftmanship among eight municipal police agencies. *Journal of Criminal Justice, 18,* 333–349.

Dantzker, M.L. (1986). Law enforcement, professionalism and a college degree. *The Justice Professional, 1,* 1–18.

———. (1995). *Understanding today's police.* Englewood Cliffs, NJ: Prentice-Hall.

Davis, M. (1991). Do cops really need a code of ethics? *Criminal Jusice Ethics, 10,* 14–27.

Manning, P.K. (1995). The police: Mandates, strategies, and appearances. In V.P. Kappeler (Ed.), *The police and society: Touchstone readings,* pp. 97–126. Prospect Heights, IL: Waveland Press.

Mecum, R.V. (1985). Police professionalism: A new look at an old topic. In H.W. More, Jr. (Ed.), *Critical issues in law enforcement* (4th ed., pp. 312–318). Cincinnati: Anderson Publishing.

Meese, E. III (1993). Community policing and the police officer. *Perspectives on policing* (15). U.S. Department of Justice.

More, H.W. Jr. (Ed.). (1985) *Critical issues in law enforcement* (4th ed.). Cincinnati: Anderson Publishing Co.

Price, B.R. (1985). Integrated professionalism: A model for controlling police practices. In H.W. More, Jr. (Ed.), *Critical issues in law enforcement* (4th ed., pp. 319–325). Cincinnati: Anderson Publishing Co.

———. (1995, June 15). Police and the quest for professionalism. *Law Enforcement News,* p. 8.

Reaves, B.A., & Smith, P.Z. (1995). *Law enforcement management and administrative statistics, 1993: Data for individual state and local agencies with 100 or more officers.* Washington, D.C.: U.S. Department of Justice.

Sessions, W.S. (1991, November). Steps toward professionalism: Crisis management training. *Police Chief,* p. 13.

Swanson, C.R., Territo, L., & Taylor, R.W. (1993). *Police administration* (3rd ed.). New York: Macmillan.

Wilson, J.Q. (1968). *Varieties of police behavior: The management of law and order in eight communities.* Cambridge, MA: Harvard University Press.

7

Professional Ethics and Policing

Elizabeth McGrath, Loyola University of Chicago

With the intense media coverage of the actions of law enforcement officers in Waco, Texas, with Rodney King, and in the investigation of the Nicole Brown Simpson-Ron Goldman murders, to cite just a few headlines from the recent past, one could easily infer that the American public has always been preoccupied with the ethical dimension of law enforcement. But the current national pastime has not always generated such widespread interest.

Historically, the public's concern with police activity has been fairly single-minded: The responsibility of the police has been to protect the public and, when crime occurs, to solve the crimes and apprehend those responsible as quickly as possible. A good police officer was expected to do whatever it took to keep society safe and secure. Since very few people seriously believed that they would ever be accused of a crime or the subject of a criminal investigation, they did not feel particularly concerned about how those who were wrongfully accused might be treated. Many believed that criminals, by their actions, relinquished many basic human rights that noncriminals enjoyed. Even today, presumption of innocence is an ideal that functions primarily on a theoretical level, not a practical one. Many people presume that a person is automatically guilty of a crime if the person has been indicted, and suspicion begins to equal guilt.

It is not surprising that widespread societal concern about the ethical treatment of those accused and those convicted of crimes were not always a matter of highest priority in the American consciousness. And these assumptions about those accused or convicted of crimes definitely colored society's views of acceptable parameters for police conduct. Police conduct, when inappropriate, usually revolves around ethics. Therefore, this chapter will examine policing and the question of ethics.

PUTTING INTO PERSPECTIVE

The evolution of society's awareness of the ethical dimension of police work was accelerated by technology and the invention of the television. The introduction of television into mainstream America and the accompanying explosion of information in the early 1960s brought new and shocking realities directly into people's homes. Demonstrations against the war in Vietnam, sit-ins on college campuses, and other graphic expressions of social unrest and rejection of traditional authorities tested the limits of the citizens' right to dissent. Academic philosophers who had previously spoken about ethics as abstract metaphysical principles began addressing specific issues of public concern, such as the morality of war, the sexual revolution, and civil rights. Courses on medical ethics, business ethics, and legal ethics sprang up in college curricula and the response, on the part of the professions, was the publication of professional codes of ethical behavior as evidence to the general public of their concern for the ethical dimension of their professional work. Social justice issues such as the justifiability of capital punishment or the scope of the exclusionary rule were argued on the academic level.

However, public concern was still slow to turn to the patrolman on the beat who had to translate these ideals into action on the street. The ethical responsibilities of judges, lawyers, or politicians still captured the public's imagination more readily and more intensely than did the concerns of the police officer confronted with domestic quarrels and street crimes.

Fortunately, the law enforcement profession did not wait for either academicians or the public at large to signal the need for concern over ethical policing. At the 1987 British conference, *Corporate Philosophy and Codes of Practice,* sponsored by the Institute of Business Ethics (Haggard, 1994), Commander L.T. Roach of the Metropolitan Police reminded his audience of law enforcement professionals that the police profession

> has a longer history of continuous ethical thinking than many others and, perhaps even more importantly, a vast experience of the problems of translating those philosophical speculations into practice. For the ethical problems of police officers are not gently debated in the cloisters of academe. They are forged in the cauldron of the inner city to be tested and refined by violent confrontation. . . . The problem is to develop and constantly to refine those ethics and then to ensure that they actually affect the behaviour and decision making of officers in a day-to-day working environment (Haggard, 1994, pp. 5–6).

The more recent emphasis on respect for and appreciation of diversity within the American culture has heightened awareness of our collective treatment of certain marginalized segments of society, among them those accused and those convicted of crimes. It is only with the realization that *all* persons, including those accused or convicted of crimes, have basic human rights that concern for their ethical treatment is even possible. A civilized society is concerned not only with the prevention of crime and the apprehension of criminals, but with the ethical means of accomplishing these goals. Examination of the U.S. Supreme Court's ongoing struggle to define what constitutes due process (ensuring the enforcement of fundamentally fair treatment/ procedures) reveals how ethical analysis is complicated by shifting societal values and cultural norms.

Our social conscience and sensitivity to ethical issues have been heightened and fine-tuned over the past few decades. However, merely becoming mindful of the importance of ethical behavior does not ensure the understanding of what ethical behavior is. The nature of "good" has been debated by philosophers for centuries. Although all segments of society share a stake in the ethical structure of the criminal justice system, not all of them understand justice to be the same thing. In situations where a crime has been committed, several sets of competing interests clash: society at large, the victim (or the victim's family), and the alleged criminals all have a different perspective on what will constitute a just response to a criminal act. Different views of the underlying causes of crime and criminal activity also dictate different responses to socially prohibited behavior. Determining the morally correct response for a police officer in any given situation requires an understanding of the role the criminal justice system is intended to play, and the diverse interests to be balanced when that officer is called to duty.

WHAT ETHICS IS ABOUT

Ethics is part of the domain of the study called philosophy. Philosophers debate issues about the meaning of life and the nature and purpose of human activity. Their theories have historically addressed very broad, sweeping issues about how we know what we know, why we act as we do, and how we should be directing our lives. Although these questions are significant for every person, the philosophers' work has generally been performed within the confines of academic settings, and only a small segment of even those well-educated in our society has addressed these issues in an intellectually systematic manner. Often theoretical ethics has remained far removed from real people and real problems. Even today, most people still look to religious institutions, family traditions, and other respected authority figures to provide answers for their day-to-day ethical dilemmas, rather than approaching these questions from a particular philosophical perspective.

Ethical dilemmas are the problems we encounter when we experience a sense that we ought to act in a particular manner, and yet are also drawn to another sort of conduct, either by some pleasure it would give us, or perhaps, due to some other conflicting sense of "ought." For example, an officer who stops a speeding vehicle, which has also ignored several stop signs, finds the driver trying to get a pregnant woman to the hospital. The officer escorts the vehicle to the emergency room and, after the woman is safe, addresses the driver's actions. One "ought" is writing several tickets, while the other "ought" is giving a stern lecture and written warnings.

Although the psychological experience of feeling that one "ought to" or "should" act in a particular way seems to be universal, the source and meaning of the experience still elude complete explanation. Many philosophers have attempted to account for what appears to be a uniquely human phenomenon, and most religions have provided their own accounts of why we are moral beings, but no single answer has yet proved satisfactory to everyone.

The problem in pinning down one meaning for "ought" is that the phrase refers to what *should be* the case, not what *is* the case. Confusion or disagreement about what *is* the case can usually be clarified and resolved by setting up tests, procedures by which we verify which state of affairs is actually the correct one. As yet, we have not devised a way of similarly settling the debates about what we consider the ideal state of affairs. To further complicate the matter, the nature of the ethical "should" is not even understood the same way by everyone. If I want to know how I *should* invest my money, we can arrive at a fairly straightforward answer once I tell you what I mean by "should." If, by "should," I mean "in order to get the largest yield within an investment period of six years," then a group of accountants and investment experts can propose investment plans and explain what each projects and why. If I want to know how I *should* act in my dealings with others, then, as with investing, I must be able to explain the context of my goal, and that entails the extraordinary task of summing up what makes life ultimately worthwhile and what makes an individual a productive human being. The context of my goal deals with the ultimate questions of why we humans are here and how we are to understand the purpose of our lives. There are as many different possible answers to those questions as there are different individuals, but in philosophy, the types of answers are grouped into different philosophies, and proponents are identified by their shared beliefs. No single school of thought (despite the beliefs of its proponents) has ever provided the final, definitive answer to life's ethical questions; each philosophy offers both strengths and weaknesses when confronting life's deepest questions.

Some philosophers, known as utilitarians, suggest that the course of action one ought to choose is that which will yield the greatest good/satisfaction for the greatest number. So, if granting immunity to the pushers on the street would help the criminal justice system successfully prosecute the one at the top of the operation, utilitarians would tend to consider it a more ethical choice to devote limited time and resources to the pursuit of the person with the most power and influence in the operation. Likewise, if the majority of the residents in a community found one type of crime—perhaps drunk driving or speeding—to be more threatening to their security and peace of mind and, so, of a higher priority than, say, gambling (the typical friendly poker game on Friday night), then a utilitarian approach would be to focus on stopping or at least successfully prosecuting the drunk driving and speeding, and devoting little, if any, time to interrupting the local poker games. The predominant strength of the utilitarian position is that it always works for a net gain in terms of human satisfaction and happiness. The weakness inherent in the view is the danger that the preferences of the majority will always overshadow those of the minority or minorities, and utilitarians run the risk of equating the concept "morally right" with "the values of the majority," as though the majority were incapable of desiring any morally unacceptable actions or institutions. If the terms "right" and "wrong" mean no more than "what the majority approves of," then, according to the history of our own nation, beating a confession out of a suspect was, at one time, morally right, as was slavery, withholding women's right to vote, and the right of the state to sterilize anyone convicted of three crimes involving moral turpitude. Ethics and morality must include some consideration of human needs, abilities, and desires, but whether they are *solely* a reflection of these fluctuating factors is a source of ongoing philosophical debate.

The group of philosophers called deontologists would recommend adopting the following formula as a guide to defining ethical behavior: (1) act in such a way that you would agree to make your rule of law universal, and (2) treat every person as having intrinsic value and never as a means to something else. Under this formula, less attention would be devoted to the wishes of, or impact on, the greatest number or the greatest happiness, and more emphasis would be placed on fairness to *each*. Consider again the example of the system that must choose between granting immunity to the pushers in order to go after the man on the top and prosecuting those whose daily activities have preyed particularly upon the poor and the young in our society. In this dilemma, deontologists would tend to emphasize the effect on society of officially overlooking the offenses of the pushers, even when this action is motivated by a desire to create the greater overall justice in the situation. The parent whose child has died as a direct result of that pusher's greed and criminal activity cannot help but be appalled at the injustice created when that person is granted immunity by the criminal justice system. The issue never boils down to numbers for a deontologist: wrongs are wrongs and must be recognized and treated as such if a system is to identify itself as a system devoted to the creation and protection of justice. They tend to treat justice as an ongoing balancing act, with every single injustice tipping the universal scale, such that some counter-force is required to restore equilibrium. Deontologists would allow for the possibility (perhaps even the probability) that, at times, the morally correct action would result in *no one* coming out ahead, in terms of greater happiness or satisfaction. While the utilitarians tie their ethics to creating the greatest good for the greatest number, the deontologists honor the principles and the rules, regardless of their impact on human happiness or misery. On a panel discussion of ethical issues in criminal justice, one psychologist, who was a deontologist, harshly criticized those in the criminal justice system who weigh a person's level of contriteness or regret when assessing the ethical quality of their actions and determining the appropriateness of punishment. He indicated that it would have made no difference to him whatsoever if Hitler had experienced a total religious conversion and had sincerely repented, vowing never to hurt a solitary soul again. The wrongs he committed cried out for punishment, and justice would not be restored in the universe until they were.

The last major group of ethical thinkers, called emotivists, would suggest that statements like, "You shouldn't kill innocent people," is just another way of saying, "I don't like it when innocent people are killed." This group would equate a culture's concept of justice with the emotional, psychological, and religious preferences of its members. At any time, and in any culture, the term "justice" reveals what the group finds comfortable or pleasurable, while actions termed "criminal" are those that they find most unpleasant and threatening. Emotivists would, for example, have little problem in explaining how beating a confession out of a person could, in a particular country at a particular time in history, be considered a just act while in that same country, at a different time, that action could be considered criminal. People's feelings about how they wish to interact and live with others change over time, so concepts of justice would naturally be expected to shift radically in response. Neither view would be *objectively* better nor worse than the other. Both would be right in the same way that it was right for you to enjoy playing with blocks at age two and equally right for you to *not* enjoy them at age forty-five. The emotivists' approach rejects the distinction between what one likes and what one considers ethically correct. The puzzle this creates is how to explain the human experience of conflict in finding one course of action desirable while believing another to be the ethically better path. If the emotivists are right, this conflict is irrational; what we prefer is precisely what we mean when we use the phrase "morally good." If you were to declare it ethically wrong to beat a confession out of a suspect, I would interpret that remark to mean that you simply don't like it when someone beats a confession out of a suspect. This approach removes the ambiguity of ethical terms, but at the cost of losing what is unique to the human experience of ethical oughts.

Ethical dilemmas are dilemmas precisely because we experience moral oughts as different from personal taste or preference. No one ever picketed another person's home or business because they disagreed as to whether chocolate cream pie or banana cream pie tasted better. If, indeed, morality is just personal taste, then how do we explain the public debate and even violent clashes over ethical issues like civil rights or the abortion issue? Either the two issues are distinct, or our experience of their separateness has been untrustworthy for hundreds of years.

Many religions explain the human experience of "ought" as humans' glimpse of the divine: it is our conscience revealing to us what our God (or gods) would want us to do. This approach removes the responsibility for formulating ethical standards from the human realm altogether; right and wrong are not determined by human preferences, values, or rules. Ethics reveals the preferences, values, and rules of the supreme being to whom we humans answer.

Whatever theory you use or goal you accept, you will find, on occasion, that your own values conflict, and your system will be at odds with your neighbor's. Acknowledging the complexity of the problem promotes patience and a realistic acknowledgment of the need for understanding and compromise as we look for a single concept of ethical professionalism that will work throughout our diverse society.

Ethics is basically a balancing act. It calls for a weighing of competing interests and the ultimate arrival at a course of action that represents a resolution to the conflict that will be morally acceptable to all. This brief explanation of ethical theories reveals how complicated the process is for even an individual to successfully resolve. Creating a unified view on a societal level is a project of tremendous complexity.

However, reaching a consensus is not necessary for peaceful coexistence. Learning to live together and respecting our differences is what ethical treatment of others is about. We may disagree sharply with our neighbors about whether or not to worship a god, how to raise our children, or how to treat our pets or property. Nevertheless, we can agree to disagree, acknowledge our differences, and still outline for ourselves and our neighbors a set of standards of conduct that we can all accept and abide by in order to create an atmosphere of freedom, safety, and respect for all.

Ethical conduct on the part of police must, likewise, be conduct that is in compliance with a set of standards that are thoughtfully formulated and consciously agreed upon by all members of the force. The process must acknowledge the various sets of personal ethical standards subscribed to by the officers as well as the members of the public with whom they interact. The standards selected will not reflect the views of every individual on the force, but they will represent a common ground on which everyone can and must be expected to comply. The sole point of agreement may actually be the acknowledgment that we share a dedication to conducting ourselves in an ethical manner and so we would realize that acceptance of some common standards would be essential to the profession, despite our personal desires or goals.

CAN ETHICS BE TAUGHT?

Certainly individuals can be taught information *about* ethics, so, in at least one sense, ethics can be taught. But if we are asking whether we can, by teaching people *about* ethics, make them actually become ethically better people for having received the education, then the answer is significantly less clear. Many theorize that it is not the presentation of new information about the difference between right and wrong and any recitation of the pertinent facts in some particularly messy moral problem that influences the listener's subsequent behavior, but rather the very act of confirming that ethics is a significant aspect of human life and a distinctly human dimension of conduct. Part of what defines us as rational beings is our ability to conceptualize, to generalize, to understand and remember what we have done, and what our actions have caused. Ethics is our way of projecting into the future how we believe our actions *should* be directed, the course they *should* follow. Implementing the plan requires more than information—an individual must not only recognize which is the correct path to follow, but also must *choose* it and commit to that, rather than another, course of action. Sometimes, choosing an ethically superior action (rather than one that is more valuable economically or socially, say) causes the individual to forgo pleasures offered by other courses of action. But showing the individual this possible path and its implications is the *first* step in guiding them in this direction. Consider the different effects when, in one group of trainees, the director emphasizes the importance to the profession of acting in a moral and ethically upright manner, while, in the second group, no mention is ever made of the ethical dimension of the profession's work. The message that the first group receives is that, regardless of what the particular ethical position may be, their director (and, by extension, the members of the profession) considers ethics to be significant enough to emphasize it in discussions about the most basic facets of the job. The second group is left to wonder whether anyone in the field is even remotely concerned about ethical issues that may arise.

The opportunity to anticipate and rehearse problematic situations and to discuss the ethical implications of possible responses provides invaluable dress rehearsals for moments when the problem arises and the new trainee has little, if any, time to reflect on the consequences of the various outcomes. Calling police officers' attention to ethical matters creates an opportunity for even the experienced officer to reflect on dimensions of the job that may have become so routine, so second-nature, that they no longer convey the same sense of ethical urgency. The best way to create and sustain appreciation for ethics is to constantly stress the service nature of police professionalism and to remind officers of the trust they hold from the society at large.

In addition to the message a code of ethics sends to police about the importance their peers place on the ethical quality of their behavior, the public also receives a strong message when the profession stresses to its members that they are expected to conform with published ethical norms. One of the defining characteristics of a profession is that it is a group that is self-governing, and this implies that they should implement a set of procedures that will outline which behaviors are required, which are prohibited, and how transgressions will be addressed by the group. The public trusts and supports the criminal justice system because it has faith that the system ultimately strives to create justice, even if it is not always successful. The continued effectiveness of the system requires this public trust. If society loses faith in the system, believes that justice is no longer being served by it, suspects that a large number of the so-called professionals are acting unethically, the public trust will be lost and criminal justice will be replaced with vigilantism.

Holding law enforcement professionals to a higher standard of conduct does not create a double standard. We are all aware that society has become increasingly concerned about the training and moral character of those who care for the most vulnerable members of our society: our children. So, too, law enforcement officers are members of a profession that uniquely supports the safety and peace of every segment of society.

DEVELOPING A CODE OF PROFESSIONAL ETHICS

Every profession faces a substantial challenge when creating a code of ethics that captures its unique function as a unit. The code must take account of the specific virtues that are most desired in professional practice and must address the vices, or at least the temptations, that form the group's collective Achilles' heel.

Law enforcement carries a responsibility unlike that of any other aspect of the criminal justice system: Law enforcement officers constantly face the possibility that they will be called upon to use force, perhaps even deadly force, in the performance of their duty. If the use of force is intrinsic to the work, then parameters must be set to distinguish ethical from unethical use of that force. If power is to be prevented from corrupting those who exercise it, then law enforcement officers must be continually reminded of the responsibility they hold to the public by virtue of their unique right to use force. How they wield their power—when and against whom—are all facets of the ethical issue. The Code of Ethics would address the broad limits on the measures police can use to effectively discharge their duties on a daily basis.

When ruling on the constitutionality of particular procedures adopted by police in the line of duty, the Supreme Court has, over the years, invoked a standard that incorporates an appeal to the collective ethical sensibility for guidance. Specifically, the Court rejects any procedures or methods that would "shock the conscience of the community." The phrase is arguably vague, but examination of the rulings provides some insight into the Court's reading of the ethical climate of the culture. Tracing the evolution of the rights of the accused in Fourth Amendment search and seizure cases reveals that the Court has followed a winding road, often doubling back on itself in response to shifts in the society's values and priorities.

Pumping a man's stomach to retrieve pills he had swallowed was determined to exceed allowable search and seizure limits in 1952 (*Rochin v. California*), but in 1985 the Court determined that similar forced intrusion of a traveler suspected of being an "alimentary canal smuggler" of drugs was an appropriate means of retrieving evidence (*United States v. Hernandez*). Staging the "Christian burial speech" to prey on an individual's mental instability and religious obsession in order to obtain a confession was determined to violate Miranda protections, even when officers asked no specific questions of the accused (*Brewer v. Williams*), but the Court ruled that Miranda warnings may be bypassed completely and officers may ask any questions they wish, later introducing their findings into evidence, if such questioning is prompted by a genuine concern for public safety (*New York v. Quarles*). The immediate concern of the Court is always to set legal limits, not moral ones, on police activity, but issues such as the limits of legitimate search and seizure touch on the ethical dimension of how all persons, criminal and noncriminal alike, are to be treated by law enforcement officers.

Legislation affecting fundamental human rights necessarily impacts, and is impacted by, the social sense of morality and values that are dominant at the time. How broadly the Court interprets particularly the Fourth and Fifth Amendments depends on how they gauge an accused's reasonable expectation of privacy. What is it that makes a person's expectations "reasonable"? That very subjective phrase reflects, at least in part, the belief system that drives the society at any one time. When economic times are good and people feel basically secure, they tend to be more understanding and sympathetic with those whose behavior deviates from social norms. When large segments of the society feel basically insecure about their jobs, their economic well-being, and their overall safety, views on how to deal with crime and criminals tend to become much more rigid and punitive. It is up to the criminal justice system to mediate the extremes and protect the society both from crime and from their own inconsistencies in reacting to it. Balancing individuals' desire for privacy and safety, and mercy and justice is a full-time challenge.

Police constantly face a tradeoff in selecting means of achieving just results. Society's interest in privacy rights and freedom of movement and association restricts police effectiveness in stopping certain sorts of crimes. Limits on the number of law enforcement officers available at any one time or in a particular location further restricts their ability to enforce the laws evenhandedly. High visibility of police presence clearly prevents a number of crimes, particularly certain types of property crimes, but not all areas can be patrolled with the same intensity and the same supply of personnel. Drug-related crimes now represent the highest proportion of criminal activity on the street, and the sheer volume of these crimes creates in the public an underlying sense of fear and vulnerability. Problems of scarcity of human resources and increasing public demands for service contribute added stress for police officers and further challenge personnel to maintain their ethical stance and to avoid shortcuts that provide practical gains but moral degeneration.

DOING JUSTICE AND APPEARING TO DO JUSTICE

Measuring the effectiveness of most professions is a fairly straightforward matter: Medicine is primarily concerned with saving lives and healing diseased bodies; financial managers either help you invest wisely (and so protect your money) or they do not. For law enforcement, however, effectiveness is as much a matter of which crimes have been prevented as which ones have been solved. It is not only the outcome of police intervention in specific criminal situations that indicates successful police work, whether solving crimes or apprehending suspects. Law enforcement officers are entrusted with the duty of maintaining order and keeping the peace. For this job to be effectively performed, police officers must hold the respect of the society they protect. For this reason, police officers hold a special duty to not only *do* what is moral in their jobs, they must also *appear* to do what is moral and just.

In terms of its social benefits, much of the value of a police force lies in its ability to create in the minds of community residents the feeling that they are safe and secure in their homes. They must also instill confidence in the society that they are responsive to the needs of *all* the residents in a community, not only the wealthy or the powerfully situated. In the marketplace people expect money to make a difference, but within a system that calls itself a criminal *justice* system, service and respect cannot be tied to the salary or position of the citizen in need, or the system will soon be recognized as a hypocritical institution no longer worthy of public trust or respect. From the law enforcement officer's point of view, the murder of a homeless person must command the same concern as the murder of a prominent politician. The person who scorns authority and voices his lack of respect must be given the same level of protection and assistance as the citizen who stands in awe of the police officer and all that he or she represents. Serving and protecting *all* members of society is a noble ideal, but one that is challenged virtually every day when insults and obscenities are hurled in response to an officer's legitimate exercise of duty. Lawyers and judges work with those accused and convicted in offices, courtrooms, and jails, where the threat of bodily harm is minimized, and where they are surrounded by the trappings of the legal system. Police officers confront suspects and criminals on the street, often in the midst of violent episodes, where training, practice, and instinct must provide split-second answers and guidance.

The following *Law Enforcement Code of Ethics* is incorporated into the curriculum of the training academy for the Chicago Police Department. Ethical issues are treated as a separate component of the curriculum, but questions about morality are also woven into pertinent topics throughout the remaining academic units.

The code covers a number of goals and aspirations, and targets those emotional and practical concerns that threaten the police officer's ethical stability. The major ethical issues can be grouped as follows: fairness, control and courtesy, collegiality

Law Enforcement Code of Ethics

AS A LAW ENFORCEMENT OFFICER, my fundamental duty is to serve the community, to safeguard lives and property, to protect the innocent against deception, the weak against oppression or intimidation and the peaceful against violence or disorder, and to respect the constitutional rights of all to liberty, equality and justice.

I WILL keep my private life unsullied as an example to all and will behave in a manner that does not bring discredit to me or my agency. I will maintain courageous calm in the face of danger, scorn or ridicule; develop self-restraint; and be constantly mindful of the welfare of others. Honest in thought and deed both in my personal and official life, I will be exemplary in obeying the law and the regulations of my department. Whatever I see or hear of a confidential nature or that is confided to me in my official capacity will be kept ever secret unless revelation is necessary in the performance of my duty.

I WILL never act officiously or permit personal feelings, prejudices, political beliefs, aspirations, animosities or friendships to influence my decisions. With no compromise for crime and with relentless prosecution of criminals, I will enforce the law courteously and appropriately without fear or favor, malice or ill will, never employing unnecessary force or violence and never accepting gratuities.

I RECOGNIZE the badge of my office as a symbol of public faith, and I accept it as a public trust to be held so long as I am true to the ethics of police service. I will never engage in acts of corruption or bribery, nor will I condone such acts by other police officers. I will cooperate with all legally authorized agencies and their representatives in the pursuit of justice.

I KNOW that I alone am responsible for my own standard of professional performance and will take every reasonable opportunity to enhance and improve my level of knowledge and competence.

I WILL constantly strive to achieve these objectives and ideals, dedicating myself before God to my chosen profession . . . law enforcement (produced and distributed by the Chicago Police Department).

(For comparison purposes, review the code of ethics provided in Chapter 6.)

and support, honesty, and autonomy and responsibility. Each of these qualities is essential in creating a just system of law enforcement, and each is challenged, on a daily basis, in a police officer's interaction with the public and with fellow police officers in the performance of his or her duty.

Fairness

The terms "justice" and "fairness" are often treated as synonymous. Treating one fairly or justly involves reference to two contexts: Treating the person fairly in response to his or her particular needs, and treating them fairly in relation to how others are treated. At times, these two goals will be easily achieved through a single action. At other times, they will be squarely at odds and no single response will satisfy them both. In those moments, the officer will need to rely on the training and experience that guide the officer's use of discretion.

Consider, for example, the classic ethical dilemma of the person who steals a loaf of bread to feed his or her starving child. If justice is truly blind, then this thief should be treated as any other would be under the law. Or consider the person who kills knowingly and willfully in the attempt to pull off the perfect crime. The action in each case fails to convey the whole story. All thieves and all murderers are not alike. Justice and fairness must take not only the deed that has been performed, but the condition of the performer as well into account. The same must be considered in all situations where discretion must be exercised. Police cannot possibly apprehend every person who breaks a law, so an officer must decide when and how to intervene in most situations that call for police attention. If the officer has encountered three instances of disorderly conduct and has elected to sternly warn the perpetrators in each case, while another officer elected to arrest similar offenders, is this fair? Officers cannot be clones of one another, and, as one judge commented when tighter sentencing guidelines were proposed in order to eliminate widely divergent sentencing practices, only computers can guarantee identical results every time. Humans differ in their judgments, attitudes, and conduct. Perhaps perfect fairness would dictate more uniform responses and less latitude for discretion, but the system would be less *human*. In the end, we may be entitled to justice, but not perfection.

The code specifically discusses protecting the innocent and the weak from those who would prey on their situation. Part of our concern with security and safety reflects our awareness that not everyone in society is capable of fully understanding and protecting themselves in their interactions with others. Our awareness is reflected in our outrage when we hear that an elderly person or a child has been attacked or injured in some way. Actions are not performed in a vacuum: we respond not only to an isolated action, but to the circumstances, the nature of the offender, and that of the victim(s) as well.

Fairness and justice are complex ideas and require a measure of objectivity as well as subjectivity. Treating everyone as though no human differences exist creates one sort of injustice, but responding only to specific circumstances and ignoring general standards of conduct creates another. Balancing the two requires a sensitivity to both extremes and a constant effort to monitor one's use of discretion.

Control and Courtesy

The majority of the American public will experience the judicial process solely by way of Court TV and rerun episodes of *Matlock* and *L.A. Law*. Only a very small number will have any direct experience of the American prison system. But almost every person has had some sort of direct experience with a police officer during his or her lifetime, whether that experience involved reporting a purse snatching, mugging, or an automobile accident or, less pleasantly, receiving a ticket for speeding. Every interaction between the public and a police officer works to either bolster or tear down the public's trust in the criminal justice system in general and law enforcement officers in particular. When an individual police officer is rude or impatient or shows disdain for a certain individual or segment of society, that behavior and attitude are attributed to *all* who wear the uniform. In a sense, a police officer never acts as a mere individual; each officer is viewed; first in the role of the police officer and only second as a person with the same human frailties and faults as any other person. More self-control and discipline *are* expected of a police officer, and this heightened sense of duty accompanies inclusion in the profession. As a citizen acting alone, John Doe has the right to become indignant and irate when another person insults him or scorns and ridicules him, but if Officer John Doe encounters that same situation while performing his duty as a police officer, he forfeits his right to return insult for insult and must not use his authority to avenge his personal honor.

Police officers are in the unique position of being perceived as public servants at the beck and call of literally every member of society. Much of their time is spent answering questions, giving directions, and offering aid that has nothing to do with solving crimes or apprehending criminals. The public turns to police for help in all sorts of situations simply because they recognize the uniform as a helpful and supportive presence. In addition to their role as general problem solvers, police officers are also expected to address every complaint and criticism that the public chooses to make of the entire criminal justice system. Responding with patience and understanding is, at times, quite challenging, but these exchanges all contribute to the society's perception of the professionalism of their police force and is an opportunity to reinforce the trust and support of the general public.

Collegiality and Support

The responsibilities of police officers are emotionally draining at times and often exact a high price in terms of stress and strain on the officers' private lives. It is difficult to constantly set aside one's personal feelings and to maintain the demeanor of a police officer. Because the lifestyle and unique duties tend to create a sense of isolation for many members of the force, it becomes critical that police officers act as emotional support for one another. The work environment itself tends to create a sense of loyalty and trust, since officers know that, at any moment, their very lives may depend on the skills and courage of their fellow officers. This level of interdependence creates a sort of camaraderie that can simultaneously support and undermine the ethical behavior of fellow officers.

As members of the same team, police officers share experiences, perceptions, and problems. The trust and confidence that are built up between officers help to counter the often undermining and even demeaning experiences on the street. Since so much of an officer's job revolves around negative or confrontational situations, acceptance and understanding from fellow officers may be the only positive reinforcement available at the end of the day for a job well done.

The ethical dilemmas arise when the officer, who understands, supports, and compliments you, also indulges in activities you know to be beyond the law, or at least beyond the ethical code. An officer is trained to cope with the actual danger that will be encountered on the street, but confronting a fellow officer is a much fuzzier, emotionally draining challenge.

Honesty

The toughest clash between ideals and reality that a police officer will grapple with in the ethical arena will be the clash between what his or her superior officers or other professionals in the field will say. Officers should not necessarily do what these same professionals would do out in the field. Theory and reality clash the moment an officer sees a fellow officer accepting free meals or other gifts after being told about the dangers of divided allegiance. The clash is all the more fierce, because the officer now must decide how to handle the information he has unwillingly received about another officer's (perhaps a friend or partner's) unethical behavior. The admonishment to tell the truth and report any wrongdoing by another officer suddenly leaves the newcomer exposed to allegations of snitching, back stabbing, and betrayal. The ethical dictate that one should be honest in all matters will, for many police officers, clash with the ethical dictate that one should support and protect one's fellow officer.

Honesty is more than a matter of telling the truth at all times. Honesty requires an officer to decline the free meal that is offered out of gratitude for a helping hand extended at a critical moment, or perhaps requires him or her to insist on paying for services extended as a courtesy by a store owner who appreciates the mere presence of the officer on the premises. Honesty is about remaining free from any sort of conflict of interest or preferential treatment. Why should it be considered dishonest to accept a free meal at the end of your shift in the neighborhood coffee shop? Because your presence *in uniform* extends service to one restaurant rather than another on the basis of *money*. You have bartered your services for a free meal, whether you call it that or not. But does it not matter that you are there on your own time and that the owner sincerely wants to give you the free meal?

If you look no further than the parties' motives in this all-too-familiar scene, you cannot help but conclude that everyone means well. However, good intentions cover only half of the ethical picture; understanding and correctly assessing the situation is the other half.

> *Illustration:*   "If I, as a private citizen, am on the beach and realize that a person is drowning nearby, I have no obligation to intervene, risking bodily injury to myself, and attempt a rescue. But if I, through some misguided sense of altruism or heroics, announce to the onlookers that *I* will affect a rescue, and so discourage others from helping, and yet I can't really swim or be of any assistance, my good intentions will justifiably land me in a lawsuit. It is not enough to mean well; one must also act in a reasonable manner. I may not mean to create an opportunity for conflicts of interest to arise or preferential treatment to be offered, but if I act in ways that can be reason-

ably expected to yield such results, then I am ethically responsible, despite my good intentions."

Very few people actually enter the profession determined to compromise themselves or to ignore considerations of ethics and morality; the distance is crossed in inches with hundreds of tiny, innocent-looking steps.

Autonomy and Responsibility

Every individual is responsible for his or her own acts or omissions. A police officer cannot hide behind the badge or the profession's code of ethics to explain away responsibility for his or her actions. No one can expect his or her fellow officers to ignore ethical transgressions out of loyalty to the badge or the group. Misplaced loyalties create ethical dilemmas for everyone and blur the distinction between being supportive and being an accomplice to an unethical act.

Throughout the span of a career, it is very easy to settle into a routine, a comfortable mindset and set of predictable reactions. Continued growth and development in the profession are a challenging ethical obligation for every police officer. A certain hardness and hopelessness become evident in those who quit growing in their professions, and burnout and apathy are often the outcome. Keeping an open mind and maintaining a willingness to approach situations with a fresh perspective requires work and dedication.

Continuing education is the chief means of maintaining a fresh outlook and warding off stagnation, but a commitment to growth and new learning requires individual interest and incentive. Programs targeting ethical issues or innovative approaches to public service will be successful to the extent that individual officers are willing to remain receptive to their message. The ethical obligation to improve one's level of knowledge and competence benefits the public at large, the entire police force, and each police officer who takes that charge seriously. For police to serve the public well, they must be aware of social and cultural events and trends, and must be realistic about the people and situations they will encounter. This requires the police officer to remain interested and involved in the society he or she has sworn to protect and serve.

POLICE CORRUPTION: NATURE OR NURTURE?

Just as every profession requires its members to develop and display certain skills and virtues in order for their work to flourish, every profession, including policing, contains the potential for certain human corruption within its culture. Whether some police are corrupted by their environment within the force or whether they enter the profession already tainted, some police officers end up involved in unethical and, at times, also illegal activities that not only affect their personal ethics, but also demean their fellow officers and the entire profession in the eyes of the general public.

Some sociologists and historians studying the history of corruption within police units blame problems of corruption on poor hiring practices, others on inadequate training, and still others on poor supervision or the "rotten apple" theory: that certain individuals are just bad people and, when they enter the police force, exhibit the qualities of bad police officers. All acknowledge the ripe opportunity for the slippery slope phenomenon. Once an officer begins to slip in small matters, accepting tips or gifts in return for doing the job, then there is a greater likelihood that the situation can escalate to the point that the officer is accepting larger and larger gifts that, at least initially, would have appeared clearly inappropriate—even worthy of the name *graft*.

> for some police, the small kindness—like making fresh coffee when the police arrive in the middle of the night—is just that. It is not like a tip for a bellhop, and it is not the beginning of a slippery slope. Since the intentions of the restaurant personnel are often equally innocent, police acceptance and appreciation are not illicit. Other police believe themselves deserving of special consideration because they feel underpaid or burdened with too much hardship in their work. If this attitude resembles self-pity, it can be a sign of vulnerability to a slippery slope. The free coffee may not cause the vulnerability, but it may, by indulging it, lead to worse things (Delattre, 1994, pp. 80–81).

Self-pity is a dangerous attitude for police to carry unresolved, because it serves as a breeding ground for resentment (toward those who continue to profit from crime and toward those whom they perceive to have more glamorous, interesting, or higher paying positions) and anger. Even if just one officer in fifty starts down the path to corruption as a result of gifts and well-intentioned tokens of appreciation, it is one officer too many, and the entire profession and the society they serve will pay the consequences.

The problem, of course, rarely remains limited to one who will remain isolated among the fifty. After a while, when gifts from merchants, free meals in restaurants, and even kickbacks from those investigated or arrested become the norm and eventually even expected, those officers who attempt to decline such offers and remain independent of their influence end up becoming the targets of suspicion by the officers who have succumbed to the temptation. Those who have resisted involvement come to fear that their fellow officers who are on the take may not help them or provide vital backup when they need it and the group invariably ends up split by the influence of what may well have started out as just a free cup of coffee from a grateful citizen.

The problem, in both its most basic and more sophisticated forms, is faced by every city. Various remedies have been fashioned in an attempt to eliminate, or at least reduce, the most destructive effects of the dilemma. Some cities, for example, encourage restaurants to provide whatever free meals or coffee they wish, but then ask these establishments to submit records of the expenses so that the city can reimburse them. This makes the city the benefactor, not the individual store or restaurant owner, and breaks the cycle of creating unhealthy debts. Some police departments attempt to enforce a policy of no free meals, gifts, etc., although that tactic is usually only moderately effective in addressing the problem. The most effective means of combating conflict of interest dilemmas comes in two forms: leading by example and a consciously created heightened sense of accountability.

The slippery slope owes its slipperiness to the fact that, once one *is allowed to* start down the path, there is usually little that can be done to interrupt the descent. It is true that many who take the first step are well-intentioned, innocent officers who simply do not anticipate their ultimate destination. Those who have a supervisory role, beginning with those active in academy training, should constantly emphasize that the initial, innocent gifts, such as the free cup of coffee or the car wash, *seem* insignificant and irrelevant but they *are* the beginnings of a conflict of interest dilemma, and, so, should simply be avoided from the beginning. If the message is repeated loudly enough and often enough, the hidden trap and the slippery slope will be avoided by everyone who is concerned enough to reflect on the principle. Placing the responsibility on each officer's shoulders to be alert to potential problems along these lines also creates greater likelihood that those who would be tempted to ignore the message themselves would, nonetheless, be concerned about accepting favors or gifts that other officers may learn about later. Silent complicity becomes the standard response of fellow officers only if those in supervisory positions offer no other realistic alternatives.

Unfortunately, there exists in many departments a level of corruption that extends far beyond the acceptance of the free cup of coffee or occasional meal. Officers who put their lives on the line daily for $30,000 per year see drug dealers who pocket that amount on a weekly basis. An officer may, during an investigation, find himself or herself in a position to receive kickbacks that would easily exceed even a generous salary, and the temptation clearly proves more than some can resist. This level of compromise poses an obvious ethical problem for the officer directly involved but, ultimately, also creates an impossible situation for the partner or fellow officer who may become privy to the situation and then must decide between involving themselves in the cover-up or risking severe repercussions from their fellow officers. In many cases, officers have committed perjury rather than informing on their fellow officers, even in cases where those officers were guilty of major felonies. Once the pressure to protect their own has become that strong, it is unlikely that courses on ethics will alter behavior significantly. Severe lapses and the accompanying cover-ups can be effectively addressed only through strong proactive measures on the part of police supervisors and trainers.

The first measure must be tight control on the recruitment and selection of new police officers. Careful screening is essential in weeding out those whose motives for inclusion on the force are likely to create more problems than they will solve. A profession that is entrusted with that degree of power and authority over the public cannot help but attract a certain number of people who care more about wielding power than about serving and protecting the public. If the screening is properly handled, a large number of problem cases will be avoided from the outset. Part of the screening process would be an introduction to the ideals and values that make up the police officer's professional virtues and would acquaint prospective members with the goals and expectations of the profession.

Once the recruitment and screening processes are completed, the leadership within the departments would have to make a concerted effort to impress upon the members of the force that corrupt practices simply would not be tolerated. Forceful statements that police professionals "shouldn't accept bribes," coupled with ambiguous dicta to "always be supportive of fellow officers" won't work. The dilemma *will* arise, and officers need to recognize in advance that they will be asked to choose between two competing virtues, honesty and loyalty. If they are not explicitly reminded that loyalty does *not* include participation in criminal cover-ups, and if supervisors continue to look the other way while officers on the take intimidate the others into a conspiracy of silence, then corruption will never stop and the screening and training will be wasted.

The effects of corruption reach far beyond the actual crimes, payoffs, and cover-ups. The problem takes a tremendous toll on the image and reputation of all law enforcement professionals and leaves the public more convinced than ever that police officers are either dishonest, power-hungry, or greedy. The profession is, by its very nature, a high-profile, highly visible one. When corrupt police officers are finally exposed and caught, their names make front-page news, because the guardians of public safety are shown to be as dangerous to the society as the worst criminals in our midst. Whether the attitude is realistic or not, there is something more insidious about a cop-turned-villain than an ordinary citizen of unknown background; there is an element of scandal and heightened fear and indignation stirred up in the community, because a special trust has been broken. Perhaps it is not realistic to expect more of the police officers than of the general public—after all, all humans are subject to temptations and character flaws—but we still hope (sometimes in vain) that those we trust will respect and honor that trust and fulfill our expectations.

In addition to the on-the-job temptations to indulge in activities that create conflicts, there are the inevitable ethical problems that accompany the onset of boredom and apathy on the job and the resulting presence of mediocrity on the force. Doing *any* job well requires attention, dedication, and a positive attitude toward the work. If an officer begins to suffer from long-term disillusionment, boredom, or disappointment, his or her level of interest and dedication will diminish.

IDEALS VS. REALITIES

For a code of ethics to be effective, it must address the realities that the professional law enforcement officer is likely to face and not make demands that are unreasonable or dangerous in the situation. In its professional code of responsibility, the legal profession has distinguished between two types of ethical dictates: Those standards of ethical conduct to which a lawyer can be held accountable, and ethical ideals for which one strives but, when falling short, will not be penalized. It is reasonable to expect police officers to display the same level of courtesy and care to all who call on them for help, but it is unrealistic to expect them to actually like all persons equally. Professional ethical standards refer to *behavior*: The officer retains the right to think and feel any way he or she wishes, provided their behavior conforms at all times to dictated professional standards. One cannot be faulted for being tempted in certain situations, but giving in to the temptation may be an ethical transgression requiring correction or discipline.

Incorporating the spirit of the code of ethics requires a concerted effort on the part of all police officers, both in remaining diligent about their own behavior, public and private, and in supplying the sort of encouragement and support that fellow officers need to enable them to remain faithful to the code.

ETHICAL EFFECTS OF THE CRIMINAL JUSTICE SYSTEM

The intent of the criminal justice system is to remove from the individuals in society the need to protect themselves against those who otherwise would be at liberty to steal from, injure, or even kill them. Weak and strong alike receive protection in return for their agreement to refrain from avenging crimes against themselves and those close to them. The system takes great pains to ensure that individuals are dealt with in an objective and rational manner. In the earliest times of the Greek judicial system, only those who knew either or both parties to a dispute were allowed to serve as jurors at the trial of the case. The presumption was made that one must know the parties involved in order to arrive at a just solution to the case. In the American judicial system, prospective jurors are carefully screened to ensure that they are not connected in any way with any party to the case at hand. We now make the opposite assumption to the one made by the Greeks: Only one who is totally dispassionate and objective is in a position to mete out true justice. To remove every possible hint of vindictiveness, we even dictate that, should an executioner have an interest in the case in which an accused person has been found guilty and sentenced to die, another executioner be brought in to perform the execution. Evidence that a judge has a vested interest in a case before him or her is automatically treated as an irreversible error; a mistrial is inevitable. If there is a single principle that has guided the development of the vast network of rules and procedures making up the criminal justice system, it is that justice requires equal treatment of all, free from the sorts of petty interests and prejudices that color our interactions out on the street. With so much at stake, it is understandable that those on the front lines must be constantly reminded that they act as part of a vast system of justice and that the success or failure of that great enterprise depends, in large part, on how they handle each situation they encounter on a daily basis. Landmark cases like *Miranda* start out as just another part of an officer's daily routine. At a minimum, doing justice involves fair and evenhanded treatment of everyone processed within the system. One judge may decide that he no longer personally believes in the ethical soundness of the exclusionary rules, or another may decide that, despite sentencing guidelines, she feels morally bound to set a sentence that flies in the face of those guidelines. These judges may both feel personally compelled to disregard the rules, but their actions will undermine the credibility of the system for all of those who expect equal treatment under the law. It is too simple to say that one must always follow the professional code or that one must always follow one's conscience; whenever the professional and personal clash, the underlying values and costs must again be weighed. No person can devote his life to work that constantly places him at odds with his conscience, and, if the conflict occurs frequently enough, one might do well to consider a long-term career change. Occasional conflicts are inevitable. No two individuals have precisely the same ethical beliefs and standards, so it is unrealistic to assume that individuals with such diverse backgrounds and personalities as those comprising a police force would always agree perfectly with one another and with the stipulations of a professional code of ethics.

CONCLUDING THOUGHTS: HANDLING CONFLICTS BETWEEN PROFESSIONAL AND PERSONAL ETHICS

The Code of Ethics paints, with broad brush strokes, the general picture of how police officers should behave, according to the collective wisdom of other members of the law enforcement profession. What does an officer do when his or her personal code of ethics clashes with the dictates of the professional code? There is no simple answer, except to point out that in every profession these conflicts inevitably arise, and the resolution is never certain, never clear, and always painful. A person cannot simply set aside his or her personal beliefs and mechanically follow a code the officer neither believes in nor accepts. Society was appalled when those charged with war crimes after World War II offered, as their defense, the plea, "I was only following orders." Ethics is never that simple, and the conflicting feelings and duties must be acknowledged, sorted, and prioritized if the individual is to have any hope of resolving the inner turmoil.

Unlike the professional code of ethics, which is created through the conscious efforts of individuals charged with this responsibility, an individual's private code of ethics is a much more nebulous blueprint for behavior. Most people are not even aware of the multitude of authorities that have had a hand in shaping their private codes of conduct. Parents, churches, teachers, and peers all influence the development of an individual's ethical sense. Reason and emotion are both mingled into the mixture, and the result is a stew that defies analysis. Often we can't identify why we think (or, in some cases, feel) that a certain action is right or wrong. We isolate a mysterious organ called a conscience that is attributed with the ability to recognize the moral quality of actions and, when we attempt to ignore the dictates of that conscience, causes us to experience a sense of guilt or shame. Until an individual unlocks the mystery of his or her own conscience and ethical development, resolving conflicts between personal conscience and professional codes of ethics will remain a frustrating and fruitless endeavor.

The values embodied by the police officer's professional code of ethics have been openly debated and consciously chosen for inclusion as critical factors in ethical law enforcement. Those charged with developing, revising, and updating the code recognize that they are guiding the actions of a complicated organism that must accommodate the faults and frailties of thousands of individuals, each bringing a unique personal history of ethical development.

Certain common standards must be established if an institution is to survive and be effective. An institution that is as complex and powerful as the criminal justice system requires the cooperation and participation of thousands of individuals who share a commitment to a common goal. This does not mean that all of these people expect to agree on every detail and facet of the system; that would be an impossible task. However, they understand that, to accomplish the larger goal of keeping the peace and creating a safe and secure environment, there will necessarily be a great deal of compromise on both small and large issues along the way. Keeping an eye on the larger goal and "big picture" issues can help an individual sort out the seriousness of the dissonance he feels between his private ethical code and his professional code.

DISCUSSION QUESTIONS

1. Discuss the variety of sources from which you learned your system of ethical beliefs. Which person, persons, or institutions influenced you the most in the formation of your personal beliefs?
2. Which aspects of justice do you consider essential, recognition of individual differences, or equal treatment of all? Why?
3. How could society create a more supportive environment for law enforcement officers and so encourage dedication to ethical ideals?
4. Can law enforcement professionals create a more supportive environment so that officers could more easily remain faithful to their professional code of ethics?
5. Is it unfair to expect law enforcement officers to maintain a higher standard of ethical behavior than we would expect from ordinary citizens? Do we, in fact, hold politicians and other public figures to higher standards as well? Is this fair?

REFERENCES

Brandt, R.B. (1992). *Morality, utilitarianism, and rights*. Cambridge, MA: Cambridge University Press.

Brewer v. Williams, 430 U.S. 387 (1977).

Delattre, E.J. (1994). *Character and cops: Ethics in policing*. Washington, D.C.: American Enterprise Institute Press.

Feinberg, J. (1984). *Harm to others: The moral limits of the criminal law*. New York: Oxford University Press.

———, & Gross, H. (1995). *Philosophy of law*. Belmont, CA: Wadsworth Publishing.

Haar, C.M., & Fessler, D.W. (1986). *Fairness and justice*. New York: Simon & Schuster.

Haggard, P. (1994). *Police ethics*. Lewiston, NY: Edwin Mellen Press.

Hansen, D.A. (1973). *Police ethics*. Springfield, IL: Charles C. Thomas.

Hunt, M. (1990). *The compassionate beast*. New York: Doubleday Anchor Books.

Katz, L. (1987). *Bad acts and guilty minds*. Chicago: University of Chicago Press.

MacIntyre, A. (1966). *A short history of ethics*. New York: Collier Books.

Malloy, E.A. (1982). *The ethics of law enforcement and criminal punishment*. New York: University Press of America.

Martineau, H. (1989). *How to observe morals and manners*. New Brunswick, NJ: Transaction Publishers.

New York v. Quarles, 467 U.S. 649 (1984).

Punch, M. (1985). *Conduct unbecoming (The social construction of police deviance and control)*. New York: Tavistick Publications.

Rawls, J. (1971). *A theory of justice*. Cambridge, MA: Harvard University Press.

Rochin v. California, 342 U.S. 165 (1952).

Shute, S., & Hurley, S. (Eds.). (1993). *On human rights: The Oxford Amnesty Lectures 1993*. New York: BasicBooks.

Singer, P. (Ed.). (1994). *Ethics*. New York: Oxford University Press.

United States v. Hernandez, 105 S.Ct. 740 (1985).

White, M. (1981). *What is and what ought to be done*. New York: Oxford University Press.

8

Criminal Analysis

Marilyn B. Peterson, Certified Criminal Analyst

Several issues in this text can be highlighted by this chapter on criminal analysis. Although not particularly new to policing, criminal analysis is just beginning to receive the attention it deserves. Criminal analysis brings a research-based perspective to police problem solving. As a result, it impacts issues of professionalism, women in policing, technology, police management, and community policing.

Because law breakers have become more sophisticated and technologically proficient, the onus has been on law enforcement to meet this challenge. While some police agencies have had low educational requirements in the past, modern police try to "work smart" rather than "work hard." In tandem with the increasing educational levels of police officers, a new profession has emerged within policing—that of the criminal analyst.

Criminal analysts are part of the new breed of police specialists. They are college educated, intellectually curious, and communicate well. They are also readily distinguishable from their "traditional" police colleagues: most are women; most have no police street experience; and most are collegial in nature, rather than protocol-driven.

These people bring a unique perspective to policing. This uniqueness has caused apprehension for some and confusion for others. Yet numerous first-class police operations not only have criminal analysis sections, but consider them critical to their day-to-day policing efforts.

Like any emerging field, criminal analysis is not completely documented or standardized. This lack of standard operating procedures (SOPs) makes it suspect to police officers, who have been taught to do things "by the book." The philosophy that underlies criminal analysis, however, is the same as that underlying problem-oriented policing: collect information, identify the problem, and arrive at solutions to the problem.

As they have progressed in law enforcement, criminal analysts have begun to standardize their operations to some degree: developing criteria for their certification, regularizing criminal analysis methods and techniques through training and documentation, and adopting some attributes of the police culture. This chapter shows what analysis is, what issues it raises, and what is being done to resolve those issues.

THE INFORMATION PROCESS

Criminal analysis was introduced in 1971 as part of the intelligence process. Godfrey and Harris note that analysis "assembles the bits and pieces of information that have been collected . . . and puts them together in such a manner as to show pattern and meaning" (1971, p. 24).

That intelligence process—collection, evaluation, collation, analysis, reporting, dissemination, and reevaluation (see Fig. 8.1)—was devised to guide law enforcement agencies through the steps data goes through during its transformation into useful information (intelligence) (Godfrey & Harris, 1971, p. 34).

Simply put, the process shows that the data are collected, their validity and relevance are evaluated, they are organized in files and indexed (collation), they are reviewed and compared to determine their meaning (analysis), the results of the analysis are put into a reporting format, that report is shared with officials who need to know them, and feedback regarding the helpfulness of the information is sought so that the efforts (and the information) can be reevaluated if necessary.

This process refers to more than the data collected to produce law enforcement intelligence. It also applies to information that is collected for investigations, or for a research project. The process applies as well outside the law enforcement environment in social sciences and other venues.

The analysis of information is vital to successful crime control. Yet the vast majority of law enforcement agencies in the United States and Canada have no analysts and no police officers with analytical training. One reason for this is the presence of unresolved or transitional issues relating to the use of analysis in law enforcement.

Figure 8.1   The Intelligence Process

ISSUES IN ANALYSIS

Issues in analysis have been recognized since the concept was brought to the attention of law enforcement early in the 1970s. Godfrey and Harris note bluntly that "The Problem of the Non-Badged Employee" would be significant (1971, p. 68). The revised *Basic Elements of Intelligence* included a chapter (6) on managing a police intelligence unit that pointed out the difficulty in getting police to accept analysis or analysts. In it, Harris comments that "Police are usually more interested in enforcement action than in sedentary work (analysis). On the other hand, there are problems in hiring civilians. Police do not want to exchange information with non-badged personnel" (1976, p. 60). This comment is reflective of the prevailing police culture as a roadblock to the understanding of the value of analysis in policing. An ancillary point in this divergence from "normal" police culture is the fact that most analysts are women and thus face the challenges encountered by most women in policing.

Another issue is the appropriate level of education, experience, and training for analysts if they are, in fact, to be treated and valued as professionals in law enforcement. Why, too, are so many analysts resisting efforts to develop certification and standards?

Police management of analysts is another critical factor in the process of having analysis accepted within policing. Civilian analysts do not qualify for the promotions and "perks" of the officers. They quite often do not respond to military or paramilitary forms of management and organization. How then can they best be managed?

Technological advances have been rapid over the past decade in many fields, particularly in policing. From sophisticated surveillance systems to computers to telefax machines and cellular phones, law enforcement has generally embraced technology but has often failed to understand its intricacies. This chapter will discuss computer technology, how analysts support technological advances in law enforcement, and how technology supports enhanced analysis.

Finally, the role of analysis in community and problem-oriented policing is reviewed. In spite of many dollars and bodies that have been dedicated to these programs over the past six years, the analytical component is absent from most programs and may spell the difference between success and failure.

These five issues will be discussed in detail in this chapter. But first, we need to arrive at an understanding of what analysis is and what analysts do.

ANALYSTS IN LAW ENFORCEMENT

There are thousands of analysts working in law enforcement today. While many are employed by federal agencies in the United States (with the Drug Enforcement Administration, the Federal Bureau of Investigation, and the Financial Crimes Enforcement Network—FinCEN—for example), others are employed at regional, state, county, and municipal levels. Analysts work in law enforcement in other countries, too, including Canada, Australia, France, England, and Israel. While their job specifics may be as individual as their assignments, there are some basic similarities among analytical jobs.

WHAT ANALYSTS DO

Criminal analysis is "the application of particular analytical methods to data collected for the purpose of criminal investigation or criminal research" (Peterson, 1994, p. 1). It is an umbrella term which encompasses specific types of analysis used in law enforcement, the military, and private security: crime analysis, investigative (tactical intelligence) analysis, and strategic (intelligence) analysis.

The 1996 edition of the *Basic Elements of Intelligence* provides an overview of analysts' duties. These include

* reading and indexing incoming reports,
* developing and maintaining files and sources of information,
* identifying information requirements,
* performing research and analysis, and
* preparing intelligence reports (Harris, 1976, pp. 27–28).

Crime Analysis

Crime analysis is

> a set of systematic, analytical processes directed at providing timely and pertinent information relative to crime patterns and trend correlations to assist operational and administrative personnel in planning the deployment of resources for the prevention and suppression of criminal activities, aiding the investigative process, and increasing apprehensions and the clearance of cases (Gottlieb, Arenberg & Singh, 1994, p. 13).

Crime analysis is used, for example, to determine if a series of burglaries that occurred were done by the same or different perpetrator(s), when the perpetrator may strike again, and where. These predictions are based on a statistical analysis of the patterns and similarities among past burglaries. Obviously, the more incidents that have occurred, the more data are available and the more likely the prediction of future activity will be accurate.

Crime analysis methods include time series analysis, crime pattern analysis, correlation analysis, regression analysis, geographic analysis, and frequency distribution analysis. These methods are used to arrive at conclusions, predictions, and recommendations relating to the occurrence of series of crimes.

> *Illustration:*   One example of a crime analysis product would be a conclusion that local fast-food restaurants that were robbed were being targeted by a group of robbers who typically strike in the late evening on Friday nights. A geographic view of the locations of robberies already committed, along with the locations of other fast-food restaurants in the affected area (and its

immediately adjacent area) would point out to agency management the possible targets of future robberies. The accompanying analytical recommendation would be to deploy additional patrol cars in the areas near possible targets on the next Friday night to fit the temporal pattern. Thus, a robbery in progress might be stopped and the robbers arrested. Police could even use this knowledge to "harden" a particular target by stepping up police presence in other fast-food places while leaving one supposedly unprotected and thus draw the robbers to that location for a quick arrest.[1]

Agencies who employ crime analysts are most often municipal or county agencies with a patrol function. Crime analysis, in general, focuses on pre-arrest aspects of policing, rather than the investigative or prosecutive aspects. In some police departments, crime analysis is used to support community policing efforts and crime prevention programs.

The most visible sign of a crime analysis unit or function is the distribution of crime bulletins that show a picture or composite of a perpetrator, along with physical descriptors and information on the perpetrator's modus operandi (Fig. 8.2). These crime bulletins (also called BOLOs—Be On the Look Out) serve an important role in making both law enforcement and the public aware of emerging crime problems. Crime analysis has been in police departments for decades. The "wanted" posters of the nineteenth century were the forerunners of today's crime bulletins.

Investigative (Tactical) Analysis

Investigative analysis is "the analysis of data collected as part of an investigation of a criminal violation" (Peterson, 1994, p. 273). It is tactical-level analysis in that it supports the investigation and prosecution of a crime. It can include crime analysis methods as well, but it goes beyond the patterns of a crime to marshal the proof needed to solve the crime and convict the perpetrator.

Using the example of fast-food robbers in the crime analysis illustration above, the investigative analyst would carry on the analytical function after the robbers had been arrested. The analyst would be responsible for receiving, analyzing, and deriving meaning from all information collected during the investigation.

The types of data to be received could vary widely. For example, at the arrest scene, patrol officers or detectives would have taken statements from witnesses and possibly the robbers. Information on the identity of the perpetrators, their residences, their employment, etc. could have been collected. In an effort to recover losses from the string of robberies, the police would then search the residences of the perpetrators. Once there, they might uncover not only currency, but also records or other information that might expand the investigation. Drug paraphernalia might be in evidence. Financial records, which showed the deposit of monies shortly after previous robberies, might be found. Maps or notes might provide links between the group and

---

[1]John Douglas describes this phenomenon as used by the Federal Bureau of Investigation in serial bank robberies (1995, p. 64).

$1,000,000 REWARD

Call
UNABOMB Task Force
1-800-701-BOMB
(1-800-701-2662)

UNABOMB CRIMES

1. University of Illinois **(1 injured)**
   at Chicago, IL 5/25/78
2. Northwestern University, **(1 injured)**
   Evanston, IL 5/9/79
3. American Airlines, Flight 444, **(12 injured)**
   Chicago, IL 11/15/79
4. President United Airlines, **(1 injured)**
   Chicago, IL 6/10/80
5. University of Utah
   Salt Lake City, UT 10/8/81
6. Vanderbilt University, **(1 injured)**
   Nashville, TN 5/5/82
7. University of California, **(1 injured)**
   Berkeley, CA 7/2/82
8. Boeing Aircraft
   Auburn, WA 5/8/85

9. University of California **(1 injured)**
   Berkeley, CA 5/15/85
10. University of Michigan, **(2 injured)**
    Ann Arbor, MI 11/15/85
11. Rentech Company, **(1 death)**
    Sacramento, CA 12/11/85
12. CAAM's, Inc., **(1 injured)**
    Salt Lake City, UT 2/20/87
13. Physician/Researcher, **(1 injured)**
    Tiburon, CA 6/22/93
14. Professor, Yale University, **(1 injured)**
    New Haven, CT 6/24/93
15. Advertising Executive **(1 death)**
    North Caldwell, NJ 12/10/94
16. President, California Forestry Association **(1 death)**
    Sacramento, CA 4/24/95

Explosive devices have been either placed at or mailed to the above locations. This activity began in 1978 and has resulted in three deaths and 23 injuries. The last device was mailed in April of 1995 from Oakland, California.

The UNABOMB task force will pay a reward of up to $1,000,000 for information leading to the identification, arrest, and conviction of the person(s) responsible for placing or mailing explosive devices at the above locations.

Do you know the UNABOMBER?
Please contact the UNABOMB Task Force at 1-800-701-BOMB/1-800-701-2662.

Figure 8.2   Crime Information Bulletin

previous robberies in this or in other jurisdictions. Personal phone books showing links between this group and other, more organized groups might be found.

All of this information would have to be culled and reviewed by analysts for its impact on the prosecution of these robbers. The data might also help clear other similar crimes that have occurred. The uncovering of these linkages might alter the charges or sentence length of the perpetrators.

Investigative analysis uses a number of techniques, including: association analysis, telephone record analysis, event flow analysis, visual investigative analysis, commodity flow analysis, case analysis, bank record analysis, and corporate record analysis. Each of these is used to review and compare records that may give insight into the motivation for or nature of the perpetrator of the crime.

Investigative analysts are found in both enforcement and prosecutorial agencies, but primarily in the former. They are used at the state and federal level for the most part, and support major crime, narcotics, organized crime, environmental crime, and white-collar crime investigations. Investigative analysis has been developed for use in law enforcement over the past quarter-century. The most publicly visible products of investigative analysis are the charts and tables used to support grand jury and trial presentations by investigators and analysts (Figs. 8.3 and 8.4).

Illustration: One example of how analysis is used involved narcotic activity by a motorcycle gang in California. Analytical techniques, including visual investigative analysis, were used by employees of the California Department of Justice to summarize and graphically chart the illegal activities of the various members of a motorcycle gang involved in methamphetamine manufacture and distribution. The charts, along with analyst testimony in court, helped convict several motorcycle gang members.

In another example, a financial analysis helped uncover the hidden assets of principals involved in a case of stock fraud. The assets were traced through foreign corporations and bank accounts. The principals pleaded guilty prior to trial.

Strategic Analysis

Strategic analysis, on the other hand, looks beyond a specific investigation and at an overview of a crime problem or a crime group (Sommers, 1986, p. 31).

Again using our fast-food restaurant robberies as an example, the information gleaned from the crime analysis and tactical (investigative) analysis might be used to complete a strategic assessment of the fast-food robbery phenomenon. This assessment would look beyond the specific perpetrators and these violations for a look at the big picture.

A survey of police departments in the area might be done to determine whether they have similar occurrences. If so, what have they found out about the perpetrators, about the patterns of time, or geography, or date? Are these robberies a multijurisdictional problem? Are the victims always fast-food places, or are they sometimes convenience stores or gas stations? Do certain groups specialize in certain types

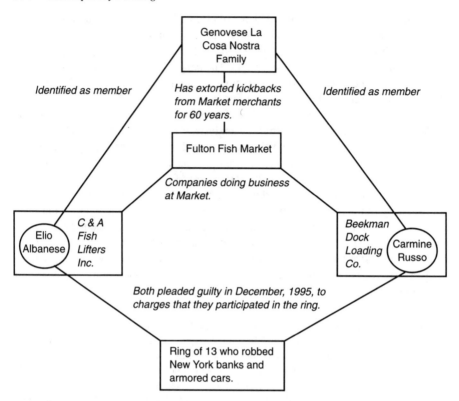

Figure 8.3   Association Chart (*Source:* Raab, Selwyn (12/31/95) "Two Fulton Market Loaders are Evicted." *New York Times,* pL-29).

of victims? What other types of crimes have the perpetrators been involved in? Are they drug dependent? What is the basis for their organization (blood relatives, neighbors, gang members, associated through school, prison, or work)?

What law enforcement techniques have been used to stop these types of robberies in other jurisdictions? How effective have they been? Is displacement a factor?

What types of crime prevention techniques have been used? What was their effectiveness? What might be changed in the operations of the fast-food/convenience stores/gas stations or in the operations of police to prevent these crimes? In other words, what could be done to deal with the overall problem of these types of robberies, as opposed to the symptoms of one, two, or four robberies? What solutions to the problem could there be? Are they law enforcement solutions, or multidisciplinary solutions? In short, strategic analysis is problem-solving policing, done at either a micro or macro level.

The concept of strategic analysis was derived from analysis done on the national and international level, but then applied to larger crime groups and problems (La Cosa Nostra, Colombian cartels, etc.). It has been performed primarily within national agencies (Federal Bureau of Investigation, Drug Enforcement Administration, U.S.

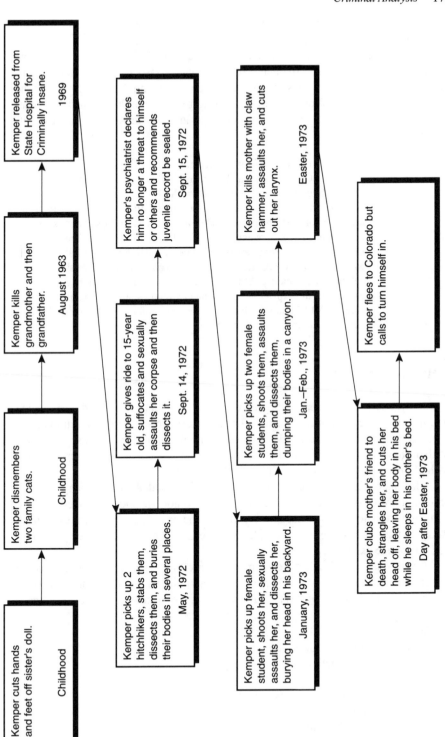

Figure 8.4 Flow of Homicides by Edward Kemper (*Source:* Douglas & Oleshaker. *Mindhunter*, pp. 106–9).

Marshal's Service) and in a few state-level enforcement agencies, such as the California Department of Justice.

Its methods and techniques may include those found in crime or investigative analysis (statistical analyses, frequency distributions, or association charts, for example) but its purpose gives these products different meaning. They help gather the information in support of long-range solutions, rather than imminent arrests or prosecutions. The most visible products of strategic analysis have been government-produced organized crime reports.

Illustration: Strategic Analysis—Threat Assessment

"While La Cosa Nostra may be battered and ailing, it is premature to write LCN's obituary. Overall, the decade of the 1990s may see a Cosa Nostra that is restructured to exclude high-profile 'Godfather' crime leaders who are easily targeted and prosecuted. It may see a Cosa Nostra that is more decentralized and more entrepreneurial than ever. . . . It may see an even more secret core organization, engaging in wider use of non-Italian associates. . . . It may see the LCN evolving into an even more diversified multinational conglomerate than it presently is . . . Pennsylvania may experience the expanding involvement within its borders not only of the New York LCN families but of the Sicilian Mafia as well" (Pennsylvania Crime Commission, 1991, p. 188).

WHO ANALYSTS ARE

Generally, analysts are people with degrees from four-year colleges who have good writing and oral communication skills. Their degrees are sometimes in criminal justice, but also can be in other social sciences, journalism, pre-law, or business. Some of them have less schooling and some more; master's degrees are common, along with a sprinkling of doctorates (Peterson, 1993, p. 51).

The range of education held by analysts is quite broad. Although many agencies require analysts to have college degrees, others promote people out of clerical positions into analytical ones or use sworn officers who have become partially disabled. Analysts may have only two-year college degrees, and a minority of analysts have had no college experience.

Godfrey and Harris identified some traits useful to analysts: a strong sense of integrity, a high intellectual level, an objective and innovative mind, and a thirst for self-education (1971, pp. 60–61). That list is further expanded by Frost to include

- intellectual curiosity,
- rapid assimilation of information,
- keen recall of information,
- tenacity,
- willingness and capacity to make judgments,
- developed writing ability,
- initiative and self-direction,

- effective personal interaction, and
- disciplined intellectual courage (Frost, 1985, pp. 6–7).

Entrance-level testing has been devised by some agencies for potential analytical hires. An average test could include writing and summarization skills, logic and inference-drawing abilities, and simple charting. No standardized testing has been developed and used by a number of agencies. According to Frost, the Central Intelligence Agency looked at giving personality tests to potential analysts but was not convinced that "such personality tests would be a useful tool for selecting persons for employment as analysts" (Frost, 1985, p. 9).

It is presumed that most entry-level analysts will need training on analytical techniques and methods, since few colleges (most notably Northeastern Missouri State University also known as Truman University, the University of Michigan, and Mercyhurst College in Erie, Pennsylvania) offer analytical classes as part of a specialization in research and intelligence. Most colleges have not yet added applied research to their criminal justice curricula although this has been recommended.

The training that is provided to new analytical hires includes segments on the intelligence process, association analysis, telephone record analysis, inference development, event flow analysis, net worth (financial) analysis, and visual investigative analysis. This training is available through agencies such as the Federal Law Enforcement Training Center in Glynco, Georgia or the New Jersey Department of Law and Public Safety in Trenton and through private vendors. Basic analytical training can last from three days to two weeks. Some federal agencies provide initial training to their analysts which can last several weeks. Some of the additional time is spent teaching the analysts how to use the in-house computer software for varied database and analytic purposes.

As a person progresses within the analytical field, additional training is available on specialized computer programs, strategic analysis, in-depth financial analysis, varied crime groups' activities, and other areas. These are often provided on an ad hoc basis, with the exception of courses developed by Anacapa Sciences (computerized analysis and financial analysis) which are available several times a year. No ongoing curriculum for advanced analytical training has been developed and accepted as standard.

One notable agency, the Royal Canadian Mounted Police (RCMP), has assembled an "Intelligence Analyst Understudy Course" for its analysts, whereby they must take certain courses and meet certain benchmarks over the 20–24 months of their employment (RCMP, 1994, p. iv). This program includes not only basic analytical training, but also report writing, presenting evidence in court, a mock trial, and various areas of specialty study.

ISSUES

There are a number of issues relating to the use of analysis and analysts in law enforcement. Among them are police culture, professionalism and standards, police management, technological advancement, and the emergence of community or problem-oriented policing.

Police Culture

The largest roadblock to analysts' being accepted as equal working members in police agencies is the clash in cultures that ensues when they begin to work with the investigative (and prosecutive) staff. Part of this is because analysts are usually female and non-sworn, and part of it is because of the lesser value placed on research-oriented work in police agencies.

The traditional police culture has valued physical strength over mental acumen and male attributes over female traits (Ortiz & Peterson, 1994). Recruits are indoctrinated with these cultural biases–including suspicion of non-police and resistance to all forms of non-technological innovation–during basic police training, and they are further reinforced on the job (Skolnick & Bayley, 1988).

Even in 1995, few police departments required a college degree as a hiring standard. Female police officers are still in the minority and are often placed in "soft" assignments, such as domestic abuse, drug education, or sex crimes units.

Resistance to change is a part of police culture. The weight of police experience and procedures drives the traditions forward and makes it difficult for change to occur. Part of this resistance comes from "bureaucratic administration personnel who have been able to do their jobs comfortably and mechanically for many years" (Sparrow, 1988, p. 7). Other resistance comes from those who feel threatened by the new views.

Work attributes that generally have had negative value in police work, such as innovation, specialization, and nonconformity, are requirements in analytical work. The experienced analyst knows that every set of facts is different and that the data should drive the analysis and response, not "the way we've always done it."

Analysts have been solitary creatures in a police environment (with the notable exceptions of the Financial Crimes Enforcement Network and the National Drug Intelligence Center, where analysts outnumber investigative personnel). In many cases, police officers have not welcomed analysts or analytical expertise with open arms. The work of analysts has been suspect, ignored, or even "stolen." Investigators loathe being upstaged by analysts who, because of their organizational abilities, can convey the gist of the case more easily than the investigators.

In 1971, Godfrey and Harris suggest teaming analysts and investigators in a "direct confrontation technique" to break down the barriers between them. This would only be effective, they note, if the analysts "rapidly prove their mettle" by providing substantive products in support of the investigation (p. 68). This has been done in several agencies, with mixed results.

Additional resistance comes from the officers' antipathy toward work that does not produce immediate arrests. "When intelligence is perceived as a 'research' effort, as opposed to an enforcement adjunct, it is generally afforded low status . . ."

(Martens, 1990, p. 5). In other words, analysis in support of arrests or prosecutions is more apt to be accepted than is a strategic analysis.

Even in agencies where analysts do provide valuable products in support of an investigation or prosecution, friction occurs if investigators view the analyst as trying to take over a case or do work that the investigator would normally do. This leads to less use of analysts by some investigators, but more use by others who are willing to accept the help the analysts can give. Ironically, some investigators who are better educated and more inclined toward analytic work themselves may be the most resistant to analyst assistance because they feel their methods of analysis are better.

Police Training and Analysis

Training is the key ingredient to changing culture within organizations (General Accounting Office, 1992). This is true because training tells the employees what the organization considers to be important and what skills and attributes the organization values.

Traditional police training has emphasized physical conditioning, the law, standard operating procedures (SOPs), and weaponry/self-defense. While each of these is critical to policing, these skills alone do not support the development of an officer working in today's police environment.

Police officers need to develop analytic and problem-solving skills. The emphasis on community-oriented, problem-solving policing requires officers who can identify problems and find solutions. This means going beyond the SOPs. Analytic and problem-solving skills include learning how to collect information, analyze it, and draw conclusions upon which recommendations can be based.

If the perception of police officers relative to analysis is to be changed, it will be through training and education of those officers. Analysis, in its simplest form, should be part of the training provided to recruits. Some agencies (such as the New Jersey Division of Criminal Justice) have a basic police course, required for all county and state investigators, which includes a 3-hour segment on analysis. Analysis should be a component of all investigative and management courses given in law enforcement. Regardless of the type of investigation or management, analytical skills are applicable.

Women in Policing

Not too many years ago, the roles of women in policing were limited primarily to clerical support. The advent of female officers has been mostly driven by affirmative action requirements, rather than a belief by police organizations that they are valuable additions to the staff.

Conversely, most analysts have been women, just as most analysts are civilians who have been paid less and have existed outside the power structure in police agencies. Thus, the role of many analysts in law enforcement has been doubly hexed—female and civilian.

Curiously, the fact that analysts are women has given them a greater degree of acceptance in some police agencies. Officers who look at the information collation and analysis function as "busy work" are more than happy to have it performed by women. They are thus relieved from tedious work.

In other cases, male officers may feel less threatened by female analysts than male ones, whose goal may be to become investigators, and thus competitors. (This may not be the case, however, when the female analysts are aggressive and experienced and may step on male egos by appearing more knowledgeable about the case than the investigating officer.)

As women have become more numerous in law enforcement agencies, however, the varied set of skills that they bring to the job have become more accepted. While it does not seem that law enforcement will ever be considered anything other than a man's field, women are bound to play an increasing role as those women who are already in place go through the ranks to become police managers.

Analysts as Specialists in Law Enforcement

Historically, police personnel are rotated through varied job assignments to create police generalists. This practice is consistent with the Japanese theory of personnel management in which the employees become experts in the company rather than in an area of the company's work. This is believed to support the retention of employees as they do not develop a specialty which can be easily transferred to another company. As Martens notes: "The current ethos prevailing among most law enforcement executives is that any police officer can do any police task" (1990, p. 16). This management style builds strong organizations rather than strong individuals.

Analysts, on the other hand, are by nature specialists. Their value lies in their complete knowledge of crime groups, local criminal activity, or the investigative use of specific computer programs. Martens continues: "The professionalism of the criminal intelligence function demands a rejection of this philosophy. Specialists are an inevitable by-product of advancing knowledge . . ." (1990, p. 16).

Analysts are often unique in their law enforcement setting, among only a few persons with that training, background, and knowledge. They cannot be replaced by any of several dozen investigators if they are transferred or leave the agency. It is for this reason that alternate means of rewarding and acknowledging analysts must be found to keep them on the job. One method of motivating analysts with several years of experience may be to rotate them to another assignment. This gives them the opportunity to learn a new set of approaches and sharpen alternate analytical skills, based on the requirements of that particular assignment. One detraction from analytical ability is the tendency, over time, to "template" analytical products or responses. Moving to another investigative area every five years or so might help combat that complacency level.

Professionalism and Standards for Analysts

Policing, with its blue-collar background and dislike of academics, has been striving toward professionalization for several years. Likewise, analysis, with its mix of academics and former clerical personnel, has also been attempting to raise its standards and become recognized as more professional. To achieve this, several organizations and certification programs have been initiated.

Organizations

As the analytical community has grown, so have the groups that serve analysts. The largest analytical organization, the International Association of Law Enforcement Intelligence Analysts (IALEIA) has a mission to "advance high standards of professionalism in law enforcement intelligence analysis at the local, state, national and international levels" (*Bylaws,* Article II, Section 1). It strives to do this through providing training, a professional journal, networking, and professional awards. Committees work to develop curricula, adopt standards, and consult with law enforcement management.[2]

A smaller analytic group, the International Association of Crime Analysts (IACA), has common goals with IALEIA but has worked, primarily, within the crime analysis community. It also holds training conferences and provides networking and other benefits to its members.[3]

Professional groups are somewhat hindered by the fact that many analysts are individualistic and not "joiners." Additionally, many of them who do join are content to receive the benefits from the organization but are loath to work for the organization. The *IALEIA Journal* is a case in point. The majority of the articles submitted and published have come from academics who are not members of the organization. Few IALEIA members have written and submitted articles. The constant complaint from the membership, however, is that the articles are too academically oriented.

Certifications

In recent years, there has been a movement toward adopting standards and certification for analysts, as a means toward the ends of quality control and status as professionals. Two certification programs have been developed. One, the Society of Certified Criminal Analysts (SCCA), offers international certification and is affiliated with IALEIA. The other, Certificate in Crime and Intelligence Analysis (CCIA), is available through certain California colleges and the California Department of Justice, and it has been affiliated with IACA.

---

[2]IALEIA can be reached at P.O. Box 2924, Miami, Florida, 33152.
[3]IACA can be reached through its president, Mark Stallo, at the Dallas, Texas Police Department (214) 670-4539.

The Society of Certified Criminal Analysts offers regular and lifetime certifications for analysts. The dividing factor is level of education and experience. Applicants for regular certification must have at least two years of college, be working as an analyst (or have worked for three years as an analyst) and have taken basic analytical training, must take a 5-hour examination including both objective questions (200) and a practical exam, and be approved by the Board of Governors.

Applicants for lifetime certification must have at least four years of college, have 10 years of analytical experience, have taken basic analytical training, and be approved by the Board of Governors. Several dozen persons have been certified under this program.[4]

The California CCIA program is not organization-based, but was developed by a crime analyst who teaches analytical courses in local colleges and then adopted by the California Department of Justice. This program requires the applicant to complete six courses in intelligence, crime, and behavioral analysis (psychological profiling) given at certain California colleges, along with a 400-hour practicum (internship). They are then given a certificate from the college and qualify for certification by the California Department of Justice. The courses given in the colleges are generally non-credit courses. Week-long versions of some of these courses have been presented in other states, making possible the adoption of this certification program in other areas by other state certifying boards. The number of persons completing this certification program has also been small, possibly due to the length of time needed to take the required courses.[5]

Alternately, it could be hypothesized that the limited interest in certification could be a result of the limited potential for professional advancement. If the analyst views his or her job as stagnant, then certification, except for personal satisfaction, has no value. On the other hand, if future advancement in that or another agency is possible and desired, then certification becomes a resume-builder.

Some agencies have moved to add certification to their qualifications for hire or promotion, including the Riverside, California Sheriff's Office (CCIA) and the Royal Canadian Mounted Police (SCCA). Once a critical mass of analysts has been certified by either program, it will become imperative for most analysts to be certified, because agencies will recognize it as a standard and will require it of their employees.

Documentation

As was noted earlier, personnel in police agencies adhere, sometimes rigidly, to standard operating procedures. One difficulty, therefore, that faces analysts in a police environment is the lack of routinely standardized, documented analytical procedures.

One of the attributes of the analytic process is that it is data-driven; that is, the information available dictates what techniques will be used and what products will

---

[4]The SCCA can be reached by writing to P. O. Box 583, Purchase, New York, 10577.
[5]The California Certification program was developed by Steve Gottlieb, who can be reached in suburban Los Angeles, California (909) 989-4366.

result. To date, no work has been published that categorizes analytic methods in an "if this fact pattern occurs, then that analytic method should be used" manner.

Individual intelligence analysis processes such as telephone record analysis, strategic analysis, link charting, and visual investigative analysis have been detailed by various authors (Andrews & Peterson, 1990; Morris, 1982; Federal Bureau of Investigation, undated). These pieces have not, however, been brought together in a coherent whole. Crime analysis techniques were for the first time detailed by Gottlieb in his 1995 book, but again as processes rather than as formalized templates.

This lack of documentation across the analytic field provides an opportunity for those in the field to produce documentation and thereby contribute to the field. Efforts to standardize techniques in an SOP manner, however, will be resisted by analysts as it is contrary to their innovative nature.

Training

There has been slightly more standardization of analytic training than there has been of procedures. As was mentioned earlier, basic training for federal, state, and local intelligence analysts in the United States is available through agencies like the Federal Law Enforcement Training Center in Glynco, Georgia, and through private vendors such as Anacapa Sciences. The latter has been providing intelligence analytic training since the 1970s and its basic course has become the informal standard.

No standardized course for crime analysis has yet been developed. One vendor of crime analysis training, the Alpha Group of Montclair, California, has been providing that training over the past several years on an occasional basis because the principal of Alpha has been employed as a crime analyst in a law enforcement agency. Likewise, no course in strategic analysis has been given often enough to be considered standard, nor have any advanced analytic courses been developed and given over a period of years or for a variety of agencies. That which has passed for advanced training has often been the demonstration of proprietary software in particular analytic applications.

Again, the lack of standardization of training and processes provides an opportunity for contribution by many people in the field. As documentation and training expand, it would be expected that non-analysts within policing would have a greater understanding of its value and processes. In fact, most of the people who take analytical training are not analysts, but are investigators and investigative supervisors. Few attorneys have studied analysis and this component also needs development.

Police Management of Analysts

The management of an analytical unit has been a difficult task since the inception of the analytical function in law enforcement. Police managers are taught to manage in the paramilitary style. Direct orders are given. Tasks assigned are generally repetitious and not complex. Evaluations are also standardized and generally quantifiable—that is, based on numbers of tickets or arrests produced.

Analysts do not respond well to military-style management or supervision. Their evaluations need to reflect the work products they produce. Some suggestions regarding effective supervision and evaluation of analysts follow. Yet, as Martens notes, "the success of the intelligence function is dependent upon a strong managerial commitment and the availability of a skilled cadre of intelligence officers/analysts. It must be perceived as a management tool . . . " (1990, p. 17). Thus, it is in the interest of police managers to embrace analysis and to know how to use it.

Supervision

Analysts do not respond well to orders or to SOPs. They are generally creative, intelligent people whose intellectual curiosity does not end at the borders of an assignment. They are more apt to ask why an officer wants them to do something than how to do it (they question authority figures).

The most pressing problem in managing analysts is in knowing how to guide their analytical work if the manager is a law enforcement officer with no analytical training or experience. This is not an impossible task, but it is daunting.

Most analysts have had supervisors or managers who have no knowledge of analysis. These individuals can range from overly supervisory (requesting status reports or products on a daily basis) to almost completely *laissez-faire*.

The best managers allow the analysts to do their jobs independently, while giving them some deadlines by which to complete the tasks. In addition, it is helpful for the analyst to know which case(s) is a priority, since they are often assigned to several cases at one time with competing time constraints.

Analytic training is available for police managers, through Anacapa Sciences or such agencies as the New Jersey Department of Law and Public Safety. People assigned to supervise or manage analysts would do well to take training if it is available or read a text on analysis that will give them an overview of it. The reference book, *Applications in Criminal Analysis* (Peterson, 1995), was designed to be read by police management and provide them with an overview of analytical work.

Evaluation

Evaluating analysts presents a difficulty in itself. Traditional police measures of success—arrests and convictions (also known as "the body count")—do not always directly result from analysis.

Trying to attribute value to the products and conclusions/recommendations of an analysis is a difficult task. An investigative lead uncovered through an analysis of bank records may, alternatively, have been uncovered through investigative interviews or other data collection. The recommendations made during a strategic analysis may or may not be followed by management. Even an analytical chart used to display evidence in the courtroom is only part of the winning prosecutive package.

Some agencies have chosen to ignore the challenge of evaluating analysts properly by using investigative (or even clerical) standards to evaluate them or by not evaluating them at all. Other agencies, more analytically based, have developed performance standards which include completing a certain number of products during the year or supporting a certain number of cases. When the latter is done, allowances have to be made for the complexity as well as the quantity of the cases or analyses.

No standardized methodology to evaluate analysts has been developed that is used across a variety of agencies or levels of government. This level of standardization is not necessary, but the development of some valid evaluation criteria is.

Technological Advancement and Analysis

A decade ago, police files were viewed as graveyards of old cases and criminal history record information. Today, more and more police agencies recognize that the vast majority of police business centers on the collection, storage, analysis, and dissemination of information. What is an investigation if it is not the collection of all the facts (data)? What is the determination of guilt if it is not an analysis of those facts—disseminated by law enforcement—by a judge or jury? As Meyer notes, "to achieve your objectives in a fast-paced, multinational, information-driven world like ours, you need to know . . . as much as possible about what's going on—and what's likely to go on . . . " (1988, p. 5).

Analysis is impacted by—and impacts—technological advances in policing. Following are a few ways this occurs.

Information Management

Today's police files are (or should be) interactive, working partners in the job to be done. Information is not just stored. It is stored so that it will be easily retrievable under all variations of search criteria that may arise. It is stored so that it can be combined and recombined with information from both public and law enforcement sources. Law enforcement managers and policy makers need analyzed data on which to base their decisions.

Sixteen years ago, computers were beyond the reach of all but federal and state police agencies. The state agencies that had computers then (mostly state police with uniform crime reporting and criminal history record-keeping responsibilities) devoted large, dust-free rooms to massive mainframe "boxes."

Today, the capabilities of a system that cost $100,000 in 1983 can be purchased for $3,000. Personal computers, connected through local area networks (LANs) is the preferred mode of computing. Laptop computers, which can be carried into the field, into briefings, or into training, have become almost as prevalent as cellular telephones.

Every aspect of policing has been influenced by computers, and analysis is no exception. The 3 × 5 card method of analytic compiling has been replaced by relational databases holding up to tens of thousands of records. While this has provided ease of data manipulation, it has created other work, because data banks are now taken on that would have previously been unthinkable. And while these "magic boxes" compile the data, it must still be analyzed by real people.

In some agencies, computers are viewed as machines which not only arrange information, but analyze it. In most cases, this is incorrect because computers are merely machines which can respond to commands programmed into it, but cannot think or intuit. Thus, agencies that initiate computerization without having analysts or investigators with analytical training to work with the computer often receive poorer information than they need. Over the last decade, law enforcement agencies have spent millions of dollars on computer systems that could not be used because the agency did not understand its needs or the capabilities of the machine. In this regard, analysts can also serve as translators who understand the needs of law enforcement and can communicate them to computer hardware and software vendors.

Computers as Analytic Tools

A symbiosis between computer software and analysis has developed out of the technological growth spawned by computers. Analysts generally have to be adept at technology since the basis of their work is information collection, management, and retrieval. They need to be conversant with how computers are used to support investigations and prosecutions through data bases (Fig. 8.5) and spreadsheets (Fig. 8.6). They know how to use the computer to arrange information in formats that are more easily understood by nontechnical people (Fig. 8.7).

They know how to use the retrieval and sorting capabilities of the computer to provide specialized reports that highlight the important data and they can easily adapt this knowledge to developing results-tracking systems that can support budget justification, manpower expansion, and annual reports.

Numerous vendors of computer software have developed programs that can assist analysts in their processes. Some involve database management, others graphics, others reporting formats, while some combine several functions to allow for automatic creation of charts from database information.

Like many computer environments, however, the reality of analytic work is far less than the possibility. State and local police agencies cannot afford much of the analytic software that is being developed. Thus, as technology advances, law enforcement gets further and further behind due to obsolescence and budget realities.

Community Policing/Problem-Oriented Policing

Community and problem-oriented policing are viewed as the underpinnings of a new era of police organization (Kelling & Moore, 1988, p. 23). Mastrofski says that "community policing . . . (is a) significant departure from the ways in which issues of role,

Name 1	Name 2	Link	Ref. #
Albanese, Elio	C & A Fish Lifters, Inc.	Owner	9
Russo, Carmine	Beekman Dock Loading Co.	Owner	9
Albanese, Elio	Genovese La Cosa Nostra	Soldier	12
Russo, Carmine	Genovese La Cosa Nostra	Soldier	14
C & A Fish Lifters	Fulton Market	Operates at	1
Beekman Dock Loading	Fulton Market	Operates at	1
Genovese LCN	Fulton Market	Kickbacks extorted 60 yrs.	15
Albanese, Elio	Ring of 13 bank robbers	Pled guilty to participating	3&4
Russo, Carmine	Ring of 13 bank robbers	Pled guilty to participating	3&4
	The database is used to extract facts from written documents		
	The "ref.#" in this case is the number of the paragraph in the		
	newspaper story.		

Figure 8.5 Database for Fulton Fish Market Chart (*Source:* Raab, Selwyn (12/31/95) "Two Fulton Market Loaders are Evicted." *New York Times*, pL_29).

Payee	Date	Ck.#	Amount	A/C#	Memo	Comments
AT&T	10/4/95	1342	$52.18	150-32-64971	555-0987	
	11/3/95	1648	$48.15	150-32-64971		
	12/6/95	1922	$39.92	150-32-64971		
			$140.25			
Cash	10/1/95	1335	$500.00	150-32-64971		
	10/15/95	1490	$200.00	150-32-64971		
	10/29/95	1553	$400.00	150-32-64971		
	11/12/95	1687	$300.00	150-32-64971		
	11/26/95	1734	$400.00	150-32-64971		
	12/10/95	1958	$500.00	150-32-64971		
	12/24/95	2055	$1,000.00	150-32-64971		Christmas
	12/31/95	2121	$1,000.00	150-32-64971		A. City trip
			$4,300.00			
Delaware National VISA	10/4/95		$150.00	150-32-64971		
	11/3/95		$200.00	150-32-64971		
	12/6/95		$250.00	150-32-64971		
			$600.00			
Hamilton Bank	10/1/95		$978.31	150-32-64971	Mortgage	
	11/1/95		$978.31	150-32-64971	Mortgage	
	12/1/95		$978.31	150-32-64971		
			$2,934.93			

Motorland	12/10/95	$3,000.00	150-32-64971	dep. 93 Honda										
		$3,000.00												
Princeton Jewelers	12/15/95	$1,254.32	150-32-64971	Marissa										
		$1,254.32												
Reston Inn	11/13/95	$623.11	150-32-64971	4 nights										
		$623.11												
		$12,852.61												
	The amounts and other information on the checks													
	are entered and then sorted and totalled to indicate													
	how much each payee receives from the account.													

Figure 8.6 Spreadsheet

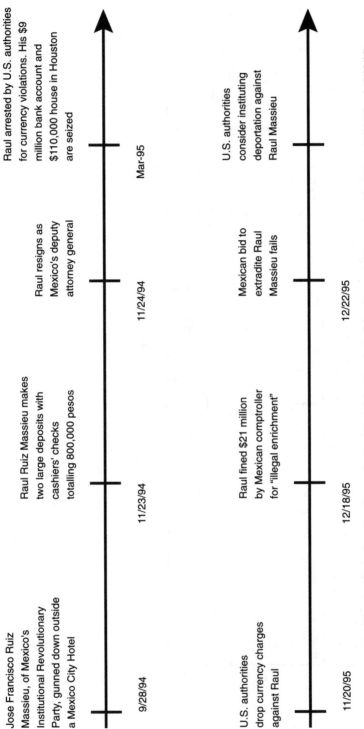

Figure 8.7 Timeline of Actions Leading to the Raul Ruiz Massieu Extradition Attempt (*Source:* Associated Press, 12/22/95 and 12/23/95).

control and legitimacy are expressed . . . policies and actions are justified . . . in terms of the sense of peace, order and security they impart" (1988, p. 47). Goldstein notes that problem-oriented policing focuses on "the problems that constitute the business of the police and how they handle them" (1990, p. 32).

As community and problem-solving policing were designed in the United States, analysis plays a critical role in both. One early version of problem-oriented policing became known as the S.A.R.A. model—Survey, Analysis, Response, and Assessment (Eck & Spelman, 1987). In Canada, a similar model called C.A.P.R.A. has evolved (Client, Analysis, Partnership, Response, Assessment).

In spite of the COP/POP design, many departments do not use analysts to support community policing efforts, nor do they train the community policing officers in analytic techniques and methods. The analysis of problems, using developed analytic methodologies should be standard operating procedures within agencies subscribing to community policing.

> Problem-solving policing implies an analytical macro approach to policing, in which violations are viewed as part of a larger problem rather than as discrete incidents. This requires the integration of the analytical function into policing . . ." (Ortiz & Peterson, 1994, p. 68).

Ultimately, the process of problem-oriented policing could and should be adopted at all levels of law enforcement.

CONCLUSIONS: POLICE ANALYSIS IN THE FUTURE

Analysis could be even more essential to law enforcement operations in the future. As the level of education by police in general rises, more acceptance for research-oriented methodologies will also rise. As more colleges and universities teach courses that explain the uses of analysis within law enforcement, more officers will come on the job with some ability to use analysis in their day-to-day police work.

More police officers will use analytic techniques and more police organizations will hire or use analysts. As the current generation of analysts retires, they will become available as consultants to smaller departments that cannot afford to hire their own analysts. Private law firms will hire analysts to support their major cases. Private security (from major corporations to security firms) will use analysts on their investigations.

With acceptance comes the institution of more standards, standardized training, and documentation. The more analysis is used, the more its value will be seen and the more impetus there will be to create higher status jobs for experienced analysts.

Analysts will be accepted as part of the team—lawyers/investigators/detective-analysts—that get the job done right. The issues described in this chapter will not disappear and others may arise. But analysis will play its critical role in effective law enforcement.

DISCUSSION QUESTIONS

1. Discuss what impact you think requiring police recruits to have four-year college degrees would have on their acceptance of criminal analysts as co-workers.
2. Given the role that analysts play in policing, what career paths would you think appropriate for their advancement in law enforcement?
3. Discuss the pros and cons of having civilian versus sworn analysts.
4. Name three ways in which computers have affected analytical work and express your opinion on the use of computers in police work.
5. Discuss the concept of policing as an information-driven concern.
6. Suggest topics for police training that would alter the police culture in favor of supporting analysis and technology.

REFERENCES

Andrews, P.P., Jr., & Peterson, M.B. (1990). *Criminal intelligence analysis.* Loomis, CA: Palmer Press.

Bylaws (1981). International Association of Law Enforcement Intelligence Analysists. South Florida, FL.

Eck, J., & Spelman, W. (1987). *Problem-oriented policing in Newport News.* Washington, D.C.: National Institute of Justice.

Federal Bureau of Investigation (undated). *Visual investigative analysis.* Washington, D.C.: U.S. Department of Justice.

Frost, C.C. (1985). Choosing good intelligence analysts: What's measurable? *Law Enforcement Intelligence Analysis Digest, 1*(1), 1–7.

General Accounting Office. (1992). *Organizational culture techniques companies use to perpetuate or change beliefs and values.* Washington, D.C.: U.S. General Accounting Office.

Godfrey, E.D., & Harris, D.R. (1971, November). *Basic elements of intelligence.* Washington, D.C.: Law Enforcement Assistance Administration.

Goldstein, H. (1990). *Problem-oriented policing.* Philadelphia: Temple University Press.

Gottlieb, S., Arenberg, S., & Singh, R. (1994). *Crime analysis: From first report to final arrest.* Montclair, CA: Alpha Publishing.

Harris, R.D. (1976). *Basic elements of intelligence—Revised.* Washington, D.C.: Law Enforcement Assistance Administration.

Kelling, G.L., & Moore, M.H. (1988). From political to reform to community: The evolving strategy of police. In J.R. Greene & S.D. Mastrofski (Eds.), *Community policing: Rhetoric or reality?* Westport, CT: Praeger.

Martens, F.T. (1990). The intelligence function. In P.P. Andrews, Jr. & M.B. Peterson (Eds.), *Criminal intelligence analysis.* Loomis, CA: Palmer Press.

Mastrofski, S.D. (1988). Community policing as reform: A cautionary tale. In J.R. Greene & S.D. Mastrofski (Eds.), *Community policing: Rhetoric or reality?* Westport, CT: Praeger.

Meyer, H.E. (1988). *Real world intelligence.* New York: Weidenfeld & Nicholson.

Morris, J. (1982). *Crime analysis charting.* Orangevale, CA: Palmer Press.

Ortiz, R.L., & Peterson, M.B. (1994, August). Police culture: A roadblock to organizational change? *Police Chief,* pp. 68–71.

Pennsylvania Crime Commission. (1991). *1990 report: Organized crime in Pennsylvania: A decade of change.* Conshohocken, PA: Pennsylvania Crime Commission.

Peterson, M.B. (1993, Summer). Analysts in the '90s: An IALEIA survey. *IALEIA Journal, 8*(1).

———. (1994). *Applications of criminal analysis: A sourcebook.* Westport, CT: Greenwood Press.

———. (1995, October). The professional law enforcement analyst. In *Intelligence—Into the 21st century* (Issues of interest to law enforcement), pp. 29–34, 51, 52. Sacramento, CA: Law Enforcement Intelligence Unit.

Royal Canadian Mounted Police. (1994). *Criminal intelligence analyst understudy course training standard.* Ottawa, Canada: Royal Canadian Mounted Police, Criminal Intelligence Directorate.

Skolnick, J.H., & Bayley, D. (1988). Community policing: Issues and practices around the world. In *NIJ Issues and Practices.* Washington, D.C.: National Institute of Justice.

Sommers, M.P. (1986). Law enforcement intelligence: A new look. *International journal of intelligence and counter-intelligence 1*(3), 25–40.

Sparrow, M. (1994). *Informing enforcement.* Westport, CT: Praeger.

———. (1988). Implementing community policing. *Perspectives in policing.* Washington, D.C.: National Institute of Justice.

9

Community Policing: Major Issues and Unanswered Questions

Arthur J. Lurigio, Loyola University of Chicago
Dennis P. Rosenbaum, University of Illinois at Chicago

We are entering a new era in policing, one in which both community leaders and reform-minded police administrators are demanding significant changes in the form and function of law enforcement agencies. Under pressure to make police officers more effective at solving neighborhood problems, at mobilizing community residents and institutions, and at preventing crime and disorder, police organizations today have elected to discard traditional structures, policies, and crime control strategies in favor of new approaches. These include experimenting with novel ways to select, deploy, supervise, and promote agency personnel under the rubric of community policing. Whether the reign of community policing will be recorded in the history books as another failed experiment in policing or whether it will produce lasting organizational reforms that significantly improve the quality of police services, remains to be seen. In the meantime, there are important questions to be asked about community policing: Is it conceptually sound (based on prior theory, research, and experience)? Can it be successfully translated from theory into practice? What kinds of positive and negative effects will community policing have on police departments, police officers, and citizens?

This chapter is about community policing and its impact on police officers. It is divided into three major sections. The first provides an overview of community policing, describing what it is as well as its various definitions and intended benefits. The second discusses the purported effects of community policing on officers; it reviews the literature on the topic and focuses on three case studies on the impact of community policing on police officers in Chicago, Aurora, and Joliet, Illinois. The third summarizes research findings and discusses their implications for community policing practices and police organizations.

INTRODUCTION TO COMMUNITY POLICING

Police departments have long been blamed for their inability to control crime and for their poor relationships with citizens. In response to these criticisms, attempts have been made to improve police responses and effectiveness through a variety of innovations and reforms. Included have been efforts to professionalize the police, to establish police–community relations units, to adapt increasingly sophisticated technological equipment to policing, and to experiment with new and modified strategies of policing (e.g., team policing, preventive patrol, and directed patrol). These initiatives have had beneficial effects on policing but rather limited success in relieving crime problems, improving community relations, or eliminating criticisms of the police. Therefore, a search for a solution to rectify these problems continues in many police departments. The most current attempt to eliminate these problems has been through projects falling under the heading of community policing. According to Sparrow,

> The concept of community policing envisages a police department striving for an absence of crime and disorder and concerned with, and sensitive to, the quality of life in the community. It perceives the community as an agent and partner in promoting security rather than as a passive audience (1988, p.1).

Community policing includes approaches to solving community problems through police-initiated, cooperative relationships between police officers and community members. In particular, the focus of such approaches is on community problems related to quality of life issues.

Community policing programs have been implemented or are being implemented in many major cities, such as Seattle; Portland, Oregon; Philadelphia; Los Angeles; Baltimore County, Maryland; San Jose, California; Chicago; and New York. The trend is not restricted to large cities. Smaller cities, such as Newport News, Virginia; McAllen, Texas; Elgin, Aurora, and Joliet, Illinois, to name just a few, are also embracing community policing. Reports from these cities include improvements in police–citizen relations, reductions in citizen fear, and less crime (McElroy, Cosgrove & Sadd, 1993; Rosenbaum, 1994a; Sparrow, Moore & Kennedy, 1990; Trojanowicz & Bucqueroux, 1990).

The preliminary success of community policing in the aforementioned cities has led other police departments to implement similar strategies. However, the implementation of community policing projects or strategies can be very difficult (Murphy, 1988; Roberg, 1994; Sparrow, 1988; Sparrow, Moore & Kennedy, 1990). As a specific model of policing, community policing has certain characteristics that are essential for effective field operations. Several issues must be confronted in order to successfully implement community policing. However, before we discuss these issues, we will attempt to define community policing.

DEFINING COMMUNITY POLICING

What is community policing and what, if anything, is so special about it? Community policing is a very trendy term with numerous definitions. The popularity and ambiguity of the concept is both a blessing and a curse. On the positive side, everyone can identify with the term (after all, who is opposed to the concept of "community," or "mother" and "apple pie" for that matter?). The nebulous nature of the concept allows people to read into it favorable attributes and unlimited possibilities for changes and reforms. On the negative side, the concept has been abused by police chiefs who use it to justify their pet programs; the cachet of community policing can produce a "halo effect" around such programs and prevent outside observers from distinguishing true police innovation from traditional policing. In addition, Goldstein (1993) maintains that the popularity of the community policing concept raises public expectations and "create[s] the impression that, somehow, on implementation, community policing will provide a panacea for not only crime, disorder, and racial tensions, but many of the other acute problems that plague our urban areas" (p. 1).

The challenge is to figure out what community policing is and is not, and to differentiate it from traditional policing. Another question is whether community policing, in practice, is truly ground-breaking or simply old wine in new bottles. Such clarification will help set the stage for critical discussions of the merits and limitations of these programs. Criminal justice scholars and police administrators have yet to articulate the full theory behind community policing or to enumerate all of its assumptions and implications. This theoretical imprecision has contributed to the criticism of community policing (e.g., Klockars, 1988; Manning, 1988; Mastrofski, 1988). As Bayley (1988) states,

> Although widely, almost universally, said to be important, [community policing] means different things to different people—public relations campaigns, shopfronts and mini-stations, rescaled patrol beats liaison with ethnic groups, permission for rank-and-file to speak to the press, Neighborhood Watch, foot patrols, patrol-detective teams, and door-to-door visits by police officers. Community policing on the ground often seems less a program than a set of aspirations wrapped in a slogan (p. 225).

Although definitional problems abound, it would be a mistake to conclude that community policing is all rhetoric and no substance or that there is no agreement regarding its core elements. Community policing has been operationalized through a variety of programs and practices, but the concept appears to be supported by a common set of guiding principles and assumptions (Eck & Spelman, 1987; Goldstein, 1990; Green & Mastrofski, 1988; Leighton, 1994; McElroy, Cosgrove & Sadd, 1993; Murphy & Muir, 1984; Rosenbaum, Yeh & Wilkinson, 1994a; Skolnick & Bayley, 1986; Sparrow, Moore & Kennedy, 1990; Toch & Grant, 1991; Trojanowicz & Bucqueroux, 1990). The frequently cited elements of community policing include a broader definition of police work, a reordering of police priorities, a greater attention to neighborhood disorder, a shift to service and shared decision making with citizens, a de-emphasizing of bureaucratic processes in favor of results, a focus on problem solving and prevention rather than on incident-driven policing, a recognition that the community plays a critical role in solving

neighborhood problems, and a restructuring and reorganization of police departments to encourage and reward a new set of police behaviors. These shared concepts and assumptions are being translated increasingly into concrete changes, such
as decentralized organizational structures, permanent beat assignments, new mechanisms for community participation and problem solving, and revamped performance evaluation systems.

Community policing, however defined, raises certain issues that must be recognized before such programs can be successful. In addressing these issues, police
departments face their biggest challenges (Dantzker, 1994; Dantzker et al., 1995).
These issues include (1) the tenets of community policing, (2) the community policing role, (3) administrative leadership and organizational support for community
policing, (4) citizen participation, and (5) community policing strategies and the community context.

Tenets of Community Policing

The successful implementation of community policing demands the acknowledgment of three primary tenets: citizen involvement, police participation, and the reduction of fear of crime and criminal activity (Murphy, 1988; Tisdale, 1989; Trojanowicz
& Bucqueroux, 1990). As noted by Trojanowicz and Bucqueroux,

> Community policing is both a philosophy and an organizational strategy that
> allows the police and community residents to work closely together in new ways to
> solve the problems of crimes, fear of crime, physical and social disorder, and
> neighborhood decay (1990, p. xiii).

Acceptance of these tenets involves both a philosophical commitment to them and
organizational strategies to actualize them.

Community Policing Role

Developing the community policing role requires changing the police culture
(Kelling, Wasserman & Williams 1988; Sparrow, 1988; Trojanowicz & Bucqueroux, 1990). The traditional police culture defines the primary role of policing as
reactive crime fighting with little concern for the underlying causes of crime.
Police officers usually deal only with the immediate problems for which their services have been requested. Community policing requires police officers to
deal with the underlying causes and sources of problems that lead to calls for services (e.g., the broken streetlights and a missing stop sign that led to an auto
accident), as well as dealing with the immediate problem (e.g., the auto accident).
This approach demands a whole new way of thinking for police officers. The role
of the community policing officer must be explicitly defined and the police culture
must be changed to incorporate values and orientations consistent with this
new role.

The community policing role necessitates other changes as well. A change to more decentralized police organizations is necessary to allow individual officers greater use of their discretionary and problem-solving skills, which often go untapped. Community policing also requires incorporating in police training curricula topics such as community problem solving, citizen mobilization, interpersonal relations, cultural awareness, and advocacy skills.

Administrative Leadership and Organizational Change

Changing management and leadership values and organizational command and control systems are other hurdles that must be conquered in order for community policing to be successful. Management through values is a crucial issue (Kelling and Moore, 1988; Sparrow, 1988; Trojanowicz & Bucqueroux, 1990). Kelling and Moore acknowledge that "it is the responsibility of police management to (1) identify values that flow from the law and the Constitution, that represent the highest norms of the profession, and that are consistent with the ideals of communities and neighborhoods, and (2) enunciate them persuasively and unambiguously" (1988, p. 3). Changing police cultures to adapt to the community policing role must involve all ranks of command and leadership and must reflect varying styles of supervision and problem solving.

Administrative and organizational provisions must be made to support community policing. We have already mentioned the importance of a more decentralized organization. In addition, the infrastructures of police organizations should provide resources; liaisons with higher level political, social, and public service sectors of the community; and a system to coordinate the activities of a community policing unit with other units of a department (e.g., patrol, traffic, detective, community relations, gang crime, narcotics, etc.).

A final issue involving administrative and organizational development is police accountability (Kelling, Waserman & Williams, 1988). Police departments and their officers are ultimately accountable to communities. Concerns with accountability in community policing are primarily a function of expanded officers' discretion, decentralized command structures, increased interaction and intimacy between police officers and citizens, and the development of patrol and police tactics by individual police officers at a neighborhood or community level, rather than within the chain of command of a police department (Kelling et al., 1988).

Under community policing, the traditional methods of ensuring centralized accountability to the community (e.g., police–community relations units or citizen advisory and review boards) are no longer acceptable. Methods that regard citizens and police as coparticipants in setting policing priorities must be established (e.g., joint committees for identifying problems and prioritizing and planning solutions) (Kelling et al., 1988). Allowing community residents to assist in setting priorities, in return, makes community policing officers more directly accountable to the community for their activities and accomplishments. In short, community policing requires greater police accountability to the community.

Community Participation

Community or citizen participation is a fundamental component of community policing—it is a broad term that must be more clearly defined by community policing programs. Community participation may be hampered more by the police than by the public. Citizens have frequently wanted to be more involved in fighting crime than by merely serving as informants. However, police departments have historically attempted to limit citizen involvement to little more than providing information that might assist in solving crimes. Community policing calls for greater citizen input and interaction with officers, not only for solving crimes, but also for identifying and solving the problems that cause crime.

Encouraging police officers to mobilize citizen involvement, on a level greater than that mandated by traditional policing methods, is a prerequisite for the success of community policing. A key factor in achieving officer participation at the level demanded by community policing is to persuade them to share problem-solving activities with private citizens on a grander scale than traditional policing has required.

A variety of tactics should be devised to mobilize citizens. Increased interaction with citizens during patrol and informal and formal visits with citizen groups and businesses are emphasized in the literature as the means through which community participation is initiated and sustained. But successful community policing programs often develop a repertoire of other strategies, including scheduling meetings with influential citizens and key community leaders and using the media to create a higher profile for the program.

Cultivating community participation necessitates defining the specific roles and responsibilities of the police and citizens. Police roles identified in the literature include community activist, mobilizing and organizing citizens; community broker, linking citizens with needed services and resources; community advocate, taking the part of citizens; and community confidante, listening to citizens' concerns and complaints. The roles that community residents should play in community policing programs are not as clearly defined as those of police officers. Informant and participant in problem identification and solving are certainly roles. But the literature also mentions "community empowerment" as an objective of community policing. However, what this means and how it translates into citizens' roles is left unspecified. Designing community policing requires a more detailed definition of both police and citizens' roles, particularly the role of citizens in community participation.

Community Context

One of the most serious failings of the community policing literature is that, while it emphasizes the importance of community context in the design and implementation of programs, it provides few details on how community context should be taken into account. However, several issues can be identified from the sparse community policing literature on this topic and from other literature that describe community context with respect to policing.

The community context in community policing is defined in terms of three community characteristics: (1) resident characteristics (e.g., demographic and socioeconomic attributes), (2) housing and land-use patterns (e.g., housing density, housing structure type, residential and business mix), and (3) overall trends in residential and business growth (Trojanowicz & Bucqueroux, 1990). An important fourth category of community characteristics should be included in this list: the social and political networks of the community (e.g., degree of neighborhood cohesion and social organization).

The literature treats these community characteristics as gross indicators of poverty, community health, racial and ethnic conflict, and other correlates of crime and deviance. Among the three categories of community characteristics, physical characteristics are frequently discussed as targets of community policing interventions (Murphy, 1988; Sparrow, Moore & Kennedy, 1990). For example, crime and fear of crime appear to be related to many factors associated with the physical environment. Fixing dilapidated buildings, towing away junk vehicles, or replacing streetlights are examples of factors that affect the quality of life in neighborhoods. Unlike traditional policing, which tends to ignore these factors, community policing tries to improve living conditions and to reduce fear.

Social network characteristics of communities should receive more attention. The literature addresses these as important resources to be mobilized for citizen involvement. But it does not explain how different types of networks relate to different community policing tactics.

COMMUNITY POLICING: APPLIED

The popularity of community policing has led to a rich source of police reform and police research (Eck & Spelman, 1987; Goldstein, 1990; Green & Mastrofski, 1988; McElroy, Cosgrove & Sadd, 1993; Murphy & Muir, 1984; Rosenbaum, 1994a; Skolnick & Bayley, 1986; Sparrow, Moore & Kennedy, 1990; Toch & Grant, 1991; Trojanowicz & Bucqueroux, 1990). Despite many uncertainties, hundreds of communities across the United States are moving "full speed ahead" with implementation. Because of a shortage of clear definitions and accepted criteria for measuring success, few carefully designed studies have examined how this multifaceted concept has been operationalized in specific locations and whether such operations have achieved desired results (Rosenbaum, 1994a).

In the early to mid-1980s, the focus of community policing was on the community. Based on the "broken windows" approach, described by Wilson and Kelling (1982), strategies for reducing the physical and psychological distance between the police and the community were often pursued. Although crime rates were rarely reduced, careful demonstration programs designed to increase foot patrol, to create local mini-stations, and to encourage police contacts with citizens had favorable effects on residents' perceptions of crime and the police (for reviews, see Rosenbaum, Hernandez & Daughtry 1991; Skogan, 1990, 1994). Policing strategies in Chicago's community policing program, for example, were reorganized around the city's 279 police beats to give officers a more visible presence in the neighborhood.

Community policing is based in the notion that crime and disorder can be effectively controlled and sometimes prevented if the police develop collaborative relationships with the community. This simple idea is based on an empirically supported premise that police are often ineffective when fighting crime alone and must rely on community resources to solve neighborhood problems (Rosenbaum, 1986). Hence, emphasis is now given to the "co-production" of public safety (Lavrakas, 1985; Murphy & Muir, 1984; Wilson & Kelling, 1982).

Research suggests that criminal activity is encouraged when neighborhoods are unable to exercise effective informal social control over their residents or to define and achieve common goals (e.g., reducing the threat of crime) (Bursik & Grasmick, 1993; Byrne & Sampson, 1986). From a policy standpoint, if communities suffer from social disorganization, then efforts should be made to strengthen social networks and bolster residents' attachment to neighborhoods.

Getting residents to work together to achieve common goals and to solve problems is one way to stimulate social interaction and to build social relationships. The involvement of local residents in anticrime or youth-oriented projects may strengthen informal social controls at the neighborhood level and may contribute to the overall aim of producing self-regulating communities (Rosenbaum, 1988). The goal of organizing local residents and encouraging more frequent social interaction is to create a social environment where people become more territorial about their neighborhoods and protective of their friends and families—a place where surveillance of suspicious behavior is high, local youths are supervised, and residents are willing to intervene to stop or deter antisocial and criminal behaviors.

At this point, the rhetoric about getting citizens involved in community policing has far exceeded the reality. For a variety of reasons, community participation in community policing has been limited in many cities (Sadd & Grinc, 1994). Nevertheless, community policing officers can pursue numerous paths toward the goal of creating self-regulated and self-defended neighborhoods, including: seeking community input and participation in defining local problems, educating the community about crime and disorder, working with citizens to develop solutions to problems, and helping identify and mobilize resources—both inside and outside the community—to respond effectively to problems.

In Chicago's community policing program, beat officers work with residents and community organizations to identify and solve neighborhood problems, while rapid response officers respond to 911 calls. To encourage communication even further, district advisory committees, consisting of police personnel and citizens, review and discuss strategic issues with each district's commander on a regular basis. At the same time, Chicago's community policing program makes greater use of municipal services to support local problem-solving efforts.

Whether the police will function well in these new roles as facilitators, coordinators, and referral agents is uncertain. It should also be noted that many of the community outreach programs that have been attempted to date were never institutionalized (i.e., they were special units grafted onto a police organization, and they often disappeared when funding was discontinued). Moreover, efforts to increase police visibility and contact with the public did not necessarily address the crime-related problems facing neighborhoods. For these and other reasons, creative police departments shifted their attention in the mid- to late 1980s to solving problems, and the problem-oriented policing model became the dominant form of police innovation (Eck & Spelman, 1987; Goldstein, 1990).

EVALUATIONS AND UNANSWERED QUESTIONS

To date, few carefully planned demonstration projects have been tied to well-designed quantitative evaluations of community policing. With a few exceptions in recent years, community policing has been studied primarily through qualitative field methods (e.g., Capowich & Roehl, 1994; Greene, Bergman & McLaughlin, 1994; Hope, 1994; McElroy, Cosgrove & Sadd, 1993; Sadd & Grinc, 1994; Skogan et al., 1995; Wilkinson & Rosenbaum, 1994). Researchers have conducted case studies of organizational processes and problem-solving activities and have occasionally supplemented them with quantitative outcome measures. The focus of qualitative evaluations has varied substantially, from general assessments of multiple police organizations (e.g., Sadd & Grinc, 1994) to detailed ethnographies of police-community dynamics in specific neighborhoods (e.g., Lyons, 1995). Field methods have demonstrated the wide range of police strategies being pursued under the rubric of community policing, the multitude of problems that emerge during program development and implementation, and the ensuing struggles to implement community policing, in organizations, target communities, and among partnership members. In short, researchers have uncovered a host of internal factors that have limited the success of community policing, ranging from rigid bureaucratic policies and procedures to a police culture that is fearful of change. There is less research on external factors, but studies suggest that developing working partnerships with the community is much harder than the police had expected, because of a history of poor relations with residents, low levels of citizen involvement, conflicting interests in the community, and ignorance on the part of both police and citizens regarding the processes inherent in problem solving and community engagement. Despite the litany of reservations about community policing described in the literature, well-documented cases of implementation success have been reported (e.g., Skogan et al., 1995; Wilkinson & Rosenbaum, 1994; Wycoff & Skogan, 1994).

The body of research on community policing has grown, but basic questions about it remain unanswered, leaving several major gaps in our current knowledge about such programs. Filling these gaps may contribute significantly to criminal justice policy and practice. Specifically, no longitudinal studies have captured the evolving implementation of community policing. (Existing studies have lasted for either one or two years.) Are observed changes in police organizations and in police–community relations long-lasting or short-lived? Will the most innovative programs or reforms be institutionalized or discontinued? Law enforcement agencies would benefit from carefully chronicled histories of how community policing evolves over several years (e.g., how serious obstacles are addressed in two different cities).

Few rigorous evaluations have examined the impact of current community policing practices on police personnel, community residents, and community problems. Qualitative case studies, which are very popular, are not sufficient to address important impact questions. What are the effects of these changes on police performance, public perceptions, levels of crime and disorder, and other important outcome measures? Extremely rare are evaluations that include the repeated measurement of key community policing constructs, indices with known reliability and validity, and carefully selected control groups.

Although many types of communities with community policing have been studied, the vast majority of rigorous evaluations have been conducted in large cities. Can the current body of knowledge about community policing be generalized to smaller cities throughout the country? Research findings from Baltimore, Chicago, Houston, Newark, New York, Oakland, Seattle, Portland, and Philadelphia would appear to have limited external validity for smaller cities in the United States and elsewhere. Yet, among municipal police departments in the United States having 100 or more full-time sworn officers, two-thirds have between 100 and 249 full-time sworn officers (Reaves, 1992).

Case studies have reported numerous examples of successful problem solving in many cities, but are these successes permanent? How are these problems treated with the passage of time? Do they remain solved or do they return? Do the police or community engage in activities to prevent recurrences of problems? Longitudinal follow-ups of selected cases that were solved three to five years earlier would provide insights into the procedures for handling neighborhood problems.

Case studies also have been used to explore organizational reforms within police agencies but less often to document the dynamics of police–community interactions, which are considered the hub of community policing in practice. There is a paucity of useful qualitative data about the nature of police–community partnerships, especially as they develop in the context of neighborhood-level and block-level meetings (see Lyons, 1995, and Skogan et al., 1995, for exceptions). More generally, the ability of police personnel to facilitate and coordinate working partnerships with schools, businesses, churches, social service agencies, and community leaders should be carefully documented so police (and other partners) know what to expect and how to face emerging challenges. Finally, the architects of community policing are presently struggling to develop new systems to evaluate police officers and to encourage new police behaviors on the street, but virtually all of these efforts have centered on developing internal performance evaluation systems. Given the importance of community needs, perceptions, knowledge, and activities in the community policing model, more attention should be given to formalizing and standardizing measures of residents' perceptions of police performance.

EFFECTS OF COMMUNITY POLICING ON OFFICERS: WHAT COMMUNITY POLICING OFFICERS DO

Community policing programs are supposed to result in a variety of favorable changes in the way police officers define and perform their jobs. Proponents of community policing claim they are working behind "a quiet revolution [that] is reshaping

American policing" (Kelling, Wasserman & Williams, 1988, p. 3) and that it will produce a "new breed" of police officers by transforming police cultures, organizations, roles, management techniques, decision-making strategies, reward systems, and training curricula (Kelling & Moore, 1988; Moore, 1992). These new reforms are designed to increase officers' knowledge and expertise in problem identification, problem solving, and community engagement tactics.

According to Ward, Taylor, and Fanning (1995), the new breed of community policing officer was envisioned as young, educated, free of the cynicism associated with the traditional police culture, open-minded, and receptive to novel ideas and approaches. In addition, the prototypic community policing officer is expected to adopt a concerned and enlightened approach to such issues as domestic violence and cultural diversity, and to be an accomplished public speaker and community organizer. The creators of community policing programs eventually realized that "such a creature did not exist," and researchers began to systematically examine the characteristics of effective community policing officers.

In general, studies have found that candidates most suitable for community policing had stable employment histories prior to their careers in policing. Those with college degrees or experience in the helping professions (e.g., social work, psychology, nursing) or with employment histories in jobs that involved a lot of contact with people were likely to be successful community policing practitioners (Ward, Taylor & Fanning, 1995). We observed earlier that no single definition of community policing fits all programs in practice or captures all that police officers actually do in those programs. The following activities, adapted from Trojanowicz and Bucqueroux (1994, pp. 756–757), describe a sample of community policing officers' responsibilities and activities:

Law Enforcement—Performs general duties common to all police patrol assignments; community policing does not mean being soft on crime.

Community Involvement—Encourages citizens and community leaders to form enduring relationships with the police and organizes them to combat crime, drugs, physical and social disorder, and neighborhood decay.

Directed Patrol—Leaves the patrol car to increase police visibility on the streets and to find opportunities to work behind the scenes, forming a bond with citizens and letting them know the police are available and caring.

Problem Solving—Takes the initiative in identifying, prioritizing, and solving neighborhood problems with citizens' assistance and creative remedies that go beyond arrests; decision making is adaptive and flexible, and involves officers at the scene, not directives from headquarters.

Communication—Communicates with other police officers, including those in special units (e.g., narcotics), and with citizens about neighborhood problems and efforts to solve those problems.

Education—Educates citizens about crime prevention and problem-solving techniques.

Conflict Resolution—Acts as a mediator, negotiator, and resolver of neighborhood problems, and challenges citizens to solve problems themselves, stressing the shared power between the police and local groups and individuals.

Referrals—Brokers neighborhood services by making referrals to city agencies (e.g., towing abandoned cars, fixing street lights, enforcing building code violations).

Proactive Projects—Works with the community on short- and long-term efforts to enhance the quality of neighborhood life and to prevent problems before they occur.

Studies on Officers' Perceptions

As a result of the aforementioned changes in their jobs and duties, community polic-ing officers are expected to experience better relationships with their supervisors and with citizens, be more satisfied with their jobs and more accountable for their work, report improvements in their relationship with citizens, and show a greater willing-ness to work with them to identify and solve crimes and other neighborhood prob-lems. What has research reported about the effects of community policing on officers' perceptions, attitudes, and behaviors?

A combination of change strategies have influenced the views of police officers in traditional departments. Studies using police surveys have shown some consistent, positive effects on officers, such as increased job satisfaction, a perceived enlarge-ment of the police role, improved relations with co-workers and citizens, and stronger beliefs about the community's role in preventing crime. In a review of several stud-ies involving police officers in twelve different cities, Lurigio and Rosenbaum (1994) conclude that "on balance, these studies have shown that community policing has exerted a positive impact on the police and on citizens' views of the police" (p. 160). For example, in one of the first investigations of the effects of community policing on officers, Boydstun and Sherry (1975) found that community policing officers in San Diego, when compared to traditional officers, reported that their jobs were more interesting and less frustrating, that they had greater knowledge of their beats, and that they had higher levels of confidence in the community.

Hayeslip and Cordner (1987) investigated officers' job satisfaction in Baltimore County, Maryland's community policing program, known as the Citizen Oriented Police Enforcement (COPE) project. Officers in COPE were compared to a control group of police officers. COPE officers reported being more satisfied with their jobs and feeling more positive about community residents. In addition, research in Cincin-nati (Schwartz & Clarren, 1977), Flint, Michigan (Trojanowicz, 1986), and Edmon-ton, Canada (Cassels, 1988) suggest that officers engaging in community policing perceived that their work was less frustrating and was more important, interesting, and rewarding than traditional policing.

Other evaluations have found that community policing officers report having more independence and control over their jobs and feeling that they are part of a team, which are crucial determinants of job satisfaction. Furthermore, community policing officers report knowing a great deal about their assigned turf, and they are more opti-mistic about the impact of their work on community problems. Finally, they tend to adopt more benign and trusting views of the public than the ones they held while doing traditional policing (Lurigio & Rosenbaum, 1994; Wycoff, 1988).

In a study of Madison, Wisconsin's decentralized police management program, Wycoff and Skogan (1993; 1994) surveyed officers at three points in time over a two-year period. Those assigned to experimental districts eventually saw themselves as working as a team, believed that their efforts were being supported by their supervisors and the department, and thought that the department was really reforming itself. They became more satisfied with their jobs and more strongly committed to the organization when compared to officers serving in other parts of the city. In addition, they were more customer oriented, invested more seriously in the principles of problem solving and community policing, and felt that they had a better relationship with the community. Officers throughout the department who believed that they were participating in organizational decisions affecting their work life were more satisfied on a wide range of outcome measures. Department records indicated that disciplinary actions, absenteeism, tardiness, and sick days went down more in the experimental area than in the rest of the city.

There is also positive—but more impressionistic—evidence from other cities that community policing can alter police officers' attitudes and perceptions. In New York City, for example, community policing officers reported that they were being exposed more to "the good people" of the community while doing their new jobs, and that they got to know residents as people and were interacting with them in a variety of situations, not just during crises (McElroy, Cosgrove & Sadd, 1993). As a result of community policing in Hayward, California, officers reported that citizens had a better understanding of the role of police and more realistic expectations about what police could actually accomplish. Officers became more attuned to community problems and more receptive to neighborhood residents' complaints. Similarly, residents there reported that the police had become more open to change and more willing to help them (Sadd & Grinc, 1994).

Studies of the effects of community policing on officers have problems: they were generally conducted during the team policing era of the 1970s or the community engagement era of the 1980s. As a result, most of the interventions were not based on the latest thinking about community policing, and therefore, were not influenced by the problem-solving model (Eck & Spelman, 1987; Goldstein, 1990), the "NIJ-Harvard Executive Sessions" (e.g., Kelling & Moore, 1988), or other recent perspectives in this area. Also, the methodological quality of these studies was uneven, and in some cases, the range of measurement was quite limited.

CHICAGO'S ALTERNATIVE POLICING STRATEGY

The most ambitious attempt at urban police reform is currently underway in Chicago and involves a wide range of strategies to enhance problem solving and community engagement while restructuring the police bureaucracy. Recognizing that many traditional policing practices are no longer effective, the city of Chicago commissioned the consulting firm of Booz, Allen, and Hamilton to study the Chicago Police Department (CPD). The firm recommended a series of operational changes designed to place more police officers on Chicago's streets to combat crime, drugs, and gang activity and to pave the way for a community policing program. Overall, they proposed a neighborhood-based strategy for CPD, which represented a transition from incident-driven policing toward community-oriented policing.

In January 1993, Mayor Richard Daley announced the creation of Chicago's Alternative Policing Strategy (CAPS), which was pilot-tested in five prototype districts chosen to reflect the diversity of Chicago's neighborhoods. At the planning stage, Chicago's community policing program had the following six basic features (Lurigio & Skogan, 1994, p. 318; Dantzker et al., 1995, pp. 47–48):

Neighborhood Orientation—CAPS gives special attention to the residents and problems of specific neighborhoods, which demands that officers know their beats (e.g., crime trends, hot spots, and community organizations and resources) and develop partnerships with the community to solve problems.

Increased Geographic Responsibility—CAPS involves organizing police services so that officers are responsible for crime control in specific areas.

Structured Response to Calls for Police Service—A system of differential responses to citizen calls frees beat team officers from the continuous demands of 911 calls.

Proactive Problem-Oriented Approach—CAPS focuses on the causes of neighborhood problems rather than on discrete incidents of crime or disturbances.

Community and City Resources for Crime Prevention and Control—CAPS assumes that police alone cannot solve the crime problem, and that they depend on the community and other city agencies to achieve success.

Emphasis on Crime Problem Analysis—CAPS requires more efficient data collection and analysis to identify crime patterns and to target areas that demand police attention.

A major evaluation of CAPS has been underway since 1993, and its preliminary results are very promising (Skogan et al., 1995). The evaluation was funded by the National Institute of Justice, the Illinois Criminal Justice Information Authority, and the MacArthur Foundation. Using a pretest-posttest control group design in the five prototype police districts, Skogan and co-workers (1995) reported significant improvements in crime rates, in neighborhood disorder and decay, and in citizens' assessments of police performance during the first 17 months of the program. Along with evidence of program impact, Skogan et al. also found several implementation problems. For example, regular beat meetings were designed as the primary vehicle to encourage citizen participation, but the traditional police leadership often hindered the development of police-citizen partnerships and problem-solving efforts. Furthermore, low participation rates in Hispanic neighborhoods suggested that the program was unable to reach this segment of the population.

CAPS' managers mounted a multipronged attack on the problem of capturing the support of rank-and-file officers. The effort itself was a departure from business as usual in a department that was dominated by very traditional, conflict-laden, labor-management relations. Many of the top brass were skeptical of the motivations of patrol officers, reflecting the department's command-and-control management style. Nonetheless, it was clear to CAPS' managers that there could be no real change in the organization unless there was a real change at the bottom (i.e., in the hearts and minds of the officers).

Before the program started, officers were surveyed about their job satisfaction, their supervisors, and their opinions regarding community policing (Lurigio & Skogan, 1994). Questionnaires were administered prior to CAPS orientation training for CPD staff assigned to the prototype districts where CAPS was pilot tested (i.e., before they had any experience with or knowledge about CAPS). They found, for example, that large percentages of officers wanted a stimulating and challenging job that allows them to exercise independent thought and action, to be creative and imaginative, and to learn new things. However, less than half felt that they had deep personal involvement in their current assignments, and only one-quarter agreed that they had any influence over their jobs and that their supervisors sought their opinions.

The pre-CAPS survey also demonstrated that large numbers of officers thought that the public failed to understand and appreciate their work, and many officers were quite pessimistic about police–community relations in Chicago. With respect to their views on community policing, officers were not enthusiastic about involving themselves in solving noncrime problems. However, a majority thought that citizens had important information to share about their beats, and that the police should be concerned about local problems.

Despite indicators of general support for a few community policing concepts, officers embarking on police work in the prototype districts were wary about adopting new tactics such as foot patrol, and they were hesitant to market their new services to the public. Furthermore, the prototype officers thought that CAPS would have little impact on the crime rate, their ability to make arrests, or the police's relationship with Chicago's minorities. Overall, however, minority officers, especially African Americans, older officers (i.e., those 45 years of age and older), female officers, and officers with higher ranks were more optimistic about CAPS and more supportive of the enterprise.

AURORA AND JOLIET DEMONSTRATION PROGRAMS

Two other major experiments with community policing are underway in the cities of Aurora and Joliet, Illinois. In 1991, these two police departments embarked on a four-year demonstration program funded by the Illinois Criminal Justice Information Authority. Rosenbaum and his colleagues at the University of Illinois-Chicago were funded to conduct a longitudinal evaluation of these initiatives. During the first two years, the program focused on building organizational capacity and retooling police personnel. The problem-oriented policing (POP) model, as promoted by the Police Executive Research Forum and Goldstein (1990), provided the theoretical and practical foundation for these reforms. Planning committees were created to address issues that are now commonplace in efforts to reform police bureaucracies, including the organizational structure, police training, performance evaluation, call management, crime analysis, interagency cooperation, and community outreach—to mention only a few. Police training became a salient feature of the community policing initiatives at these sites. In addition, street-level policing was operationalized within special units of officers assigned to target neighborhoods to engage in problem solving.

Using a nonequivalent, pretest-posttest control group design, the initial evaluation examined changes in officers' attitudes, perceptions, and behaviors after 10 months and 22 months (Rosenbaum, Yeh & Wilkinson, 1994a; 1994b). In both departments, some positive changes were observed after 10 months. For example, officers in the special units reported significantly more opportunities to work closely with other employees and greater familiarity with problem-oriented policing when compared to other officers in the department. After 22 months, officers in Joliet's special unit continued to report more skills in problem solving relative to other officers. They also reported more informal contacts with citizens and more hours on foot patrol. Aurora officers showed a different pattern of responses after 22 months: Officers *not* in Aurora's special unit reported the most gains during this period, including greater knowledge and efficacy regarding problem solving and more hours on foot patrol compared to the special unit. However, some diffusion of community policing ideas beyond the special units was observed in both departments.

These findings should not be taken out of context. As the researchers note, "the fact remains that the absence of change was the norm rather than the exception" (Rosenbaum, Yeh & Wilkinson, 1994c, p. 349). On a wide variety of outcome measures, the police officers in both departments reported no changes over time. Several explanations could be offered for these results, but based on extensive fieldwork, the researchers concluded that full-scale implementation had yet to occur at the time of data collection. Moving from special units to department-wide implementation is a multiyear process. Fortunately, both the reform efforts and the evaluation research have continued, so the complete story, including changes in crime rates and community responses, has yet to be told.

SUMMARY

The implementation of community policing is a battle for the hearts and minds of police officers (Lurigio & Skogan, 1994). Police departments are centralized, low-technology, human service organizations where the motivations and skills of operational staff are paramount. Community policing calls for significant changes in the delivery of police services at the street level as well as sweeping revisions in departments' philosophies, structures, policies, procedures, and deployment strategies. These demands can often lead to a struggle; typically, police officers are dubious about so-called innovative programs and policing reforms. Failing to alter their basic perceptions and attitudes, and neglecting to prepare them fully for the unique rigors and demands of community policing risks "program failure due to apathy, frustration, resentment, perceived inequality, fear of change, and other factors that militate against the successful implementation of community policing" (Lurigio & Rosenbaum, 1994, p. 147).

In the final analysis, police officers on the street are the key to the future success of community policing. Nonetheless, many of the directives of community policing are beyond their current capacities and roles; they were initially selected and trained to perform only basic law enforcement activities: patrolling in cars, conducting investigations, making arrests, and writing reports. Community policing requires police officers to do many of their old jobs in novel ways and to engage in unfamiliar and challenging tasks that may have been missing from the police academy curriculum. They are expected to identify and solve a broad range of problems, to reach out to elements of the community that were previously outside their orbit, and to put their careers in jeopardy by taking on unfamiliar and challenging responsibilities.

Police officers can be quite resistant to change. They would rather do "what they signed up for," usually a combination of fighting crime and delivering emergency services. In many instances, their first response to community policing is to repudiate it scornfully as "social work" and certainly not "real police work." Commenting on police officers' reactions to community policing in Houston, former Houston Police Chief Betsy Watson was said to have lamented that: "they [police officers] somehow have equated neighborhood-oriented policing with social work rather than tough law enforcement—and they've missed the point."

Most personnel in police departments are content with the status quo because it allows them to draw on predictable rules and expectations on how to serve their superiors and their constituents (i.e., the public). Community policing forces officers to develop new relationships within their agencies and with the community-at-large—an undertaking that is time-consuming and uncertain. Community policing demands creativity: officers who are accustomed to "going by the book" will be hard pressed to devise responses that are specific to neighborhood problems and needs. Community policing requires officers to accept greater levels of authority and responsibility for identifying and solving community problems with the input and cooperation of citizens. Finally, community policing requires skills to exploit a broad range of resources and to communicate effectively with other city and governmental agencies (Ward, Taylor & Fanning, 1995). In essence, advocates of reform have high expectations for police personnel, and some of these may be unreasonable under present conditions with present personnel. (For a discussion of questionable assumptions underlying community policing, see Riechers & Roberg, 1990; Roberg, 1994.)

CONCLUSIONS: ORGANIZATIONAL CHANGE

Whether police organizations direct their attention to problem solving, community involvement, or both, administrators have recently discovered a serious problem: insufficient attention has been paid to the organizational, administrative, and personnel changes needed to create, expand, and institutionalize community policing. In this regard, community policing efforts are sometimes characterized as a "cart-before-the-horse" movement (Rosenbaum, Yeh & Wilkinson, 1994c). Model programs have been tried without the organizational infrastructure needed to sustain them on a larger scale. Nonetheless, demonstration programs have been quite useful in showing that problem-solving or community mobilization strategies, when conscientiously implemented, can have favorable impacts on neighborhoods (see Eck & Rosenbaum, 1994). One of the central questions facing police administrators today is how to create an organization that will systemically support and sustain these changes.

Police departments have been given considerable advice about the types of reforms that are needed to redefine police organizations in order to make community policing a reality (Eck & Spelman, 1987; Geller, 1985; Goldstein, 1979; Kelling & Bratton, 1993; Kelling & Moore, 1988; Moore & Stephens, 1991; Sparrow, Moore & Kennedy, 1990). The need for a fresh "organizational climate" is widely recommended, including new goals and objectives that reformulate the purposes of police departments. Experts have called for changes in organizational values, management styles, operational strategies, performance evaluation criteria, and dispatch systems. In a nutshell, community policing promises to replace ineffective, reactive, quasi-military bureaucracies with modern organizations that are responsive to both the needs of their employees and the communities they serve. Many police administrators now believe that when adequate internal changes have been introduced and pilot-tested on a small scale, their organization is ready to move ahead with full-scale, department-wide implementation.

Community policing calls for organizational and management changes similar to those already present in the private sector and grounded in decades of research on organizational behavior (Roberg & Kuykendall, 1990; Sorensen & Baum, 1977). Organizational theories suggest that employees are more productive, happy, and motivated when the organization meets their individual needs for independence, recognition, responsibility, challenge, accomplishment, participation, and compensation. At the heart of community policing is a plan to remove the organizational shackles from police officers in order to stimulate creative thinking, discretion, and problem solving at the street level. Community policing recognizes that officers need more than freedom; they also need departmental support. In theory, this can be achieved through supervisory feedback and encouragement, improved communications with other units, reduced responsibilities from 911 calls, geographic-based deployment, fair standards for evaluating performance, and above all, the knowledge and skills to function effectively in new roles.

Having conducted extensive fieldwork on the implementation of community policing, we have learned that police reform is often a protracted and painful process that requires strong police leadership and consistent community support. Unfortunately, the politics of local city government produce a high rate of turnover among police chiefs, which in turn severely restricts their ability to oversee serious organizational changes. This type of job insecurity, especially in the context of strong police unions, suggests that the future of community policing remains uncertain. Despite a promising start, the jury is still out. Today, it is difficult to predict whether this period of reform will be sustained long enough to have a permanent impact on the nature and effectiveness of the police service delivery system.

DISCUSSION QUESTIONS

1. How would you define community policing? What would be the main focus of your definition? Why?
2. What would you identify as the primary characteristics of community policing?
3. Most current evaluations of community policing were conducted after relatively short periods of time. How much time do you think is sufficient before an evaluation should be done? Why?
4. Why do you think community policing tends to positively affect police officers? How is community policing different from "traditional" policing?
5. Do you think the effects of community policing found in cities such as Chicago, Aurora, and Joliet, Illinois, are similar to those in other cities? If the philosophy is the same, should you expect that all cities practicing community policing will experience positive outcomes?
6. If police officers fail to embrace community policing, should police departments abandon it, or find ways to persuade officers to adopt it?

REFERENCES

Bayley, D.H. (1988). Community policing: A report from the devil's advocate. In J.R. Greene & S.D. Mastrofski (Eds.), *Community policing: Rhetoric or reality?* pp. 225–238. New York: Praeger.

Boydstun, J.E., & Sherry, M.E. (1975). *San Diego community profile: Final report.* Washington, D.C.: Police Foundation.

Bursik, R.J., & Grasmick, H.G. (1993). *Neighborhoods and crime: The dimensions of effective community control.* New York: Lexington.

Byrne, J.M., & Sampson, R.J. (Eds.). (1986). *The social ecology of crime.* New York: Springer.

Capowich, G.E., & Roehl, J.A. (1994). Problem-oriented policing: Actions and effectiveness in San Diego. In D.P. Rosenbaum (Ed.), *The challenge of community policing: Testing the promises,* pp. 127–146. Thousand Oaks, CA: Sage.

Cassels, D. (1988). *The Edmonton police department neighborhood foot patrol project: Preliminary report.* Edmonton, Alberta: Edmonton Police Department.

Dantzker, G.D., Lurigio, A.J., Hartnett, S., Houmes, S., Davidsdottir, S., & Donovan, K. (1995). Preparing police officers for community policing: An evaluation of training for Chicago's alternative policing strategy. *Police Studies, 18*(1), 45–69.

Dantzker, M.L. (1994). The future of municipal community-oriented policing: Suggestions for implementation. *Texas Police Journal, 42*(4), 15–17.

Eck, J.E., & Rosenbaum, D.P. (1994). The new police order: Effectiveness, equity, and efficiency in community policing. In D.P. Rosenbaum (Ed.), *The challenge of community policing: Testing the promises,* pp. 3–23. Newbury Park, CA: Sage.

Eck, J.E., & Spelman, W. (1987). *Problem solving: Problem-oriented policing in Newport News.* Washington, D.C.: Police Executive Research Forum.

Geller, W.A. (Ed.). (1985). *Police leadership in America: Crisis and opportunity.* New York: Praeger.

Goldstein, H. (1979). Improving policing: A problem-oriented approach. *Crime and Delinquency, 25,* 236–258.

Goldstein, H. (1990). *Problem-oriented policing.* New York: McGraw-Hill.

Goldstein, H. (1993, August 24). *The new policing: Confronting complexity.* Paper delivered at the Conference on Community Policing, National Institute of Justice, Washington, D.C.

Greene, J.R., Bergman, W.T., & McLaughlin, E.J. (1994). Implementing community policing: Cultural and structural change in police organizations. In D.P. Rosenbaum (Ed.), *The challenge of community policing: Testing the promises,* pp. 92–109. Newbury Park, CA: Sage.

Greene, J.R., & Mastrofski, S.D. (Eds.). (1988). *Community policing: Rhetoric or reality?* New York: Praeger.

Hayeslip, D.W., & Cordner, G.W. (1987). The effects of community-oriented patrol on police officer attitudes. *American Journal of Police, 4,* 95–119.

Hope, T.J. (1994). Problem-oriented policing and drug market locations: Three case studies. In R.V. Clarke (Ed.). *Crime prevention studies,* pp. 5–31. Monsey, NY: Criminal Justice Press.

Kelling, G.L., & Bratton, J.J. (1993, July). Implementing community policing: The administrative problem. *Perspectives on Policing,* No. 17. Washington, D.C.: National Institute of Justice.

Kelling, G.L., & Moore, M.H. (1988, November). The evolving strategy of policing. *Perspectives in Policing,* No. 4. Washington, D.C.: U.S. Department of Justice.

Kelling, G.L., Wasserman, R., & Williams, H. (1988, November). Police accountability and community policing. *Perspectives on Policing, 7.* Washington, D.C.: U.S. Department of Justice.

Klockars, C.B. (1988). The rhetoric of community policing. In J.R. Greene & S.D. Mastrofski (Eds.), *Community policing: Rhetoric or reality?* pp. 239–258. New York: Praeger.

Lavrakas, P.J. (1985). Citizen self-help and neighborhood crime prevention policy. In L.A. Curtis (Ed.), *American violence and public policy,* pp. 47–63. New Haven, CT: Yale University Press.

Leighton, B.N. (1994). Community policing in Canada: An overview of experience and evaluations. In D.P. Rosenbaum (Ed.), *The challenge of community policing: Testing the promises,* pp. 209–223. Newbury Park, CA: Sage.

Lurigio, A.J., & Rosenbaum, D.P. (1994). The impact of community policing on police personnel: A review of the literature. In D.P. Rosenbaum (Ed.), *The challenge of community policing: Testing the promises,* pp. 147–163. Newbury Park, CA: Sage.

Lurigio, A.J., & Skogan, W.G. (1994). Winning the hearts and minds of police officers: An assessment of staff perceptions of community policing in Chicago. *Crime and Delinquency, 40,* 315–330.

Lyons, B. (1995, June 1–4). *Responsiveness and reciprocity: Community policing in southeast Seattle.* Paper presented at the 1995 Annual Meetings of the Law and Society Association, Toronto, Canada. Seattle, WA: University of Washington Department of Political Science.

Manning, P.K. (1988). Community policing as a drama of control. In J.R. Greene & S.D. Mastrofski (Eds.), *Community policing: Rhetoric or reality?* pp. 27–46. New York: Praeger.

Mastrofski, S.D. (1988). Community policing as reform: A cautionary tale. In J.R. Green & S.D. Mastrofski (Eds.), *Community policing: Rhetoric or reality?* pp. 47–68. New York: Praeger.

McElroy, J.E., Cosgrove, C.A., & Sadd, S. (1993). *Community policing: The CPOP in New York.* Newbury Park, CA: Sage.

Moore, M.H. (1992). Problem-solving and community policing. In M. Tonry & N. Morris (Eds.), *Crime and justice: A review of research,* vol. 15, pp. 99–158. Chicago: University of Chicago Press.

Moore, M.H., & Stephens, D. (1991). *Police organization and management: Towards a new managerial orthodoxy.* Washington, D.C.: Police Executive Research Forum.

Murphy, C. (1988). Community problems, problem communities and community policing in Toronto. *Journal of Research in Crime and Delinquency, 25*(4), 392–410.

Murphy, C. (1988). The development, impact, and implications of community policing in Canada. In J.R. Greene & S.D. Mastrofski (Eds.), *Community policing: Rhetoric or reality?* pp. 177–189. New York: Praeger.

Murphy, C., & Muir, G. (1984). *Community-based policing: A review of the critical issues.* Ottawa: Solicitor General of Canada.

Reaves, B.A. (1992). *Law enforcement management and administrative statistics, 1990: Data for individual state and local agencies with 100 or more officers* (NCJ-134436). Washington, D.C.: U.S. Department of Justice, Bureau of Justice Statistics.

Riechers, L., & Roberg, R.R. (1990). Community policing: A critical review of underlying assumptions. *Journal of Police Science and Administration, 17,* 105–114.

Roberg, R.R. (1994). Can today's police organizations effectively implement community policing? In D.P. Rosenbaum (Ed.), *The challenge of community policing: Testing the promises,* pp. 249–257. Thousand Oaks, CA: Sage.

Roberg, R., & Kuykendall, J. (1990). *Police organization and management.* Pacific Grove, CA: Brooks/Cole.

Rosenbaum, D.P. (1986). *Community crime prevention: Does it work?* Beverly Hills, CA: Sage.

Rosenbaum, D.P. (1988). Community crime prevention: A review and synthesis of the literature. *Justice Quarterly, 5,* 323–395.

Rosenbaum, D.P. (1994a). *The challenge of community policing: Testing the promises.* Thousand Oaks, CA: Sage.

Rosenbaum, D.P., Hernandez, E., & Daughtry, S., Jr. (1991). Crime prevention, fear reduction, and the community. In W.A. Geller (Ed.), *Local government police management* (Golden Anniversary Ed., pp. 96–130). Washington, D.C.: International City Management Association.

Rosenbaum, D.P., Yeh, S., & Wilkinson, D.L. (1994a). *Community policing in Joliet: Impact on police personnel and community residents.* Final Report (vol. 2) submitted to the Illinois Criminal Justice Information Authority. Chicago: University of Illinois at Chicago, Center for Research in Law and Justice.

———. (1994b). *Community policing in Aurora: Impact on police personnel and community residents.* Final report (vol. 2) submitted to the Illinois Criminal Justice Information Authority. Chicago: University of Illinois at Chicago, Center for Research in Law and Justice.

———. (1994c). Impact of community policing on police personnel: A quasi-experimental test. *Crime and Delinquency, 40,* 331–353.

Sadd, S., & Grinc, R. (1994). Innovative neighborhood oriented policing: An evaluation of community policing programs in eight cities. In D.P. Rosenbaum (Ed.), *The challenge of community policing: Testing the promises,* pp. 27–52. Newbury Park, CA: Sage.

Schwartz, A.I., & Clarren, S.N. (1977). *The Cincinnati team policing experiment: A summary report.* Washington, D.C.: Urban Institute and Police Foundation.

Skogan, W.G. (1990). *Disorder and community decline: Crime and the spiral of decay in American neighborhoods.* New York: Free Press.

Skogan, W.G. (1994). The impact of community policing on neighborhood residents: A cross-site analysis. In D.P. Rosenbaum (Ed.), *The challenge of community policing: Testing the promises,* pp. 167–181. Thousand Oaks, CA: Sage.

Skogan, W.G., Hartnett, S.M., Lovig, J.H., DuBois, J., Houmes, S., Davidsdottir, S., Van-Stedum, R., Kaiser, M., Cole, D., Gonzalez, N., Bennett, S.F., Lavrakas, P.J., Lurigio, A.J., Block, R.L., Rosenbaum, D.P., Althaus, S., Whelan, D., Johnson, T.R., & Higgins,

L. (1995). *Community policing in Chicago, year two: An interim report.* Chicago: Illinois Criminal Justice Information Authority.

Skolnick, J., & Bayley, D. (1986). *The new blue line: Police innovation in six American cities.* New York: Free Press.

Sorensen, P.F., Jr., & Baum, B.H. (Eds.). (1977). *Perspectives on organizational behavior.* Champaign, IL: Stipes.

Sparrow, M.K. (1988, November). Implementing community policing. *Perspectives on Policing,* 9, U.S. Department of Justice.

Sparrow, M.K., Moore, M.H., & Kennedy, D.M. (1990). *Beyond 911: A new era for policing.* New York: BasicBooks.

Tisdale, W.T. (1989, October). Community policing: The current state of common characteristics. A paper presented at the annual meeting of the Southwestern Association of Criminal Justice Educators. Corpus Christi, Texas.

Toch, H., & Grant, J.D. (1991). *Police as problem solvers.* New York: Plenum.

Trojanowicz, R.C. (1986). Evaluating a neighborhood foot patrol program: The Flint, Michigan project. In D.P. Rosenbaum (Ed.), *Community crime prevention: Does it work?* pp. 157–178. Beverly Hills, CA: Sage.

Trojanowicz, R.C., & Bucqueroux, B. (1990). *Community policing: A contemporary perspective.* Cincinnati, OH: Anderson.

Trojanowicz, R.C. (1994). *Community policing: How to get started.* Cincinnati, OH: Anderson.

Ward, R.H., Taylor, N.J., & Fanning, P. (1995). *Community policing for law enforcement managers.* Chicago: Illinois Criminal Justice Information Authority.

Wilkinson, D., & Rosenbaum, D.P. (1994). The effects of organizational structure on community policing: A comparison of two cities. In D.P. Rosenbaum (Ed.), *The challenge of community policing: Testing the promises,* pp. 110–126. Newbury Park, CA: Sage.

Wilson, J.Q., & Kelling G.L. (1982, March). Broken windows: The police and neighborhood safety. *Atlantic Monthly,* pp. 29–38.

Wycoff, M.A. (1988). The benefits of community policing: Evidence and conjecture. In J.R. Greene & S.D. Mastrofski (Eds.), *Community Policing: Rhetoric or reality?* pp. 103–120. New York: Praeger.

10

Use of Force: A Matter of Control

Lorie Fridell and *Antony M. Pate, Florida State University*

The vast majority of citizens adhere to the law, either because of the success of the informal means of social control, or because of concern about the consequences that might result from being caught as a violator. A very few individuals, however, insist on violating laws, providing the impetus for bringing society's sanctions upon the wrongdoers. In order to impose these sanctions, against the will of the violators, it is often necessary to utilize force, thus literally to *enforce* the law. Within the last 175 years, modern governments have entrusted the authority to utilize appropriate levels of force to police officers. Thus, it is reasonable to expect that police will, and *must,* use force as an integral part of their job.

It is precisely because the *appropriate* use of force is the defining characteristic of policing that Kerstetter (1985, p. 149) says, "the inappropriate use of coercive force is the central problem of contemporary police misconduct." Indeed, we would go further, to argue that the history of policing has been characterized by a dynamic search for the means by which to *optimize* the use of legitimate force: utilizing it as necessary to maintain order, but not to the extent that it is excessive and abusive.

Concern about the need to control the use of force exercised by government authority is at least as old as the Roman question, "Who will guard the guardians themselves?" Similarly, much of the Magna Carta dealt with means of controlling abuse of power by the sheriffs, bailiffs, and constables of the thirteenth century. Today's headlines are rife with the consequences of concerns about police use of force, including militia activism in reaction to alleged excessive force used at Ruby Ridge and Waco, cases being dropped in Philadelphia on the grounds of police brutality, and disallowing evidence because police in Harlem were known to be abusive and violent.

Two events surrounding the recent riots in Los Angeles represent the tenuous bounds within which the optimal use of force must be calibrated. That is, the first represents the *excessive* use of force and the second, the *insufficient* use.

> ***Illustration One:*** At approximately 12:40 A.M. on March 3, 1991, a California Highway Patrol unit observed a white Hyundai being driven at excessive

217

speed on a freeway. Although the cruiser activated its roof lights, the car sought to escape, leading to a chase involving several police vehicles and a helicopter, which finally ended at the intersection of Florence and Normandie avenues in South Central Los Angeles. The officers at the scene were undoubtedly authorized to exercise force in order to secure the compliance of the driver, Rodney King, a 38-year-old African American, with their directives. However, in a scene preserved by amateur video photographer George Holliday, King was beaten repeatedly by several police officers at the scene. Criminal indictments were issued against one sergeant and three police officers, all of them white, shown beating King on the video tape.

As a result of the above event, a commission, headed by Warren Christopher, was created to investigate use of force by the Los Angeles Police Department. The report of the Independent Commission of the LAPD (or "Christopher Commission Report"), issued on July 9, 1991, concluded that the department suffered from a siege mentality, accentuated by indications of racism, and that a relatively small number of officers accounted for an inordinate number of allegations of excessive force but went unpunished (Independent Commission of the LAPD, 1991).

Illustration Two: At 3:10 on the afternoon of April 29, 1992, the jury (none of whom were African-American) trying the police officers in the beating of Rodney King reached "not guilty" verdicts. Within minutes, angry crowds gathered in South Central Los Angeles to protest the verdicts. A riot lasting six days ensued, leading to the damage or destruction of more than $1 billion in property and the deaths of 52 persons.

This event led to another commission, headed by William Webster, which was constituted to study the causes of the riot and the city's response to it. The commission found, despite weeks of intense focus on the trial, that the police department had failed to plan and prepare for unrest, had been put completely on the defensive, had failed to respond effectively to the initial scenes of disorder, and had therefore "lost all control over the mobs of demonstrators," allowing them to loot and burn at will (Webster Commission, 1992).

There is nothing unique about Los Angeles. Allegations of excessive force and insufficient force have likewise been made in many jurisdictions. Decisions about the optimal use of force must be made by individual police officers and law enforcement agencies throughout the nation every day. It is not surprising that many police officers lament that, "We're damned if we do, and we're damned if we don't" when it comes to the use of force.

It is also not surprising that, since a disproportionate number of crimes and arrests occur, in low-income areas of our major cities, frequently inhabited largely by African Americans and Hispanics, that racial and ethnic tensions are often exacerbated by allegations of use of excessive force, or, conversely, the use of too little force.

We will start this chapter by defining "force" and "excessive force," and by presenting what is known about the extent to which police use and misuse force. In later sections we will describe why optimizing the use of force is critical for law enforcement departments, describe what is known about the correlates of police use and misuse of force, and describe what departments can do to effectively control their officers' use of force.

DEFINING "FORCE" AND "EXCESSIVE FORCE"

"'Force' has been defined as the exertion of power to compel or restrain the behavior of others" (Kania & Mackey, 1977, p. 29). Police force can be classified in several ways. In terms of level of force, it can be classified as "deadly" or "less than lethal." *Deadly force* is, by definition, "likely to cause death or serious bodily harm." *Less-than-lethal force* is *not* likely to cause death or serious bodily harm. There are variations across department policies and court cases as to what types of force are considered "likely to cause death or serious bodily harm." Thus, although all departments consider shooting a firearm at a citizen to be "deadly force," department policies vary, for instance, as to whether a choke hold is "likely to cause death or serious bodily harm."

Many use-of-force continua recognize even nonphysical actions on the part of police as "force." For instance, the use-of-force model presented by Desmedt (1984), portrayed in Figure 10.1, includes officer presence and verbal direction as ways in which officers can compel or restrain the behavior of others.

Force can also be classified in terms of its appropriate use; that is, force is classified as "justifiable force" or "excessive force." Legally, force by police is excessive "when it is used for other than lawful purposes or when it is used out of proportion to the need" (Cheh, 1995, p. 234). Or, as stated by Kania and Mackey (1977, p. 29), excessive force is "violence of a degree that is more than necessary or justified to effect a legitimate police function." Figure 10.1, which indicates the level of force an officer may use to respond to specific behaviors on the part of opponents, also conveys when officer force is "excessive" and when it is "ineffective."

Departments use the "reasonable" versus "excessive" classifications to determine if an officer's use of force requires disciplinary action. Fyfe (1987), however, expands the conceptualization of which uses of force are appropriate by acknowledging that even lawful force can be, in some instances, "unnecessary." Fyfe is referring here to force that is, legally speaking, "reasonable," but *could have been avoided.* He explains that unnecessary force "occurs when well-meaning officers lack the skills to resolve problems with as little violence as possible, and, instead, resort to force that might otherwise have been avoided" (Fyfe, 1987, p. 6). The distinction Fyfe makes has also been referred to as the difference between "use of excessive force" and "excessive use of (legal) force" (Adams, 1995, p. 65). As covered below, more and more departments are training their officers to better use tactical and verbal techniques to keep incidents from escalating into force situations. That is, these departments are training officers to reduce *unnecessary* force as well as *excessive* force.

Although on paper it is fairly easy to classify force in various ways, the real-life application is tremendously more difficult. Because it is not possible to articulate the specific appropriate force responses of officers for every conceivable situation,

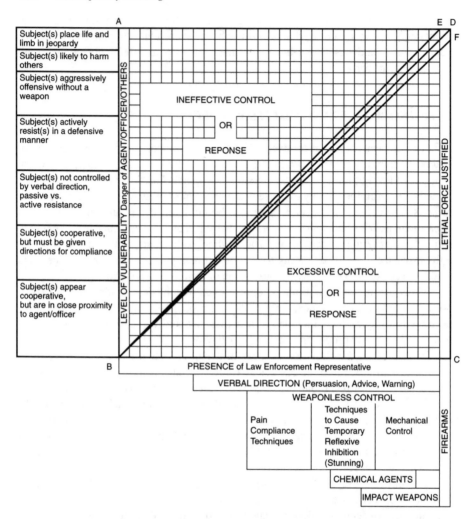

Figure 10.1   Desmedt's Use-of-Force Model (Reprinted from *Journal of Police Science and Administration,* Vol. 12, No. 2, page 173, 1984. Copyright held by the International Association of Chiefs of Police, 515 N. Washington Street, Alexandria, VA 22314, USA. Further reproduction without express written permission from IACP is strictly prohibited).

officers are usually trained and evaluated in accordance with the "reasonableness standard." That is, officers are told they can use that amount of force which is reasonably necessary to effect their lawful function. As Alpert and Smith (1994, p. 481) note, there is an "unrealistic expectation which is placed on police to understand, interpret, and follow vague 'reasonableness' guidelines." The officers are asked to find that narrow line, portrayed in Figure 10.1, that "wobbles between proper practice and excessive violence" (Manning, 1980, p. 140).

Legal parameters are somewhat clearer for deadly force than for less-than-lethal force. Though both are judged by the "reasonableness" standard, the U.S. Supreme

Court has provided more specific parameters of reasonableness for the use of deadly force, particularly in the context of using deadly force to arrest. In *Tennessee v. Garner* the U.S. Supreme Court held that the police shooting of an escaping, apparently unarmed 15-year-old boy was an unconstitutional seizure. Basically, the Court said that police can use deadly force to arrest only *dangerous* fleeing felons, not *non*dangerous fleeing felons. That is, officers can use deadly force to effect an arrest only when they have "probable cause to believe that the suspect poses a threat of serious physical harm, either to the officer or to others" (471 U.S. 1, 11, 1985).

EXTENT TO WHICH POLICE USE AND MISUSE FORCE

It is very difficult to determine the extent to which police use and misuse force. In this section, we describe the work of researchers who have attempted this determination, using various methodologies such as observation, survey, and utilization of departmental records. We will follow the presentation of this research with a discussion of the drawbacks to each of the various methodologies and describe the national force reporting system which is being created by the federal government.

Deadly Force

Police authority to use deadly force against citizens represents one of the most dramatic, most ominous powers of government. Despite the importance of this police response, there are no reliable national data regarding the frequency of its occurrence. Most research on police use of deadly force has relied on the data provided directly by various individual law enforcement agencies. These piecemeal data provide the basis for some tentative estimates of national figures. In *Deadly Force: What We Know*, Geller and Scott (1992) estimated that deadly force is used against approximately thirty-six hundred citizens each year. Of these thirty-six hundred, they estimated that six hundred (17 percent) are killed, twelve hundred (33 percent) are wounded, and eighteen hundred (50 percent) escape injury due to officer misses.

A study of United States cities with populations of more than 250,000 provided some interesting figures that reflect two important points regarding the frequencies of police killings of citizens: (1) there are vast differences across cities in the rates at which police kill citizens, and (2) even in the cities with high rates, most officers will never kill a citizen. Specifically, Sherman et al. reports (1986, p. 1) that

> Police in all cities kill rarely, but at widely varying rates. The average Jacksonville police officer would have to work 139 years before killing anyone. In New York City, the wait would be 694 years. It would be 1,299 in Milwaukee and 7,692 years in Honolulu. All based on 1980–1984 rates of killing.

The above study looked only at police *killings* excluding deadly force incidents that resulted in *wounds or misses*. In fact, several authors have criticized research that purports to examine "deadly force," but focuses merely on police-caused *homicides* (see, e.g., Fridell, 1989; Fyfe, 1978). However, until relatively recently, departments did not maintain aggregate statistical records on non-fatal deadly force incidents and thus data were not available to researchers. However, increasingly, departments are collecting detailed information regarding officer firearms discharges (Pate & Fridell, 1993). In fact, by 1991, 100 percent of the state agencies, 92 percent of the sheriffs' departments, and 95 percent of the municipal departments had policies requiring that their officers report not just shots that killed or wounded but also discharges at citizens that missed (Pate & Fridell, 1993).

Pate and Fridell (1993) collected information on the use of deadly force for the year 1991 from more than 1,000 sheriffs' departments, municipal police departments, and state agencies. For the one-year period there were 8.5 incidents involving deadly force for every 1,000 sworn sheriff personnel; 4.1 for every 1,000 sworn municipal officers; and 2.6 for every 1,000 sworn state officers. Overall, approximately 17 percent of the incidents involving deadly force resulted in citizens' deaths. (Note that this matches exactly the Geller and Scott estimate on the previous page.)

It is interesting to note that the number of persons slain by police has been on the decline for two decades. The study of "Big Cities" (Sherman et al., 1986) found that police in 50 of these cities killed 353 citizens in 1971 compared to 172 in 1984 (the last year for which they collected data). This represents a 51 percent reduction in citizens slain. Geller and Scott (1992) confirmed this overall downward trend, but noted that there has been an "upward turn in the frequency of police-involved shootings in several major American cities during the late 1980s" (p. 62). Clashes between law enforcement and minority communities over police use and misuse of force led to major changes in deadly force policies during the last two decades and likely contributed greatly to the significant reduction in the police use of deadly force (Alpert & Fridell, 1992). A study sponsored by the Urban League (Mendez, 1983) found that the decrease in the number of citizens killed was due in very large part to a decrease in shootings of African American citizens, rather than whites. In 1971, seven African American citizens were killed by police for every one white citizen. By 1979, this ratio had dropped to 2.8 African American citizens killed for every white citizen killed. It is important to note, as the author did, that African American arrests *did not* decrease during this time period.

Less-Than-Lethal Force

Departmental collection of information regarding less-than-lethal force is much less advanced than that for deadly force (Pate & Fridell, 1993). It is only within the past 10 years or so that departments have begun to systematically collect from their officers information on incidents in which non-lethal force is used (e.g., use of batons, dogs, electrical devices, chemical sprays, fists/feet). Without these departmental data, researchers had relied on observational studies and surveys of citizens and police officers to assess the extent to which reasonable and excessive force were used.

Below we describe these studies as well as the more recent studies that utilize departmental data.

Observational Studies. Some researchers have attempted to assess the extent to which officers use force by placing trained observers in the field with police to document law enforcement behavior. Overall, data from these observational studies indicate that police use force in 4 to 8 percent of the high-risk police–citizen contacts (that is, contacts which involve suspects—as opposed to non-suspect citizens—or have the "potential for violence") and that in one-third of these incidents the force is excessive. For instance, Black and Reiss (1967) collected information on more than thirty-eight hundred police-citizen encounters in three cities during the summer of 1966. Using these data, Reiss (1971, and Friedrich, 1980, using the same data) determined that force was used in 5 percent of the 1,565 incidents "in which police came into contact with citizens they regarded as at least potential offenders" (Friedrich, 1980, p. 86). In the small proportion of incidents in which force was used, the force was determined to be *reasonable* in two-thirds of those incidents and *excessive* in one-third.

Bayley and Garofalo (1987, 1989) report that out of 467 *potentially violent* encounters observed between police and citizens, police used force in 37 (8 percent). No assessment was made with regard to whether the force was justified or excessive. Worden (1995a) conducted secondary analyses on observational data collected for the Police Services Study in 1977. Data were collected on nearly fifty-seven hundred police–citizen encounters by trained observers on 900 patrol shifts in 24 police departments in three metropolitan areas. Worden reports that police used force in just over 1 percent of *all* of the police–citizen encounters. In one-third of the encounters in which force was used, the observer adjudged the force to be excessive or unnecessary. Among the subset of encounters that *involved suspects* (that is, this subset excluded encounters with citizens who were not suspects), *reasonable force* was used in less than 3 percent of the encounters and *improper force* was used in about 1 percent. The remaining 96 percent of the incidents involving suspects did not involve force.

Surveys of Citizens. Focusing specifically on police "brutality," various studies have surveyed citizens to determine whether they have been the subject of, seen, or heard from acquaintances about police use of excessive force. It is important to note that these studies relied on the subjects' interpretations of which police behavior qualified as "excessive force."

Overall, the studies indicate that 1 to 15 percent of respondents in various racial subgroups perceive themselves to have been victims of police excessive force. African Americans and persons with Spanish surnames report this more frequently than Caucasians.

For instance, a survey conducted for the National Advisory Commission on Civil Disorders (Campbell & Schuman, 1969) asked citizens in 15 cities about their negative experiences with law enforcement. Seven percent of the African Americans and 2 percent of the whites claimed that police had "roughed them up."

Just over 800 citizens of Denver were asked about their experiences *and* their friends' and neighbors' experiences with police brutality (Bayley & Mendelsohn,

1969). Four percent of the Caucasians, 9 percent of the African Americans, and 15 percent of the persons with Spanish surnames claimed to have personally experienced police brutality. Thirty percent of the African Americans, compared to 4 percent of the Caucasians and 12 percent of the persons with Spanish surnames, reported that they had heard of charges of police brutality from their friends or neighbors.

Twenty percent of the persons responding to a Gallup poll conducted in March of 1991 (after the Rodney King incident) claimed to know someone "who has been physically mistreated or abused by police" (Gallup, 1991, p. 79). Eight percent reported that someone in their own household had been "physically mistreated or abused by the police" and 5 percent reported that they themselves had been so treated. Consistently the highest percentages of affirmative responses to the questions regarding self, household, and others were for African Americans, males, persons living in large cities, and persons between 18 and 29 years of age. For instance, whereas (as reported above) 20 percent of the respondents overall claimed to know someone who had been abused by the police, this included 40 percent of the African American respondents and just 17 percent of the white.

Surveys of Police Officers.   Some researchers have surveyed law enforcement personnel to gauge the extent to which police use excessive force. For instance, Bayley and Mendelsohn (1969) asked 100 officers of the Denver Police Department whether they had witnessed an "incident that *someone* might consider to constitute police brutality" (p. 128, emphasis added). Over half of the officers (53 percent), responded in the affirmative. Twenty-seven percent of the officers maintained that they witnessed incidents which, *in their opinion,* involved "harassment or the excessive use of force" (p. 129).

Forty-three officers in a small southern city were asked by Barker (1978) to estimate the percent of their fellow officers who had used "excessive force on a prisoner." On the average, officers reported that 40 percent of their fellow officers had used excessive force on a prisoner. This was perceived as prevalent as sleeping on duty and more prevalent than perjury, sex on duty, and drinking on duty.

Departmental Records.   Some researchers have taken advantage of the increased utilization by departments of use-of-force forms to determine the extent to which police use force. These and other researchers have also used department records to document the extent to which citizens lodge complaints of excessive force.

Use-of-Force Forms

Overall, researchers using departmental force forms as their source of data report that for every 1,000 calls for service or calls "requiring reports," between 0.5 and 2 of those incidents reportedly involve force. The rates vary by type of call. For instance, Croft and Austin (1987) used departmental use-of-force forms to determine the extent of this action on the part of officers in both Rochester and Syracuse, New York. Calculating the rates of force per call for service, Croft and Austin reported approximately two use-of-force reports in Rochester for every 1,000 calls for service and about 1.5 use-of-force reports in Syracuse for every 1,000 calls for service. No assessment was made regarding the justifiability of the force for purposes of the research project.

McLaughlin (1992) analyzed the 133 use-of-force forms completed by Savannah officers in 1989. He reports that force is used in 0.65 of every 1,000 incidents in which written police reports are required. (Though not clear, it would seem that written reports are required for all "dispatched and officer-initiated calls," p. 44.) This researcher was able to present the rate at which force is used within various categories of incidents. Thus, for instance, McLaughlin reports that during 1989 force was used by Savannah police officers in 4.6 of every 1,000 incidents involving domestic disputes, in 3.6 of every 1,000 incidents involving robbery, in 1.5 of every 1,000 incidents involving arrest warrants, and in 0.7 of every 1,000 traffic stops.

For two recent studies it is not surprising that the rates produced are higher than those reported above, because these studies focused on the subgroup of calls for service which *resulted in arrests* (instead of looking at *all* calls for service). For instance, the Virginia Association of Chiefs of Police (1994) determined through a survey of law enforcement agencies in Virginia that force was used in 150 of every 1,000 arrests in 1993. In 1992, only 30 of every 1,000 arrests had resulted in the use of force. A 1994 Phoenix study (Garner & Buchanan, 1995) determined that force is used in 220 of every 1,000 adult custody arrests.

The survey conducted by Pate and Fridell (1993), mentioned above, collected information from a stratified random sample of more than 1,000 law enforcement departments on force reporting requirements, reported use of force, receipt of excessive force complaints, and the processing of citizen complaints. Sheriffs' departments, municipal departments and state agencies provided information regarding the amount of force reported by their officers during the 1991 calendar year for 18 types of force. (It is important to keep in mind that within these agencies the officers are not necessarily *required to report* all incidents of the various types of force, and thus the department records would not reflect *all* uses of force.) Handcuffing and bodily force were the most frequently reported types of force used by officers within all three agency types (sheriffs' departments, municipal departments, and state agencies). Both municipal departments and sheriffs' departments also reported high rates of use of chemical weapons (e.g., mace, capstun) and "come alongs." Municipal departments reported high rates of baton use, flashlight use (as a weapon), twist locks or wrist locks, swarms, and firm grips.

Complaints of Excessive Force

Researchers with access to information regarding complaints lodged by citizens (e.g., Brooks, 1965; Chevigny, 1969; Walker & Bumphus, 1992; Kerstetter, 1985; Dugan & Breda, 1991) have calculated *rates* of complaints received by various departments. It is difficult to compare the figures across studies because of the variation in the units being counted. For instance, some derive percentages using *excessive force* complaints in the numerator while others use *all complaints* of misconduct. Used as denominators in various studies are all police–citizen encounters, all encounters involving force, all encounters resulting in arrest, number of police officers, and so forth.

Croft and Austin (1987) report that of *all* use-of-force incidents, less than 5 percent result in complaints of excessive force. Focusing on all complaints of police misconduct, and using all police–citizen interactions in the denominator, Walker and Bumphus (1992, citing a finding of the New York City Civilian Complaint Investigative Bureau, 1990) reported that, in 1990, misconduct complaints in New York City occurred in fewer than 0.05 percent of all police–citizen encounters.

Several studies have calculated the average number of complaints received per officer per year. They all indicate between 0.3 and one misconduct complaint per officer per year. Kerstetter (1985) calculated rates of complaints per officer for four cities using data collected by Perez (1978). Interestingly, for three of the cities—Kansas City, Oakland, and Chicago, the rates were exactly the same: 0.5 complaints per officer. For Berkeley he reported approximately one complaint (0.95 complaints) per officer. (See also, New York City Police Department Civilian Complaint Review Board, 1986.) Dugan and Breda (1991) calculated the rate of complaints per year for 165 agencies in the state of Washington. They report 0.3 complaints for every "public-contact enforcement officer in the agency" (p. 166).

Pate and Fridell (1993) produced rates of *excessive force* complaints per officer (as opposed to rates for *all complaints of misconduct,* as reported above) and compared these rates across types of law enforcement agencies. City police departments had the highest rate of complaints, at 0.05 complaints of excessive force per sworn officer in 1991. Sheriffs' departments and state agencies both reported 0.02 excessive force complaints per sworn officer.

Percentages of total complaints that were *excessive force* complaints ranged from 18 in Dugan and Breda's (1991) study of 168 Washington state departments to 66 in "Metro City" studied by Wagner (1980). Twenty-one percent of the misconduct complaints in Detroit in 1975 were for excessive force (Littlejohn, 1981). The corresponding figure for all five cities studied by Perez (1978) was 25 percent (Kerstetter, 1985; see also, New York City Police Department, 1986).

Researchers studying complaints also frequently assess the extent to which departments *sustain* the allegations against officers, that is, determine the proportion of complaints found to be true following departmental review. Overall, these researchers report sustained rates of between 1 and 25 percent for complaints of police misconduct (which includes, but is not limited to, excessive force complaints). For instance, Dugan and Breda (1991) found that 25 percent of the complaints received by the 165 Washington state agencies responding to their survey were sustained. For excessive force complaints in particular, however, the percentage sustained was only 11.6. This is consistent with the findings of Wagner (1980), who found that excessive force complaints were the type of complaint least likely to be sustained. In his study, only 2.1 percent of the excessive force complaints were sustained.

The Independent Commission of the LAPD (1991) found that only 2 percent (42 of 2,152) of the excessive force complaints filed between 1986 and 1990 in the city of Los Angeles were sustained. This was one-fifth of the percentage of sustained complaints that Pate and Fridell (1993) found for municipal agencies. Specifically, 10 percent of the excessive force complaints filed against the municipal departments responding to the national survey were sustained. This compares to 12 percent for state agencies and 6 percent for sheriffs' departments.

Limitations of Data Sources

As described above, researchers have used various methodologies in an attempt to measure the use and misuse of force. We cannot, using any of these methods, be confident that the results truly measure the amount of police force used because there are drawbacks to each.

Observational studies are very time-consuming and thus very expensive. For instance, consider the Bayley and Garafalo (1989) study described above. Each of six student observers received more than 30 hours of training and then this group observed police on 350 8-hour tours. Out of this approximately 2,800-hour investment of observation time in the high-police-activity areas of a major metropolitan area, the students observed 37 instances in which police used force against citizens (primarily grabbing and restraining). This is an investment of 81 training and observation hours for every incident of force observed. Because of the large investment involved in gathering data, most observational studies cannot generate sufficient data for generalizing to other areas or departments.

Another major problem with observational studies is that they suffer from the probable reactivity of the officers to being the subject of observation. As Mastrofski and Parks (1990, p. 476) point out: "officers are known for their concern with secrecy and protection from misinterpretation of their actions." Even though observers are generally admonished to be passive and non-intrusive, it is likely that their presence affects the behavior of the officers under observation. As such, they are not measuring officers acting as they normally would.

Data on community surveys on the incidence and prevalence of police use of force can tap into *unreported* incidents of excessive force in the way official records cannot. However, these surveys measure only individual *perceptions* of excessive force, and not necessarily force that is *legally defined* as excessive. That citizens differ in their perceptions of what is "reasonable" force was evident in the two different decisions by two juries in the trials of the officers who used force against Rodney King. The findings reported above—that more minority citizens than Caucasian citizens report being the victims of or being acquainted with a victim of excessive force—could reflect the greater victimization by police of minority persons or broader definitions of "excessive force" held by minority persons.

Surveys of police officers also reflect only perceptions. Indeed, officers (rightly or wrongly) may have much narrower conceptions than citizens regarding what is "excessive force" and certainly might respond to surveys in a way that puts them and their profession in the best possible light.

Data collected from agency records have drawbacks, as well. First of all, official data from any government agency reflects the agency perspective and may or may not fully represent reality. Second, information from departmental records on force is frequently incomplete and variations in reporting requirements across departments may be so great that it could be inappropriate to assume that the data from an individual department, or several departments, is representative of other departments. Third, the department records do not contain information on police use of force that officers chose not to report for whatever reason. Finally, researchers who have studied force within individual departments most likely achieved access to the most progressive departments, which were more amenable to scrutiny.

In terms of excessive force, departments can only provide data on *complaints* of excessive force or *sustained* complaints of excessive force, neither of which can be considered a valid measure of the extent to which departments use excessive force. Two citizen surveys found that only one-third of the persons who believed they had been mistreated by police lodged a complaint with the department (Whitaker, 1983; Winick, 1987). In contrast, Adams (1995) speculates that only 3 percent of incidents perceived by citizens to be excessive are reported. Furthermore, the rate of complaints received by a jurisdiction may be as much a product of citizen confidence in the complaint process as any other factor (see Pate & Fridell, 1993). On this point, West (1988, p. 113) comments that

> Frequently assumed to provide a measure of police performance, the complaints rate is one of the most badly abused police-based statistics. Thus, an increasing number of complaints filed with a particular agency may not reflect a deterioration in standards of officer behavior, but could be interpreted as indicating a sign of increasing citizen confidence in the complaints system.

Several researchers have found support for the contention that more complaints are received by complaint systems that are most accessible or in which citizens have confidence (Jolin & Gibbons, 1984; Kahn, 1975; Kerstetter, 1985; Littlejohn, 1981; Perez, 1978). It is also important to note that, while lack of reporting leads to an *underestimate* of excessive force, illegitimate complaints could lead to an *overestimation*. Finally, the proportion of complaints that are sustained by a department may convey more information about a department's complaint review system than the extent to which excessive force is used by its personnel (Pate & Fridell, 1993).

The New National Reporting System

Over the years a number of researchers have called for a national reporting system for police use of force. In their earliest forms, these calls were for collecting national data on the police use of deadly force (e.g., Alpert & Fridell, 1992; Blumberg, 1985; Fridell, 1989; Sherman & Langworthy, 1979; Sherman et al., 1986). More recently, various scholars (e.g., Adams, 1995; Geller & Scott, 1992; Geller & Toch, 1995; Pate & Fridell, 1993; Ross, 1994), practitioners (police chiefs from various large cities; see, e.g., James, 1991), and interest groups (e.g., the American Civil Liberties Union and Americans for Effective Law Enforcement) have called for a national police use-of-force reporting system which would encompass less-than-lethal, as well as deadly, force (see Geller & Scott, 1992).

The Violent Crime Control and Law Enforcement Act of 1994 has provided the long-awaited impetus for a national reporting system on the police use of force. This federal legislation requires that the Attorney General collect data "about the use of *excessive* force by law enforcement officers" (Title XXI, Subtitle D, Police Pattern or Practice, Section 210402, emphasis added). A use-of-force workshop convened in 1995 by both the National Institute of Justice (NIJ) and the Bureau of Justice Statistics (BJS) brought together more than 40 use-of-force experts, including law enforcement representatives, researchers (including the two authors of this chapter), and lawyers. Discussions from that meeting were instrumental in formulating plans for collecting national data on the use of force by officers. Recognizing that each method of counting force has drawbacks and that in order to measure *excessive force* we must first be able to measure *force*. NIJ and BJS are, at the time of this writing, moving forward with a two-pronged data collection system. One component of this system is the establishment of a National Use of Force Database Center within the International Association of Chiefs of Police (IACP) which will involve the collection of data from police departments on use-of-force incidents. For the second component, questions are being developed for inclusion in the National Crime Survey, which would elicit information from respondents regarding their encounters with police, including information regarding force which was used during that incident. These two methodologies will, for the first time, provide for nationwide measures of both the reported and unreported use of force by law enforcement officers.

THE USE AND MISUSE OF FORCE: DEPARTMENTAL ISSUES

The goal of departments should not be to *eliminate* the police use of force. Reducing police use of force to a frequency of zero, would, of course, lead to harm to many officers and reduce drastically law enforcement's ability to enforce the law. Police must be able to use force to effectively do their jobs. Instead, a departmental goal should be to *optimize* the use of police force; that is, to have police use force only when no other nonviolent means would be effective and to use only that amount of force which is reasonably necessary to effectuate a legitimate police function. In this section we discuss *why* it is important for departments to optimize their use of force, and as key components of that "optimization," reduce the amount of excessive and unnecessary force used by their officers.

The Fourth Amendment

The Articles of the U.S. Constitution set forth the powers of the federal government. The Bill of Rights imparts power to the citizens by restricting the power of government. Specifically, these provisions state what the government *cannot do* vis-a-vis citizens (e.g., restrict speech, legislate religion) and indicates what the government *must do* when processing a citizen through the criminal justice system (e.g., provide a public trial with an impartial jury). Our early political leaders wrote these provisions in an attempt to avoid the governmental repression the colonists had experienced under Great Britain.

An important "government can't" provision is the Fourth Amendment, which reads:

> The right of the people to be secure in their persons, houses, papers and effects against unreasonable searches and seizures, shall not be violated, and no Warrants shall issue, but upon probable cause, supported by Oath or affirmation, and particularly describing the place to be searched and the person or things to be seized.

This amendment, though restricting all government officials, has particular relevance to police. It governs police ability to search persons, places, and things and to seize evidence and people (e.g., make arrests or detain people). This amendment to the U.S. Constitution is the source of the standard of "reasonableness" (*Tennessee v. Garner,* 1985; *Graham v. Connor,* 1989), and therefore any use of excessive (that is, unreasonable) force is a violation of a constitutional right. One would hope that there exists within departmental cultures the moral imperative to abide by our country's founding document as well as the federal and state laws which similarly restrict force. Lacking this moral imperative, the Fourth Amendment could still impact law enforcement departments in that, as discussed below, constitutional and statutory violations provide the basis of lawsuits against police.

Police–Community Relations

The citizen surveys described above solicited specific information from respondents about incidents of police abuse that they (or their family members or acquaintances) had experienced. These and other surveys have also asked respondents whether they believed that police in their areas used excessive force frequently (e.g., Komarnicki & Doble, 1985; Urban Studies Center, 1982). Providing findings that are fairly consistent with other studies, a 1985 poll by the *New York Daily News* (cited in Flanagan & Vaughn, 1995) determined that while only 7 percent of the *white* respondents believed that police "often use too much force," a full 26 percent of the *African American and Hispanic* respondents believed that too much force was used by police. A *New York Times* poll in 1987 (cited in Flanagan & Vaughn, 1995) determined that 70 percent of the African American respondents think that "New York City police often engage in brutality against blacks." Only 19 percent of the whites thought that police "often" used excessive force against whites.

The police use of force generally, and use of deadly force particularly, have played a significant role in the history of both police policy reform and police-community relations. Essential to this history is this perception on the part of ethnic minority communities that police use force excessively against them. Especially during the 1960s and 1970s, this perception had a great impact on the relationship between police and minority communities across the country. According to Alpert and Fridell (1992, p. 141),

> A great deal of effort has been expended to determine whether or not the dispro-portionate representation of black subjects of police shootings is the result of police bias. However, for purposes of analyzing the forces of change in the area of deadly force with firearms, the precise answer to that question is less important than public perception. Regardless of whether or not the police have "one trigger finger for blacks and one for whites," this perception has been reality for a large segment of the minority community. Indeed, the consequences of these perceptions have been critical, not just for police use of deadly force policies and practices, but for policing in general.

As reported by Gilbert G. Pompa, Director of the Federal Department of Justice Community Relations Service (CRS), at a convention in 1980,

> During recent years, charges of police use of excessive force have grown to replace school desegregation as the issue that most dominates the caseload of the CRS. Not even the Ku Klux Klan promotes more community resentment or minor-ity/white hostilities, or has more potential for sparking open community violence than allegations that police use force excessively against minorities.

This "open community violence" includes many of the riots during the last 35 years. Miami during the 1980s experienced a series of civil disturbances that were caused by police use of deadly force against members of the minority community (see Alpert, 1989). Additionally, police shooting incidents have led to violence during the 1980s and 1990s in cities such as Los Angeles, St. Louis, Brooklyn, Birmingham, Paterson (NJ), and San Francisco. However, the hostility between the police and minority communities was most intense during the 1960s, and Walker (1980) reports that a police encounter with a minority citizen was the precipitating event for at least 84 of the 136 major riots during this decade.

Alpert and Fridell (1992) discuss how the perceptions on the part of minority communities regarding the excessive use of force, particularly deadly force, on the part of police led to major changes in both policy and practice across the country. However, as indicated by the relatively recent poll results described above, the per-ception still exists on the part of ethnic minorities that they are the frequent targets of police use of excessive force.

Particularly in this era of community policing, this strained relationship between the police and the minority community has costs beyond the tragedy of civil distur-bances. As Bayley (1995, p. 270) notes, "the fear of police brutality might affect calls for police service, readiness to assist the police, levels of emotion in police contacts, avoidance of police contact, latent disrespect, repressed anger, and inclination to believe the worst about the police." Bayley explains that the fear of brutality might, in fact, lead to more brutality, which is consistent with the discussion below of the transactional nature of force incidents. For instance, an African American male who believes police are racist and brutal may be disinclined to cooperate with police and show the deference that many police expect. The police may, in turn, resort to more force than is reasonably necessary in the face of this resistance.

At a broader level, Bayley (1995, p. 276) points out that brutality is a problem of "political legitimacy." The perception of police as lawless can lead to an overall lack of respect for government and rule of law. At a more practical level for the police, the lack of community support may lead to reduced budgets and other support.

Lawsuits

Certainly it is devastating to a law enforcement department to have an officer charged criminally for using excessive force. But much more common than criminal charges against officers accused of excessive force are lawsuits filed against officers, and frequently against their supervisors and their departments, as well (Pate & Fridell, 1993). Federal law provides that citizens can sue government officials for deprivation of constitutional rights, and most states permit civil law suits against law enforcement for excessive use of force and other misconduct (Cheh, 1995). State laws vary as to when the officer's supervisor or the department, as well as the officer, may be liable. Under federal law, the supervisor can be liable for an officer's misconduct if the supervisor was negligent in his training of, directing, supervising, hiring, disciplining, or assigning the officer (del Carmen, 1995). An officer's department (or city) may be liable for his or her misconduct if the behavior of the officer was caused by a written or unwritten departmental policy (*Monell v. Department of Social Services,* 1988).

Although the data for police liability is not easy to obtain, some efforts have provided a brief picture of the financial aspects of police lawsuits. For example, Newell, Pollock, and Tweedy (1992) report (from data collected in 1990) that the highest liability claim was $36 million; the average cost for outside legal counsel was $16,500 and the maximum settlement was $2.5 million. More specifically related to force lawsuits, Pate and Fridell (1993) asked departments to indicate the number of civil suits filed against them in 1991 that alleged excessive force. The resolutions of the completed suits, including amounts paid to litigants, was also requested. Unfortunately, less than 30 percent of the departments provided this information. Some indicated that they did not keep annual statistics on this information and others stated that they were unable or unwilling to release such information, out of concern that it might prove to be politically controversial or would provoke additional inquiries from litigants. Based on the limited information provided by the responding agencies, Pate and Fridell determined that in 1991 the rates of civil suits alleging excessive force per 1,000 sworn officers were 23.7 for municipal police departments, 14.5 for sheriffs' departments, and 5.9 for state agencies.

Most information on civil suits is available only at the departmental level. For instance, del Carmen (1993) reports that the city of Los Angeles paid $11 million and $13 million in 1990 and 1991, respectively, in damage awards for police misconduct. New York spent $44 million to settle misconduct suits between 1986 and 1992, and, according to the *Miami Herald,* Miami Beach, during 1986 and 1992 paid to litigants an average of $11,254 per sworn officer (cited in del Carmen, 1993). Clearly, these statistics indicate that departments have a lot to lose financially if they do not work to optimize their officers' use of force.

Officer Injuries and Deaths

We have described why departments need to reduce the amount of excessive and unnecessary force used by their officers. However, as noted in the introduction to this chapter, limiting officers' capabilities of using reasonable and necessary force has many ramifications for departments, too. Arguably, most of the approximately 80,000 assaults against officers each year and the 60 to 75 felonious killings of officers annually (see Fridell & Pate, 1995) are the result of insufficient force used by officers to take control of their encounters with citizens. Added onto the intangible costs associated with these deaths and injuries are financial costs in the form of death benefits, insurance, and the temporary or permanent loss of trained personnel. Further, as indicated dramatically by the Los Angeles riots following the first verdict in the Rodney King case, the underutilization of force reduces the department's ability to enforce the law.

Maintaining the Balance

Obviously, a department with frequent incidents involving misuse of force incurs costs in the form of perceived legitimacy, public relations and public support, and lawsuits. On the other hand, a department with frequent incidents in which reasonable and necessary force is underutilized is less able to effectively enforce the law and incurs deaths and injuries to officers and the financial, morale, and emotional costs associated therewith.

Earlier we discussed how an officer applying the force continuum must find that narrow line separating excessive force and insufficient force. A department attempting to optimize its force is also balancing on that thin line with great costs associated with leanings to either side.

CORRELATES OF THE USE AND MISUSE OF FORCE

In previous sections, we have presented information regarding the extent to which police use and misuse force and discussed the ramifications to departments of the overutilization or underutilization of force. For departments to effectively intervene to optimize the use of force by their officers, they need information regarding the factors which researchers have identified as correlates of the use and misuse of force. The extent to which *reasonable force* is used by police could be a product of many factors *outside* the police department, as well as of factors *within* the department. For instance, characteristics of the community such as crime rates, citizen attitudes toward police, and availability of guns could affect the degree to which officers need to use force to effectuate legitimate police functions. On the other hand, we argue that the extent to which this force is *excessive* can only be explained by factors internal to the department, for instance, the type of officer employed, the socialization and training of those officers, the extent to which officers are disciplined for misusing force.

In this section, we focus on the individual, situational, and departmental factors that have been found to be associated with the use and misuse of force. We begin by presenting what researchers have found with regard to the characteristics of officers who use and misuse force and the justifications provided by officers for their use of force. Those justifications help explain how and why incidents involving certain police officers and certain groups of citizens are at increased risk of becoming violent. Also in this section we discuss how policy restrictiveness and policy enforcement can affect the extent to which reasonable and excessive force is used in departments.

Officer Characteristics and the Use of Force

Toch (1969, 1985, 1995) claims that there exist violence-prone individuals who "invite violence-prone interactions" (1995, p. 225). Similarly, the Independent Commission of the Los Angeles Police Department (1991), which was charged with investigating the LAPD following the Rodney King incident, found that a small number of officers were responsible for a large proportion of excessive force complaints. Research has attempted to identify the individual characteristics that differentiate these officers who do and do not use excessive force. Croft (1985) used use-of-force forms to compare Rochester, New York, officers who used force frequently with officers who did not, controlling for duty assignment and arrest exposure. She found that officers who used more force were significantly younger and, relatedly, had fewer years of service. Similarly, studying *complaints* of excessive force, Cohen and Chaiken (1972) found that younger officers had more complaints filed against them. However, Friedrich (1980, p. 89) reported that "there is only the slightest indication that more experienced officers use force more reasonably and less excessively than less experienced officers."

The results regarding education levels and use of force or use of excessive force are mixed, depending on whether the research is looking at force reported to the department, observed excessive force, or complaints of excessive force. Croft (1985) found no effect of education on the extent to which force is used; however, several researchers reported that the less educated officers have more citizen complaints (Cascio, 1977; Cohen & Chaiken, 1972; Pate & Fridell, 1993). (Though Pate and Fridell only found this for sheriffs' departments, not for municipal police or state law enforcement agencies.) Possibly tying those results together, Worden (1995a, using observational data) found that officers with at least a bachelor's degree were more likely to use force, but less likely to use improper force.

On the subject of race, using observational data, both Friedrich (1980) and Worden (1995a) report that African American officers were more likely to use *reason-*

able force, but less likely to use *excessive* force. Paralleling the reasonable force finding is the deadly force research that has found that African American officers use more deadly force than white officers (e.g., Fyfe, 1981; Geller & Karales, 1981). This has been attributed to the assignment of African American officers to the higher crime areas and to the greater propensity for African American officers to live in the higher crime neighborhoods (see, e.g., Fyfe, 1981; Geller & Karales, 1981).

On the subject of racism, the Independent Commission of the LAPD made a point of the one-quarter of the 650 officers surveyed who believed that "an officer's prejudice towards the suspect's race may lead to the use of excessive force" (1991, p. 69). Toch (1995), on the other hand, made a point of the 57 percent of the respondents to this survey who believed that this was *not* true. Black and Reiss (1967) and Friedrich (1980) came to different conclusions regarding the role of racial prejudice in officers' use of force against African Americans, though they used the same source of data. The officers' attitudes toward African Americans were assessed based on the conversations between the observers and officers during their lengthy interactions. Reiss (1971) reported that, though more than 75 percent of the officers made prejudiced statements about African Americans during the period of observation, the police did not assault African American persons unnecessarily or treat African American persons "uncivilly" more often than they did whites. On the other hand, Friedrich (1980) claimed that although the differences across prejudiced and non-prejudiced officers were small, "the more prejudiced the police are, the more likely they are to use force against black offenders" (p. 90).

Worden (1995a, 1995b) uses his data on officer attitudes and the existing literature on typologies of police officers to identify "composite types" of officers who "appear to differ in their propensities to use force" (1995a, p. 34). For instance, Wordon speculates that the type of officer *least* likely to misuse force is the "problem solver." He describes the problem solver this way (1995b, pp. 59–60):

> They regard their clientele as people who endure tragedies not of their own making. These officers see themselves as a positive force, "offering assistance in solving whatever kind of problem . . . [their clientele] face." For problem-solvers, then, the scope of legitimate police duties encompasses much more than crime control. . . . They are skeptical of traditional police methods, as they are unable to reconcile the use of coercive measures with their moral code. Consequently, although they are willing to invoke the law when situations demand it, they prefer informal approaches (citations omitted).

In contrast, the "tough cops," according to Worden (1995a) are the *most* likely to misuse force. He describes this type of officer as follows (1995b, pp. 58–59):

> Tough cops have a cynic perspective and an integrated morality. Their cynicism may lead them to define the police role as one of controlling crime; they see themselves as a principally negative force in people's lives. They do not (or refuse to) empathize with their clientele; they believe that the citizenry is hostile to police, and they are insensitive to the myriad forces that impel people to behave as they do. . . . They believe in an aggressive style of patrol, that legal restrictions do more

harm than good, and that the "brass" are "out of touch with the reality of the street. . . ." They believe in the utility of force and the effectiveness of "curbstone justice" (citations omitted).

Officer Justifications for the Use of Force

The officers' characteristics described above are hypothesized to affect police use or misuse of force, depending on the characteristics of the situation in which an officer finds himself or herself. That is, to explain and understand use of force, we need to conceive of police–citizen encounters as transactional in nature. This becomes especially apparent when looking at the research on officers' motives for using force, especially excessive force, as it pertains to disenfranchised groups of citizens in society.

In an early study, Westley (1970) found that officers felt illegal force was acceptable to obtain the respect of citizens or, if necessary, to make a "good pinch" (arrest). Regarding the former, when asked to name the instances when "roughing someone up" might be justified, the largest response category referred to instances where a citizen was showing disrespect for police. Thirty-nine percent of the officers gave this as their primary or secondary response. This expectation of deference on the part of officers, and its relation to police violence, has been discussed by other authors and is consistent with the classic literature on the effect of citizen demeanor on police actions (Black & Reiss, 1967; Lundman, Sykes & Clark, 1978; Petersen, 1972; Piliavin & Briar, 1964). Toch (1985, p. 10) explains, "A recurrently established finding in the police violence literature is that brutality is a response to perceived challenges by citizens of the officer's right to 'control' their encounter." (See, e.g., Worden, 1995a.) Or, as Sykes and Clark (1975, p. 93) state, "Officers learn to expect others to acknowledge their status and power, for most citizens extend them compliance and deference. . . . When citizen interaction falls below their standard, they utilize corrective sanctions."

Forms of this citizen defiance might include merely speech (see, e.g., the results of Chevigny, 1969), or might involve failing to move along, ripping up a traffic ticket, recording an officer's badge number, or something much more serious. Several of the widely broadcast videotaped beatings of citizens by police followed on the heels of citizen defiance in the form of failing to stop a vehicle. Police pursuit of vehicles preceded the videotaped beating of Rodney King by the LAPD, the undocumented immigrants by Riverside County law enforcement, and a lone female motorist in South Carolina. Worden's (1995a) finding that the use of improper force was significantly more likely in incidents involving car chases supports the notion that leading police in a vehicle pursuit is a particularly potent form of "contempt of cop," and fits the defiance hypothesis quite well.

This officer demand for respect can lead to particular troubles with segments of the population that are not inclined to show deference to the police. Further, officers' expectations regarding the lack of deference they *expect* from particular groups can lead to an "over assertion" of authority, which might *elicit* the expected negative response whether or not it was originally forthcoming (see especially, Smith &

Hawkins, 1973, as well as Westley, 1953, and Skolnick, 1966). Conversely, citizen *expectation* of an uncivil (or even brutal) response from police might prematurely elicit defiance. [Relevant here is a recent judicial ruling—subsequently reversed—that it was reasonable (and thus, not suspicious) for persons to run from police in a particular area of New York City where cops were known to be very corrupt and violent.]

The high-risk scenario described above, involving an officer who wants respect and a citizen disinclined to provide it, may help to explain the complaint (e.g., Pate & Fridell, 1993), self-report (e.g., Bayley & Mendelsohn, 1969), and observational data (Worden, 1995a) that indicate that young males and minority group members are disproportionately the victims of misuse of force by police.

The second major justification that Westley's subjects offered for excessive force was to put a criminal behind bars. Specifically, the emphasis was on using excessive force to get information to facilitate the apprehension or conviction of a criminal. Twenty-three percent of Westley's subjects mentioned this justification as primary or secondary responses to the question regarding when "roughing someone up" was justified. Westley explains (1970, p. 128),

> The use of force against the suspect is justified by the men on the basis that they are acting in the interests of the community. They feel that they are only using the methods of the suspect, and that in doing so they frequently apprehend men who are a danger to the people in the community.

This reflects the moral dilemma of police referred to by Klockars (1980) as "the Dirty Harry problem." Specifically, this moral dilemma exists "when the ends to be achieved are urgent and unquestionably good and only dirty means will work to achieve them" (p. 33). The three criteria for a "Dirty Harry problem," according to Klockars are that (1) the ends are, in fact, "good"; (2) the dirty means will result in the good end; and (3) the dirty means are the only means to achieve the good end. This type of dilemma, he explains, manifests itself in police decisions to detain people, search people, use excessive force, and so forth. If the dirty means are ends in themselves—for instance, the police take it upon themselves to "punish" the guilty person—there is no moral dilemma. Klockars (1980, p. 40) explains,

> Dirty Harry problems of this type can no longer be read as cases of dirty means employed to the achievement of good ends. For unless we are willing to admit that in a democratic society a police arrogates to itself the task of punishing those who they think are guilty, we are forced to conclude that Dirty Harry problems represent cases of employing dirty means to dirty ends, in which case, nobody, not the police and certainly not us, is left with any kind of moral dilemma.

To prevent police using dirty means to achieve good ends and dirty means to achieve dirty ends, Klockars says we must "punish those who use them and the agency which endorses their use" (p. 33).

This means–ends dilemma (or maybe small sample size) might be responsible for the distressing results found by Barker (1978) in his survey of officers regarding deviant activities. This survey was mentioned above with regard to officers' beliefs regarding the prevalence of police perjury, sex on duty, drinking on duty, sleeping on duty, and excessive force on a prisoner. The officers were also asked to indicate, using a scale of zero to nine, how "wrong" each activity was. Finally, each officer was asked to indicate for each deviant behavior whether a fellow officer would "always," "sometimes," "rarely," or "never" report a colleague. Forty-six percent of the officers indicated that their fellow officers would "rarely" or "never" turn in another officer for excessive force against a prisoner. They report, instead, that officers are more likely to be turned in for sleeping or drinking on duty. Police brutality was perceived by the officer respondents to be the least "wrong" of the five activities studied! On the ten-point scale (0–9, with nine indicating the "most wrong"), officers rated excessive force against a prisoner as 6.7, compared to 7.5 for sex on duty, 8.0 for sleeping on duty, 8.6 for perjury, and 8.7 for drinking on duty.

Policy Restrictiveness and the Use of Force

Not surprisingly, research indicates that policy restrictiveness affects the extent to which members of a department use force. The earliest published study was conducted by Uelman (1973) who collected information from 50 police agencies in Los Angeles County to assess policy, content, effectiveness, and enforcement. He found great diversity across jurisdictions in terms of policies regarding the use of deadly force against fleeing felons and found, as one would expect, that shooting rates correlate with policy restrictiveness. Furthermore, he found that the departments in the most restrictive policy category had approximately one-half the shooting rates of departments with the least restrictive policies. Not surprising, the greatest difference in policies was whether or not the department allowed for the shooting of persons fleeing from a felony, and, indeed, the shooting of fleeing felons accounted for a large part of the differences in rates. However, Uelman also found departments with more restrictive policies had fewer defense of life shootings, as well, even though all departments (with and without "restrictive" policies) allow for this type of shooting. This indicated that more restrictive policies produced an overall reduction in police shootings at citizens, even beyond the reductions which would be expected by the specific limitations posed by the policies.

Several years later Fyfe (1978) assessed the effects of a new shooting policy and new shooting review procedures in New York City. In 1972, the New York City Police Department implemented a policy that further limited the situations in which officers could shoot citizens and provided for a Firearms Discharge Review Board to investigate and evaluate all discharges by department police. Thus, simultaneously, the department reduced officers' power to use deadly force and implemented a policy enforcement mechanism. Fyfe studied all police discharges in that city between January 1, 1971, and December 31, 1975, to document the effect on the "frequency, nature, and consequences of police shooting in New York City" of the new policy and new review board (p. 312). He found a "considerable reduction" in police firearms discharges following the policy modifications. The greatest reduction was in the "most controversial shootings," that is, those involving fleeing felons or the prevention or termination of a crime. Reductions in shooting rates followed implementation of more restrictive policies in Los Angeles (Meyer, 1980), Atlanta, Kansas City (Missouri) (Sherman, 1983), Oakland (see Geller & Scott, 1992), and Omaha (Walker & Fridell, 1993).

One unintended consequence of more restrictive policies could be greater danger to police officers. As such, it is important to note that the studies that documented decreases in shooting rates following the adoptions of more restrictive policies did not find that officers were harmed at greater rates.

Policy Enforcement and the Use of Force

The content of a policy may have little impact on police behavior if the policy is not enforced by the department. As mentioned above, Fyfe noted the importance, not only of the new, more restrictive shooting policy in New York City, but also the establishment of the Firearms Discharge Review Board for policy enforcement. Uchida (1982) assessed the effectiveness of Operation Rollout in Los Angeles in the 1970s, which changed the way police-involved shootings were investigated. It was hypothesized that the involvement of the Los Angeles District Attorney's Office in the at-the-scene as well as follow-up investigations would provide a more "full, fair, objective, independent, and timely" review process which would reduce the frequency of police shootings (p. 189). In fact, Uchida's data indicates that police use of deadly force decreased following the implementation of Operation Rollout, though he cautioned that "it cannot be said with certainty how much of that change was a result of Rollout" (p. 272).

The existence and strength of enforcement units such as those described above are components of a department's "administrative posture" regarding force policy adherence. Investigating the Los Angeles Police Department after the Rodney King beating, the Independent Commission of the Los Angeles Police Department reported that, "The problem of excessive force in the LAPD is fundamentally a problem of supervision, management, and leadership" (1991, p. 32). This statement highlights that not just the *content* of policies, but the *administrative commitment* to those policies is key to controlling force. That polices and procedures are insufficient in the absence of an administrative posture demanding compliance is also indicated in an American Civil Liberties Union report on "Police Brutality and its Remedies." The report states (1991, p. 6): "When incidents of brutality, misconduct or racism occur, the chief's immediate reaction to these incidents will have a great impact on whether the incident will be repeated in the future."

Skolnick and Fyfe (1993) describe events in several cities in which the contents of restrictive written shooting policies were overwhelmed by the much more lax unwritten policies of the top administrators. Similarly, Sherman (1983) maintained that findings of reduced shootings following policy adoption in the cities he looked at

> do not suggest that these results can be achieved by the mere invocation of a written policy. The policy changes in each of these cities were all accompanied by

intense public criticism of the police and an increasingly severe administrative and disciplinary posture toward shooting (p. 123).

Waegel (1984) assessed the compliance of the Philadelphia Police Department with a 1973 statutory change in deadly force law by examining police shootings between 1970 and 1978. The primary effect of the statutory revision was to restrict officers' abilities to shoot nondangerous fleeing felons. Waegel found "a substantial noncompliance" with the new law. He reported that 20 percent of the shooting incidents after the statute changed were unlawful, suggesting that "statutory change alone may not be sufficient to bring about desired changes in police behavior" (p. 136). Instead, he argued that without an administrative stance that the law will be complied with, the changes in behavior called for by a statutory revision will not occur.

Geller and Scott (1992), too, argue that "a written policy must have 'teeth' put into it through various administrative initiatives" (p. 278). They describe the stiff penalties for brutality imposed by Chief Steven Bishop in Kansas City shortly after his arrival. Geller and Scott (1992, p. 278) state that "such decisions often send police employees powerful messages about the importance of restraint in the use of force, and insiders believe these discipline cases help explain the drop in use of deadly force."

The administrative posture in a department may encompass much more than the chief's attitude toward use of force. It may reflect an overall attitude toward the role and style of law enforcement. For instance, the report of the Los Angeles Independent Commission, in its attempt to determine the causes of misuse of force, identified the police department's "assertive style of law enforcement" as leading to "aggressive confrontations with the public" (1991, p. 97). They described a reward structure in which aggressive policing produced the greatest reinforcements for officers. In discussing Los Angeles, Toch (1985, p. 103) points out that "the motives of violence-prone officers tend to be compatible with hard-nosed ('let's go get 'em') organizational goals."

DEPARTMENTAL INTERVENTIONS TO OPTIMIZE THE USE OF FORCE

The research results presented in the previous section indicate that officer characteristics, departmental policies regarding force, and departmental commitment to enforcing those policies are essential to understanding the extent to which force is used and, especially, misused. That information will be related in this section to departmental policies and procedures that can be used to reduce officer use of excessive and unnecessary force.

Employment Screening

As noted above, some preliminary research indicates that a few officers are responsible for a large proportion of incidents involving excessive force. One question is whether this tendency to use excessive force is a result of (1) characteristics that the officer brought to the job, (2) a result of socialization within the police department, or (3) both. Assuming that this propensity to use force is a result of *both* characteristics brought to the job and socialization/norms within the police department, we discuss here how employment screening might be able to address the former and below we address how training and policy enforcement might address the latter.

It is probable that the persons who use excessive force frequently came into the job with personality characteristics or values that inclined him or her toward this behavior. The great challenge for researchers and policy makers is to identify these characteristics and values and develop ways to screen for them at the hiring stage.

Grant and Grant (1995) report that there are no studies that *effectively* assess the link between screening mechanisms and the *use or misuse of force*. There is some literature, however, that addresses more generally the ability of screening mechanisms to screen out "undesirable" officers. They report (1995, p. 151) that "a review of the studies suggests that recruit screening, at least as it is done at present, is not a very effective way to weed out bad or incompetent police officers." The New York State Commission reported (1987, p. 306): "Early identification and screening of applicants that are or may be violence prone are . . . problematic. In order to develop methods to do so, it is necessary . . . [t]o isolate those personality characteristics that are predictive of violent behavior." This commission suggested that additional research be conducted which could lead to the development of screening devices to identify violence-prone persons. Recognizing the tremendous challenge of predicting violent behavior based on psychological tests, they also recommended that background investigations be especially vigorous as *past behavior* is the best predictor of *future behavior.*

Similarly, the Independent Commission of the LAPD highlighted the importance of assessing *violent histories* of applicants. The members were disturbed that the LAPD, during background investigations, paid much more attention to drug use and sexual orientation than violent tendencies. They reported (1991, p. 11),

> according to the Personnel Department, the investigators often ask intensely personal and pointed follow-up questions regarding sexual history and use of drugs, while not pursuing a candidate's responses to the questions on violence. As a result, the investigators may not effectively screen out individuals with violent tendencies.

The LAPD commission, like the New York State Commission, recommended that, during employment screening, more attention should be given to past behavior and less to test and interview results. The members expressed concern in their report that psychological screening devices may not be able to "test for . . . subtle abnormalities which may make an individual ill-suited to be a police officer, such as poor impulse control and the proclivity toward violence" (p. 110).

Most departments do provide for some form of psychological evaluation of applicants. Sixty to 90 percent of the various types of law enforcement departments have psychological evaluations for applicants. Specifically, Pate and Fridell (1993) report that about 60 percent of the sheriffs' departments, 70 percent of the municipal police departments, and 90 percent of the state agencies give psychological or psychiatric evaluations to prospective officers. Larger agencies were more likely than smaller agencies to have this type of assessment. Consistent with these results, Scrivner (1994) found that 71 percent of the police psychologists who responded to her survey reported that preemployment screening of law enforcement applicants was one of their major functions.

Employee Monitoring and Early Warning

The commission on the LAPD emphasized that, in addition to preselection screening, departments should retest officers periodically during employment to detect problems. For two decades, law enforcement agencies have used various methods to monitor their officers. This monitoring might focus broadly on detecting psychological/emotional problems or might, more specifically, attempt to identify officers who are prone to or using excessive force (Federal Bureau of Investigation, 1991).

Grant and Grant (1995), however, suggest that these psychological tests are no more effective in predicting misuse of force *after selection* than they are *before selection*. Instead, they claim that the greatest potential of psychological tests would be to detect the onset of personal problems or work stress which could negatively affect an officer's overall performance capabilities. Along these lines, they recommend that departments "divert mental health resources from selection decision-making to support services" for both recruits and in-service employees (see also, Scrivner, 1994).

As stated earlier, more and more departments are enhancing their monitoring capabilities by adopting use-of-force forms on which officers report and describe incidents in which force was used. It should also be noted that departments that do not use use-of-force forms, may still require force reporting in *regular* incident reports. Further, departments may only require that certain types of force be reported *every* time it is used and that other types of force be reported only, for instance, when an injury results from that use. Thus, while virtually all (though, interestingly, not *all*) law enforcement departments have policies requiring that officers report incidents in which citizens are shot and killed, approximately 80 percent of all sheriffs' departments and municipal police departments require that their officers report the use of batons or the use of flashlights as weapons, and 70 percent required the reporting of incidents in which chemical agents (e.g., Mace, Capstun) are used (Pate & Fridell, 1993).

A number of researchers (e.g., Geller & Toch, 1995; Klockars, 1995; Pate & Fridell, 1993) call for all departments to adopt use-of-force reports. Klockars (1995) states that although collecting information on *each and every* use of force by police is ideal, this comprehensive collection is not practical. Instead, he advocates that all uses of force that "cause death or bodily injury or involve the use of police equipment such as firearms, batons, chemical irritants, stun devices, and attack dogs" be reported, as well as those lower level uses of force that cause injury or may potentially lead to a complaint (as indicated by the reaction of the person against whom the force was used).

Klockars suggests that—in addition to dates, times, locations, and identities of all officers, subjects, and witnesses—these reports should contain "a detailed description of the type and amount of force used; a description of the incident and relevant events that led up to and followed it; and a description of the injuries sustained by any and all parties" (1995, pp. 23–24). He suggests that supervisors, not the officers involved, complete these forms. If the forms contain a checklist, as well as a narrative section, then the former section can be utilized to produce a computerized data set.

To be effective force-monitoring mechanisms, the reports must themselves be monitored. Or, as Klockars (1995, p. 24) states, "From the point of view of controlling the excessive use of force, it is pointless to report a use of force without evaluating it." That is, these reports should be regularly reviewed as they are submitted or computerized to provide for an assessment of officer and department use of force over time. The Pate and Fridell (1993) survey found that between 56 and 70 percent of sheriffs' departments, municipal police departments, and state law enforcement agencies reviewed *all* reports of force.

Geller and Toch (1995) report that most departments only pay attention to certain categories of force. Specifically, departments generally attend to unreasonable use of force and commendable force—punishing the former and rewarding the latter. However, departments generally do not reward commendable restraint (when officers reasonably refrain from using force, though it might have been justified) or provide feedback to officers who use unnecessary force in situations in which more skilled officers might have been able to avoid force. Klockars (1995) points out that, by punishing only *excessive* force and ignoring *unnecessary* force, the department is thereby setting a minimum standard of "no unreasonable force," instead of aspiring to a higher standard of "no unreasonable *nor* unnecessary force." He argues that departments ought to attend to (though not necessarily with punishment) officers' uses of unnecessary force that come to the departments' attention through force reports.

The force review process that Klockars recommends would start with the supervisor preparing the use-of-force form and determining whether the force was (1) necessary and appropriate, (2) reasonable but unnecessary, or (3) in violation of department policy. The report and supervisor's assessment should be passed up the chain of command and the officer should receive feedback from this review within 48 hours, which either (1) acknowledges his or her appropriate (maybe even commendable) use of necessary and reasonable force; (2) informs him or her that the incident has been referred to Internal Affairs, because the reviewing agents believed the force to be excessive; or (3) informs the officer that, though the force used might have been reasonable, it appeared to have been unnecessary. Klockars does not advocate punishment for this latter outcome, but rather a brief retraining session, for instance, whereby "a senior, skilled, and experienced police officer explains to (the) fellow officer in detail how that officer might have conducted himself in a way that might have avoided the need to use force or minimized its actual use" (p. 26).

Information beyond use-of-force forms/reports contained within personnel files can be used as part of an "early warning" system designed to help identify violence-prone officers. Materials maintained in personnel files which would be pertinent to an "early warning" system might include

- The number of times an officer is assaulted or resisted in the course of making an arrest, as well as the number of injuries sustained by an officer or citizen in confrontations between the two;
- The number and outcome of citizen complaints lodged against an officer, alleging abusive behavior or unwarranted use of force. Many such complaints are groundless, and many that would be well-founded are never made; nevertheless, the accumulation of a large number of complaints against an officer may reveal something about that officer's style of policing;
- The number of shootings or [firearms] discharges involving an officer; and
- The picture of the officer presented in supervisory evaluations, interdepartmental memoranda, letters, and other reports (U.S. Commission on Civil Rights, 1981, p. 81).

An assessment of these indicators should take into consideration the nature of the officer's assignment, and his or her productivity (e.g., number of felony arrests).

After the Rodney King incident, the Christopher Commission called for an early warning system to be implemented in Los Angeles. The New York State Commission (1987) reported that 29 of the 30 New York agencies that responded to their survey indicated that they had some form of early intervention system in place.

Some more-aggressive monitoring programs were established in Salt Lake City and Bakersfield, California. In Salt Lake City, officer performance was "inspected" periodically by the department. An inspector interviewed persons with whom the officer had recently interacted—including suspects, witnesses, victims, and so forth. If the inspector came across negative comments, she or he interviewed at least five more citizens. Officers were informed of the outcome of the inspection and given constructive feedback regarding positive and negative points. If serious problems were found, in-person counseling would follow. Complaints against police dropped from five per day to an average of five per month within one year of policy implementation (Smith, 1974).

In 1967, as a result of citizen complaints of officer discourtesy, the Bakersfield Police Department required that officers tape record all of their officer-citizen contacts. Complaints of discourtesy dropped to near zero (Broadaway, 1974).

Complaint Review System

In an earlier section, we emphasized the importance of a strong administrative stance or message that excessive (and maybe even unnecessary) force will not be tolerated. This message can be conveyed in a number of ways, including via the force review system described above. Another form of that message is the existence of a strong, effective complaint review system. The Independent Commission of the LAPD claimed that, absent the video recording, the officers in the Rodney King incident would never have been held accountable for their behavior. The commission report (1991) stated,

The efforts of King's brother, Paul, to file a complaint were frustrated, and the report of the involved officers was falsified. Even if there had been an investigation, our case-by-case review of the handling of over 700 complaints indicates that without the Holliday videotape the complaint might have been adjudged to be "not sustained," because the officers' version conflicted with the account by King and his two passengers, who typically would have been viewed as not "independent."

(As an aside, it is also interesting to note that George Holliday attempted to bring the video to the attention of the LAPD, thinking that they would be interested in investigating this civilian beating. Subsequent to their communication of disinterest, Holliday turned the tape over to a local television station.)

A department that is not interested in controlling the use and misuse of force can very easily make the complaint review process a frustrating and ineffectual one. Adams (1995), Kamau (n.d.), and Pate and Fridell (1993) summarize the methods police use to do this. The police can make filing a complaint inconvenient or even impossible, or threaten or intimidate a citizen into not filing. Police can charge the potential complainant with resisting arrest. This charge can serve to undermine the citizen's credibility or be used later to bargain with the citizen to drop the complaint. Further, citizen witnesses may also be charged so as to undermine their credibility, as well. Police might warn a complainant that they could be charged with filing a false report if the complaint is not substantiated by the department.

Even if a department allows complaints to be filed, the investigation process might be weak or intimidating to complainants (see Pate & Fridell, 1993). For instance, Walker and Bumphus (1992, citing New York City Civilian Complaint Investigative Bureau, 1990) reported that one-third of the complaints filed during a 12-month period in New York City were dropped because either the citizen withdrew the complaint or the citizen was unavailable or refused to cooperate with the investigation. Walker and Bumphus noted that this citizen behavior may be the result, at least in part, of investigators' behavior. They suggested that "complaint processing officials may discourage citizens through indifference, rudeness, or failure to act on complaints in a timely fashion" (p. 13).

The LAPD Independent Commission found that the investigations of complaints were inadequate. They found "for example, [that] in a number of complaint files . . . there was no indication that the investigators had attempted to identify or locate independent witnesses, or if identified, to interview them" (1991, p. xix). Similarly, the Management Review Team of the Boston Police Department reported lengthy delays in the investigations of citizen complaints, insufficient "supervision or oversight to ensure thorough investigations" (p. 123) by the Internal Affairs unit, and "an appalling lack of documentation and record-keeping by IAD investigators" (St. Clair, 1992, p. 126).

The report on the Los Angeles Sheriff's Department (LASD) indicated that a number of complaints were never investigated and that the investigations into a significant number of complaints were closed prior to completion "at times under highly suspicious circumstances" (Kolts, 1992, p. 100). Those that were investigated were investigated in a "deficient" manner. In close to 100 of nearly 800 complaint files reviewed "there was no attempt to interview witnesses identified by LASD officers or the complainant" (Kolts, 1992, p. 111).

Perez and Muir (1995) review three general models of complaint review: internal review, civilian review board, and civilian monitor. Most departments have complaint review processes that are entirely internal (Pate & Fridell, 1993). Generally, under this model complaints are investigated by sworn personnel within the department, and this investigation is reviewed by the officers' immediate supervisor or the top administrator in the agency (e.g., chief, sheriff, commissioner). Increasingly, cities are adopting Civilian Review Boards (Walker, 1995), which incorporate citizens into the process. This type of citizen-run board might oversee the investigation, as well as review, of the complaints of misconduct brought to them. Perez refers to a mild form of civilian review as "civilian monitor." Under this model, the police investigate the complaints, but a civilian "monitors those investigations and (acts) as citizens' advocates" (p. 206). (See Pate & Fridell, 1993, for information regarding how departments nationwide investigate and review complaints of misconduct.)

A number of authors have reviewed the positive and negative aspects of incorporating civilians into the complaint review process (see, e.g., Brown, 1983; Gellhorn, 1966; Hensley, 1988; Hudson, 1971; Terrill, 1982, 1990). Proponents of some form of civilian review argue that it is required to ensure objective investigation and disposition of complaints and to enhance the credibility of the process (see, e.g., American Civil Liberties Union, 1991). Additional arguments are that civilian participation will make the system appear less intimidating, and thus more accessible, provide for more thorough investigations, and provide for more appropriate dispositions of misconduct complaints (see, e.g., Brown, 1983; Kerstetter, 1985; Skolnick & Fyfe, 1993).

Conversely, opponents claim that only law enforcement personnel have the expertise to evaluate police behavior and that citizens have recourse in the forms of criminal prosecution or civil suit if they are not satisfied with the departmental review (see Brown, 1983; Terrill, 1982). They express concern that the restraint imposed on police by an external review process would result in police becoming "so concerned about possible disciplinary action that they would be ineffective in their assigned duties" (Kerstetter, 1985, p. 161).

Perez conducted case studies in Oakland, Berkeley, and Kansas City, which had internal review, a civilian review board, and a civilian monitor, respectively. He concludes that there are positive and negative aspects of all three models. His research shows that citizens filing complaints would prefer to lodge them at a location other than the police station and speak to a civilian about their complaint. Although Perez reports that any of the models is capable of producing thorough investigations, citizens have the most faith in systems that incorporate some form of citizen review/oversight. And while internal systems will generally have greater expertise in determining what is misconduct, the systems with citizen involvement may in fact have the greater objectivity.

Though Perez claims that "external systems are less effective in influencing police behavior in several ways" (p. 218), he did not find that citizen involvement in complaint review was unacceptable to police. In a survey of police, he found that 35 percent preferred a combination of citizens and law enforcement officers serving as investigators. Even more surprising, 62 percent of the officers surveyed believed that a hearing board should consist of both police and civilians.

Finally, in looking at costs, Perez found the civilian review model to be the most expensive, even "so costly as to be prohibitive in most jurisdictions." [This would seem to correspond with Walker's finding (1995) that civilian review boards frequently are provided with staffing that is inadequate for carrying out their mandate.] Perez' conclusion was that, on balance, the civilian monitor system had the greatest potential for most departments.

Training

It is clear that training can positively impact all aspects of police work, including the use of force by police. The training of officers in the area of deadly force has greatly improved in recent years (see Alpert & Fridell, 1992) and much of that progress has ramifications for the use of less-than-lethal force, as well. A major advancement in the deadly force area was the increased emphasis in training on *when* to shoot, not just *how* to shoot. The corresponding application for less-than-lethal force is training, not just on less-than-lethal tactics and weapons, but on their appropriate utilization in various types of police-citizen encounters.

Further, progressive departments are training officers to avoid or defuse violence with smart tactics and strong communication skills. As Geller and Toch (1995, p. 319) explain, "Conflict management training essentially helps officers enhance their oral communication skills and use their mouths and minds as the primary tools for controlling potentially violent people." Various forms of conflict management training focus on reducing officer stress in potentially violent circumstances, on reducing the fear that police generate in citizens, and on approach tactics that reduce officer vulnerability (Geller & Scott, 1992; Geller & Toch, 1995). The Independent Commission of the LAPD recognized the need for these types of skills following their review of the academy, field, and in-service training in Los Angeles. The commission determined that "in each phase of training additional emphasis is needed on the use of verbal skills rather than physical force to control potentially volatile situations and on the development of human relationship skills to better serve Los Angeles' increasingly diverse population" (1991, p. 121).

The Metro-Dade Violence Reduction Project, developed by Fyfe, used role-playing of police-citizen encounters to "enhance patrol officers' skills in defusing the potentially violent situations they encounter every day" (1987, p. 1). The officers role-played perpetrators, bystanders, and officers as they learned and applied not just safety tactics, but officer sensitivity and politeness when dealing with citizens in order to avoid escalation to violence. Fyfe and his colleagues report that this training has been followed by substantial (30 to 50 percent) reductions in injuries to officers, officers' use of force, and citizens' complaints of abuse (Fyfe, 1995, citing Skolnick and Fyfe, 1993).

The emphasis on tactics by the Metro-Dade training and other models is consistent with the phase conceptualization of potentially violent encounters developed by Binder and Scharf (see, e.g., Binder & Scharf, 1980 and Scharf & Binder, 1983). These researchers point out that training should not focus so heavily on the final decision in a potentially violent encounter to use force or not use force, but rather, should give attention to decisions made early in such an encounter which may increase or decrease the likelihood of a force response. This involves conceptualizing potentially violent encounters, not merely as "split-second decisions" made by officers, but as incidents involving multiple decisions made by both opponents and officers where early decisions in an encounter affect the options available at a later point. Or as Binder and Scharf (1980, p. 111) explained, "the violent police-citizen encounter . . . is . . . a developmental process in which successive decisions and behaviors by either police officer or citizen, or both, make the violent outcome more or less likely." New tactical training, like that developed in Metro-Dade, "attempts to influence officer decision making well before the decision to (use force)" (Scharf & Binder, 1983, p. 207).

Additionally, in more recent years departments have emphasized cultural sensitivity training. This type of training has the potential to improve the overall quality of interaction among police and various segments of a jurisdiction's population. Geller and Toch (1995) explain the potential impact of this type of training on officer use and misuse of force: "By enhancing officers' understanding of the backgrounds and life circumstances of people with whom they interact, cultural awareness training can help officers avoid misreading and overreacting to the degree of danger in their encounters with potential opponents" (p. 308). These authors also point out that this training can inform police as to how their behavior may be interpreted, which could lead to "misreading and overreacting" on the part of citizens. (For instance, they point out that some persons of Southeast Asian descent would believe that a police request to kneel and place their hands behind their heads was a prelude to assassination and could lead to violent resistance; p. 312.) Consistent with the transactional nature of police–citizen encounters, Geller and Toch (1995) note that reducing hostility and bigotry on the part of officers could reduce the hostile response police get back. Thus, in fact, we could reduce the perceived need for violence on both the part of officer and citizen.

Changing Departmental Reward Structures

Training is not limited to the academy classroom, or even to the Field Training Officer experience or in-service courses. In fact, there is much training going on when an officer learns that, though the department policy says one thing, his peers, immediate supervisor, or agency head reward and reinforce another (see, e.g., Fyfe, 1995). That is, there is as much or more informal training (or socializing) occurring as formal training, and the former may in many instances have more impact than the latter. This highlights the theme of this section on departmental interventions: The key to optimizing the use of force by the department is a clear message conveyed to sworn personnel that excessive force and unnecessary force will not be tolerated. This message can be conveyed through applicant screening procedures, by monitoring employees' use of force, by implementing a strong and effective complaint review system, by educating officers on cultural differences, and training officers to use communication skills and tactics to defuse or avoid violence.

Officers should not only expect and receive punishment for excessive force and retraining for unnecessary force but, just as important, officers should expect and receive reinforcements for appropriate behavior. As noted previously, Geller and Toch (1995) suggest that departments need to use incentives, as well as punishment. They state (p. 282) that

> Except for a small number of officers who knowingly and wilfully misuse force—and who deserve punishment and probably separation from the agency if the necessary evidence can be compiled—we believe the best results in upgrading the use-of-force decision making and tactical skills of most officers will be obtained through positive incentives rather than through punishments.

Specifically, these researchers note the importance of rewarding commendable use of force and commendable restraint.

In a similar vein, Toch (1995) highlights the importance of reinforcing officers for the successful resolution of volatile interactions without force and argues that violence in police–citizen interactions can be reduced by "changing an agency's philosophy and its reward system to emphasize positive involvements with citizens" (p. 111). He contrasts this reward system to "crime-fighting" agencies where aggressive officers are held in high esteem and where recruits soon learn "that they will earn the respect of their veteran coworkers not by observing legal niceties in using force, but by being 'aggressive' and using whatever force is necessary in a given situation" (Hunt, 1985: p. 318, cited in Toch, 1995).

CONCLUSION

As this chapter conclusion is being written, the news is still abuzz with the recent beating of two suspected undocumented immigrants by Riverside County sheriffs' deputies. On the heels of an 80-mile chase of a rusting pickup carrying more than 20 persons, these officers were caught on videotape delivering baton blows to a man lying face down on the ground and to a woman pulled by her hair from the truck.

This chapter asks how often and why incidents like this happen and seeks to set forth remedies that departments might undertake to control the use of force. In trying to understand incidents such as these, we ask what is it about *these officers* that when placed in this *these circumstances* leads to the use of excessive force? What is it about the culture and atmosphere of law enforcement generally or the officers' departments in particular that made them think that they could treat persons in this fashion? We could ask these questions about the beating of Rodney King, the police murder of Malice Green in Detroit, the murder of Adolph Archie in Crescent City, Louisiana, the fatal beating of Arthur McDuffie in Miami, and many others (see De Santis, 1994).

Indeed, the misuse of force by police is a critical problem facing virtually all law enforcement departments in the United States. This problem is costing police departments millions of dollars, as well as reducing greatly their ability to work with the public to enforce the law. For the citizens of this country, as well, the costs are great. Police brutality reduces citizens' respect for the government and the rule of law and reduces to mere words the protections set forth in our Constitution. Brutality reduces our trust of and support for police and aggravates racial tensions. Brutality leads to fear, injury, and even loss of human life.

On the other hand the underutilization of reasonable and necessary force leads to 200 officers being assaulted each day and one officer feloniously killed each week. It can lead to underenforcement of the law, including tragic riots in our nation's streets.

Optimizing force is the challenge of every law enforcement department in this nation. Particularly potent are the pressures to reduce the excessive and unnecessary use of force by officers. Though there are major barriers to change, including the code of silence and deep-set, long-standing values and attitudes, there *are* ways to reduce these types of force in the departments which have the will to do so.

On the national level, there may be room for some optimism. Across the nation, researchers, citizens, police administrators, and policy makers are paying greater attention to the problem of police abuse. An increasing number of departments are beginning to monitor more closely the use of force by their officers. A new two-pronged national force-reporting system is being implemented. There are an increasing number of departments incorporating civilians into their complaint review process. More and more departments—under the rubric of community policing—are establishing strong, cooperative, respectful partnerships with the communities they serve. These and other changes, which have been taking place across the country, could be the seeds of major reform in this area.

DISCUSSION QUESTIONS

1. What is the difference between "excessive force" and "unnecessary force"? Which of these need to be controlled?
2. What do the authors mean when they refer to departments "optimizing" their officers' use of force? What are the drawbacks of too much force? Of too little force?
3. Why, according to the authors, is it important for departments to optimize their officers' use of force? Which of the reasons provided is/are most compelling to you?
4. Describe the type of department that would likely have very frequent uses of excessive force.
5. What are some of the promising mechanisms for optimizing police use of force? What mechanism or mechanisms are least promising?
6. What types of departmental interventions have been found to be associated with the reduced use of either force or excessive force?

REFERENCES

Adams, K. (1995). Measuring the prevalence of police abuse of force. In W.A. Geller & H. Toch (Eds.), *And justice for all: Understanding and controlling police abuse of force*, pp. 61–97. Washington, D.C.: Police Executive Research Forum.

Alpert, G.P., (1989). Police use of deadly force: The Miami experience. In R.G. Dunham & G.P. Alpert (Eds.), *Critical issues in policing: Contemporary readings*, pp. 480–495. Prospect Heights, IL: Waveland Press.

Alpert, G.P., & Fridell, L.A. (1992). *Police vehicles and firearms: Instruments of deadly force*. Prospect Heights, IL: Waveland Press.

———, & Smith, W. (1994). How reasonable is the reasonable man?: Police and excessive force. *Journal of Criminal Law and Criminology, 85*(2), 481–501.

American Civil Liberties Union. (1991). *On the line: Police brutality and its remedies*. New York: ACLU.

Barker, T. (1978). An empirical study of police deviance other than corruption. *Journal of Police Science and Administration, 6*(3), 264–272. Reprinted in T. Barker & D.L. Carter, (Eds.). (1991). *Police Deviance* 2nd Ed., pp. 123–138. Cincinnati: Anderson.

Bayley, D.H. (1995). Police brutality abroad. In W.A. Geller & H. Toch (Eds.), *And justice for all: Understanding and controlling police abuse of force*, pp. 261–276. Washington, D.C.: Police Executive Research Forum.

Bayley, D.H., & Mendelsohn, H. (1969). *Minorities and the police: Confrontation in America*. New York: Free Press.

———, & Garofalo, J. (1987). Patrol officer effectiveness in managing conflict during police–citizen encounters. In *Report to the Governor* (vol. III, pp. B–i to B–88). Albany: New York State Commission on Criminal Justice and the Use of Force.

———. (1989). The management of violence by police patrol officers. *Criminology, 27*(1), 1–25.

———, & Scharf, P. (1980). The violent police–citizen encounter. *Annals of the American Academy of Political and Social Science, 452,* 111–121.

Black, D.J., & Reiss, A.J., Jr. (1967). *Patterns of behavior in police and citizen transactions.* Field surveys III, studies in crime and law enforcement in major metropolitan areas, Vol. 2. Washington, D.C.: Government Printing Office.

Blumberg, M. (1985). Research on police use of deadly force: The state of the art. In A.S. Blumberg & E. Niederhoffer (Eds.), *The ambivalent force: Perspectives on the police*, 3rd ed., pp. 340–350. New York: Holt, Rinehart, and Winston.

Broadaway, F.M. (1974). Police misconduct: Positive alternatives. *Journal of Police Science and Administration, 2*(2), 210–218.

Brooks, T.R. (1965, December 5). Police brutality? *New York Times Magazine,* pp. 60–61, 63, 65–66, 68.

Brown, D.C. (1983). *Civilian review of complaints against the police: A survey of the United States literature.* London: Home Office, Research and Planning Unit, Paper 19.

Campbell, A., & Schuman, H. (1969). Racial attitudes in fifteen American cities. *Supplemental Studies for the National Advisory Commission on Civil Disorders.* Washington, D.C.: U.S. Government Printing Office.

Cascio, W.F. (1977). Formal education and police officer performance. *Journal of Police Science and Administration, 5*(1), 89–96.

Cheh, M.M. (1995). Are law suits an answer to police brutality? In W.A. Geller & H. Toch (Eds.), *And justice for all: Understanding and controlling police abuse of force*, pp. 233–259. Washington, D.C.: Police Executive Research Forum.

Chevigny, P. (1969). *Police power: Police abuses in New York City.* New York: Pantheon Books.

Cohen, E.B., & Chaiken, J.M. (1972). *Police background characteristics and performance: Summary.* New York: Rand Institute.

Croft, E.B. (1985). Police use of force: An empirical analysis. An unpublished doctoral dissertation, State University of New York at Albany.

Croft, E.B., & Austin, B.A. (1987). Police use of force in Rochester and Syracuse, New York 1984 and 1985. In *Report to the Governor* (vol. III, pp. C–i to C–128). Albany, NY: New York State Commission on Criminal Justice and the Use of Force.

del Carmen, R. (1993). Civil liabilities in law enforcement: Where are we and where should we go from here?, *American Journal of Police, 11*(4), 87–99.

———. (1995). *Criminal procedure: Law and practice,* 3rd ed. Belmont, CA: Wadsworth Publishing Company.

De Santis, J. (1994). The new untouchables: How America sanctions police violence. Chicago: The Noble Press, Inc.

Desmedt, J.C. (1984). Use of force paradigm for law enforcement. *Journal of Police Science and Administration, 12*(2), 170–176.

Dugan, J.R., & Breda, D.R. (1991). Complaints about police officers: A comparison among types and agencies. *Journal of Criminal Justice, 19*(2), 165–171.

Federal Bureau of Investigation. (1991). Use of unauthorized force by law. Washington, D.C.: Author.

Flanagan, T.J., & Vaughn, M.S. (1995). Public opinion about police abuse of force. In W.A. Geller & H. Toch (Eds.), *And justice for all: Understanding and controlling police abuse of force,* pp. 113–131. Washington, D.C.: Police Executive Research Forum.

Fridell, L.A. (1989). Justifiable use of measures in research on deadly force. *Journal of Criminal Justice, 17,* 157–165.

Fridell, L.A., & Pate, A.M. (1995). Death on patrol: Felonious homicides of American police officers. Final report submitted to the National Institute of Justice, Washington, D.C. (#91-IJ-CX-K025).

Friedrich, R.J. (1980, November). Police use of force: Individuals, situations, and organizations. *Annals of the American Academy of Political and Social Science, 452,* 82–97.

Fyfe, J.J. (1978). Shots fired: Examination of New York City police firearms discharges. Unpublished doctoral dissertation, State University of New York, Albany.

———. (1981). Who shoots? A look at officer race and police shooting. *Journal of Police Science and Administration, 9,* 367–382.

———. (1987). The Metro-Dade police/citizen violence reduction project. An unpublished report submitted to the Metro-Dade Police Department by the Police Foundation.

———. (1995). Training to reduce police–civilian violence. In W.A. Geller & H. Toch (Eds.), *And justice for all: Understanding and controlling police abuse of force,* pp. 163–175. Washington, D.C.: Police Executive Research Forum.

Gallup, A.M. (1991). Americans say police brutality frequent—But not locally. *Gallup Poll News Service, 55,* 42b.

Garner, J.H., & Buchanan, J. (1995). *Executive summary: Understanding the use of force by and against the police.* Washington, D.C.: National Institute of Justice.

Geller, W.A., & Karales, K.J. (1981). *Split-second decisions: Shootings of and by Chicago police.* Chicago: Chicago Law Enforcement Study Group.

———, & Scott, M. (1992). *Deadly Force: What we know—A practitioner's desk reference on police-involved shootings in the United States.* Washington, D.C.: Police Executive Research Forum.

Geller, W.A., & Toch, H. (Eds.). (1995). Improving our understanding and control of police abuse of force: Recommendations for research and action. In *And justice for all: Understanding and controlling police abuse of force*, pp. 277–337. Washington, D.C.: Police Executive Research Forum.

———. (Eds.). (1995). *And justice for all: Understanding and controlling police abuse of force*. Washington, D.C.: Police Executive Research Forum.

Gellhorm, W. (1966). Police review boards: Hoax or hope? *Columbia University Forum,* Summer, 5–10.

Graham v. Connor, 490 U.S. 386 (1989).

Grant, J.D., & Grant, J. (1995). Officer selection and the prevention of abuse of force. In W.A. Geller & H. Toch (Eds.), *And justice for all: Understanding and controlling police abuse of force*, pp. 151–162. Washington, D.C.: Police Executive Research Forum.

Hensley, T. (1988, September). Civilian review boards: A means to police accountability. *Police Chief,* pp. 45–47.

Hudson, J.R. (1971). Police review boards and police accountability. *Law and Contemporary Problems, 36,* 515–538.

Hunt, J. (1985). Police accounts of normal force. *Urban Life: A Journal of Ethnographic Research, 13*(4), 315–341.

Independent Commission of the Los Angeles Police Department. (1991). *Report of the Independent Commission of the Los Angeles Police Department.* Los Angeles, CA: Author.

James, G. (1991, April 17). Police chiefs call for U.S. to study force. *New York Times,* B3.

Jolin, A.I., & Gibbons, D.C. (1984). Policing the police: The Portland experience. *Journal of Police Science and Administration, 12*(3), 315–322.

Kahn, R. (1975). Urban reform and police accountability in New York City: 1950–1974. In R. Lineberry (Ed.), *Urban problems and public policy.* Lexington, MA: Lexington Books.

Kamau, D. (no date). Unpublished press release.

Kania, R.R.E., & Mackey, W.C. (1977). Police violence as a function of community characteristics. *Criminology, 15*(1), 27–48.

Kerstetter, W.A. (1985). Who disciplines the police? Who should? In W.A. Geller (Ed.), *Police leadership in America: Crisis and opportunity,* pp. 149–182. New York: Praeger.

Klockars, C. (1980, November). The Dirty Harry problem. *Annals of the American Academy of Political and Social Science, 452,* 33–47.

———. (1995). A theory of excessive force and its control. In W.A. Geller & H. Toch (Eds.), *And justice for all: Understanding and controlling police abuse of force,* pp. 11–29. Washington, D.C.: Police Executive Research Forum.

Kolts, J.G. (1992). *The Los Angeles County Sheriff's Department.* Presented to the Board of Supervisors of Los Angeles County. Los Angeles, CA: Author.

Komarnicki, M., & Doble, J. (1985). *Crime and corrections: A review of public opinion data since 1975.* New York: Public Agenda Foundation.

Littlejohn, E.J. (1981). The civilian police commission: A deterrent of police misconduct. *Journal of Urban Law, 59*(5), 5–62.

Lundman, R., Sykes, R.E., & Clark, J.P. (1978). Police control of juveniles. *Journal of Research in Crime and Delinquency, 15*(1), 74–91.

Manning, P.K. (1980, November). Violence and the police role. *Annals of the American Academy of Political and Social Science, 452,* 135–144.

Mastrofski, S.D., & Parks, R.B. (1990). Improving observational studies of police. *Criminology, 28,* 475–496.

McLaughlin, V. (1992). *Police and the use of force: The Savannah study.* Westport, CT: Praeger.

Mendez, G.A., Jr. (1983). *The role of race and ethnicity in the incidence of police use of deadly force.* New York: National Urban League.

Meyer, M.W. (1980). Police shootings at minorities: The case of Los Angeles. *Annals of the American Academy of Political and Social Sciences, 452,* 98–110.

Monnell v. Department of Social Services, 436 U.S. 658 (1988).

Newell, C., Pollock, J., & Tweedy, J. (1992). Financial aspects of police liability. *Baseline Data Report, 24*(2), 1–8.

New York City Civilian Complaint Investigative Bureau. (1990). *Annual Report.* New York: Author.

New York City Police Department Civilian Complaint Review Board. (1986). *Nationwide survey of civilian complaint systems.* New York: Author.

New York State Commission on Criminal Justice and the Use of Force. (1987). *Report to the Governor,* volumes I–IV. New York: New York State.

Pate, A.M., & Fridell, L.A. (1993). *Police use of force: Official reports, citizen complaints, and legal consequences.* Washington, D.C.: Police Foundation.

Perez, D. (1978). Police accountability: A question of balance. An unpublished doctoral dissertation, University of California, Berkeley.

Perez, D., & Muir, W.K. (1995). Administrative review of alleged police brutality. In W.A. Geller & H. Toch (Eds.), *And justice for all: Understanding and controlling police abuse of force,* pp. 205–222. Washington, D.C.: Police Executive Research Forum.

Petersen, D.M. (1972). Police disposition of the petty offender. *Sociology and Social Research, 56*(3), 320–330.

Piliavin, I., & Briar, S. (1964, September). Police encounters with juveniles. *American Journal of Sociology, 70,* 206–214.

Pompa, G.G. (1980). Police use of force: How citizens think it should be dealt with. Paper presented at the 1980 National Convention of the League of United Latin American Citizens.

Reiss, A.J. Jr. (1971). *The police and the public.* New Haven, CT: Yale University Press.

Ross, J.I. (1994, Summer). The future of municipal police violence in advanced industrialized democracies: Towards a structural causal model. *Police Studies: The International Review of Police Development 17*(2), 1–27.

Scharf, P., & Binder, A. (1983). *The badge and the bullet: Police use of deadly force.* New York: Praeger.

Scrivner, E.M. (1994). *The role of police psychology in controlling excessive force.* A National Institute of Justice "Research Report." Washington, D.C.: National Institute of Justice.

Sherman, L.W., & Langworthy, R. (1979). Measuring homicide by police officers. *Journal of Criminal Law and Criminology, 70,* 546–560.

———. (1983). Reducing police gun use: Critical events, administrative policy and organizational change. In M. Punch (Ed.), *The management and control of police organizations,* pp. 98–125. Cambridge, MA: Massachusetts Institute of Technology Press.

Sherman, L. W., Cohn, E.G., Gartin, P.R., Hamilton, E.E., & Rogan, D.P. (1986). *Citizens killed by big city police, 1970–1984.* Washington, D.C.: Crime Control Institute.

Skolnick, J.H. (1966). *Justice without trial: Law enforcement in democratic society.* New York: John Wiley & Sons.

Skolnick, J.H., & Fyfe, J.J. (1993). *Above the law: Police and the excessive use of force.* New York: Free Press.

Smith, J.L. (1974, February). Police inspection and complaint reception procedures. *FBI Law Enforcement Bulletin,* pp. 12–15.

Smith, P.E., & Hawkins, R.O. (1973). Victimization, types of citizen-police contacts, and attitudes toward the police. *Law and Society Review, 8,* 135–152.

St. Clair, J.D. (1992). *Report of the Boston police department management review committee.* Unpublished report submitted to Major Raymond L. Flynn, January 14.

Sykes, R., & Clark, J.P. (1975). A theory of deference exchange in police–civilian encounters. *American Journal of Sociology, 81*(3), 584–600.

Tennessee v. Garner, 471 U.S. 1, 11 (1985).

Terrill, R.J. (1982). Complaint procedures: Variations on the theme of civilian participation. *Journal of Police Science and Administration, 10*(4), 398–407.

———. (1990). Alternative perceptions of independence in civilian oversight. *Journal of Police Science and Administration, 17,* 77–83.

Toch, H. (1969). *Violent men: An inquiry into the psychology of violence.* Chicago: Aldine. (Revised edition, 1984, Cambridge) MA: Schenkman.

———. (1985). The catalytic situation in the violence equation. *Journal of Applied Social Psychology, 15*(2), 105–123.

———. (1995). The "violence-prone" police officer. In W.A. Geller & H. Toch (Eds.), *And justice for all: Understanding and controlling police abuse of force,* pp. 99–112. Washington, D.C.: Police Executive Research Forum.

Uchida, C.D. (1982). Controlling police use of deadly force: Organizational change in Los Angeles. An unpublished doctoral dissertation, State University of New York at Albany.

Uelman, G.F. (1973). Varieties of public policy: A study of policy regarding the use of deadly force in Los Angeles County. *University of Loyola at Los Angeles Law Review, 6,* 1–65.

United States Commission on Civil Rights. (1981). *Who is guarding the guardians? A report on police practices.* Washington, D.C.: Government Printing Office.

Urban Studies Center. (1982, March). Jefferson County Survey. Louisville: University of Louisville.

Virginia Association of Chiefs of Police. (1994). *Use of force report.* Richmond, VA.

Waegel, W.B. (1984). The use of lethal force by police: The effect of statutory change. *Crime and Delinquency, 31,* 121–140.

Wagner, A.E. (1980). Citizen complaints against the police: The complainant. *Journal of Police Science and Administration, 8,* 247–252.

Walker, S. (1980). *Popular justice: A history of American criminal justice.* New York: Oxford University Press.

———. (1995). *Citizen review resource manual.* Washington, D.C.: Police Executive Research Forum.

Walker, S., & Bumphus, V.W. (1992). The effectiveness of civilian review: Observations on recent trends and new issues regarding the civilian review of the police. *American Journal of Police, XI*(4), 1–26.

———, & Fridell, L. (1993). Forces of change in police policy: The impact of *Tennessee v. Garner* on deadly force policy. *American Journal of Police, 11*(3), 97–112.

Webster Commission. A report by the special advisor to the board of police commissioners on the civil disorder in Los Angeles (1992). *The city in crisis.* Los Angeles.

Westley, W.A. (1953, July). Violence and the police. *American Journal of Sociology, 59,* 34–41.

———. (1970). *Violence and the police: A sociological study of law, custom, and morality.* Cambridge, MA: Massachusetts Institute of Technology Press.

West, P. (1988). Investigation of complaints against the police: Summary report of a national survey. *American Journal of Police, 7*(2), 101–121.

Whitaker, G.P. (1983). Police department size and the quality and cost of police services. In S. Nagel, E. Fairchild, & A. Champagne (Eds.), *The political science of criminal justice.* Springfield, IL: Charles C. Thomas.

Winick, C. (1987). Public opinion on police misuse of force: A New York study. *Report to the Governor* (vol. III, pp. A–i to A–70). Albany: New York State Commission on Criminal Justice and the Use of Force.

Worden, R.E. (1995a). The "causes" of police brutality: Theory and evidence on police use of force. In W.A. Geller & H. Toch (Eds.), *Justice for all: Understanding and controlling police abuse of force,* pp. 31–60. Washington, D.C.: Police Executive Research Forum.

———. (1995b). Police officers' belief systems: A framework for analysis. *American Journal of Police, XIV*(1), 49–81.

11

Re-Blueing the Police*: Technological Changes and Law Enforcement Practices

Jeffery T. Walker, University of Arkansas at Little Rock

The history of major changes in police practices often centers on technological changes of the time. The invention and widespread adoption of the repeating gun, telephone, radio, and automobile all dramatically changed the way law enforcement agencies carried out their duties.

The proliferation of computers has once again changed the way law enforcement agencies perform their duties—and it is changing at an ever-increasing pace. The Automated Fingerprint Identification System (AFIS) and its big brother, the Automated Video Identification System (AVIS) have greatly increased the ability of the police to store, retrieve, and make investigative searches of suspected criminals. Computer Aided Dispatch (CAD), pagers, and cellular telephones allow closer contact, provide more information, and require officers to carry more equipment than ever before. Geomapping and computer crime analysis bombards officers with information about their areas of responsibility and the people in those areas. In almost every facet of their work, technological changes in society have altered the pattern of law enforcement operations.

Technological advances not only benefit law enforcement, however. Computers and technology are also being employed by criminals in their efforts to outwit the police. Computer crimes and criminals who use technology to aid illegal activities are more prevalent that ever before. Because of the growing number of criminals relying on technology to enhance their illegal enterprises, law enforcement must stay abreast of technological advances and incorporate them into their methods of law enforcement. They must take advantage of new methods of tracking, identifying, and dealing with criminals; they must be able to recognize when criminal enterprises are making use of computers and other forms of technology; and they must be able to deal with these uses.

---

*Re-blueing is the practice of reconditioning the outside of the worn barrel of a weapon to bring it back to its original condition and luster.

Remaining current, however, is not without problems. High cost, resistance to change, and fear of computers all work to slow the adoption of technology in law enforcement. These stumbling blocks were once a severe limitation on the use of technology in law enforcement. They are becoming less of an issue, however, and may soon no longer hinder effective use of computers and technology.

This chapter will provide an overview of the technological changes that have shaped the way law enforcement is carried out in America. The history of technological changes prior to the computer revolution will be discussed to provide a basis for gauging changes that have occurred in the past twenty years. A discussion of current computer and other technological innovations and practices will provide the reader with a snapshot of how such changes have altered the practices of modern policing. It also briefly discusses how technology is advancing criminal activities, and discusses what law enforcement officers might expect to encounter, even when dealing with street-level criminals. The attitude of officers toward technological changes and problems associated with these changes will also be discussed, as well as what law enforcement agencies can do to ease the transition to new methods of law enforcement. Finally, we will take a look at the future and how "techno-policing" may be carried out in the twenty-first century.

THE HISTORY OF TECHNOLOGICAL CHANGE IN LAW ENFORCEMENT

In the beginning, things were simple. Tribal law enforcement consisted mainly of convincing people that they were in violation of the supreme being or ruler's will (Breasted, 1938). This form of control did not change much through the thirteenth century, although it became easier to persuade people with the development of the spear, the mace, and the bow.

Weaponry

The first significant technological advancement that would affect law enforcement came with the development of the hand cannon in the fourteenth century (Greener, 1967). Using gunpowder to propel projectiles, and based on early artillery-type weapons, this weapon brought the power of fire and projectiles to an individual.

The advantages of firearms for citizens and standing armies that represented law enforcement increased with the development of the "matchlock," the "wheellock," and the "flintlock." Subsequent developments of magazine-fed rifles and multi-barreled repeating rifles further increased the firing capacity of those charged with maintaining order (Greener, 1967).

By the time the city of Charleston, South Carolina, implemented its city guard in 1807, technology had advanced to the point that muskets could be breach-loaded and charges could be held in self-contained steel thimble-like chambers. By the time the United States saw its first state police agency (the Texas Rangers) in 1835, the revolver, made popular by Colonel Samuel Colt, had taken the weapons industry by storm (Kopel, 1992). With its light weight and the ability to launch six projectiles without reloading, the Colt revolver was considered by many to be the perfect weapon.

Following the Civil War, weapons technology made probably its greatest advancement for law enforcement. Tested in the Civil War, the Winchester repeating rifle placed a self-contained, high capacity weapon in the hands of law enforcement officials in the west.

Although technological changes in weaponry have continued to play a part in law enforcement, especially if one considers the debate between revolvers and semi-automatic pistols, most advances have been simple refinements or changes pertaining to personal preference, rather than true technological changes in the way law enforcement functions are performed.

The next major events to occur in law enforcement centered on the ability of law enforcement officers to move and communicate with each other. This development saw the adoption of the patrol car, telephone, and eventually the radio for law enforcement use.

Communications and Mobility

One of the enduring problems of early law enforcement was a lack of communication, both between officers and between citizens and the police. Usually the only way to make contact with law enforcement officers in the early years of policing was to meet them face to face. Communication was such a problem, in fact, that during the early nineteenth century sergeants in Philadelphia and Brooklyn were called "roundsmen" because most of their time was spent riding around on a horse keeping track of officers (Rubinstein, 1973).

The earliest advancements in communication came with the development of telegraphs in the 1850s. While this allowed officers to receive messages, it was lacking in both promptness and the ability to reach officers wherever they were.

This problem was somewhat reduced with the invention of police "call boxes." The first call boxes allowed an officer to pull a switch and alert the headquarters that he needed assistance. Although it did not allow direct communication, it at least provided a relatively quick link between the officer and the station.

The combination of the telephone with the call box in 1880 revolutionized police communications (Rubinstein, 1973). Now law enforcement officers had the ability to communicate directly with supervisors at the police station. Although there was no way to call the officer directly, at least an officer could check in on a regular basis and contact his supervisor if the need arose.

The technological advancement that has probably had the greatest impact on law enforcement came just prior to World War I. Developments made in the automobile allowed the police to more rapidly dispatch a larger number of officers to a larger portion of the city than ever before (Walker, 1977). By the 1920s the patrol car was considered by many to be an essential component of the law enforcement function (Vollmer, 1936). The use of automobiles in law enforcement was so important, in fact, that August Vollmer continually expressed its necessity in his quintessential book on policing (1936) and is reported to have claimed credit for making the Berkeley Police Department the first fully motorized police department in America (Walker, 1977).

The police car soon merged with the telephone to provide better communications between police officers and headquarters. Although there was no direct link between the police and headquarters, now police driving in the city could at least call head-quarters from a call box if the need arose. This led to ingenious ways to contact offi-cers in the field (prior to the development of the radio). Cities used lights or sirens mounted strategically throughout the city (on water towers, for example) to alert offi-cers that they should call the police station. The telephone also revolutionized law enforcement by enhancing the ability of citizens to contact the police.

The next significant development in police technology was the development and adoption of the use of radios in patrol cars. At first, radios did not resemble the cur-rent state of wireless communication. The first radio-equipped patrol cars relied on the public radio to pass along information (Scheetz, 1989). The cry of "calling all cars . . ." was first heard along with music and news on fledgling radio stations in America. By 1921, it is reported that the first patrol car equipped with a non-public radio was fielded in Detroit, Michigan (Rubinstein, 1973). These radios, however, were only one-way, so an officer receiving a call from headquarters would have to stop and use the telephone if more information were required (Scheetz, 1989). It was almost a decade later that two-way radios began to be commonplace in patrol cars (Rubinstein, 1973).

The final piece of the communications puzzle was added around 1950. Adapted from the war in Korea, walkie-talkies were provided to police officers so they could communicate when they were away from their patrol cars (Scheetz, 1989). This invention meant that officers did not have to be cut off from other officers at any time; this technology would remain essentially unchanged to the present.

THE SECOND "ICE" AGE: INFORMATION, COMMUNICATIONS, AND ELECTRONICS

The modern ICE age can be said to have begun in the early 1940s. Based on Charles Babbage's "analytical machine" developed in 1830, scientists at Pennsylvania's Moore School of Electrical Engineering produced the first electronic digital computer. This 30-ton machine, which took up approximately 1,500 square feet of floor space, was able to make calculations at the blinding speed of 300 multiplications per second (by comparison, current personal computers are often rated at over one million instructions per second). This machine, called ENIAC (Electronic Numerical Inte-grator And Calculator), was a significant improvement over any calculating machine available at that time, which could only muster about one multiplication per second.

The ICE age moved from the polar cap of scientific computing and into business with the second generation of computers (1959–1964). These computers were smaller (about the size of a car), less expensive, and easier to maintain. These computers still had to be hand programmed, however, and were very limited in the functions that they could perform. It was during this time that police departments began to use computers. Their uses, however, were very limited and generally restricted to accounting or similar mathematical functions.

Although difficult to determine, it is reported (Rosen, 1982) that the New Orleans Police Department (NOPD) was the first police agency in the country to utilize a computer in police work. NOPD installed an electronic data processing machine in 1955 to make summaries of arrests and warrants. Chicago soon followed in 1956 by installing an electromechanical accounting machine to compile statistics on traffic accidents (Rosen, 1982).

The ICE age further encroached on policing with the third generation of computers (1964–1970). The use of miniature integrated circuits further reduced the physical size of computers and greatly increased their processing speed, reliability, and accuracy. At this point, computers moved from specialized, one-of-a-kind machines built for a specific purpose to general-purpose machines.

It was during this time that computer networks linking police departments began to spring up (Rosen, 1982). The National Law Enforcement Telecommunications System (NLETS) was developed in 1966 to link all state police computers (except Hawaii). This was designed to facilitate the exchange of information between law enforcement agencies.

NLETS was followed in 1967 by the development of the first national law enforcement data base of crime and criminal information. The National Crime Information Center (NCIC), operated by the FBI, provided information on stolen property, guns, and wanted persons to all fifty states, Canada, the Virgin Islands, and Puerto Rico.

The fourth generation of computers (1970–present) has enabled law enforcement to seriously utilize computer technology. Fourth-generation computers are most often characterized by the explosion of personal computers that are inexpensive, relatively easy to operate, and possess more power and capabilities than early mainframes at a fraction of the cost.

By 1972, the first computers were added to patrol cars. Although not a computer in the classical sense, a mobile printer developed by Xerox could be attached to radios and would record all messages sent. This forerunner of the Mobile Digital Terminal (MDT) allowed officers to receive, retrieve, and recheck calls that they may have missed.

Until the mid-1980s, most police departments that utilized computer technology operated from central, mainframe computers, either operated solely by the police department or, more likely, as part of a central government data processing center. Although law enforcement was well advanced in other areas of technology by this time (communications, patrol cars, etc.), computer usage was still quite primitive and usually limited to basic accounting and record keeping. This would soon change for many police departments, however.

With the spread of PCs in the mid-1980s, police departments began to look to distributed networks that officers could access directly, and they began to discover law enforcement functions that could be handled more effectively with computer assistance. For example, many police departments began to automate their dispatching system through the use of computer assisted dispatch (CAD). Not only did this create a more efficient method of dispatching officers, it allowed officers and supervisors to view upcoming calls, determine the backlog of calls, and determine the location of a call more quickly and accurately.

The added bonus of CAD was that it provided officers with information about patterns of crime in their patrol areas. Since calls for service were entered into a computer, they could be grouped in different ways so that an officer, for example, could see the pattern of burglaries in his or her patrol area for a given month. This allowed officers to plan crime prevention efforts and assisted in criminal investigations.

Law enforcement agencies also began to turn to the Internet by the mid-1990s. Although much of the utilization of the Internet by law enforcement agencies was limited to a few officers or "cops talking to cops," some agencies realized genuine value from the Internet. Probably the greatest direct benefit came from the access that law enforcement officers had to information pertinent to their function. Not only could officers now get information on criminals through NCIC, they could also get information about hiring practices, new computer programs, or laws affecting their duties from such sources as the International Association of Chiefs of Police (IACP Net) or the National Institute of Justice bulletin board service. Some agencies also realized the public relations opportunity of the Internet. As a result, a growing number of agencies began to create their own World Wide Web (www) pages that provided the public with information about the agency and facilitated the interaction between the police and others who had an interest in law enforcement.

NOT ROBOCOP YET: POLICE TECHNOLOGY IN THE 1990s

The 1990s showed a significant increase in law enforcement's use of computers. As more programs began to be written for law enforcement applications, as more service and equipment providers began to realize the potential market in law enforcement, and as more officers began to become computer literate, the more law enforcement embraced computer technology and the more they demanded that law enforcement functions become computerized.

In this portion of the chapter, the focus turns to a discussion of the current state of law enforcement technology. Two qualifiers should be mentioned, however. First, this section will focus primarily on the current state of computer technology in law enforcement. Police technology, especially in current discussions, has become synonymous with computers, since communications, weapons, and patrol cars have not changed significantly since the time frame of the discussion above, while computer technology is expanding at an ever-increasing rate. The second qualifier is that this section will not cover all of the technological or computer applications that are currently being used in law enforcement. With more than 17,000 police agencies in America, computers are being used in many different ways in different agencies. This portion of the discussion will focus, then, on a few of the major or more popular uses of computer technology.

Computer Applications Aiding Investigations

Probably the greatest focus of law enforcement on computer technology in the first half of the 1990s has been on applications that aid investigations. This is not to say that it is the most widespread technology; that honor would probably go to the applications used by patrol or support functions of law enforcement agencies. The need to solve crimes, however, has focused emphasis on technological developments that aid criminal investigations.

Easily the best-received technological advancement in this area is the Automated Fingerprint Identification System (AFIS). The advantages of this kind of technology for law enforcement are evident, even for the most skeptical officer.

> *Illustration:* When testing an AFIS system for possible purchase by the Little Rock, Arkansas, police department, twenty cases, some unsolved for over a decade, got new leads when fingerprints found at the scenes of crimes were finally matched to a person. Officers had been unable to determine who had left the prints using the traditional 10-print cards and non-computer assisted examination because of the time it would have taken to compare the prints to the thousands of 10-print cards held by the department.

Although the method of classifying and storing fingerprint images may vary among systems (see below), the basic procedures of an AFIS system are that fingerprints of a person are taken and entered into the computer, usually via some method of scanning the 10-print card. After the prints are in the computer, other prints can be entered and the computer used to find matches to that print.

The AFIS system has not been without its problems, however. AFIS is still limited as a law enforcement tool because of compatibility between systems. At the present time, there are several methods of classification and storage used, depending on the system chosen. For example, some AFIS systems convert the characteristics of fingerprints (loops, whorls, etc.) to a numerical representation by using a mathematical plotting system, while others store the images more as pictures that can be compared. As a result, police departments in nearby cities may find themselves in a situation where they cannot exchange fingerprint information because their systems use different methods of storing and retrieving the prints. This problem will begin to diminish, however, as scanning and printing technology increases to the point that law enforcement agencies can print, mail, and re-scan fingerprints (or transfer the images directly between computers) with little or no loss of clarity.

Advancements in the AFIS system that are beginning to emerge in law enforcement include what is known as "live digital fingerprinting." This system involves taking laser images directly from the finger. This technology allows officers to take a clearer and more accurate picture of the fingerprint with less possibility of the smudging common in traditional methods of fingerprinting.

Closely related to automated fingerprinting is a system of automated mug shots and rap sheets. These systems are commonly called Automated Video Identification Systems or AVIS. These systems involve digitizing a picture or video of a person and storing it, along with physical and other information about the person, in a computer. The information can then be retrieved in a number of ways that aid identification of a suspect. At the most basic level, a victim or witness could reduce the number of photographs that they are required to review by eliminating pictures that do not match the characteristics of the suspect (hair color, age, etc.). This system can also be used to produce suspects when only vague information is known about the person. For example, if, at the scene of a robbery, a witnesses said that a white woman with a tattoo on her neck was the robber, the officer could type "female, white, mark on neck" into the computer and get only those mug shots that fit the description provided by the witness. Instead of the witnesses having to plow through tons of mug shots, possibly clouding their memory of the suspect, an officer can narrow the selection to only those that meet relevant criteria—and the searches can be done in seconds at the scene of the crime. Even if the only thing a witness knew was that it was a white female, the search could be narrowed based on the area or crime type, and the number of mug shots that the victim or witness would have to view could be reduced dramatically.

Other technological advancements that aid investigations include computer programs that can enhance photographs or video images for clearer identification, and dozens of database programs that track different kinds of offenders and activities. Though none of these technological advancements can replace the criminal investigator, they can make the job that he or she does easier and quicker.

Computer Applications Aiding Patrol Functions

While not as flashy as technological advancements aiding investigations, computer applications aiding patrol functions have increased the ability of law enforcement officers to perform their duties under increasing workloads. Most of the technology aiding patrol was spawned from the CAD systems which became so popular a decade or so previously, and are primarily focused on the efficiency and effectiveness of responding to calls for service.

One of the earliest computer programs designed specifically for law enforcement was the Patrol Car Application Program. This program, and many others that have followed it, were designed to assist law enforcement supervisors in distributing patrol cars throughout the area of operation. Although these programs differ in what they do, the basic design is to take data on calls for service, crime, area of coverage, etc. and determine the optimal way to distribute the available patrol units. Programs such as these have also been used by law enforcement managers to explore issues such as one- versus two-person patrols and shift rotation.

The same programming logic can be used to allocate and schedule personnel. Scheduling law enforcement personnel is much more difficult than in most organizations. Even those organizations that have to schedule 24-hour shifts do not have to deal with the issues of time off for court (both through time off while on duty and comp time for court appearances during off-duty hours), scheduling training for the officers, etc. Even with these complicating factors, law enforcement supervisors still must schedule enough personnel to adequately cover the city with law enforcement service.

Probably the most beneficial computer application directly affecting the patrol (and investigation) function of law enforcement was the development and spread of geographic information systems (GIS). GIS takes data drawn from a CAD system or other information and represents it graphically on computer-generated maps. This is a computerized version of the long-used "pin maps." The difference is that GIS maps contain much more information and can be created with many different views of the same information. GIS information greatly increases the ability of officers and detectives to plan crime prevention, understand the dynamics of crime in his or her area, and to aid in criminal investigations. GIS information also aids law enforcement by putting in graphical form crime analysis that had previously only been available in a somewhat cryptic form. With GIS, then, an officer can simply look at a map (and ask for additional maps of different information) rather than having to pore over mounds of crime analysis data.

A final technological/computer advancement that has aided the patrol function of law enforcement is the Mobile Digital Terminal (MDT). MDTs are very small computers that can either be mounted in a patrol car or carried by an officer. MDTs do not actually provide a separate function or capability for officers, but they do provide the most advanced link between the officer and any computer technology of the agency. For example, most MDTs provide information to the officer from the dispatch system. The officer can also run records checks from the MDT, or, if the department is operating an AVIS system, the officer may even be able to access that information. Finally, most MDTs allow automated ticket writing. Again, the MDT does not add technological advances for the officer, but it does allow greater freedom in accessing the computer capabilities of the agency.

Computers Supporting Law Enforcement Activities

Although the more important computer programs may support the line or patrol function of law enforcement, there are programs that operate on the periphery of law enforcement duties that are nonetheless important to law enforcement officers. These programs are typically adapted from other fields and usually enter law enforcement through the insight of a particular officer who can see the application for law enforcement functions.

One of the more interesting technological advancements that aids law enforcement is the use of computer aided design. This process uses computers to more accurately draw and lay out situations such as crime scenes, traffic accidents, and buildings. With this technology, for example, a SWAT team commander would have information far beyond a blueprint of a building in which to guide entry teams; or an investigator could illustrate the actions at a crime scene to show a jury how a particular crime was committed.

Another computer application that supports law enforcement activities is a program that tracks evidence. One of the major responsibilities of law enforcement at the scene of a crime or an arrest is making sure that any evidence to be used in court is properly searched for and seized and that the evidence is securely stored and protected from the time it is seized until it is presented in court. Many cases have been lost because the police could not find evidence crucial to the case after it had been seized or because the so-called "chain of custody" was somehow breached.

Evidence-tracking programs can facilitate maintaining the chain of custody by more accurately recording and tracking the evidence once it is in law enforcement hands (Hamilton, 1991). For example, at the scene of an arrest, a house is searched and a great deal of evidence is taken into custody. When an officer seizes the evidence, he or she brings it to an officer who is operating the evidence program. That officer will place a bar code sticker on the evidence, scan the bar code to initialize the program and then enter a description of the evidence and how it was seized. From that point on, each time someone moves the evidence, the bar code can be scanned and the details of the move can be entered into the database. When the evidence arrives in court, a detailed account of the seizure and each movement of the evidence can also be presented.

A similar program can be used for processing prisoners and tracking their movement. When a prisoner is booked, he or she can be given a bracelet with a bar code on it. The bar code can be scanned and the information concerning the prisoner, including where he or she will be kept, can be entered into a database. From that point on, each time the prisoner is moved (e.g., taken to court) the bar code can be read and the whereabouts of the prisoner entered. Although the movement of a prisoner is not as important as that of evidence, a law enforcement agency that is responsible for hundreds or thousands of prisoners can greatly benefit from a program that aids in knowing exactly where each prisoner is supposed to be at a given time.

Other Current Technology

Not all of the current technological aids for law enforcement are computer related. Some are adapted from the military or other fields and have great value for law enforcement.

One of the more interesting developments was popularized by operations in Desert Storm. Used in specialized law enforcement situations (e.g., scanning buildings for meth labs) for a number of years, thermal imaging (infrared) systems are now finding their way from the tanks of Desert Storm to the patrol cars of law enforcement officers. Instead of a hand-held configuration, however, this system uses a heat-sensitive infrared camera mounted to the top of a patrol car to scan the darkness around the officer. This camera is excellent for finding people in dark corners and alleys, and can even pick up such things as fresh tire tracks left from cars or guns that are still giving off heat from human contact (McMillan, 1994).

Another system under development adapts technology from submarines to assist officers in identifying the existence and location of gunshots in a city. The system works by mounting a small device on utility poles or other structures. The device has an acoustic sensor and a transmitter that can differentiate between gunshots and various sounds in the city. If the device detects gunshots, it transmits a signal to the police.

Since several of the devices will send a signal from the same gunshots, triangulation can be used to place the location of the gunshots fairly accurately.

Finally, technological advancements have greatly increased the effectiveness of operations that law enforcement officers have undertaken for years. For instance, current technology allows officers to use lasers and chemicals to take fingerprints from objects that they never would have been able to view with traditional fingerprint dusting. Such technology, for example, made it possible to get a conviction based on a thumb print taken from a banana that a burglar ate while burglarizing a house.

Fifth Generation Computers in Law Enforcement

The next generation of computers is the fifth generation. Fifth generation computers use new systems of logic not restricted to the linear commands of previous generations. The term most closely associated with fifth generation computers is "artificial intelligence." This is a capability that allows a computer to process a large amount of information and then make decisions based on the combined knowledge. Artificial intelligence also allows a computer to learn from its mistakes.

Although use of fifth generation computer technology is still in its infancy in law enforcement, the Federal Bureau of Investigation has begun to use artificial intelligence in the form of "expert systems." In the late 1970s the FBI began to consider the need for expert systems to assist investigators (Bayse & Morris, 1990). By the mid-1980s the Bureau had developed and implemented expert systems to assist in organized crime, narcotics, and terrorism investigations.

Artificial intelligence (expert systems) work in law enforcement by teaching a computer how to "think" like an investigator. For example, those considered expert in a particular area may be interviewed to determine how they investigate crimes and what rules of thumb or information those investigators rely on. This information can then be coded into a computer in a series of if/then statements that can guide the computer in analyzing investigative information for a particular case. The advantage of this kind of expert system over a human expert is that the computer can draw on each of the rules of thumb independently and in combination to reach conclusions, whereas most investigators use a more simplified paradigm. The drawback to artificial intelligence expert systems, at least for the time being, is that the computers cannot play the hunches and rely on the life experiences of human investigators. As a result, these systems will not replace investigators and can only be used to aid a trained investigator in his or her work.

NOT JUST FOR POLICE ANYMORE: CRIMINAL USES OF TECHNOLOGY AND COMPUTERS

In many ways, policing has always had to react to new ways of committing crimes. The invention and development of firearms forced new policing methods; when trains became prevalent on the western frontier, police adapted with new techniques. The same has happened with computer technology.

Criminals were perhaps slow to see the value of using computers and other technology in the commission of crimes; that time is no more. In addition to crimes involving computers (e.g., stolen computer equipment), criminals are beginning to use computers in the commission of their crimes. As Georgette Bennett (1987) proposed in her futuristic look at crime, "computers, cashless money, technological secrets will become new booty" for criminals that will radically change the way police will investigate many crimes (p. xiv).

Computer crimes can be placed into two main categories of illegal activities: those where the computer is the target and those where the computer is the instrument. Where the computer is the target, the most common computer crimes are theft or destruction of computers or software, illicit use of software, and viruses that destroy data. Using a computer as an instrument is typically exhibited in "hacking" or the more serious computer espionage. Computers can also contain valuable information about criminal activities, such as when drug dealers record sales and clients or use a computer for accounting purposes in their illegal activities.

Crimes Against Computers

The most basic crimes involving computers are those where the computer itself is the target. The size of personal computers and components makes them easy targets for theft. Furthermore, the standardization of computer parts, combined with ease of removal and installation, makes computers among the easiest of all consumer goods to strip and resell with little ability to trace its origin. Computers may also be the objects of sabotage. Disgruntled employees or ex-employees seeking revenge often destroy computer equipment.

This type of activity is currently under the jurisdiction of law enforcement agencies at all levels of government. Since most of these crimes are treated simply as thefts, traditional investigation methods can be employed by law enforcement officers, and there is usually no real need for specialized training.

Viruses.   Viruses are the "street crime" of computer crimes. Like street crimes, they are the most unpredictable—even those who create and spread the viruses do not know the extent of the damage or who will be affected. Also like street crimes, they often afflict those who are least able to pay for the damage. Because of these factors, viruses, like street crimes, are the most fearsome for computer users. Because of the seriousness of possible damage from viruses, several national organizations have been created with the purpose of providing security against viruses.

A virus is a program written to operate within other computer programs. Computers work through "executable programs" that are a series of statements telling the computer to perform certain functions. Viruses cause the computer to function in ways other than what the operator desires. Viruses spread when programs within which the virus is embedded are copied from computer to computer.

For the most part, law enforcement is not concerned with this type of crime at this time. As stated above, there are several national organizations that have primary concern and responsibility for keeping track of viruses, for providing virus alerts, and for dealing with viruses once they have hit. As this type of crime becomes more prevalent and more of a problem to society, however, law enforcement will no doubt be required to begin detection and investigation of these kinds of illegal behaviors.

Hackers. Hacking is the archetypal form of computer crime. It may come in the form of unauthorized use of a computer, fraudulent alteration of information (deleting unfavorable information) or destruction of data. It may also include theft by a computer (in banking transactions, for example).

While hacking may be perpetrated by the stereotypical computer whiz breaking into a company's computer to explore or cause damage, more often hacking is an effort to steal money, services, or other goods of value from the company (e.g., stocks). As such, financial institutions are more likely targets of pure hacking than are other companies.

Unlike other computer crimes where law enforcement may have a limited interest and role in investigation, law enforcement must deal with these kinds of crimes. Although many of these crimes fall more under the jurisdiction of federal law enforcement agencies, who are more likely to have some expertise in this area, there are instances where local law enforcement will be required to deal with these kinds of crimes. As such, law enforcement agencies are beginning to see the need to have some of their officers trained in computer crime investigations.

Another concern of law enforcement in this area is internal security of law enforcement computers. There are many people who would like to have access to or be able to alter law enforcement records. Security of law enforcement computers should, therefore, be a primary concern of law enforcement managers and supervisors.

Computer Espionage. Hacking in which information in the computer is the target is considered computer espionage. As companies rely more on computers in their operations, it is easier to gain information about the company or products by tapping into their computers. Many people, therefore, are making it their business to tap into company computers and steal information.

Although this kind of activity is serious and illegal, it seldom becomes the concern of law enforcement except at the federal level. Espionage by its definition usually entails illegal activities that would fall under the jurisdiction of the FBI or another federal law enforcement agency. State and local law enforcement agencies, however, must at least have enough of an understanding in this area to know what has happened and when it is appropriate to turn the matter over to another agency.

Computer Criminals

Most computer crimes are perpetrated by people who take advantage of their access to a computer or information. In contrast to popular opinions that all computer criminals are whiz kids, the profile of a typical computer criminal is a person who is an employee of the victimized agency, who was in a position of trust (at least with a computer), not necessarily a computer specialist, had good job ratings, and no prior record of criminal activity. However, with the growth of computers, any average person or previous non-computer literate criminal could use a computer for criminal purposes.

Illustration: There continues to be an increasing number of news stories describing criminal actions that were completed because of the computer: On a college campus outside Chicago, a disabled woman is sexually assaulted by a man she met through the computer. A few months later, a young boy is lured from his home by a man he met through the computer. Fortunately, in both cases the perpetrators were apprehended.

The skills and abilities of investigators, as discussed below, do not necessarily require significant computer skills to catch this kind of criminal. Sound investigative skills of an experienced investigator will typically result in a successful investigation; however, computer skills do aid in this type of law enforcement activity and are a requirement in some hacking/espionage cases.

Investigating Computer Crimes

Most computer crime is detected by accident or discovery, like other crimes. As such, computer crime investigations are also conducted like other crimes. Because computers are structured, logic machines, computer criminals must follow patterns, practices, and courses of action that assist in the detection and investigation of computer crimes. For example, a computer that is accessible by modem is susceptible to hacking from outsiders, while information taken from a computer that has no outside links and which is protected by passwords points to someone who has access to the information as a part of their employment.

Likewise, computer crime detectives do not all have to have a full understanding of computer operations. Many computer crimes are solved by examining sources of information other than the computer. For example, a great deal of information can be obtained by determining employees who are isolated in their job in a way that they could commit the crime without detection or by determining if any employees have a grudge against the company. All of these activities could be undertaken by an officer with no computer skills; however, such investigations are aided when the officer has a good understanding of computers and their operation.

HINDRANCES AND SOLUTIONS TO TECHNOLOGICAL CHANGE

Police and technology have an interesting and often enigmatic relationship. On the one hand, law enforcement agencies and officers are generally quick to adopt the newest gadgets that enter the law enforcement arena. New cars, new lighting equipment, stun guns, pepper spray, the list could go on and on. When it comes to computer technology, however, law enforcement has lagged far behind comparable organizations and have only relatively recently begun to use computers for specialized or advanced law enforcement operations. This portion of the chapter will look at some of the hindrances that have kept law enforcement from adopting computer technology as quickly as other parts of society.

Probably the greatest factor that has limited the use of computer technology for law enforcement is the fact that many agency heads are not computer literate. As in so many other organizations, it is the new, younger officers who have been introduced to computer technology, while supervisors and agency heads consider computer technology at best a fad and at worst something that would only have to be understood by the "bean counters" of the organization. Coincidentally, this is the same attitude that exists in many university settings. Because of this technophobia, many police managers refuse to consider adopting computer technology or drag their feet when adopting these changes.

Technophobia does not stop at management in law enforcement agencies, however. While many officers are embracing computer technology at an ever-increasing rate, many others are fighting it to the bitter end. In many law enforcement agencies, computer literacy has fallen to a few officers who use computers more as a hobby than as a serious method of change for law enforcement. As a result, many agencies now have World Wide Web sites for their agencies that are actually run almost as a hobby by one or a few of the officers.

Much of the fear/distrust on the part of law enforcement officers is warranted and stems from early interaction with computers. As discussed above, computers were limited for many years to scientific and then business applications. As a result, most of the very early application of computers to policing came only in the form of accounting or other managerial functions, often from city hall or another governing body. The antagonism between law enforcement managers and these departments many times spilled over into dislike for computers, which was often a source of conflict between the two groups.

The distrust of computers was only exacerbated when computer technology moved into more traditional law enforcement areas. First- and second-generation languages operating on second- and third-generation computers often resulted in applications that produced more agony than productivity for law enforcement personnel. For instance, early attempts at crime analysis (see Chapter 8) were often focused more on crime counting than on readily retrievable information that could be used by line-level officers. Combine this with the problem that the officers and those operating the computers did not speak the same language and the result was a typical exasperation by an officer that "the computer can't give me what I need and it takes too long to even get me what I can't use!" This set the stage for a long battle between officers and computers/computer personnel that has followed those officers as they have moved into management positions in law enforcement agencies.

Also producing technophobia in law enforcement officers was the flat learning curve of computers (the common phrase of a steep learning curve is actually incorrect). Early computers in law enforcement still required a fair amount of computer knowledge and were often difficult to program. Officers who were reluctant to use a typewriter to type reports were certainly not going to use word processing programs that would be considered difficult to operate in comparison with current software, but, were often the most easily operated programs available in law enforcement at that time.

Another problem that has hampered the use of computer technology in law enforcement has been the cost. Until relatively recently, the cost of computer automation for any law enforcement function often exceeded the annual budget of even the largest law enforcement agencies. If the city, county, or state government did not provide additional funds for the purchase of computers, or did not at least allow the law enforcement agency to share time on a central computer, such technological advancements were out of the reach of many law enforcement agencies. While the cost of computerization has been reduced dramatically with advancements in personal computers, some smaller agencies even today have difficulty finding funding to automate their agencies. I have spoken to many chiefs of small agencies who exclaim, "I don't have enough money to hire the extra officer I need or to keep my patrol cars running; how can I afford to buy thousands of dollars of computer equipment?"

Finally, a significant problem in the use of computer technology in law enforcement has been the lack of application programs suitable for law enforcement. For many years, law enforcement agencies who wished to use computer technology in their operations had two choices: try to adapt a program not designed for law enforcement or have the programs custom designed. Neither of these options endeared computer applications to law enforcement.

While programs existed that could aid law enforcement agencies, most of them were adapted from business applications and had only limited service in true law enforcement functions. For example, while it was easy to purchase an accounting application that worked for law enforcement agencies, attempting to adapt an off-the-shelf program for crime analysis was more difficult and about as effective as consulting a Ouija board.

As law enforcement agencies began to become more involved in computer technology, companies began to support law enforcement functions. This was not the holy grail that law enforcement was looking for, however. While many of these programs were effective at automating law enforcement functions, they had two drawbacks. First, they were generally very expensive. Since these programs required a code to be written for each specific application, there was little economy of scale to bring the price of such programs into a range that law enforcement agencies could afford. More damning, however, was that these programs generally could not be altered without the company who provided the software reprogramming it for new functions. As a result, once a police agency bought a program and began to use it, it often could not be changed without a significant outlay of funds. For example, a law enforcement agency that wished to add a field to a criminal investigation program would have to return to the vendor to reprogram the software. This would be expensive at best, and many times the software company went out of business, stranding the agency to operate with a program that was outdated and ineffective.

There was also the problem that the software engineers rarely had an adequate understanding of law enforcement needs. This resulted in many software programs that did not exactly fit the needs of the agency and reinforced the view that "the computer cannot give me what I need."

To get around this problem, some law enforcement agencies tried to write their programs internally, getting an officer who was considered a computer expert in the agency to write the program. While these officers certainly understood the needs of the agency, they were often deficient in the computer planning, design, and programming that is needed to ensure properly operating software. The end result of these problems was a continued agreement among police managers and officers that computers were just not appropriate for law enforcement functions. This attitude would remain in many law enforcement agencies long after software became available that was inexpensive yet effective for law enforcement applications.

Solutions

Many of the solutions to the problems discussed above have already appeared—at least partially. Others will only occur with the passage of time and the changing attitude of society as a whole.

Most of the problem with applications' not being available for law enforcement functions or only being written at a high cost by specialty software companies has been resolved. While many law enforcement agencies are still turning to specialty software companies for their programs (and for some applications this is still necessary) many of the current off-the-shelf software programs can be easily adapted to law enforcement functions. For example, any of the current database management programs can be configured for law enforcement applications. Even if a law enforcement agency does not have the in-house expertise to do the initial programming, software companies or local universities may be able to do this. After training and some work with these programs, in-house personnel can easily change or add to these databases to keep them current and useful in aiding law enforcement operations.

Although the cost of computer equipment and programs is still prohibitive for many agencies, it is becoming less of a problem. Even the smallest agencies are better able to purchase at least one PC and enough software that they can computerize some of their law enforcement functions. Costs will continue to be less of a factor as technological advancements increase.

Also, advancements in computer programs have greatly increased the user-friendliness of programs. Where once an officer would essentially have to program any function that he or she wanted to perform, now that officer can probably just click on a button or type a few words to get what he or she needs. Officers who can quickly learn a program and get the information that they need become confident with the computer's ability and will utilize it more. As computer programs become more user-friendly, the technophobia will subside to a level about where VCRs are now (the time may still be flashing, but at least a person can play a tape and record a program).

With the advancements in software that allow law enforcement agencies to do their programming in-house, more user-friendly programs that promote greater use by officers, and a reduced cost that allows law enforcement agencies to purchase their own computers, the friction that once existed between law enforcement agencies and data processing departments is also being reduced. Since law enforcement agencies have to rely on data processing departments less, the mystique that once surrounded computers is gone and the value of computer technology is increasingly being recognized.

This brings us to the last problem: distrust/fear of computers exhibited by officers and management personnel. For many law enforcement agencies, the solutions discussed above have reduced or eliminated the distrust of computers by management and officers, resulting in increased awareness and adoption of computer technology. Just like some university professors who refuse to give up their typewriters, however, some law enforcement officers and managers refuse to cave in to computer technology. Only time and an increased acceptance of computers in society will solve this problem and make way for a full acceptance and utilization of computers in law enforcement.

THE FUTURE

Many futurists predict that the world will become a cashless society in the first quarter of the twenty-first century—all transactions in this new society will take place through electronic funds transfers. Should this occur, the use of computers to steal, redirect, and alter electronic funds will become the number one crime throughout the world—far outpacing any threat of theft or embezzlement that currently exists. It can safely be said, then, that when the world gets to the twenty-first century, criminals will be waiting there.

If computers are the source of crime that is expected by futurists, then computers are also in the future for law enforcement. In fact, law enforcement may expect to rely on computers more than the general population or most other nonscientific organizations. This is because the police will undoubtedly follow patterns of increased computer use exhibited by society and other organizations; plus law enforcement will be expected to possess an understanding of computers sufficient to allow them to detect, investigate, and prevent computer crime. This will require law enforcement agencies to greatly increase their computer skills and, for a number of officers, acquire computer skills that will rival the business and scientific fields. In fact, there may come a time in the not-too-distant future that larger law enforcement agencies will begin to seriously draw personnel from the scientific and business fields.

This does not mean, however, that all computer/technological advancements for law enforcement will be restricted to personnel and personnel issues. In fact, there are still a large number of technological advancements on the horizon that will greatly affect the way some law enforcement agencies and officers perform their duties.

We are only beginning to see the tip of what artificial intelligence and expert systems can do for law enforcement. As this technology advances (and becomes more reasonably priced), law enforcement will increasingly turn to artificial intelligence to aid in police work. This technology will not be limited to aiding investigators in high-profile crimes, however. It is likely that artificial intelligence will also be used for such tasks as modeling the time and place where more officers are needed for traffic enforcement and working wrecks, modeling patrol car assignments for fluid coverage of a city, based on expected calls for service, or even estimating the time and place of the occurrence of crimes in order to increase the police presence. The opportunities for use of artificial intelligence in law enforcement are endless and will no doubt alter police operations in the future.

Other technological advancements may also aid law enforcement in functions that they currently perform. For example, law enforcement is beginning to use technology called "biochips" in detecting bombs. Biochips are a form of computer hardware that can detect and identify particular elements in the air. Current use of this application is mostly in bomb-sniffing equipment; however, this technology could easily be adapted for use as drug sniffers or in identifying a range of illegal items.

Finally, law enforcement will no doubt be aided by technological advancements meant for other fields but which can be adapted to law enforcement functions. For example, technological advancements in Charged Coupled Devices (CCD) make it possible to see eighty times better than with photographic film. This technology can easily be adapted to law enforcement to increase the effectiveness of surveillance activities.

CONCLUSION

Since the earliest forms of law enforcement, this field has been directed by and continues to react to changes in technology. The development of the gun, the automobile, the radio, and, most recently, the computer, have all changed the way law enforcement operates.

The development and proliferation of personal computers has brought computer technology within the grasp of law enforcement in the 1990s. Furthermore, the ease with which computers can now be operated and the ability to program these computers for the kinds of information and operations that officers need has brought an attitude of respect and usefulness to this once-scorned technology. As systems such as AFIS, AVIS, and artificial intelligence become more commonplace, law enforcement officers will increasingly accept what technology has to offer.

While computer technology will not replace law enforcement officers, it will continue to become an increasing part of the law enforcement function. As crime moves from street robberies to fraud by computer, the police will advance their skills and wield new weapons to fight twenty-first century crime.

DISCUSSION QUESTIONS

1. Apart from those discussed in the chapter, what are other technological and societal events that have significantly changed the way the police do business?
2. Who has been more affected by law enforcement technology, law enforcement officers, supervisors, or management-level personnel?
3. Which form of technology (firearms, communications and mobility, or computers) has been more important in defining law enforcement as we know it today?

4. What do you see as the future of technology in law enforcement?
5. Do you ever see a time when law enforcement officers will be replaced by technology or other people controlling technology?

REFERENCES

Bayse, W.A., & Morris, C.G. (1990, June). Automated systems' reasoning capabilities a boon to law enforcement. *Police Chief, 57*(6), 48–52.

Bennett, G. (1987). *Crime warps: The future of crime in America.* Garden City, NY: Anchor Press/Doubleday.

Breasted, J.H. (1938). *The conquest of civilization.* New York: Harper & Brothers.

Greener, W.W. (1967). *The gun and its development.* New York: Bonanza Books.

Hamilton, T.S. (1991, April). Developing an automated evidence tracking system. *Police Chief,* 146–149.

Kopel, D.B. (1992). *The samurai, the mountie, and the cowboy: Should America adopt the gun controls of other democracies?* Buffalo, NY: Prometheus Books.

McMillan, M. (1994, August). High tech enters the field of view. *Police Chief,* 29–34.

Rosen, M.D. (1982, September). Police and computers: The revolution that never happened. *Police Magazine,* 9–18.

Rubinstein, J. (1973). *City police.* New York: Farrar, Straus, and Giroux.

Scheetz, R.E. (1989, July). Calling all cars. . . . *Police Chief,* 61–63.

Vollmer, A. (1936). *The police and modern society.* Berkeley, CA: University of California Press.

Walker, S. (1977). *A critical history of police reform: The emergence of professionalism.* Lexington, MA: Lexington Books.

Index